Political Unification Revisited

Political Unification Revisited

Revisited

On Building Supranational Communities

Amitai Etzioni

LEXINGTON BOOKS
Lanham • Boulder • New York • Oxford

LEXINGTON BOOKS

Published in the United States of America
by Lexington Books
4720 Boston Way, Lanham, Maryland 20706

12 Hid's Copse Road
Cumnor Hill, Oxford OX2 9JJ, England

British Library Cataloguing in Publication Information Available

Library of Congress Cataloging-in-Publication Data

Etzioni, Amitai.
   Political unification revisited : on building supranational communities /
Amitai Etzioni.
      p.   cm.
   Includes bibliographical information and index.
   ISBN 0-7391-0272-9 (cloth : alk. paper)—ISBN 0-7391-0273-7 (pbk. : alk.
paper)
   1. International organization. 2. World politics. 3. Supranationalism. I. Title.
JZ5566 .E88   2001
   327.1—dc21   2001029635

Printed in the United States of America

⊗ ™ The paper used in this publication meets the minimum requirements of
American National Standard for Information Sciences—Permanence of Paper
for Printed Library Materials, ANSI/NISO Z39.48–1992.

FOR M.M.M.

Defenceless under the night
Our world in stupour lies;
Yet, dotted everywhere,
Ironic points of light
Flash out wherever the Just
Exchange their messages;
May I, composed like them
Of Eros and of dust,
Beleaguered by the same
Negation and despair,
Show an affirming flame.

—*W. H. Auden*

Introduction to Political Unification Revisited*

————•◆•————

1. TOWARD A NEW WORLD ARCHITECTURE?

Ever since I was a student, 50 years ago, references to world government or world community were dismissed as sheerly rhetorical, meaningless phrases or, worse, as naively idealistic. They were treated as off-the-wall notions held by a few dew-eyed visionaries, such as members of the United World Federalists and UN enthusiasts.

This long and much dismissed vision needs now to be seriously reexamined. The reasons for this are numerous, but most come down to new manifestations of an age-old problem, that of alienation. Ever since the beginning of modernization, "man" has unleashed technological and economic forces that were supposed to serve him but instead have lorded over him. Ever since, man has been trying to "come out on top," to develop political institutions that would allow his values to govern, but all such efforts have largely failed. All too often, instruments twist purposes rather than serving them.

Alienation's new form is the globalization of technological and economic forces that used to be mainly domestic. Collective self-determination, to the extent that it existed a generation ago, is increasingly threatened by transnational developments. Weapons of mass destruction (and installations to build them) are bought and sold across national borders. Hate materials banned in one country

* I am indebted to Andrew Volmert for numerous comments on previous drafts and for research assistance, as well as to Jason Marsh, and for very valuable criticism of a previous draft by Joel Rosenthal and to Alexander Wendt.

are easily reached via the Internet in others. Civil war in one country threatens others with massive immigration, which is difficult to curb by means democratic societies find tolerable. Crime is increasingly organized across state lines and is on the rise.[1] Women and children are sold into slavery for sex and forced labor.[2] National governments are helpless when a nuclear accident in Chernobyl rains radioactive material on their territories. A currency collapse in Russia, Thailand, or Indonesia rattles the financial markets of the world. A computer virus set loose in the Philippines causes worldwide disruptions. Supranational corporations shift capital and jobs from one nation to another, circumventing national policies.

Although these problems and others like them differ greatly from one another, they have one common denominator: the national institutions that are supposed to express people's preferences in these matters are woefully inadequate in coping with them. Alienation has become distinctly international.

How may we subject transnational processes to our collective or aggregated purposes? (By *collective purposes*, I mean shared worldwide goals such as stopping a plague; by *aggregated*, I mean goals that are at least initially national and even subnational but can be only or best served transnationally-trade, for instance.) Given that building any institution that even remotely resembles a national government and society on a global scale is demanding beyond what most people can imagine, before such an approach can even be seriously considered, we must first examine other possibilities.

2. THE OLD INTERNATIONAL SYSTEM IS OVERLOADED

Such an examination starts with asking whether the rising transnational problems may be handled the old system of intergovernmental relations, combining international efforts by single national governments, various joint efforts by such governments, and interna-

---

[1] National Intelligence Council, "Global Trends 2015: A Dialogue about the Future with Nongovernment Experts," December 2000.
[2] Joseph Kahn and Judith Miller, "Getting Tough on Gangsters, High Tech and Global," *New York Times*, 15 December 2000, A9.

tional organizations that are governed by national states. (For here on, the old system). However, even a cursory examination of the problems listed above strongly suggests that the old system is overloaded, that it is not well suited for a *high* and *rising* volume of *significant* activities. I will not examine the details of these problems because I consider the increase in transnational problems to be well established.

Although it is true that sometimes the old system does make some significant progress on one important front or another, especially on certain economic matters such as international trade and finance, it has makes little progress on many others (as the list introduced above serves to remind). I write *significant* because those keen to build a record of success point either to agreements on *relatively* insignificant matters, such as limiting the hunting of whales, or to limited agreements that address only one aspect of a major issue. For instance, the 1994 U.S. agreement with North Korea in which it agreed to stop developing nuclear weapons in exchange for two energy-providing nuclear reactors was hailed at the time as a significant step toward curbing proliferation. While such advances at the margin are often preferable compared to inaction, they should not be used to deny that the backlog of untreated and undertreated transnational problems is growing.

The main reasons the old system is increasingly inadequate are well known: it is too formal, too cumbersome, and too slow. Currently, worldwide policies are frequently formed through negotiations, via accredited diplomats or other national representatives, involving scores of nations, sometimes nearly two hundred in all. Diplomats must consult with and receive instructions from home-based authorities (the State Department, the White House, or their equivalents in other countries).

To provide but one illustrative example: the WHO was concerned that due to the Internet people have access to all kinds of sites that represent themselves as medical sources but are highly misleading if not dangerous. It wanted to formulate some standards such sources would have to follow-worldwide. However, it soon realized that given the highly different ideas of what constitutes health and medical treatment, such a task was impossible to carry out. If this was the case for a relatively limited and innocuous issue, one can readily see what happens when the nations of the world have to agree about matters of greater complexity and import.

Moreover, when agreements finally are reached, they are often not honored or are openly breached; the mechanisms for enforcement often either do not exist or are themselves cumbersome, slow, weak, and able to carry only a small volume of traffic. The argument may be made that intergovernmental efforts to promote trade have worked quite well.[3] However, one should note that trade is different in character from most other transnational issues,[4] and it would be a mistake to generalize from the experience of trade treaties to other transnational organizations.[5]

3. "GOVERNANCE WITHOUT GOVERNMENT"

In examining potential treatments for transnational problems other than the old system but less demanding than a world government, much attention has recently been paid to "governance without government",[6] especially to "nonstate" actors, in particular interna-

[3] Robert E. Hudec, *Enforcing International Trade Law: The Evolution of the Modern GATT Legal System* (Austin, Tex.: Butterworth Legal Publishers, 1991); Alec Stone Sweet, "The New GATT: Dispute Resolution and Judicialization of the Trade Regime," in Mary L. Volcansek, ed., *Law above Nations: Supranational Courts and the Legalization of Politics* (Gainesville: University of Florida Press, 1997): 118–141; Hudec, "The New WTO Dispute Settlement Procedure: An Overview of the First Three Years," *Minnesota Journal of Global Trade* 8 (Winter 1999): 1–53.

[4] A study of the special factors involved would take us far afield. Briefly trade seems to be supported by supranational corporations that have no similar investment in the treatment of many other problems, and it promises to pay off for all parties in relatively short order.

[5] The EU also had the fewest difficulties, although far from none, when it was largely a freer trade association, and this is still its strongest suit.

[6] See for instance James N. Rosenau and Ernst-Otto Czempiel, eds., *Governance without Government: Order and Change in World Politics* (Cambridge: Cambridge University Press, 1992); Oran R. Young, *Governance in World Affairs* (Ithaca, N.Y.: Cornell University Press, 1999); Thomas G. Weiss and Leon Gordenker, eds., *NGOs, the UN, and Global Governance* (Boulder, Colo.: Lynne Rienner Publishers, 1996); Wolfgang H. Reinicke, *Global Public Policy: Governing without Government?* (Washington, D.C.: Brookings Institution Press, 1998).

tional nongovernmental organizations (I-NGOs), which have grown rapidly since 1990, and transnational networks. Sometimes the term global civil society is used to refer to the evolving social fabric developed by these bodies, in clear distinction to a world state or government. In a few extreme expressions, governance without government is associated with the old dream of abolishing all states and replacing them with communitarian bonds and bodies. Most of the time, nonstate actors are merely expected to help significantly to deal with the transnational problems the old system seems unable to cope with.

There has been a fair measure of optimism as to the capabilities of nonstate actors. This position is so well captured in the following quote that it can stand for all others: Lester M. Salamon writes, "A striking upsurge is under way around the globe in organized voluntary activity and the creation of private, nonprofit or nongovernmental organizations. . . . The scope and scale of this phenomenon are immense. Indeed, we are in the midst of a global 'associational revolution' that may prove to be as significant to the latter twentieth century as the rise of the nation-state was to the latter nineteenth."[7] Salamon also writes that there is a "crisis of confidence in the capability of the state. Broad historical changes have thus opened the way for alternative institutions that can respond more effectively to human needs. With their small scale, flexibility and capacity to engage grass-roots energies, private nonprofit organizations have been ideally suited to fill the resulting gap. The consequence is a sweeping process of change . . ."[8]

The discussion turns next to examine the extent to which nonstate actors can fill the gap. It focuses on what I shall call transnational communitarian bodies (TCBs)-mainly I-NGOs, social movements, and public interest lobbies-because they tend to have a set of shared beliefs and affective bonds that binds their leaders and staff as well

[7] "The Rise of the Nonprofit Sector," *Foreign Affairs* 73 (July/August 1994): 109. See Jessica Mathews, "Power Shift," *Foreign Affairs* 76 (January/February 1997): 50–66; Peter Spiro, "New Global Communities: Nongovernmental Organizations in International Decision-Making Institutions," *Washington Quarterly* 18 (Winter 1995): 45–56; and James N. Rosenau, "Governance in the Twenty-first Century," *Global Governance* 1 (Winter 1995): 13–43.
[8] "The Rise of the Nonprofit Sector": 110.

as some of their members. That is, they have some of the attributes
of real, or at least imagined, communities. I avoid discussing transnational corporations and trade associations because they are largely
part of that which needs to be treated rather than a source of treatment if the goal is to find ways for political and normative choices
to control the use of technological and economic means.

Because TCBs are familiar, I only discuss them briefly, with an
eye toward evaluating rather than describing them. I cannot stress
enough that the examples given next seek to illustrate the points
made and to remind the reader of widely known information rather
than to prove anything.

Before I proceed, a general comment. Historically, much has been
made of the role of (domestic) civil society in protecting citizens
from excessive intrusion by the state, and ensuring that the state will
not weaken communities, voluntary associations, and families by
preempting their functions. In short, civil society has been viewed
largely as a counterweight to a potentially overpowering state.

Less has been made in recent work (unlike the work of earlier
social philosophers) of the benefits that civil society derives from the
state. This is true, in part, because it is obvious that society benefits
from the state, for instance by curbing intergroup and interpersonal
violence. It also reflects the fact that there are relatively few empirical studies that examine the relationship between a community's
ability to rely on its norms and informal controls and the availability
of laws and public authorities to back up these communal norms and
controls. Especially in view of past totalitarianism and authoritarian-
ism, more attention has been paid to protecting society from the state
than to the state's nurturing of civil society.

In discussing the evolving global civil society, it is worth keeping
in mind that domestic civil society does benefit from and rely upon
the state. This suggests that there may be considerable limitations to
how far global civil society can evolve without a global state.

A. I-NGOs

A critical assessment of I-NGOs suggests that while they can and
do help handle several transnational problems, they very often rely

on getting more mileage out of the old system, which ultimately limits what they can deliver.

I-NGOs have been particularly effective in setting transnational agendas, mobilizing public opinion in general and that of concerned groups in particular, acting as public interest groups that lobby various international organizations and thus act as an important counterweight to private interest lobbies, and developing transnational values and norms. Note, though, that most of these activities are aimed at changing public policies (i.e., those of the state), seeking to activate the state where it is neglectful and to monitor its work rather than carrying out the tasks themselves. And this means that there must be a state to act on. The typical targets of I-NGOs are most often national states (for instance, pushing them to endorse a treaty banning landmines) or international organizations (for instance, pushing the WHO to pay more attention to AIDS). But here we come full circle: these are the old systems that are unable to cope with rising transnational problems. Flogging them does some good, but it cannot make up for the absence of a supranational authority and welfare state.

The same holds when I-NGOs work as the kernel of a protest movement that raises the public consciousness and changes people's values, at which they can be very effective. However, their work is often much more consequential if it results in institutionalization, in the enactment of new laws and court rulings and action by government agencies. Such institutionalization is the key reason the environmental, civil rights, and women's movements have been so effective. However, when there are no transnational institutions that can enact and enforce the needed laws and no new such agencies can be created-that is, when these movements try to work transnationally without some form of transnational govern*ment*-their longer-run effectiveness is limited. They tend to dissipate or fall back on the overloaded old system.

In addition to activating the state, NGOs can handle some problems on their own or make significant contributions to their resolutions. For instance, Benjamin Barber points to a movement to affix "Good Housekeeping seals" to food (e.g., dolphin-safe tuna) and rugs (made without child labor).[9] And when a natural disaster strikes, I-NGOs (working with local organizations) can take care of the victims and their families. However, typically the situation is akin to the domestic welfare *state:* I-NGOs cannot take over its duties but only some of its burdens. Thus, as important as voluntary firefighters are in the United States, they cannot do the job without state resources and state-paid firefighters. The same holds internationally: Doctors Without Borders does a very commendable job, but it cannot begin to tackle all that cries out for service. In short, these communitarian bodies can be important partners with the state but cannot replace it, and hence when they are supposed to govern (transnationally) without a government, they lack the government partner.

In addition, I-NGOs as a rule cannot handle those matters that are the essence of the state's functions, matters dealing with legitimate use of violence (international courts, law enforcement, jails, peacekeeping, etc.), regulation, and revenue collection. They cannot deal directly with international drug traffic, terrorism, and people smuggling, among other issues. (I write "directly" because a case can be made that I-NGOs can deal with the root cause of these problems. But such treatments are at best slow, and it is as a rule far from sufficient unless direct treatment is also provided.)

Although it may be true that new technologies allow for flatter hierarchies and more sharing of information, there continue to be numerous issues in which decision making will continue to require differential application of power and force. This cannot be avoided in a world in which terrorists roam, armies march across borders, and women are smuggled across national boundaries to be locked into brothels.[10] This is not to suggest that one should overlook the importance of "soft" laws in international relations or of the rise of what are being called international "regimes" and norms. Although they can significantly reduce the burden on "hard" laws (and the powers needed to back them up), they cannot replace them and are themselves diminished if no such enforcement is available.

[9] Benjamin R. Barber, "Globalizing Democracy," *The American Prospect*, 11 September 2000, 16.

[10] Cf. Kenneth W. Abbott and Duncan Snidal, "Hard and Soft Law in International Governance," *International Organization* 54, no. 3 (2000): 421–456.

Also, I-NGOs cannot engage in peacekeeping activities, a major challenge for any international system. Mediation (for instance, of the kind provided by former president Jimmy Carter and his associates), informal meetings of opponents arranged by I-NGOs (for instance, a camp for Israeli and Palestinian youth in the United States), and education for peace are all of value but are far from being commensurate with the problems at hand.

And voluntary assessments cannot, in the long run, replace mandatory contributions and tax collections needed to finance supranational work. A comparison of the amounts of donations collected by UNICEF, CARE, and thousands of other such groups that provide foreign aid to the dues paid by governments to the UN, grants and loans provided by the World Bank and the IMF, and by national governments to third world countries, indicates the relatively limited scope of voluntary assessments. The relatively small amounts are significant in that they build a communitarian awareness of transnational needs, allow individuals and civic groups to express their commitments to helping others above and beyond what governments do, and add resources, but their scope is relatively small.

Lastly, many of the I-NGOs themselves are structured like international, not supranational, bodies. They have national "chapters" that pass resolutions and instruct their representatives on positions to be taken in international meetings, although these instructions generally are not as detailed or strict as those provided by national governments. (For example, the International Federation of Red Cross and Red Crescent Societies, which is one of the governing institutions of the International Red Cross, is composed of national delegations.) Negotiations among these representatives are not, on average, as complex and prolonged as those among governmental representatives, but they are typically quite burdensome, and slower and more complex than those among members of a supranational body. And, of course, the resolutions are neither truly binding nor enforceable.

All said and done: I-NGOs can handle some transnational tasks on their own; they can help in discharging others by prodding national states and international organizations to change course and act more vigorously. However, without some new transnational authority and resources, they have little to work with but the authority and resources already available in the old system. (To sharpen the point, imagine that the UN were a true world government that could collect taxes and issue regulations above and beyond those provided by the national states.)

I do not mean to denigrate the work of I-NGOS. Acts that save human lives, even if the number is small compared to those endangered, or provide relief during major disasters, and so on, are worthy and commendable. But they also serve to highlight-if one examines the totality of the need in whatever issue is being faced-how much remains uncovered, unregulated, unserved. And the question stands: how are these to be better attended to?

B. TRANSNATIONAL NETWORKS

Another form transnational governance is reported to take is transnational networks. In these, civil servants, experts, and select policy makers from several countries form *informal* networks, which entail a measure of interpersonal bonding and provide a reference group against which participants can measure their own performance and that commands some loyalty.[11] (Hence, up to a point, the network's priorities may trump participants' commitments to those of their own nation.) These networks can ease the pressure of transnational work, as when police officers of various countries exchange more information than they are supposed to, work around official policies that are less accommodating to what members of the network believe ought to be done, and so on. (Among those who have depicted such networks are Wolfgang H. Reinicke and Peter Evans.)[12]

Such networks seem helpful on the face of it, but so far there is little evidence that they can handle significant issues on their own. Studies of these networks typically point to their undeniable merits in facilitating the exchange of information, enhancing cooperation, and so on, but there seems to be very little documentation that these

[11] Robert O. Keohane and Joseph S. Nye, "Transgovernmental Relations and International Organizations," *World Politics* 27 (October 1974): 39–62.

[12] Wolfgang H. Reinicke, "The Other World Wide Web: Global Public Policy Networks, *Foreign Policy*, Winter 1999/2000: 44–57; Peter Evans, "Fighting Marginalization with Transnational Networks: Counter-Hegemonic Globalization," *Contemporary Sociology* 29, no. 1 (2000): 230–241.

networks can step in and cope with matters that are too difficult for other institutions to handle. Thus, while there is anecdotal evidence that here or there smugglers of drugs or sex slaves or illegal immigrants have been caught because of informal cooperation among the agents of various nations, few claim that as a result this traffic has been curtailed. Moreover, while such networks may to some extent soften or harden national policies, they are basically limited to working within the framework of these policies and within the old system, which limits their contributions.

Some scholars envision stronger versions of these networks that amount to "transgovernmental" agencies-a transnational agency for fighting terrorism, for public health, for human rights, and so on-but without a crowning government, without an elected prime minister or president, and without being accountable to and overseen by any elected transnational parliament. (This view is sometimes referred to as "functionalist.")[13]

Because these transnational agencies would be composed of national agencies and networks of representatives of the various national governments, they would face difficulties similar to those now evident in the WHO, the ILO, and other such organizations. (Indeed, because they would have greater duties, they could only encompass, at best, a small number of countries that already shared a considerable body of interests and values. Examples given by Slaughter include the Basle Committee of Central Bankers and cooperation between the Antitrust Division of the U.S. Department of Justice and the EU's European Commission.[14] Reports on the enormous difficulties NATO faced during the 1999 bombing campaign against Yugoslavia when 19 representatives of the 19 member nations had to agree on specific military issues, such as expanding the target list, a relatively straightforward matter, illustrate the point at hand.)

Transnational bodies that are built on and around the old government-based system are either limited in the significance and volume of the missions they can undertake, or in the number and variety of

[13] See David Mitrany, *A Working Peace System* (London: Royal Institute of International Affairs, 1943).
[14] Slaughter, "The Real New World Order," *Foreign Affairs* 76 (September/October 1997), 190.

the nations they can encompass. (Making non-binding and unen-
forceable decisions, which are treated mainly as expressions of sentiment, falls into the first category, of having limited significance.)

*   *   *

Taken together, transnational bodies and various kinds of networks so far have been unable to cope with transnational problems
as is evident from their continued increase. It might be said that even
well-formed nation-states have been unable to solve many domestic
problems, from drug abuse to curbing the spread of HIV. Indeed,
for that reason I systematically avoided the term *solving* of social
problems. They are almost never solved. But well-formed nation-
states-which often do a rather poor job on numerous social fronts-
have been much more effective than the stateless transnational system. Reallocation of wealth, for instance, which is meager domestically, is minuscule internationally. Curbing HIV by national public
health authorities in well-formed nation-states has not been highly
effective, but much more than attempts to prevent its flow from nation to nation and to provide international help to countries that are
unable to cope with it on their own. Most important, a point to which
I shall return below, a major reason nation-states' capacities are woefully insufficient is that problems are handled nation by nation rather
than globally. But the old system, even augmented by various nonstate actors, often does not come close to what nation-states were able
to do, which was far from adequate.

4. SUPRANATIONALITY: SMALL STEPS TOWARD A NEW WORLD ARCHITECTURE

To round off this review of recent attempts to cope with rising
transnational problems and the inadequacies of the old system, I turn
to examine supranational bodies that are constructed, in part or in
whole, on a fundamentally different set of principles than both the
old intergovernmental system and the transnational communitarian
bodies (the TCBs). I first deal with matters of definition; then I review existing limited supranational bodies; then I review the great
difficulties in developing full-blown supranationality; the discussion

turns next to explore whether an intermediary level of supranationality (higher than limited but lower than full) can be stabilized, trying to learn from the most advanced supranational body, the European Union; the discussion closes with an examination of questions concerning democratization of global bodies.

A. SUPRANATIONALITY DEFINED

It is useful to think about supranationality as a composite of several elements. Hence one cannot only have more of each element but also a body that contains a larger number of elements. One "supranational" element is decision making carried out by a governing body not composed of national representatives, a body that follows its own rules, policies, and values rather than being "instructed" by national governments. (For an institution to qualify as supranational, its decisions must concern significant matters because all international organizations can make some minor decisions on their own, as long as they fall within the boundaries and limits set by the governments represented.) This often allows them to move with more agility and speed than international organizations.

Another element is that the nations encompassed by these entities-as well as their citizens and member-units such as corporations and labor unions-are expected to follow the rulings by these bodies (rather than requiring separate decisions by the national governments whose people are affected). In addition, supranational bodies may have some kind of effective enforcement capacity of their own, such as the ability to fine corporations within the member states directly or order them to desist from some action rather than fine the governments or ask them to rein in the corporations. That is, they have more bite than networks or NGOs. To put it differently, supranationality presumes some surrender of sovereignty by the member nations.

Supranational bodies differ from TCBs in that they have several if not all of the powers of a state. These may include the abilities to raise taxes, enact laws and enforce them, sign treaties, and so on.

B. LIMITED SUPRANATIONAL INSTITUTIONS

An example of a supranational institution is the International Criminal Tribunal for the former Yugoslavia at The Hague, where judges rule on cases not on the basis of specific or general instructions from individual nations but based on international law.[15] Rulings do not require approval of individual nations. The court has enforcement powers including the imprisonment of those convicted of crimes against humanity.[16] (I am not suggesting that the court is fully neutral; it may reflect Western values and powers or those of democratic societies. To be supranational does not mean to be without a normative or political profile, but rather not to have one that is tied to the specific values and instructions of the nations involved.)[17]

Some scholars characterize the WTO as a supranational body. For instance, Alec Stone Sweet concludes his examination of the WTO with the statement: "More generally, it can be argued that the WTO is a supranational constitutional polity and that the SAB [Standing Appellate Body] is nothing less than a [supranational] constitutional court."[18] He elaborates, "The SAB['s] . . . function is to interpret and apply fixed norms of reference. These norms are supranational, and they take precedence in any conflict with national norms."[19]

Others have viewed the WTO as only partially supranational, suggesting that it often acts more like a traditional intergovernmental body. For instance, Mary L. Volcansek argues that the WTO judicial structure has only some of the characteristics of a supranational

[15] Radmila May, "The Yugoslav War Crimes Tribunal: Part Two," *Contemporary Review* 275, (October 1999): 174–179.

[16] Sean D. Murphy, "Progress and Jurisprudence of the International Criminal Tribunal for the Former Yugoslavia," *The American Journal of International Law* 93 (January 1999): 57–97.

[17] For other developments in international laws and courts and in their relationships with national laws and courts see Joseph H. H. Weiler, "The Democracy Deficit of Transnational Governance: What Role for Technology?" presented at the International Political Science Association congress in Quebec City, August 1–5, 2000. For a detailed discussion of the importance of enforcement capabilities of supranational bodies, their development in the EU, and the implications for world courts, see Anne-Marie Slaughter and Laurence R. Helfer, "Toward a Theory of Effective Supranational Adjudication," *Yale Law Journal* 107 (November 1997): 273–328; and also Slaughter, "Fourtieth Anniversary Perspective: Judicial Globalization," *Virginia Journal of International Law* 40 (Summer 2000): 1103–1123; Slaughter, "The Real New World Order"; William J. Aceves, "Liberalism and International Legal Scholarship: The Pinochet Case and the Move Toward a Universal System of Transnational Law Litigation," *Harvard International Law Journal* 41, no. 1 (2000): 129–184; Volcansek, ed., *Law above Nations*.

[18] "The New GATT," 139.

[19] Ibid.

court.[20] She concludes that it is sitting "at the margins" of supranationality.[21] In addition, the WTO General Council and Ministerial Conferences are less supranational than WTO judicial bodies because they are composed of national representatives. However, these bodies are supranational in that their decisions are binding on national governments. Scholars generally accord the WTO at least some supranational features.

ICANN (the Internet Corporation for Assigned Names and Numbers) is often characterized as a supranational body and one that has been quite effective in facilitating the Internet in select matters.[22] Transnational business associations, such as the International Chamber of Commerce, are somewhat supranational in that the commercial codes they formulate and commercial arbitration they provide, while voluntarily agreed to by industry, have become, through laws or norms, somewhat authoritative. The EU supranational authorities are much more encompassing in scope and require separate treatment, which is given below.

These bodies have made significant contributions, but still limited ones. To give but one example, the UN's International Criminal Tribunal for the former Yugoslavia is limited to dealing with the cases emanating out of the former Yugoslavia, and the International Criminal Tribunal for Rwanda is similarly limited to cases from Rwanda. This leaves most crimes against humanity outside these courts' jurisdictions. Attempts to form the International Criminal Court that the Rome Conference laid the foundation for in 1998 have been stalled.

* * *

There are two basic different ways to view these limited supranational bodies. One is to view them as self-standing attempts to supplement the old system and attend to those numerous tasks neither TCBs nor networks can cope with. If viewed in this way, the question of

---

[20] "Supranational Courts in a Political Context," in *Law Above Nations*, ed. Volcansek, 1–19.

[21] Ibid, 3.

[22] It is not clear to what extent ICANN is truly supranational. According to the former chairman of ICANN's board of directors, Esther Dyson, many of the board members were chosen by their national governments and instructed closely as to which positions to take (private communications with Dyson, 1/1/01).

the legitimacy of these bodies arises, especially if they are effective, because they are not accountable to anyone. To the extent that they are supranational, they are not accountable to national representatives (and hence at least indirectly to their parliaments and electorates), nor to any supranational electorate. Moreover, they directly challenge national sovereignty and democracy at the national level.

Another view is to see these supranational bodies as building blocks for a new world architecture that would have some form of accountability to some kind of world parliament, to global public opinion, and to transnational parties and interest groups. But this raises the question of what such a full-blown supranational body would entail and, above all, what would be required to stabilize it.

c. The Extraordinary Prerequisites for Full Supranationality

My analysis of the prerequisites of full supranationality draws on the observations about four attempts to absorb nations into encompassing supranational entities that provide the body of this book, as well as many other case studies and analyses cited below. The findings basically are that to form full-fledged supranational unions (a term I use to refer to the combination of a supranational government and a community) requires three capabilities on the supranational level: legitimate control of the means of violence, which must exceed that of the member units; allocation of resources among the member units; and command of political loyalties that exceed those accorded to member units. The three are additive in the sense that each requires the other two and all three are required to form a stable supranational union.

The availability of these three capabilities goes to the heart of current limitations of transnational bodies. If the rulings of a supranational body cannot be enforced unless they are endorsed by national governments-if a supranational body cannot implement its policies independently of national governments, or cannot command sufficient resources to produce significant effects-then its ability to deal with transnational problems more effectively than old-fashioned international bodies will be greatly impaired. The same holds for loyalties; if the people of various nations regularly side with their nation when a conflict arises between it and the supranational body, this greatly hinders what the body can accomplish and undermines its stability. Moreover, the three capabilities are interrelated: weak enforcement capability or a weak ability to provide resources undermines loyalty, and weak loyalty is a major reason that the ability to enforce and reallocate is limited (at least as long as we are dealing with relatively democratic entities rather than with empires).

According to this analysis, what is required to attain full supranationality is not merely split and layered sovereignty but for the supranational layer to "crown" the national entities encompassed, in the sense that in a case of conflict between the layers, the supranational layer will trump the national layers. Not to mince words, the findings in the body of this book suggest that the structure of a full-fledged supranational union must be that of a federation (rather than a confederation or some looser form of constitutional relations) and that loyalties to the supranational community must be stronger than those to the member national communities when these two come into conflict. (I add this last provision because not all federations per se meet the third criterion, of commanding superior loyalty.)

There are a considerable number of sociological assumptions behind the preceding statement that need not be spelled out here. Basically, it is assumed that intracommunity processes deeply affect political loyalties. (As Alexander Wendt puts it, "without changes in identity the most we can expect is behavioral cooperation, not community.")[23] Hence, when communities consider a government not to be legitimate or are loyal to other political authorities that conflict with the government in question-whether this loyalty is to a foreign government, to a lower, local level of government; or to some other body, whether religious or ideological-the government in question will be unable to command the three capabilities needed for a stable union. Or, in the terms used here, there must be considerable overlap between community and government to make for a stable national as well as supranational polity.

The United States for instance, was from the beginning a federation, but until after the Civil War did not command superior political

[23] Alexander Wendt, "Collective Identity Formation and the International State," *American Political Science Review* 88, no. 2 (1994): 384.

loyalty.[24] Similarly, a lower level of bonding, as the findings in this book suggest, did not suffice to contain divisive centrifugal forces in other unions. Since the cases encompassed in this book were studied, other examples have arisen. The USSR long controlled the means of violence and economic means of its 15 member republics in much more force and completeness than any of those supranational governments studied here, but its inability to command the loyalty of the people of these republics became one major reason, arguably the reason, that these republics chose to break away from the USSR when its government weakened.

Similarly, the absence of such loyalty destroyed Yugoslavia despite the fact that, at the end of the Tito regime, it had full control of the military, the police, and the courts as well as a very considerable ability to reallocate resources. The main reason Québec was considering pulling out of Canada was not Canada's lack of control of the means of violence or an inability to reallocate resources, but because Anglo-dominated Canada does not command sufficient loyalty from many of the people in Franco-dominated Québec. Israel long controlled the means of violence and the economy of the West Bank, but not the loyalty of its Palestinian community, with obvious results. Hence, as demanding as this requirement is, the thesis of this book is that without forming a supranational community in the full sense of this term, rather than merely a supranational government, it is impossible to sustain full-fledged supranational unions with the ability to cope with problems as nations once were able to do. The bar that must be cleared to form a stable world government is indeed set very high.

5. THE EU AS A TEST CASE OF HALFWAY SUPRANATIONALITY[25]

Given that full supranational integration of even two nations, let alone a larger group, is very difficult to achieve, and limited suprana-

---

[24] Lawrence Lessig, *Code and Other Laws of Cyberspace* (New York: Basic Books, 1999), 225–226.

[25] For general reading on the EU, see William James Adams, ed., *Singular Europe: Economy and Polity of the European Community after 1992* (Ann Arbor: University of Michigan Press, 1992); Robert Keohane and Stanley Hoff-

tionality is woefully insufficient, one is bound to revisit a question
this book raised some 36 years ago: can "halfway" integration suffice for coping with transnational problems, and is such a level of
integration sustainable? *Halfway integration* is defined as giving the
nations involved full or nearly full autonomy in some important matters while providing full or nearly full control to a supranational
authority on other important matters.

The findings reported in this book show that two of the four attempts to form supranational states, the United Arab Republic and
the Federation of the West Indies, did not develop to any significant
extent any of the three capabilities the theory suggested are needed
for such an integration to be stable. As expected, both collapsed in
short order. The third attempt, the Nordic Council, developed only
low integrative capabilities but survived by doing little transnational
work, leaving high autonomy to the member nations in practically
all matters.

The fourth case, and by far the most relevant one for the issue at
hand, was the European Coal and Steel Community, the precursor of
the EU. From the viewpoint of the hypothesis advanced here, and
for all interested in designing halfway supranational states, the EU
provides the most telling experiment. The EU is trying to largely
integrate the economies of the different nations involved, but at least
for the near future basically maintain their political independence. If
such a halfway integration could be stabilized, it might well be preferred to the much more onerous task of forming a full-fledged supranational European Union.

To put it metaphorically, can the EU, as a developing, supranational community, stand *between two steps*? Can it maintain a level
of integration that falls between a low level of integration limited
to a few sectors (e.g., trade and cultural exchanges) and full union
(integration of the national political structures and the formation of
a core of communal values and bonds. I refer to a core because a full

---

man, eds., *The New European Community: Decisionmaking and Institutional
Change* (Boulder, Colo.: Westview Press, 1991); Alberta Sbragia, ed., *Euro-
Politics: Institutions and Policymaking in the "New" European Community*
(Washington, D.C.: Brookings Institution, 1992); Dennis Swann, ed., *The Single
European Market and Beyond: A Study of the Wider Implications of the Single
European Act* (New York: Routledge, 1992).

integration of the political culture is not needed even for a full-blown supranational union).[26]

What I mean by this metaphor is that obviously nations can sustain a low level of integration, that there are no apparent internal contradictions in such a limited cross-national bonding, say, the way the Nordic countries or the Benelux ones related to one another before the formation of the EU. Also, if a group of nations manages to merge into one encompassing community (as the colonies did in the United States and cities and regional states did in Germany and Italy),[27] clearly this high level of integration can be sustained. The question the EU now faces is whether it is possible to supranationalize quite fully only several *important* sectors (especially related to the free flow of goods and services, to capital and labor, and to financial policy), while keeping political integration at a rather low level. (This very issue was explicitly raised in the summer of 2000 in a public exchange between the Germans and the French. Germany's foreign minister, Joschka Fischer, called for a fully integrated "federalist" Europe [a United States of Europe] while the French warned against this. Jean Pierre Chevenement, France's interior minister, accused Germany of having imperialistic ambitions and trying to establish a new Holy Roman Empire. Although the French government backed off from such harsh language, it continued to oppose any path to a European federation, with Prime Minister Jacques Chirac calling Fischer's suggestion divisive.)[28]

To explore this question, one must separate those who genuinely believe that integration can be stabilized at a halfway level in the long run and those who realize that their ultimate goal must be full integration but believe that it is necessary not to acknowledge it so openly. The latter are concerned that the numerous people who iden-

[26] For discussion of this point, see Amitai Etzioni, "Pluralism within Unity," Chapter 7 of *The New Golden Rule: Community and Morality in a Democratic Society* (New York: Basic Books, 1996): 189–216.

[27] Note though that neither of the entities involved was a nation in the full sense of the term and that in all cases force was used in bringing about the merger or sustaining it.

[28] Denis Staunton, "Fischer Denies German Vision of a Federal Europe Is a Form of Imperialism," *Irish Times*, 22 June 2000, World News, 13; John Lichfield, "Chirac Spurns 'Divisive' German Vision of European Federation," *The Independent* (London), 31 May 2000, Foreign News, 18.

tify with their nation will strongly oppose even economic integration if they fear it will lead to loss of political sovereignty. Hence their strategy is to proceed with economic integration and hope that it by itself will lead their people to be willing to embrace political integration or make such integration inevitable, without acknowledging this or forming a consensus up front. I next explore first why *halfway integration in my view cannot be stabilized* and then why *the process of fuller integration must involve open and inclusive consensus building.*

The basic reason halfway, mainly economic, integration is not sustainable is that the libertarian model is erroneous. Society is not composed of individuals seeking to maximize their pleasure or profit, and society will not, as libertarians suggest, naturally gravitate to a system that, by rationalizing the allocation of economic resources, will enhance those individuals' income and wealth. Nor are markets self-controlling (guided by an invisible hand).

The first quite elementary point is that people are not merely traders and consumers but also citizens whose sense of self is involved in their nation. Hence, when economic integration that benefits their pocketbook threatens their national identity, people will tend to balk. (The exact level of economic integration at which nationalist opposition rises to a level sufficient to undermine that economic integration depends on numerous factors, including how strong national identity is to begin with and when people realize that higher levels of economic integration undermine their nation's ability to guide its own policies.)

Moreover, halfway integration, especially high economic integration combined with low political integration, cannot be sustained because markets-and, more generally, economies-are not freestanding systems with their own distinct dynamics but are integrally tied to the polity and society of which they are a part. Indeed, economies cannot function well without the capsule provided by political institutions and societal values and bonds.[29] Moreover, in free societies, major economic policy decisions must be made in line with a na-

[29] Amitai Etzioni, "In Conclusion: Policy and Moral Implications," Chapter 14 of *The Moral Dimension: Toward a New Economics* (New York: Free Press, 1988): 237–51.

tion's values and politically worked-out consensus-or by other institutions that have acquired the legitimacy previously commanded by the national institutions. Otherwise the sense of alienation will increase to a level that will endanger the sustainability of the regime.

One may argue that, despite various delays and setbacks, the economic integration of the EU has proceeded to ever higher levels with little political integration and even less formation of a shared creed. However, opposition to integration has been growing recently, as seen in the refusal of countries such as Britain and Denmark to adopt the euro, in Ireland's 2001 rejection of the Nice treaty, and in a recent anti-EU petition in Austria, intended to force a referendum on EU membership, that collected almost 200,000 signatures.[30] More indirectly, this opposition is one force that propels numerous and rising right-wing groups in many EU members.

In addition, some special historical conditions that favored the EU are unlikely to persist, and in effect are already changing. Until the turn of the century, the creed of one of the two major powers in the EU, Germany, was strongly "European" and antinational and hence abnormally supportive of the EU. However, roughly since the advent of the new century, Germany has been moving to view itself as and demand to be treated as a "normal" national-state, and hence one must assume that in the future it will be more insistent that its values and preferences be taken into account. France, the other major power, favored the EU as long as, in effect, France dominated it and the EU helped protect France from German hegemony. However, it always maintained a strong nationalist policy. In short, the special conditions that tolerated a high level of economic integration combined with a low level of political integration are eroding.

Moreover, so far the level of economic integration has not been as high as has often been claimed. While the liberalization of trade and the coordination of fiscal policy have been quite extensive, the proportion of nations' budgets controlled by the EU is still very small. In the year 2000, the ceiling on the EU budget was a mere

[30] Allan Hall, "Austrian Bid to Drop Out of EU," *The Scotsman*, 30 November 2000, 13; Michael Leidig, "Austrian Anti-EU Group Forces Debate by MPs," *Daily Telegraph* (London), 8 December 2000, 20.

1.27 percent of members' gross domestic product.[31] This is of special importance because high proportions of national GDP are processed by the national governments (on average, taxes and social costs in the EU compose 42.4 percent of national GDP).[32] However, by the year 2000, the EU was moving closer to the level of economic integration at which the unsustainability of halfway integration will be tested. Can it continue to extend its economic integration without developing a higher level of political integration? Or will it be pushed back to lower levels of economic integration?

To avoid a misunderstanding: the argument advanced here is not that the EU is not politically integrated at all. After all, there is a European Parliament, a Commission, a Council of Ministers, a European flag, and some other shared symbols. However, the powers of these institutions and symbols are very limited compared to the national ones, by practically any measure. The European Parliament is weak compared to the far-from-powerful national ones; the Commission is weak compared to the national governments; and the European flag evokes little sentiment among most people. That is, they do not meet the important crowning criterion of supranationality-that the supranational layer be stronger than the national one.

Also important is that these European bodies are largely international ones and not truly supranational ones. The Commission is composed of national representatives. Although, theoretically, the transnational parties of the Parliament represent like-minded Europeans across national lines regarding European issues, in reality these parties are largely controlled by the national parties that compose them. These national parties are reported to "exploit" European elections for "immediate, domestic purposes"[33] rather than promote Europe-wide platforms. (This is not to deny that these transnational parties have made some strides in organizing national parties at the European level and in adapting to the structure of the

---

[31] Simon Serfaty, "Europe 2007: From Nation-States to Member States," *The Washington Quarterly* 23, no. 4 (2000): 19.

[32] Dan Bilefsky, "Belgian Budget Prioritises Cuts in Tax and Social Costs," *Financial Times*, 19 October 2000, World News, 10.

[33] Thomas Jansen, *The European People's Party: Origins and Development*, trans. Barbara Steen (New York: St. Martin's Press, 1998), 19.

EU.)[34] Although the European Parliament may be a bit more supra-national than the Commission and the Council of Ministers, it is not strongly so and is by far the weakest of the three bodies.

In short, while there is a measure of political integration, it is much lower than the level of economic integration. And for reasons already discussed and others to follow, while economic integration is growing, political integration may be about to retrogress.

As already mentioned, several European leaders seem to hold that the best way to achieve fuller integration is not to construct a supra-national political authority, say, through a constitutional assembly of the kind that preceded the formation of the United States, but rather to continue to increase economic integration. This, it is said, would lead numerous groups within each nation to realize that their inter-ests have become supranational rather than simply national, and hence gradually to shift their lobbying, politicking, and loyalties to the supranational union and its institutions. Thus, gradually, instead of national governments vying over EU policies, it is envisioned that the farmers of several countries, federations of European labor unions, and coalitions of EU industrialists would vie with one an-other. This in turn would pressure the EU to develop more EU-wide political powers to work out these differences, which in turn would build the legitimacy of an EU government. Call it a syndicalist inte-gration leading to a full-fledged supranational one. The idea is, in-stead of a frontal attack and a bold attempt to jump from many nations into a United States of Europe that would face the full brunt of nationalist opposition, allow processes to unfold gradually, ac-cording people time to adjust to the new supranational realities and for their new loyalties to evolve.

The fact is, though, that such a syndicalist integration is occurring only to a surprisingly limited degree. Most times, farmers, workers, and businesses find it more effective to lobby their national govern-

---

[34] Christopher Lord, introduction to *Transnational Parties in the European Union*, ed. David S. Bell and Christopher Lord (Aldershot, England: Ashgate, 1998), 5; Julie Smith, "How European Are European Elections," in *Political Parties and the European Union*, ed. John Gaffney (London: Routledge, 1996): 275–290.

ments for special considerations (farm subsidies, for instance) than to lobby the EU Commission, not to mention the EU Parliament.

The continued high level of national rather than syndicalist commitments was dramatized in the year 2000, when the EU leaders met to reconsider the unanimity rule in light of their plan to increase EU membership. The difficult negotiations were about how many votes each nation would be allotted-not each European party. (Indeed, if the main players were EU-wide interest groups, the number of votes allotted to each nation would be a relatively small matter, and the access of interest groups to EU legislators and the Commission would have been the key issue.) Moreover, the political integration scenario based on syndicalist integration ignores the fact that by itself syndicalization cannot provide the needed core of shared values, legitimacy, and consensus building. (See the discussion below of moral dialogues as to what is needed.)

All said and done, it is my hypothesis that halfway integration cannot be sustained and that the EU will either have to move to a high level of supranationality or fall back to a lower one. If it is true that regional communities cannot be integrated and stabilized unless they move to a high level of supranationality, the same may well hold for attempts to form a world union. This is *not* to argue that it is possible to obtain such a high level of integration on either the regional or the world level, only that halfway integration seems to be unsustainable. Ergo, if low levels of integration are insufficient for attaining the primacy of purposes over means, to curb alienation, then either we shall not effectively cope with transnational problems or we must find a way to attain a high level of supranationality.

With this conclusion in mind, and because the EU represents the most advanced attempt to form a true supranational community in more than fifty years, the question arises: what would it require for the EU to move to a higher level of supranationality, to achieve political integration? The major factors that agitate against community building in the EU are the absence of effective EU-wide moral dialogues and the commitment to increase the membership of the community before it is well solidified.

6. MORAL DIALOGUES ESSENTIAL FOR HIGHER SUPRANATIONALITY

Moral dialogues occur when a group of people engage in a process of sorting out the values that should guide their lives. They face questions such as: should the vision of a color-blind society or reverse discrimination shape our employment policies? Should society recognize gay marriages? Should the death penalty continue to be imposed? and so on. Moral dialogues are often messy, they meander and have no fixed beginnings or endings. Nevertheless, they often deeply affect people's beliefs and actions, what people consider virtuous, and the habits of their heart.

Moral dialogues assume that societies need shared formulations of the good and that they cannot function on the basis of only negotiated settlements of differences among individual and subgroup formulations of the good. Moreover, moral dialogues concern values and are not merely deliberations over empirical facts or the logic of a position.[35] Moral dialogues are not only a matter of reasonable people coming to terms, but of people of divergent convictions finding a common normative ground.

It is easy to demonstrate that such dialogues take place constantly in well-formed national societies, which most democracies are, and that frequently they result (albeit sometimes only after prolonged dialogues) in a new affirmed direction for the respective societies. For instance, in the United States, we have had intensive moral dialogues on environmentalism, civil rights, and welfare policy. While Americans continue to debate differences over details of these public policies, the basic orientation has shifted following these dialogues.

But can moral dialogues take place transnationally and to what effect? Moral dialogues occurring across national lines are much more limited in scope, intensity, conclusion, and effect than intranational ones. Nevertheless, they begin to provide a thicker shared moral base, political culture, and legitimacy for supranational institutions than currently exist. For example, there are transnational dia-

---

[35] For a justification of this point, see Etzioni, *New Golden Rule*, 102–104, 227–31.

logues about the extent to which "we" ought to respect the environment. True, such dialogues are affected by numerous nonnormative considerations, often dressed up as normative claims. However, dialogues do affect what people of different nationalities consider morally appropriate. Thus, one reason most countries try to avoid being perceived as environmentally irresponsible is that they do not wish to be seen as acting illegitimately in the eyes of nations other than their own.[36] (Indeed, transnational moral dialogues occur on three levels: should the people of one culture "judge" those of others? If yes, which values should guide such judgments? And what means should be employed beyond speech and symbolic gestures to undergird these values? Thus, some who opposed Saddam Hussein's regime or the ethnic cleansing of Kosovo still opposed the economic sanctions imposed on Iraq and the bombing of Serbia.)

Although there have been exchanges among the intellectual and political elites about the need for a European supranational community since World War II, the public at large has not been deeply engaged. As a result, there is no public acceptance of a core of shared European values, nor is there a sense that Europe's shared political institutions would be legitimate if their role were expanded. One of the reasons that the right wing's influence is rising in several European countries is that the pace of unification is more rapid than is supported by the public.[37] Simon Serfaty refers to a "top down" integration.[38] And, one may add, the dialogue about unification has not reached very far down. In effect, the opposite has happened. The Commission's legitimacy, insofar as it has any, has been diminished by charges of corruption, nepotism, and undemocratic conduct, and the EU Parliament has acquired a reputation for being highly ineffectual.

The rulings by the European Court of Justice illustrate both the limits of the EU's supranationality and the lack of sufficient moral

[36] Gareth Porter and Janet Welsh Brown, *Global Environmental Politics* (Westview Press: 1996), 69–105; Beth Simmons, "International Law and State Behavior: Commitment and Compliance in International Monetary Affairs," *American Political Science Review* 94, no. 4 (2000): 819–835.

[37] See Timothy Garton Ash, *History of the Present: Essays, Sketches, and Dispatches from Europe in the 1990s* (New York: Random House, 1999).

[38] Serfaty, "Europe 2007," 19.

dialogues. The Court has been engaging in judicial activism, in effect making social policy on numerous issues about which the EU government has not passed legislation. And national judges have increasingly drawn on rulings by the Court of Justice in their deliberations and rulings.

Because the Court's rulings are based on its own deliberations rather than on national representation, it is truly a supranational court. At the same time, it has a very limited capacity to monitor and enforce its rulings; for these it must rely on national governments, which highlights the shortcomings of limited supranationality.

The initial result has been an "enforcement deficit"[39] in which several EU members do not enforce the Court's rulings and citizens of those that do feel cheated. In reaction, the EU institutions have exerted growing pressure on the national governments to enforce more fully the Court's rulings, leading one expert to conclude these developments would result in federation building.[40] He compared the Court of Justice to the U.S. Supreme Court of the 1960s, which increased the federal government's role over the states in minting numerous rights (concerning affirmative action, the environment, and women's choice), which resulted in stronger federal power.

The comparison is a telling one, although the story being told is open to a different interpretation. To the extent that the increased centralism of the '60s was not prepared for or followed by moral dialogues through which the public came to support these actions-it led in the United States to a conservative countermovement. Gradually, a GOP-dominated Congress and a new conservative majority in the Supreme Court have reversed or thinned out many of the changes of the '60s. Hence one would expect that unless moral dialogues support the directions the Court of Justice is taking the EU, these moves will also face countermoves. Moreover, here they are more likely to take the form of opposing the very development of the EU's supranational powers, rather than of seeking to reverse specific policies established by these powers. There is, indeed, evidence of

---

[39] R. Daniel Kelemen, "Regulatory Federalism: EU Environmental Regulation in Comparative Perspective," *Journal of Public Policy* 20, (May-August 2000): 133–167.

[40] Kelemen, "Regulatory Federalism."

growing opposition to the supranational authority of the Court in response to its rulings on matters such as the introduction of the metric system in the United Kingdom.

The argument is not that the Court of Justice has no degree of freedom or is powerless. It can, indeed, rule on many individual issues and have its ruling heeded to some extent. However, when such rulings in accumulation offend people's deeply held values without moral dialogues to engage in and change these values, then sooner or later such an approach will backfire. It seems that by 2001, that sooner is no longer later.

Recently, much attention has been paid by students of international relations and legal scholars to the formation of transnational "norms,"[41] a term once largely the province of sociologists. Such a development is indeed occurring and has all the merits and difficulties that these scholars attribute to norms. One should, however, note that there are norms on at least two rather different levels: those that are limited to shared conceptions among judges and lawyers (and other elites),[42] and those also shared by the publics involved. Without the latter, there is no solid community building, and the latter will not mature without moral dialogues.

A major reason moral dialogues have not flourished in the EU community is that numerous political leaders have deliberately avoided them. Many leaders who may realize that political integration is unavoidable if a higher level of economic integration is to be sustainable believe that it is impolitic to openly acknowledge the need for political unification. The fact that international relations are often developed with much less transparency than domestic policies encourages politicians to posture and play to existing national prejudices rather than attempt to change them. The rise of nationalist opposition, both in a relatively moderate form (for instance, the opposition Tony Blair faced from the Tories when he ran for reelection in 2001) and in a stronger form from the rise of right-wing parties and leaders (in Italy, Austria, France, and Germany), has

[41] Amitai Etzioni, "Social Norms: The Rubicon of Social Science," in *The Monochrome Society* (Princeton, N.J.: Princeton University Press, 2001), 163–185.
[42] Helfer and Slaughter, "Toward a Theory of Effective Supranational Adjudication"; Slaughter, "Fourtieth Anniversary Perspective: Judicial Globalization."

made it better politics not to face head-on the issues raised by supra-national integration.

Indeed, many integrative steps were taken following deliberations that, in effect, took place behind closed doors, because they were conducted in highly complex and technical language, and the resulting agreements were similarly obscure. For instance, the Maastricht treaty, which created the European Union, is almost 250 pages long.[43] It was described by Jacques Chirac (then the leader of France's Rally for the Republic) as "abstruse, badly put together, long, complex, and ambiguous."[44]

To put it differently, while the first part of my thesis is that high levels of economic integration require the integration of political institutions and culture, the second part is that such integration cannot be attained merely by EU-wide functionalism (although it can be a helping factor) and that such integration is hindered by what often in effect amounts to closed decision making. A shared creed and legitimacy must be developed, and the only way to do so in an age in which the public cannot be excluded is via intensive and prolonged moral dialogues.

To push the point, I suggest that even if tomorrow the EU had a constitutional assembly and formed a democratic federation, emulating the founding assembly of the United States, moral dialogues would still be essential both for the assembly to succeed and for the people of Europe not to rebel against it. It should be noted that the American constitutional assembly occurred in a very small society, with a population smaller than quite a few single European cities now have. In addition, in those days, large segments of the population were not politically engaged. This is no longer the case.

All this is not to suggest that EU integration must cease until moral dialogues mature, only that they are currently the lagging element, that there is a severe moral dialogue deficit. My thesis is merely that the EU cannot allow the gap between economic, institutional, and judicial integration, on one hand, and moral integration,

[43] Larry Elliott, "Maastricht: That Treaty Explained," *The Guardian* (London), 17 May 1993, E9.
[44] Andrew Gumbel, "Mitterand Urged to Hold Referendum on Maastricht Treaty," *The Herald* (Glasgow), 16 April 1992, 4.

on the other, to grow much larger. Political integration entails more than institution building. Building the normative foundations of legitimacy is an inevitable part of the process.

One may argue that one cannot prove a positive by a negative; even if the EU atrophies or retreats, amounting to little more than a glorified trade union, this does not prove that political integration would have been possible, or that if it had been achieved it would have saved the EU. However, the experience of nations built out of previously autonomous political bodies in the United States, Germany, Italy, and several African countries adds a measure of credence to the thesis that full integration can be achieved and stabilized, although these nations arose under rather different historical conditions than the EU currently faces. In addition, whatever the future of the EU will teach us, so far there are no stable halfway integrations in any other region.

7. MEMBERSHIP SIZE: A FURTHER HINDRANCE

The EU grand experiment in supranational integration, of great importance in its own right and for those interested in community building among nations elsewhere, is greatly endangered, and its results will be further muddled (a great disadvantage of natural experiments as compared to laboratory ones) because the EU aims to *increase its membership* while it is trying to cope with the issues that arise from an attempt at political unification. This is a most unfortunate occurrence from the viewpoint of at least this sociologist. If there is an iron law of community building, it is that the larger the number of members, especially the more heterogeneous they are, the more difficult integration of any kind and especially of the political kind is. Moving from 15 to 27 nations may well be enough to severely threaten any supranational community already developed. The fact that the members to be added include several former communist states (and particularly hard-core ones such as Romania), a semi-Muslim state (Turkey), and several nations with rather different cultures from those prevailing in Western Europe, overburdens political integration to the point that it will be, at best, extremely challenging.

One could argue that not including more Eastern European nations in the EU community would have several disadvantages, ranging from creating hostile blocs to keeping these nations poorer. An examination of these claims would take us far afield, requiring the consideration of such questions as what truly makes for international hostility (note that democratic nations do not initiate war against one another) and for international inequality and how these conditions may be treated. But there is an essential fact that cannot be ignored: if the EU expands before its community is further solidified, there may well be no community to join. It comes down to the question of which risk one prefers, but whatever the conclusion, rapid expansion poses a threat to community building. Or, to put it the other way around: it is in the very nature of communities to exclude. It is both an unattractive and an unavoidable feature of these social creatures.

Also, to form a smaller community does not necessarily mean that there would be no attractive options for outsiders. They can form their own community, and two different (Eastern and Western) European communities could form a supra-association together. The Council of Europe is a very small step in that direction. (See below for additional discussion of building communities of communities.)

What holds for the EU holds for other budding regional communities. Nurturing moral dialogues and keeping the number of members small is crucial during their formative stage. Later I turn to the question of whether such "small" regional communities, presuming they will be fully supranational, will hinder the formation of a world community or serve as building blocks.

8. FACILITATING FACTORS

A. A FAMILIAR LIST

Although the task of building supranational communities on a regional or even more encompassing level is daunting at best, there are several developments that facilitate such community building.

As these have often been depicted, they are merely listed here for the completeness of the record and for balance. They include the development of English as a de facto lingua franca (approximately 1.6 billion people, almost one-third of the world's population, use English in some form),[45] the rise of worldwide communication systems, the great increase in international trade and travel, the development of worldwide news (e.g., CNN), and the already cited development of transnational civil and legal institutions and norms. Although these factors do not suffice to cope with transnational problems, they can facilitate the development of a worldwide government and global community.

Also, well-designed political institutions can ease the tensions created by new supranational governments. For instance, the creation of two parliamentary levels can help to provide small states some extra representation on one level, protecting them from the tyranny of the majority, while also helping protect on another level the more populated states from a tyranny of minorities. The values and interests of smaller states are protected in that way to some extent not only in the U.S. Senate and in the British House of Lords but also in effect in the UN Security Council, in the EU Commission, and in the complex directorate of the World Bank. The interests of the more populated states are better represented in the U.S. House, the UN General Assembly, and so on. Although all these institutional architectures are far from flawless, the bicameral conception can contribute to allaying some of the fears of increased supranationalization.

Another source of protection from new community-wide demands is provided by region-wide (European) and worldwide (UN) declarations of human rights, which increasingly acquire some of the power of constitutions. A major earmark of the specific communitarian position presented here is that it argues that a respect for universal individual (and minority) rights can be combined with a strong commitment to particularistic, community-specific, values.[46]

Also helpful from the viewpoint of easing the transition to fuller

[45] Joshua A. Fishman, "The New Linguistic Order," *Foreign Policy* 113 (Winter 1998–1999): 26.

[46] For more discussion, see Amitai Etzioni, "The Final Arbiters of Community's Values," Chapter 8 of *New Golden Rule*: 217–257.

supranationality is a particularly ingenious accommodating legal device, "mutual recognition," which the EU developed. Under this policy, various licences and degrees (e.g., M.D. and Ph.D.) from any member country are accorded full status in other EU countries as long as they meet some agreed-upon minimum standards. These are much easier to agree upon than having to agree what constitutes the proper basis for licences, degrees, titles, and so on.

B. A SPECIAL KIND OF SUBSIDIARITY

The concept of subsidiarity also eases the formation of supranational communities. Although a supranational community must possess the three "crowning" capabilities described earlier, it need not command full control of any of them. Indeed, it can delegate (or leave to begin with) considerable control in each of these areas to lower-level entities including national and local governments, communities, and voluntary associations. Supranational communities can provide a context, a framework, for a group of nations, but they need not seek to replace these states or to abolish their autonomy. Crowning, though, refers not to any and all kinds of subsidiarity, nor to any division of control or functions within a state, but to the capacity of the encompassing entity to have the final say in cases of conflict, no matter how much power and resources are delegated to the smaller entities encompassed.

The United States provides an illustrative example. Many powers and rights are reserved, by the Constitution, for the member states and are honored in numerous ways. The *Federal* Bureau of Investigation has not replaced the local and state police, and the U.S. military has not replaced the *National* Guard, which is state controlled. However, in the rare occasions in which national and local priorities clash, the nation has taken precedent. The Constitution explicitly states the "supremacy" of the federation over the states. This has often been tested not merely in courts of law but also most dramatically (since the Civil War) during the move to desegregate schools in Little Rock, Arkansas. It was a crowning use of force. And as is well known that although numerous issues are disposed of by local and state courts, the U.S. Supreme Court is the forum for the final appeal. And it rules on matters that concern conflicts between the 50 states and the national government.

And although states and local governments and communities can collect taxes and other revenues and allocate those according to their preferences, very large amounts of revenue are collected by the federal government and then allotted to the states, localities, and communities (for instance, religious groups). *Numerous* suggestions to transfer to states the right to collect these revenues have been rejected-to maintain the federal ability to set rules that affect the use of these funds, that is, to maintain the federal crowning effect in this area.

Loyalties, too, are divided between states (and regions such as the South and the West) and the nation. However, following the Civil War, commitments to the nation tend to prevail when these come into conflict with those to states and localities.

In addition, numerous other matters are handled by nationwide bodies that cut across state lines but are not governmental bodies. These include many thousands of nonresidential communities, especially ethnic and racial groups, as well as a large number of voluntary associations. But, again, they are contextuated by the federal government and society-wide values. For instance, none of these bodies can violate the Constitution, which reflects both the ultimate legal crowning authority and the shared values of national society. All this shows that the U.S. political architecture suggests that the difficulties involved in building supranational community can be eased by crowning subsidiarity, a form of federalism.

Policies that make room for cultural privileges are a good example of ways to avoid overloading the higher level of government. These policies are justified because they make it easier for people who must give up part of their national sovereignty to maintain a strong sense of distinct social identity and community.

c. A CULTURAL EXCEPTION

Cultural exceptions to international agreements, a topic that by itself is not of the highest importance, illustrate the approach that combines building up additional layers of communities of communities (or communities of the third order) while respecting the member communities' particular values. The question is whether cultural products (such as magazines and movies) should be treated in the same manner as other goods and services or should be accorded an exception to free trade agreements. It is a complex subject due to the de facto universal access to cultural products created by the Internet and other technological devices.

For the purpose at hand, it suffices to note that to the extent that some cultural products are of special import for sustaining member communities' distinctive identity, they should be exempt from some parts of free trade agreements (which, of course, would involve rene-gotiating them). The underlying reason for this is that identity and sense of self are nourished by cultural products. If these are under-mined, nationalism is likely to run rampant. This will not necessarily occur if widgets, cranes, and ball bearings are imported. Although any product from airplanes to sports cars can be turned into a matter of national pride, cultural products are much more likely to carry a richer and more authentic symbolic content. Certain images and word choices are integral to certain cultures, which can hardly be said about the pieces used to make a plane or a car, whose origin is likely to be mixed and multinational to begin with.

Providing cultural exceptions need not be an all-encompassing policy. For instance, a community may be allowed to provide subsid-ies for local filmmakers and for productions of plays (as a way to support the local culture) but not allowed to place import controls on magazines and films (excluding other cultures).

Similarly, there seems to be no reason to oppose academies of languages trying to come up with national terms for new objects from computers to satellites, rather than relying on English words. Language is a major part of a culture, and people are correctly con-cerned about protecting it from an excessive absorption of foreign terms (although this has occurred throughout history). However, to the extent that these efforts do not attack the rapid development of English as a *second* language, they are justified according to the criteria applied here. English is on its way to becoming the language of the third layer community, the lingua franca. Nurturing national languages is compatible with nurturing English as a second language.

It is possible to combine the protection of national culture with openness to the world. This is evident from the significant cultural differences that exist between communities within the same nation-for instance, Bavaria and northwest Germany, Sicily and Milan, Manhattan and Louisiana.

D. THE ADVANTAGE OF BEING WORLDWIDE

One may ask: why expect supranational bodies to be able to handle problems that national governments have not been able to handle at the national level? For instance, national governments have had difficulty stemming the flow of controlled substances, at least without resorting to extreme, undemocratic measures of the kind employed by Singapore and Malaysia. In response, one notes that a major reason nations are unable to cope with many challenges they face is that there are no effective cross-national bodies to deal with them. When pollution flows from country A into country B, there is often little B can do to stop it. If a nation purchases or produces ten million additional highly polluting cars, their effect on the climate cannot be stopped by other countries. When country A sells missiles and weapons of mass destruction to country B, which threatens country C, C and its allies often have little recourse. True, countries can try to make the offending countries desist, either by compensating, imposing sanctions, or appealing to their better natures. Sometimes, for some matters, after much give-and-take, there is some measure of success. However, there is a vast disproportionality between what is achieved this way and what is needed to make it possible for national governments to govern effectively.

Under supranational governments, none of the problems would disappear, but they would be greatly curtailed-without the national governments having to spend a penny or hire a cop. To highlight this point, an examination of trading in cigarettes might be useful. It is merely a mental experiment that stands for numerous other public policy issues. When the United States tried to discourage smoking, several states raised their taxes on cigarettes-but they were greatly held back by the fact that neighboring states raised their taxes much less. If all 50 states would raise taxes to the same level, this would enhance tax enforcement although cigarettes would still be smuggled in from Mexico (as they are on a large scale from the United States to Canada).[47] However, if a North American body or, better, one that encompasses all nations in the Western hemisphere or, best, world-wide would levy a similar amount of taxes, the ability to impose taxes on cigarettes would be greatly enhanced, without any increase in policing. True, the problem would not disappear. Nations would differ in the level of law enforcement, and if taxes were high, local contraband would be produced. However, all said and done, the abil-ity to cope with this and numerous other problems would be signifi-cantly increased merely by fashioning regional or, best, worldwide policies and enforcement.

It goes without saying that if there were worldwide governing bodies that were as effective as national ones (not necessarily as the most effective ones but, say, an average one), many international problems would be easier to deal with because, obviously, there would be no place outside the reach of the government where nuclear bombs, missiles, submarines, and other arms could be bought or sold; where factories could cause radiation or acid rain that spills across state lines; where sex slaves could be bought or sold; or where tax evaders could find a haven. I am not claiming that curbing na-tional and transnational problems would become easy; I am only suggesting that dealing with them would be significantly more effec-tive than it is currently.

9. REGIONAL COMMUNITIES AS BUILDING BLOCKS

The argument has been made that forming supranational unions, which have been, as a rule, regional communities, will hinder the formation of a world community. For instance, it is feared that the development of regional trade blocs will undermine worldwide free

[47] Scott Morrison, "The Tobacco Moguls and Canada's Dollars 1 Billion Charge of Smuggling," *Financial Times*, 6 January 2000, World News, 14.

trade.[48] It should be granted that this could be the case, especially if regional communities are formed on the basis of antagonism toward other communities. However, there is no reason that such antagonism must develop. For instance, while the growth of the EU has caused some minor tensions with North American NAFTA, it has caused no serious difficulties with the United States, Canada, or Mexico, or for other worldwide organizations' dealings with the EU, say, in the UN. The same holds for Mercosur, the world's third-biggest trade bloc, which contains six South American nations, in its dealings with other blocs.

In effect, the opposite seems to be the case. Instead of having to negotiate with 15 European countries on issues such as the reduction of farm subsidies, the other countries and regional associations now can increasingly deal with one representative.

As far as a world community is concerned, it is difficult to imagine that it could evolve out of the give-and-take of moral dialogues among some 200 nations. True, after years of complicated negotiations, even such a large number of nations can reach some limited, narrowly crafted, very poorly enforced agreements. However, because of the sociological reasons already cited, if instead these nations first formed a much smaller number of regional bodies-a United States of Europe, a Union of Latin American States, of Southeast Asia, and so on-interactions among communities would be much simpler, making possible the formation of a more encompassing community, a community of communities. After all, the formation of the EU is based on the coming together of two blocs (the inner six and the outer seven), which benefited from the preexistent bonds among the Benelux countries. Moreover, it is widely recognized that until the U.S. Civil War the South and the North were rather separate societies, and that the American society congealed mainly after the 1890s-out of two regional "blocs."

If one accepts the building blocks approach to community building, rather than the one-time jump from the many to the one, it is possible to imagine the formation of an additional supraregional level (say, North and South America, or the United States and the

[48] "Responsible Regionalism," *Economist*, 22 December 2000, 19.

EU in the form of a revived Atlantic Alliance). Perhaps a world government might follow this, in contrast to moving directly from regional blocs to a worldwide one.

Because for so long the very mention of a world government has been scorned by serious scholars, it might be useful to provide an imaginary scenario of how a world government might be hurried along. (I write hurried along rather than initiated because some initiatives have already been undertaken in this direction, such as the UN Declaration of Human Rights and the development of worldwide moral dialogues.[49]) The scenario builds on the long-established notion that people tend most to unite when they face a common enemy. Indeed, many utopian scenarios of world government start with an attack by an alien or with a worldwide threat by some asteroid or plague. (These threats are the moral equivalent of war.)

Imagine that a nuclear war has occurred between India and Pakistan resulting in 100 million casualties and turning most of Kashmir and adjacent regions into a radioactive desert. The tensions between Iraq and Israel are mounting and intelligence reports suggest that these two countries might be close to nuclear blows that might spill over into other countries in the region, including those with large oil fields. At this point, world public opinion would strongly favor worldwide nuclear disarmament. However, on recognizing that the superpowers are unwilling to lay down their nuclear weapons, the public is likely to support a less just and less democratic but relatively effective treatment of the immediate issue at hand: it would support (the way cities awash with crime support strong armed police) a UN action (backed by a coalition of superpowers, say, the members of a restructured Security Council) to demand that all small nuclear powers give up their nuclear arms and submit to inspection. In return, their borders will be guarded by UN forces. (Another possible scenario would concern the spread of a plague across national borders, such as a stronger mutant of HIV that the "have" countries could not handle domestically.)

These scenarios share one attribute: it is relatively self-evident that the people of the world face a clear and present danger that

[49] Etzioni, "The Final Arbiters of Community's Values."

urgently requires handling and that cannot be effectively treated the old-fashioned way. The gravity of these situations justifies action on its own, rather than because they were preceded by moral dialogues, consensus building, and democratic decision making specifically related to the events at hand.

Once such a world government proves effective in handling such a clear and present danger, it might gradually expand to tackle a *limited* set of other transnational problems, expanding its crowning capabilities, as well as becoming more democratic (a point to which I will return shortly). However, it is essential that it initially be narrowly construed and limited to purposes whose merit seems self-evident to most people.

The scenario assumes two previous developments: one is a design of a world government that is on the shelf, so to speak, to be taken down when a consensus develops that the world is ready for it. Experience suggests that even when catastrophes hit, if no thought-out designs are available, the mobilizing effects of the catastrophes dissipate or people embrace less effective or unsustainable designs.

Second, worldwide moral dialogues have matured to the point of developing a political culture favorable to a narrow world government. A small step in this direction would occur if there were to be a growing acceptance of Secretary-General Kofi Annan's doctrine that UN intervention in the internal affairs of nation-states is justified if massive violations of human rights occur. This would constitute a significant expansion of the purpose of the UN, which was founded to stop wars between states rather than within them.[50] (These two points are complementary-moral dialogues would benefit from the proffering of designs around which they could congeal.)

Indeed, if the development of world government designs and moral dialogues were well advanced, it is conceivable that such a government might be embraced merely out of the anticipation of a nuclear war or some other major catastrophe before it actually struck, and thus it could be avoided.

[50] Robert Wright, "The Peace That's within Our Grasp," *New York Times*, 12 September 2000, A27; Tracy Rubin, "Kofi's World: The UN Leader's Dangerous Ambitions," *Pittsburgh Post-Gazette*, 8 September 2000, A23; Maggie Farley, "Millennium Summit at UN to Draw 150 Leaders," *Los Angeles Times*, 4 September 2000, A1.

*   *   *

Perhaps it is possible to imagine a narrow world government, but some might argue that a global community truly challenges the imagination. People often associate community with local residential social entities in which people know one another personally. It is further assumed that for informal social controls to work, which is so important in establishing social order, people must both bond with one another and have a shared moral culture. However, it has been long established that nations can acquire some features of community.[51] But what about a worldwide "we"? Are not communities typically defined in separation from some other people? Can there be a "we" without a "they"? My response is that the new "they" could be a virus or a weapon of mass destruction or some other such "enemy." After all, we have long seen people uniting to fight a runaway fire or flooding rivers.

One should also note that current worldwide moral dialogues are already leading to the formation of some global mores, the beginnings of a shared political culture and shared values.[52] This is evident in the very widespread opposition to totalitarianism, support of freer markets, and even a measure of legal and political rights, as well as more specific opposition to land mines, sex slaves, whale hunting, trade in ivory, the destruction of the environment, and much else.

One earmark of communities is that people adjust their behavior to some extent to prevailing norms in order to preserve or enhance their reputation. Increasingly, it seems that nations (for a mixture of motives) do things that are considered humanitarian or proenvironment, show respect for individual rights, and so on-because of a budding commitment to an inchoate global community. (Lawrence Lessig, a major legal scholar, far from considered a dew-eyed visionary, wrote recently, "We stand today just a few years before where

[51] Benedict R. O. G. Anderson, *Imagined Communities: Reflections on the Origin and Spread of Nationalism* (London: Verso, 1983).

[23] Martha Finnemore, "Norms, Culture, and World Politics: Insights from Sociology's Institutionalism," *International Organization* 50 (Spring 1996): 325–348; Etzioni, "The Final Arbiters of Community's Values"; Volker Rittberger, ed., *Regime Theory and International Relations* (Oxford: Clarendon Press, 1993); Peter J. Katzenstein, ed., *The Culture of National Security: Norms and Identity in World Politics* (New York: Columbia University Press, 1996).

Webster stood in 1850. We stand on the brink of being able to say, 'I speak as a citizen of the world,' without the ordinary person thinking, 'What a nut.' ")[53]

The discussion focused on territorial building blocks of a world community, arguing that, initially, supranational communities could not encompass two hundred nations, but would instead be smaller, regional communities (that themselves might be grouped into communities of communities). Other building blocks are provided by the many thousands of transnational associations, networks, and institutions often grouped together as nonstate actors or as "governance." That is, although-as I argued above-they will be insufficient in themselves to cope with swelling transnational problems, they can provide very important components of a much larger edifice, that is, they can help the development of a world government and global community.

10. POWER PROFILE AND DEMOCRATIZATION

As in other communitarian analyses, it is implied in the preceding discussion that when a large number of lives are directly endangered, public safety and public health take priority over other considerations.[54] Hence one should openly acknowledge that in its initial stage, the world government might well not be a fully democratic one. Moreover, there can be little doubt that on most issues that do not concern avoiding a nuclear war or stopping a plague, most "have" countries would refuse to submit to a world government in which "have-less" countries would have a strong majority (somewhat like the UN assembly), and most countries would refuse to submit to a government in which, initially, the superpowers would have considerable say (somewhat like they now have in the Security Council).

At the same time, one should expect that each nation and group of nations will attempt to get the evolving world government to serve

[53] Lessig, *Code*, 226.
[54] Amitai Etzioni, *The Limits of Privacy* (New York: Basic Books, 1999), especially Chapter 6, "A Contemporary Conception of Privacy," 183–215.

its purposes, from imposing legal and political rights (which the West would favor) to reallocating wealth (which many if not all "have-not" nations would favor), from protecting local cultures to protecting the environment. In addition, specific interest groups are likely to pressure the world government to impose whatever they desire or believe in. However, little would be more detrimental to the development of a world government than if, in its first stages, it were overloaded in this way. The resulting differences of viewpoint and conflicts of interests and values would be extremely likely to undermine all efforts to significantly increase the scope of supranationality.

The opposite strategy is called for: limiting the world government to narrowly focused albeit significant, indeed vital, issues, ones that most people can readily see as legitimate. As the world government expands its scope and legitimacy, it will also have to grow more democratic (through some kind of bi- or multicameral system).

This is not to suggest that democratization is not essential. On the contrary, one of the main arguments used against increasing supranationality on a regional and world level is that supranational bodies are *not accountable to the public, to elected officials*, and hence are illegitimate. This criticism has been leveled against NAFTA, the WTO, the UN, and the EU, as well as some I-NGOs. My only argument is that supranational democratization, which entails surrendering a considerable degree of national sovereignty, cannot proceed far without building up the legitimacy of supranational political institutions.

One may argue that we have here a typical chicken-and-egg problem: for a supranational government to grow, people must trust it; for them to trust it, they must consider it legitimate. If one examines the ways national democratic governments evolved out of smaller entities (e.g., the original U.S. colonies), we see that first their effectiveness was enhanced and, only later, their democratization. (For instance, the right of people without property to run for office and of women and African-Americans to vote came only slowly and long after the formation of the U.S. federation.)

It seems that a world government might evolve in a similar way. The UN's effectiveness arguably has grown over the decades (its Declaration of Human Rights has gained respect and is followed in more countries over the years, and its peacekeeping efforts have improved), but it did not grow significantly more democratic. Major decisions are made by the Security Council, and the power of the General Assembly is very limited.

These empirical observations should not be taken as antidemocratic sentiments; it is essential for developing the legitimacy of the world government for it to be democratic. However, given that world government is most likely to develop when the world faces a clear and present danger, a condition under which even fully democratic nations declare a state of emergency and suspend their constitutions (as Britain did in effect when faced with the threat of a Nazi invasion), one should realize that one may face a tough choice between tolerating a less democratic government for a transition period or not dealing with a direct threat to the lives of hundreds of millions of people all over the world.

In conclusion, I argue that transnational problems are increasing and that the treatment of these problems by the current mix of intergovernmental and transnational bodies will be found unsatisfactory by more and more people in different parts of the world. To try to cope better with these problems, three options are available: more of the same (including more limited supranationality and low-level, especially trade, regional, and even worldwide architecture); halfway supranationality in regional and interregional bodies; or a narrow world government and global community with a high degree of devolution.

I argued that as difficult, even elusive, as the world government option might be, only it might be able to provide adequate treatment for worldwide threats such as nuclear wars and plagues. I am not arguing that even such a limited world authority is feasible. I am merely suggesting that lesser designs will not cut it, and that it is useful to develop worldwide designs in case a catastrophe creates a strong political will to proceed, in the hope that the extensive considerations of such a design might help implement it before a catastrophe strikes. Much is required for such a development to occur. Beyond adding more building blocks (which include a variety of networks, I-NGOs, and limited supranational bodies) and strengthening them-we above all need supranational moral dialogues to develop a limited set of shared values and bonds, and to develop legitimacy for a new world order.

The examination in the following pages provides a much closer look at the factors and processes involved in forming supranational communities, what worked and what failed, in an attempt to move toward a general theory on the subject. It aims to cast some light on regional communities, the building blocks of a world community, as well as assist more directly in examining the conditions under which some kind of a global community and world authority might be formed.

CONTENTS

FOREWORD

Relations between states are in our era described as "international." This is eloquent testimony to the widely held belief that there is constantly a state for every nation, and that where there is not, a right of national self-determination exists. The fact is that states have made nations far more often than nations have made states. In particular, most states today were colonial provinces in yesterday's empires. Roman public administration left its mark in the state boundaries of modern Europe. Latin American nations are the product of Spanish colonial administration and the vice-royalties Spain created in the New World. Old tribal loyalties have been sundered in the emergence of the new "nations" of Africa. What are the prospects for combination or recombination among the perhaps one hundred twenty-five sovereignties of the 1960s?

Seemingly opposite tendencies are at work today. Within the North American-West European "zone of peace" there are vital impulses toward building supranational institutions; within the Soviet bloc there have been some "mirror-image" institutions created, of which the Warsaw Treaty Organization and the Council of Mutual Economic Assistance are examples. Elsewhere, the process of multiplying sovereignties goes on apace, so that, for example, by 1965 tiny Gambia has won its independence.

Common sense—and the United States' experience is welding one political community out of 13 ex-colonies—suggests that many of the post–World War II sovereignties ought to combine. They hardly meet the old League of Nations standard for mandates graduating to independence—the ability to "stand alone under the strenuous conditions of the modern world." Will Gambia, for example, finds its security and its welfare by joining its one neighbor, Senegal? The example of Tanzania (Tanganyika and Zanzibar) to the contrary notwithstanding, a century and a half of Latin American history hardly suggests that "common sense" will prevail any more in Africa, the Middle East, and Southeast Asia than it has so far in Latin America. A greater awareness of the factors making for and the factors hindering political unification may, however, modify the prospect.

Whether one is interested in the present limited but genuine unification among the states of the Europeanized world, or in the ambitious but premature efforts of the new nations of Africa and Asia to unify, or in the possibilities of unification to lead to genuinely viable states in the same two continents, Professor Etzioni's study will be welcomed. We really know very little about what does and what does not make for political unification in our time. What little we do know is rarely stated comparatively. Amitai Etzioni's paradigm for comparative analysis, his four case studies, and his tentative findings are exercises at the frontier of contemporary international relations research.

The political sociology of international relations can become as important an area for collaboration and discussion between the political scientist and the sociologist as has the political sociology of domestic politics. This book, and especially the hypotheses that the four case studies test, will generate a dialogue that can only be to the advantage of political scientist and sociologist alike.

The paradigm for the study of political unification in the first three chapters is by design rather elaborate. It is more complex than is needed for the four case studies and for the comparative observations that conclude the book. This is all to the good. The paradigm and the propositions on pages 94–96 are invitations to further case studies, not only by Professor Etzioni but also by others who find them stimulating and find in the four case studies evidence of the utility of both paradigm and propositions.

William T. R. Fox

Director
Institute of War and Peace Studies
Columbia University

PREFACE

————————•◦•◦•————————

An understanding of regional institutions is an integral part of the field of international relations. This book not only examines the successes and failures of regional associations in four areas of the contemporary world, but also suggests a general framework for the study of regionalism. Hopefully it will enhance our understanding of the mechanisms of political unification in areas other than those examined here.

At the same time this book illustrates a sociological approach to international relations, a subject that is more often examined from a historical or legal viewpoint. The sociological approach focuses on relations as we know them now rather than on those that existed among states in earlier periods; to the degree that the sociology of earlier periods is explored, it is with an eye to what we might learn from these periods to broaden our understanding of contemporary international relations. Moreover, this sociological approach is concerned with social, political, and economic forces; the formal structures of institutions are studied, but always in relation to the social forces that created the institutions and always with the question in mind: How well do these institutions fit international reality? Our approach combines a traditional power analysis with the Parsonian theory of action and with conceptions of cybernetics and communication theory introduced by Karl Deutsch. Thus even a reader who has no specific interest in regionalism may find these pages of value, for they illustrate a new and rising approach to political science in general and international relations in particular.

The research methodology used in this study illustrates the efficacy of combining techniques. Data were obtained through statistical computations, interviews, textual analysis, and observations; for our purposes, at least, no single technique could cull all the data that seemed available and relevant. To the degree that any one technique is preferred, it is that of secondary analysis—the reexamination of data to derive and support propositions not explored by whoever was first to use the particular body of evidence. Thus this volume might also be viewed as making a case for a particular approach to research—the favoring of "mixing" over purer methods. We hope to show in a future publication that the need to combine research techniques goes beyond the demands of this or any other single study.

The study of regional communities, whether of states, cities, or tribes, has gained growing attention from political scientists, students of public administration, sociologists, and economists. The success of the European Economic Community has provided added interest. In every part of the world efforts are being made to develop broader political communities, and studies of the factors that make for the success or failure of these communities are a new and expanding specialty. Regular sessions are devoted to regionalism at meetings of national and international associations and in seminars at leading universities. In addition to the publishing of a journal specifically reporting on common market studies, other journals are devoting increasing space to the subject of regionalism. All these developments indicate the growing volume of work in this area.

A closely related subject, of much more traditional standing, is the study of federal institutions. Sometimes treated as if it were a world apart, federalism actually covers much the same ground as regionalism, though from a more institutional perspective. Federalism is largely concerned with the conditions under which diverse social units find their place in one political community. The study of regionalism differs from that of federalism only in that the former does not presuppose that the institutional framework in which the community will express itself will necessarily be federal.

For this author, the most compelling appeal of regionalism is that the rise of regional communities may provide a stepping-stone on the way from a world of a hundred-odd states to a world of a stable and just peace. Such an achievement seems to require the establishment of a world political community. The rise of a world community is by no means assured; at best it will be a long and difficult process. Nor does the evolution of every regional community serve to advance the cause of a world community. And one must note that, so far, for every regional association that has succeeded, several have failed. But the increase in the number of regional communities and their growing success seems to indicate that the one avenue by which a world community—and not a world empire—might rise is the growth of regionalism. The studies of regionalism and of war and peace are, hence, closely related.

This study would not have been possible without the support of the Institute of War and Peace Studies. It was initiated, conducted, and completed under the Institute's auspices. The Institute is supportive without being directive; it is stimulating without being intrusive; it blends the traditions of social and political science without doing violence to either. The credit for this atmosphere and for making this work possible rests fully with its director, Professor William T. R. Fox. My warm thanks are extended also to the associate director of the Institute, Professor Leland M. Goodrich, for his advice and continuous interest. In addition to the assistance provided by the Institute from a Ford Foundation grant, I have had indispensable support from the Rockefeller Institute. The help of both foundations is gratefully acknowledged.

At various stages of the project I was assisted by Martha McConnell, Jane McFadden, Philip Shellhaas, Audrey Slesinger, and Martin Wenglinsky. Ethna Lehman and Robert McGeehan stayed with the project from beginning to end. I am especially indebted for their help. Three of my colleagues commended on earlier versions of the manuscript: William A. Glaser, Leon N. Lindberg, and Immanuel M. Wallerstein. On the U.A.R. case study I benefited from the comments of Richard H. Dekmejian and George Haggar; on the Nordic case study from those of Carl Bolang, Gunnar Leistikow, John Wuorinen, Eric V. Youngquist, and, in particular, Stanley V. Anderson; and on the West Indian case study from those of Noel Brown, Lambros E. Comitas, Sidney Martin Greenfield, William A. Richardson, and Vera Rubin. Part One is a much expanded and revised version of an article published in the October 1962 issue of *World Politics.*

A. E.

New York City
February 1965

INTRODUCTION

It is easier to see the limitations of the nation-state than it is to determine what can be done realistically to overcome them. Few observers believe that a global-state can be the next step in the development of political institutions. Many, however, view regional unions as a way of augmenting and eventually replacing the nation-state. Others have warned that the region-states might serve as a barrier on the way to one global-state. Whatever course one wishes history to take or expects the future to follow, there is much to be learned from contemporary efforts to form new, more encompassing polities. The conditions under which political unification *is* (not should be or could be) initiated are the subject of this study. Less attention is paid here to historical cases of unification both because they have been studied with relative frequency and success and because the projection of findings from past periods, especially prenationalist ones, into the future is risky and difficult. Hence, this study focuses on contemporary attempts at unification.

Contemporary unions of states, it soon becomes clear, are hard to initiate and even more difficult to sustain. Emotional commitment to the nation-state is so intense and widespread and concern with national interests so encompassing that contemporary unions are largely limited to efforts to serve the nation more effectively by regional arrangements rather than to replace it. It is true that, to some degree, the very establishment of multinational and especially supranational organizations arouses additional support for regional unions, but we found, in our study of contemporary unification, not one instance of a significant conflict between nationalism and supranationalism in which the latter orientation carried the day. This might be accounted for in part by the fact that contemporary unions are at or just beyond the initiation stage. Moreover, there are many more stillborn unions than unions that continue to increase their level and scope of integration. Our study reflects this state of affairs: two of the unions failed—the Federation of the West Indies (1958–1962) and the United Arab Republic (1958–1961); one has grown but slightly—the Nordic union (1953–1964); and only one is thriving—the European Economic Community (1958–1964). Even the last union we study, though more successful than the others, is still in its infancy. Hence our study deals with the initiation of unions, some successful and some that failed, but not with contemporary unifications that have been completed.

The study of unification has a relevance beyond that of the diagnosis and prognosis of inter-state relations. By treating the kind of identification of citizens with their polity as a variable rather than as a given, our analysis is relevant both to polities that are nations and those that are not; we are actually studying the conditions under which social units join to form new entities. Much of the analytical framework that serves the study of regional unification also serves the study of the formation of a nation out of tribes, villages, or feudal fiefs or the merger of two suburbs, corporations, or ethnic groups. Put into its widest framework, this is a study of the unification of social units, and not just of nation-states.

The first part of the book unrolls a wide canvas on which we chart a large number of systematic related factors used to formulate questions that studies of unification need to answer. Searching the literature, it soon became evident that for most answers supported by a given authority with some reasoning and some data there is a counterposition presented by some other authority and supported by similarly valid reasoning and evidence. Often, for any given question, there are more than two answers. By the end of the first part of our endeavor to analyze the process of unification, many questions remain but there are few answers. These questions are recorded for what such an overview is worth.

From this large number of questions, a few are chosen for detailed consideration. The second part of this volume explores unification from a limited perspective: *we seek to establish who led a particular unification effort, under what conditions, by what means, and with what results.* In other words, what kinds of leadership armed with what kinds of powers are more or less successful in initiating unification. (More technically, the nature of the integrating power and that of the elite-units are our independent variables and the level and scope of integration attained are our dependent ones.)

Four contemporary unification efforts are examined from these perspectives: the Federation of the West Indies, the United Arab Republic, the Nordic union,[1] and the European Economic Community. The cases differ considerably on many counts. The Federation of the West Indies was one of the most limited federations ever founded in terms of those functions that were "federalized"; the United Arab Republic was a unitary state; the Nordic Council is a multinational organization; the European Economic Community blends supranational and multinational forms of unification. No less significant are their differences from many other viewpoints: two are in developing regions, two in developed ones; one is a union of states adjacent to each other; two are separated by the sea, and one by hostile countries. In one the population is almost exclusively Moslem, in another Lutheran; a third is largely Catholic, and the last is mainly Anglican. The list of divergences could readily be extended. This provides us with a richer context than would a single case study in which to explore the relationships among leadership, forces, and level of integration attained, though it necessarily limits the attention each case can be given.[2]

The volume closes with a comparison of the four cases. Comparative analysis in general helps to guard against ethnocentric bias and culture-bound interpretations and helps one to view factors in perspective. Often what is considered impossible in one instance is found to be successful in another setting. Thus, comparative analysis serves to indicate both the large number of possible combinations of factors and the relative and hence tentative nature of all statements made.

Special care was taken, though this effort was far from an un-

[1] The study focuses on the period since the formation of the Nordic Council in 1953. Earlier developments of the Nordic union are examined only insofar as they affect the union in the period under consideration.

[2] A more detailed discussion of the reason for studying more than one case and for selecting these particular ones is given below; for a summary of the propositions tested, see the concluding section of chap. 3; and for conclusions, see chap. 8. A glossary of terms used is provided at the end of the volume.

equivocal success, to limit the conceptual apparatus as much as possible without damaging the analysis. This is not a new dictionary or list of concepts for the study of unification, though the first pages might seem so; it is rather an attempt to raise questions and provide some answers that hopefully are of interest both to those concerned with better understanding unification and for those concerned with understanding how better to unify.

Part One

A PARADIGM FOR THE STUDY OF POLITICAL UNIFICATION

A paradigm is more than a perspective but less than a theory. It provides a set of interrelated questions, but no account of validated propositions. It provides a "language," a net of variables, but it does not specify the relationships among those variables. It is less vague than a mere perspective, providing a systematic, specific, and often logically exhaustive set of foci for research and speculation. A paradigm is often a stage on the way from an old perspective to a new theory.[1]

The test of a paradigm is not only that of the validity of the theories constructed through its application, but also its fruitfulness in terms of the spectrum of significant problems whose study is facilitated by it. We begin by delineating the subject matter of this paradigm, and then present the paradigm itself. The major objective of this section is to indicate kinds of problems that can be handled by the use of our paradigm. At the same time we endeavor to point out some of the questions that must be answered if the understanding of political unification is to be advanced.

[1] Two paradigms that had a lasting impact on sociology have been constructed by Robert K. Merton, one for functional analysis and one for the study of the sociology of knowledge. See his *Social Theory and Social Structure,* revised edition. New York: The Free Press of Glencoe, 1957.

Part One is an expanded and revised version of an article published in *World Politics,* October 1962.

CHAPTER 1

Delineation of the Subject and of Elementary Concepts

————————◆•◆•◆————————

Our paradigm provides a set of dimensions for the study of a process, specifically one that affects the relations among units, as contrasted to their internal structure.[1] To the degree that the net effect of the process is to increase or strengthen the bonds among the units, we refer to it as unification; to the degree that it reduces such bonds, de-unification is used, in absence of a better term. We are particularly interested in the unification of already existing nations, but the paradigm applies also to the development of other unifications, such as the evolution of national bonds among tribes, villages, or feudal fiefs.[2]

[1] *Unit* is used in the formal sense, i.e., as a single constituent of a whole; what it substantively is—a nation, a village, etc.—depends on the system-reference. It is a nation for a supranational community, a village for a rural region, etc. Units become systems and systems, units as the analyst changes the level of analysis or the problem he wishes to study.

[2] Although this cannot be demonstrated here, we would like to suggest that the paradigm advanced here applies to a study of the changing relationship between the federal and state governments in the United States, as effectively outlined by Daniel J. Elazar, *The American Partnership.* Chicago: University of Chicago Press, 1962, and to the relationship between a national church movement and the member-societies, as presented by Paul Harrison in his *Authority and Power in the Free Church Tradition.* Princeton, N.J.: Princeton University Press, 1959. See also Leo Moulin, "Le Fédéralisme dans l'Organisation Politique des Ordres Religieux," paper presented at the Sixième Congres Mondial, Association Internationale de Science Politique, Génève, September 21–25, 1964; Frank W. Young, "Location and Reputation in a Mexican Inter-Village Network," *Human Organization,* vol. 23 (1964), pp. 36–41; and Philip E. Jacob and James V. Toscano (eds.), *The Integration of Political Communities.* Philadelphia: J. B. Lippincott Company, 1964.

Not every increase or strengthening of the bonds that relate social units to each other brings them to the point of development at which they constitute one community. A *community* is established only when it has self-sufficient integrative mechanisms; that is, when the maintenance of its existence and form[3] is provided for by its own processes and is not dependent upon those of external systems or member-units. A *political community* is a community that possesses three kinds of integration: (a) it has an effective control over the use of the means of violence (though it may "delegate" some of this control to member-units); (b) it has a center of a decision-making that is able to affect significantly the allocation of resources and rewards throughout the community; and (c) it is the dominant focus of political identification for the large majority of politically aware citizens.

A political community is thus a state, an administrative-economic unit, and a focal point of identification. The control of means of violence distinguishes a political community from other communities, such as religious and ethnic ones. It safeguards the community from the arbitrary interference of subgroups; it makes the community the ultimate arbitrator among these groups; it serves to counter secessionist pressures and it makes the political community the focus of defense against outside aggression.

The ability to affect allocation of resources is required to finance the activities of the community, especially those of its internal and external security forces and of its administrative machinery. This capacity is also needed for the peaceful adjustment of the distribution of resources throughout the community to the changing power relations among the various member groups. Finally, it serves to shift public attention and that of interest groups from the component units to the community; it leads to the formation of cleavages that cut

[3] Most functional models deal only with the conditions under which a community survives. The need to study the conditions under which a community (or, for that matter, any social unit) maintains its form or structure is spelled out elsewhere. A community might survive while its structure is changing; i.e., one form is lost and a new one is established. See "Two Approaches to Organizational Analysis: A Critique and a Suggestion," *Administrative Science Quarterly,* vol. 5 (1960), pp. 257–278. This point is further elaborated in the author's *Modern Organizations.* Englewood Cliffs, N.J.: Prentice-Hall, Inc., 1964, pp. 17–19.

across the member-units and create community-wide interest groups, thus countervailing centrifugal forces. In the United States, for instance, the national organization of labor unions reduced the states' role in regulating labor-management relations and strengthened that of the federal government.

Dominant identification with the community serves to prevent a separation, and hence a potential conflict, between the unit of force and administration on the one hand and the unit of identification on the other hand. Most national states meet this requirement of community, while empires—especially after the rise of nationalism—have not. The identification of some Slavic groups in the Austro-Hungarian Empire with two ethnic groups in Russia, the Ukrainians and the Poles, in the years preceding World War I is a case in point.[4]

Identification with the community is necessary only in political matters. Identification in other areas, such as the religious, might be less or more encompassing without necessarily undermining the integration of the community. This is the case only so long as the religious focus of identification of most of the citizens is apolitical or compatible with the dominant political orientation. In political matters, identification with subgroups, such as political parties, is not dysfunctional so long as identification with the community is dominant; that is, in case of conflict identification with the community is more powerful than that with a subgroup. This is not to imply that every subgroup so identifies with the community in which it exists. (The Black Muslims, for instance, seem to identify politically with their group, its leaders and symbols, ore than with those of the United States.) Rather, the statement suggests that the greater the attraction of such egocentric subgroups existing within a community, the less integrated that community is likely to be; and that as such dominant identification with subgroups spreads, a limit may be reached beyond which the community cannot continue to maintain its structure (for example, its democratic form of government).

[4] Robert A. Kann, *The Habsburg Empire.* New York: Frederick A. Praeger, Inc., 1957, pp. 49ff. Cf. I. Wallerstein, "Ethnicity and National Integration in West Africa," *Cahiers D'Etudes Africaines,* no. 3, October 1960, pp. 129–139.

The level of political integration[5] is the main characteristic that distinguishes political communities from other political systems. *System* is the more encompassing concept, indicating that changes in the action of one (or more) unit(s) affect actions in one (or more) other units, and that these latter changes in turn have repercussions on the unit or units in which or from which the change was initiated.[6] While the parts of a system are, by definition, interrelated, its level of integration—on each of the three counts specified above—might be high or low. One cannot, for instance, deduce from the fact that the USSR and the United States have become part of one global system—because they affect each other—anything about the integrative level of this relationship.[7] Even countries engaged in war are parts of one system. In short, units of systems are interdependent; members of communities are integrated.[8]

Interdependence might be either self-maintained or sustained by

[5] We shall refer below to the state of the system, with respect to the three properties discussed, as its "level of integration." It should be noted, though, that we are dealing with political integration, not with religious, economic, or general integration. Karl W. Deutsch *et al.* use "integration" to refer to the relationship among countries that no longer anticipate engaging in war with one another (*Political Community and the North Atlantic Area.* Princeton, N.J.: Princeton University Press, 1957, p. 31). Canada and the United States, for instance, are "integrated." This is of course a different definition, one that has a lower threshold than ours. Ernst B. Haas uses "political integration" to refer to "the process whereby political actors in several distinct national settings are persuaded to shift their loyalties, expectations, and political activities toward a new center, whose institutions possess or demand jurisdiction over the preexisting national states." (*The Uniting of Europe.* Stanford, Calif.: Stanford University Press, 1958, p. 16.) The threshold of this definition is higher than that of Deutsch *et al.* but not as high as ours. (Cf. Haas' discussion of "political community," pp. 4–11.) In particular, it does not require the ability of the "institutions" to significantly affect the allocation of resources throughout the community as does our definition. Note also that Haas uses "integration" to refer to a process while we use it to refer to a condition (Deutsch uses the concept to refer to both). Our reasons for following a particular usage of the term will become evident below.

[6] See Morton A. Kaplan, *System and Process in International Politics.* New York: John Wiley & Sons, Inc., 1957, p. 4.

[7] Cf. Talcott Parsons, "Polarization and the Problem of International Order," *Berkeley Journal of Sociology,* vol. 6 (1961), pp. 130ff. Reprinted in Eva and Amitai Etzioni (eds.), *Social Change: Sources, Patterns, and Consequences.* New York: Basic Books, Inc., 1964.

[8] Integration is the more inclusive term: all that are integrated are also interdependent, but not all that are interdependent are integrated.

the component units (such as member-nations); or it might be a product of the external environment (forced, for example, by a superior power, not a member of the system). Integration of the members of a community is *self*-maintained by definition; it distinguishes the concept of community from the more encompassing one of systems.

Several of the most frequently used terms in the literature on international relations can be viewed as applying to international systems which differ consistently in their degree of integration. International organizations,[9] blocs, and empires are all international systems but they are less integrated than political communities. They can be fruitfully ordered according to their relative position on the three dimensions of integration. First let us consider the effective control of means of violence. Monofunctional organizations as a rule command no such means at all, let alone an effective control over their use. Members of blocs (and alliances) often coordinate their military efforts (as did the Allied forces in World War II), but the forces remain chiefly under the control of the member-units, the nations. Empires have armed forces of their own, but their monopoly of the means of violence is frequently challenged by member-units. Only the control of means of violence by political communities is both effective and comparatively noncontested.

All of these types of international systems have some common decision-making center, but they differ greatly in the capacity, scope, and saliency of that center. The great majority of monofunctional organizations (in our specific use of that term) are consultative bodies whose decision-making powers are sharply limited either by the rule of unanimity, or by the non-bonding nature of the resolutions passed, or by both; and whose decision-making scope is limited to

[9] The term *international organizations* is used in two quite different ways in the literature on international relations. One, a more encompassing use, refers to every interstate relationship that is organized, including both monofunctional (such as the International Civil Aviation Organization) and multifunctional (such as the United Nations). The term is also used more restrictively, to refer to organizations that are largely monofunctional in nature and whose decision-making organs are limited to an advisory capacity, such as the International Labor Organization and the World Health Organization. The League of Nations and the UN differ on so many counts from most international organizations that they should be treated as a distinct category. We use the concept monofunctional organizations in order to avoid confusion.

one or a few spheres (such as postal services, or health, or labor) and to functions that are not essential to the survival of the member-units or their ability to pursue their national interests. The decision-making of blocs (and alliances) tends to be consultative, like that of monofunctional organizations, but their scope is larger. They are often multifunctional (for example, political and military; cultural and economic), and the functions affected are regarded as more salient by the member-societies than those served by most international organizations. Empires have a considerable amount of decision-making power that binds member-units, that is, their decisions are enforceable. Their scope is larger than that of blocs, frequently encompassing political, military, and economic functions as well as communicational, cultural, educational, and other functions. The spheres affected are at least as salient as those affected by blocs. The decision-making centers of empires are less encompassing than those of political communities, not in regard to their power, but in the legitimation of the decisions made. Since membership in empires is not usually voluntary, and responsiveness to the needs of member-units is not high, it might well be said that empires rely less on legitimation, and hence less on authority, but relatively more on "naked" power.[10]

Finally, monofunctional organizations rarely serve as a focus of political identification. Blocs, historically, have been lacking in this criterion, although since World War I blocs have acquired increasing ideological meaning (for example, the contemporary "Free World"). Empires, on the whole, are not much more integrated on this score than blocs, but they usually have at least one core unit (Rome, Britain) which strongly identifies with the empire, a commitment only

[10] *Power* is a unit's capacity to induce or influence another unit to carry out directives or any other norms it (the first unit) supports. This definition of power differs from those commonly used in that it does not assume that the norms supported are necessarily those of the person who exercises the power. A policeman, for instance, is expected to enforce the law of the country, regardless of whether that law concurs with his own personal norms. In 1964, the United States threatened to cut off assistance to atomic research for peaceful usages in third countries unless they adhere to the regulations set by and allowing inspection by the International Atomic Energy Agency. *Authority* is defined, following Max Weber, as legitimate power; that is, as power whose exercise is viewed as just by those subject to its application. See discussion of imbalanced integration below.

approximated but not matched by bloc-leaders. There was a mixture of exploitation and responsibility in the orientation of the core-country of empires to those subordinated to it; the orientation of bloc "superpowers"[11] to other bloc members tends to be governed primarily by expediency. The core-countries used to view the empire as an extension of their own polities; they often attempted to assimilate the subordinate units into the core-country; they even granted citizenship to some of the indigenous populations. The modern bloc superpower, on the other hand, usually views the bloc as a limited partnership with outsiders. (The Soviet system comes closer to an empire than a bloc from this viewpoint.[12]) At least some local elites in the subordinate countries responded by identifying with the empire,[13] a phenomenon less intensively reproduced in the attitude of members of blocs to the superpower.[14] In short, empires seem to have drawn relatively more identification than blocs do, but neither has attracted the kind of encompassing and intensive identification that political communities command. Thus, in regard to the three dimensions, monofunctional organizations are less integrated than blocs, blocs less than empires, and empires less than political communities.

The concepts of monofunctional organization, bloc, empire, and political community are used in the literature of international relations only approximately as they are defined here. Since these concepts are originally used by historians and journalists, they do not constitute part of a formal language or theory. Hence it is not sur-

---

[11] "Superpower" is used throughout this volume as in William T. R. Fox, *The Super-Powers.* New York: Harcourt, Brace & World Inc., 1944.

[12] See Zbigniew K. Brzezinski, "The Organization of the Communist Camp," *World Politics,* vol. 13 (1961), pp. 175–209, and *The Soviet Bloc.* Cambridge, Mass.: Harvard University Press, 1960. Cf. George Modelski, *The Communist International System.* Center of International Studies, Princeton University, 1960; R. J. Mitchell, "A Theoretical Approach to the Study of Communist International Organizations," *Stanford Studies of the Communist System.* Stanford University, 1964; and Andrzej Korbonski, "Comecon," *International Conciliation,* no. 549, September, 1964.

[13] Quincy Wright, "Empires and World Governments Before 1918," *Current History* (1960), p. 66.

[14] In this sense the two concepts are historically bound. Blocs are usually units of contemporary history composed of nations; while empires—at least the classical ones—are largely made up of political units with whom the citizens identify less strongly than with nation-states.

prising that when these are defined deductively and viewed as positions in a multidimensional space some discrepancies between their definition and their traditional usage occur. By our definition, as already noted, the Soviet bloc between 1945 and 1953—at least some parts of it—was not a "bloc" but an empire; parts of the Roman Empire, at least in its heyday, were not an "empire" but a political community. It would be futile to search for deductive definitions that will fit exactly concrete cases or inductive concepts. Actually it is a point in favor of a deductive approach that it calls attention to the fact that behind the commonly used labels lie analytically different phenomena. By using deductive definitions, statements can be made that would not be possible with the traditional concepts. Thus, one can ask if, since 1953, the East European part of the Communist system (with the exception of Albania) has moved from an empire system to a system somewhat closer to that of a political community. This is more fruitful than stating that the Soviet system—all of it— was and is a bloc. Similarly, it might be useful to state that the Roman system during its heyday came much closer to being a political community—at least for the countries other than those at its periphery—than, let us say, the Ottoman system, which was chiefly an empire. Such statements require keeping our definition analytically pure, and viewing reality as being composed of various configurations and approximations of our analytical concepts.

Statements about the level of integration of a particular international system are in effect a composite score of the three dimensions of integration: monopolization of force, allocation of resources, and dominant identification. Precise measurements are rare, but it is generally possible to determine the comparative position of a particular international entity by using these dimensions. For instance, there will be little disagreement that NATO has more control of the military forces of its member countries than SEATO has of hers, and that the USSR has more control of the Warsaw Treaty Organization than the United States has of NATO. Public opinion polls are helpful in comparing the identification of citizens of various countries with various international organs (for example, the French, as compared to the West Germans, identify *relatively* more strongly with the European Economic Community than with NATO).[15]

Further elaboration of this approach would require an extensive study of *unbalanced systems,* that is, systems in which integration on one score is significantly higher than on the other two, such as identification over monopolization of force (typical to commonwealth types of international systems) or force over identification (common to military organizations). In general we would expect such imbalances to be dysfunctional; that is, strain would be caused that would undermine the structure of the particular system under study. The nature of the imbalance should allow prediction of the nature of the strains. For example, when control of force is higher than focusing of identification, alienation of the member units—or at least some of them—is likely to be high. We shall see below that for certain purposes it suffices to state that integration, as a composite score, is high, lower, or medium, while for other purposes, the composition of the score will have to be determined. Two systems whose integration is "medium" might be quite different, one drawing largely on military, the other on administrative-economic integration.

A reexamination of the major types of international systems[16] examined above suggests that there is a close association between the composite level of political integration and the social scope of the international system. *Scope* is measured in terms of the number of social sectors[17] of the member-units that the shared system penetrates (such as only military or both military and economic) and in terms of the importance of these sectors to the survival of the units and the realization of their interests (for example, postal service versus defense alliance). It seems that, in general, *the higher the level*

[15] Daniel Lerner and Morton Gorden, "European Community and Atlantic Security in the World Arena." Cambridge, Mass.: Massachusetts Institute of Technology, n.d., passim.

[16] International systems refers to systems whose member-units are nations, but no implication is made that all nations are members as when one alludes to "the international system."

[17] Social sector refers to all the activities of a social unit that serve a particular function for that unit. For instance, the religious sector of a society is composed of religious activities in churches, schools, families, etc.

of integration the broader the scope. Monofunctional organizations are low on both counts; communities, high on both; blocs and empires, medium. Note that no causality is assumed; the level of integration and scope of a system, we suggest, change together (though there is no tight one-to-one relationship between them). Moreover, both changes are probably largely the consequence of the operation of various unification processes, rather than of the effect of each upon the other. Putting it more technically, the level of integration is our central dependent variable; various unification factors and the conditions under which they emerge are our independent factors; and the conditions under which they emerge are our independent variables. Scope is a second dependent variable whose relationship to the central dependent variable is examined, not assumed.

Our paradigm serves not so much to study this or that state of integration or scope but rather to examine the process of unification, a process through which integration is increased and scope tends to grow. Since systems that *increased* their level of integration and scope are often confused with those that have *reached* a community level—as when one refers to the present West European or Scandinavian system as a political community—we introduce a concept to avoid this ambiguity. We use the term *unions* to refer to international systems whose level of integration and scope is higher than that of a typical international organization and lower than that of an established political community.[18] A union is a group of countries that acts in unison, on a continuous rather than an *ad hoc* basis, on a wide range of matters, and on matters more important to its interest than is the case in typical international organizations. The concept of union is used here, it should be noted, as a sociopolitical concept and not a legal term. No particular institutional form is assumed.[19] The Scandinavian countries, we shall see, constitute a union by this definition, though legally they are a set of fully sovereign states and in this sense are less related than Iceland and Turkey, two members of NATO that have pooled some of their sovereignty. On the other

[18] Note that *union* might hence be used to refer to systems whose level of integration and scope is increasing, decreasing, or stable; *unification* refers to the process of increasing, *de-unification* to the decrease.

[19] For a similar use of the term, see Deutsch, *et al., Political Community,* p. 7.

hand, the Union of African States is not a union despite its legal title, since the treaty of Ghana, Guinea, and Mali to form a union has not to date led to the buildup of military, economic, administrative, or psychological bonds among the three countries stronger than those common to members of a monofunctional organization, nor has the treaty affected most social sectors of those countries. In the same sense, a federation may be disbanded but a union continue to exist, or a federation may be formed without the prior existence of a union.[20]

[20] For a recent survey of research and theory on these questions, see Carl J. Friedrich, "New Tendencies in Federal Theory and Practice," General report to the Sixth World Congress International Political Science Association, Geneva, Sept. 21–25, 1964. See, by the same author, *Man and His Government*, New York: McGraw-Hill, Inc., 1963, chap. 2. For earlier works by other authors, see William Anderson, *The Nation and the States, Rivals or Partners?* Minneapolis: University of Minnesota Press, 1955; Arthur W. Macmahen, *Federalism, Mature and Emergent*. Garden City, New York: Doubleday & Company, Inc., 1955; and William S. Livingston, *Federalism and Constitutional Change*. Oxford: Clarendon Press, 1956; Walter Hartwell Bennett, *American Theories of Federalism*. University of Alabama Press, 1964.

CHAPTER 2

Political Unification

————————•••••————————

Four major questions can be asked about every process: Under what conditions is it initiated? What forces direct its development? What path does it take? And what is the state of the system affected by the process once it is terminated? We use this paradigm of processes to construct one for the study of unification, especially for the study of the unification of nations. We ask, first, what is the state of the various units and the relations among them when the unification process is initiated and which factors enhance and which hinder this initiation. Once the process has been initiated, we ask what powers are applied to control unification and how these powers are distributed among the various participants. What pattern does unification itself follow? Do all societal sectors unify simultaneously or successively, and if successively, in what order, that is, which sector comes first and which later? Finally, we ask, once unification is interrupted or ceased, what level of integration has the system reached, how encompassing has its scope become, and what new function does it serve?

Whatever the independent variable—background conditions, integrating powers, retarding factors—we turn to the same dependent variables: the level and scope of integration; that is, we wish to outline the problems involved in determining the effect these various factors have on the success or failure of unification.[1]

[1] "Success" and "failure" are used throughout the volume as referring to the accomplishments of a unification effort, as reflected in a later state of the system compared with an earlier point in time. No implication is made that unification is desirable, or de-unification undesirable.

14

More specifically, our paradigm includes the following dimensions:[2]

THE PREUNIFICATION STATE
Unit Properties
Individual Properties
Analytical Properties
Environment Properties
Nonsocial (Ecological) Properties
Social Properties
System Properties
Shared Properties (Other Than Integration)
Preunification Integration

THE UNIFICATION PROCESS: A. INTEGRATING POWER
Effective Compositions[3]
Differences in Kind
Differences in Quantities
The Communication Factor
Effective Distributions
Degree of Elitism
Degree of Internalization

THE UNIFICATION PROCESS: B. INTEGRATED SECTORS
The First Stage: Take-Off
Determinants of Take-Off
The Take-Off Sector
Expansion of the Union's Scope
A Stable Scope
Sequences of Unification

THE TERMINATION STATE
Level and Scope
The Dominant Function

[2] This should not be viewed as a table of contents since conceptual digressions are not included.
[3] "Effective" refers to a union's ability to maintain its level of integration and scope if it is in a termination state, or to increase its level of integration and scope if it is in a unifying stage.

THE PREUNIFICATION STATE

The question of the conditions under which the process of unification is initiated is considered from four viewpoints. First, what is the state of each societal unit that is to become a member of a particular union: is it likely to resist unification or to support it? Second, what is the nature of the aggregate of these units: are most or all units "ready" to unify or are only a few ready? Third, are environmental factors favorable for unification? Finally, to what degree was there interdependence and integration before a specific process of unification was initiated? Many specific questions have to be answered before these general questions can be fully considered. In the following pages, no attempt is made to exhaust the specific problems or to provide an inventory of all the various issues involved. Each of the basic four perspectives is illustrated by discussing one or two of the specific questions raised in the effort to establish the conditions which existed before unification began, or as a process of unification is initiated.

Unit Properties

Individual Properties: Integration and Resistance to Unification

The unification process is one in which control of the means of violence, the capacity to allocate resources and rewards, and the locus of identification are transferred from member-units to the system in which they are members. This obviously involves at least some reduction of the integration of the member-units as they become increasingly incorporated into the system. It would appear, therefore, that the degree to which these units are initially internally integrated would greatly affect their potential resistance to unification and therefore the success of any specific unification effort. The question is, what level (or levels) of unit-integration are most conducive to the initiation and development of unification? One possibility is low level unit-integration. The integration of Malaya, for instance, is believed to have been enhanced by the fact that racial groups were

so dispersed among ecological units that unit-identification was low.[4]
It should be noted that it is the existence of tensions among the racial
groups in each ecological unit, not simply the plurality of groups,
which makes for low unit-integration. For instance, the existence of
an organized labor movement side by side with a manufacturing
association in Great Britain does not reduce the association's integration so long as institutionalized avenues of conflict (such as collective bargaining, arbitration) are available and so long as the level
of conflict does not exceed the amount these avenues can successfully channel off.

Another possibility is that low unit-integration impedes unifications. Countries that fall apart, like the Republic of the Congo in the
early 1960s, can hardly form a union with other countries. Brazil, in
the early sixties, was so overwhelmed with internal problems that
few resources and little manpower and attention were available to
be devoted to leadership of a regional union. At least one authority
suggested that underdeveloped countries in general are less likely to
form unions than developed ones.[5] Thus, lack of unit integration
might hinder system integration.

Other possibilities also are to be entertained until research answers these questions. A medium level of unit-integration might be
the most favorable condition for unification; such a unit would be
sufficiently integrated to confer enough stability on the unit for it to
participate in and contribute to the unification effort, and would not
be so well-integrated as to be able to neutralize pressures to share
more and more bonds of the evolving union. Or, high unit-
integration might be conducive to the first state of unification; low
unit-integration for later stages. Or, high unit-integration in countries
that favor unification, and low in those resisting it.

The study of the further specification of effects of unit-integration
might proceed by examining the effects of differences in the degree
of integration along the dimensions spelled out above. For instance,
we may need to know how much control over the means of violence

---

[4] Max Beloff, "The 'Federal' Solution in Its Application to Europe, Asia, and
Africa," *Political Studies,* vol. 1 (1953), p. 118.
[5] Lincoln Gordon, "Economic Regionalism Reconsidered," *World Politics,*
vol. 13 (1961), pp. 235–236.

the government of a member-nation has, how responsive the national center of decision-making is to various groups within the population, and how legitimate the government of a member-unit is considered to be. What is the nature of the unit-legitimation: is it chiefly religious or secular? In either case, is it national (as the tradition of the Church of England or the American "heritage") or comparatively cosmopolitan (as Roman Catholicism and Communism are)? What effect do those differences have on unification?

The term international is used rather misleadingly to refer to relations among states that are not nations. In this way one possible value of a variable, namely a high degree of identification of politically conscious citizens with their states (which characterizes nation-states), is included in the mere definition of the system. Actually, many past *and* contemporary unions have been initiated among units whose politically active citizens either were expressing their nationalist sentiments by creating the union (for example, Germany and Italy) or took place before such sentiments significantly affected either the units or the system (for example, the federation of Canada).[6] In short, unification might be initiated in a prenationalist period, in a postnationalist one, or be, itself, an expression of nationalism. It might seem obvious that postnationalist unifications would be more difficult to attain than the other two kinds, and that a unification that expresses nationalism would be the easiest to accomplish. But, as we shall see, the two most successful contemporary unions—the Scandinavian one and the West European one—are postnationalist.[7] One of the most successful unions of developing countries is also one that takes place among established nations—the Central American Common Market.[8] Thus, this question, too, must be left open for further research.

[6] Similarly, the term, "supranational authorities" should be reserved to refer to centers whose decisions are binding on units that are nations, not merely states.

[7] "Postnationalist" refers to the fact that unification was initiated after the member-units were exposed to nationalism; it is not implied that unification was an expression of a postnationalist ideology.

[8] See "Progress Report CACM," *Latin American Business Highlights,* vol. 13 (1963), pp. 8–15. See also Raymond Mikesell, "Movement Toward Regional Trading Groups in Latin America," in Albert O. Hirsschman (ed.), *Latin American Issues: Essays and Comments.* New York: Twentieth Century Fund, 1961, pp. 125–151.

Analytical Properties: Heterogeneity and Unification

Analytical properties are not properties of any single unit but are derived from a study of the distribution of unit-attributes.[9] Unlike unit-properties or relational properties, analytical properties cannot be observed. They are "second order" abstractions.

The most important analytical property for the study of the pre-requisites of unification seems to be the degree of heterogeneity of the member units. On the one hand, it has been suggested that the less homogeneous a group, whether it is a small group, a community, or a nation, the less likely it is to be highly integrated. For instance, it has been shown that the greater the diversity of opinions people have, the less likely they are to become and stay friends.[10] On the other hand, there are reports of instances in which this relationship between homogeneity and integration did not hold. Seashore found that differences in education and age of workers did not relate to the degree of integration of their groups.[11] Blau and Scott found that homogeneity in age, sex, and religion did not relate to the integration of the groups of social workers he studied.[12]

It seems that not all background characteristics are of the same relevance to integration. Some may have great effect while others have very little or no effect; moreover, we shall see that the existence of some heterogeneity might enhance rather than undermine integration. The study of the effects of heterogeneity must hence proceed by examining the effects of the diversity of each major background

[9] Paul F. Lazarsfeld and Herbert Menzel, "On the Relation Between Individual and Collective Properties," in Amitai Etzioni (ed.), *Complex Organization: A Sociological Reader.* New York: Holt, Rinehart and Winston, Inc., 1961, pp. 422–440, esp. p. 427.

[10] T. M. Newcomb, "An Approach to the Study of Communicative Acts," *Psychological Review,* vol. 60 (1953), pp. 393–404. Paul F. Lazarsfeld and Robert K. Merton, "Friendship as Social Process: A Substantive and Methodological Analysis," in M. Berger, T. Abel, and C. H. Page (eds.), *Freedom and Control in Modern Society.* New York: D. Van Nostrand Company, Inc., 1954, pp. 18–66.

[11] Small group studies use the term cohesion to refer to the same *analytical* quality defined above as integration. Stanley E. Seashore, *Group Cohesiveness in the Industrial Work Group.* Ann Arbor, Mich.: Institute for Social Research, University of Michigan, 1954, p. 82.

[12] Peter M. Blau and W. Richard Scott, *Formal Organizations.* San Francisco: Chandler Publishing Company, 1962, p. 109.

characteristic on integration, in addition to examining the effects of this variable holistically. At this stage of our research it is far from clear what those effects are.

In the economic sphere, the composition of the production of the merging units and their comparative wealth are of great interest. It is almost universally assumed that countries that *differ* in the composition of their economies will integrate more easily than those that have similar economies. One of the foundations of the British Commonwealth, for instance, is a complementary heterogeneity of agricultural and industrial economies. Thus, New Zealand's exports to Britain have been almost exclusively farm products such as wool, dairy products, and meat; and Britain's exports to New Zealand have consisted largely of manufactured goods. But actually there are few international unions built on such complementary heterogeneity. All six countries of the European Economic Community are industrial in the sense that 50 percent or more of their labor force is engaged in nonagricultural production. Moreover, the Treaty of Rome limited the Common Market for the first five years largely to nonagricultural products. Hence agricultural-industrial exchange could hardly account for the successful initiation of the EEC. Similarly, the Latin American Free Trade Area and the various African custom unions are composed of countries fairly similar in their economies to one another. Thus it might seem that economic homogeneity enhances the initiation of unification.

Two or more industrial countries might complement each other in the type of industries whose products they export, for example, light and heavy industries; lesser distinctions, such as trucks and passenger cars, long and short cotton grain, etc., may similarly serve as complements. Some differences are to be found in the products of any two units, even those in the same economy, if only in the name of the brand. Moreover, under a certain distribution of tastes, as found now in the EEC, some citizens of one country have a preference for certain products of another country, even if their own country produces a rather similar product. Thus the Germans drink French wines, the Italians drive German cars, and the French like Italian refrigerators.[13]

[13] *Time*, September 14, 1962.

But complementary becomes a meaningless concept if it is applied to products that can be readily substituted for each other. More important, we find significant reasons, both in theory and in practice, for countries to engage in economic unification when their products are similar and they have no taste for each others' bananas, coffee, cotton, oil, steel, etc. One reason is the desire of some important industries to form international cartels to protect prices and to allocate markets for their products. This is more easily done in integrated economies than in those separated by national boundaries. Similarly such integrations are believed to help small countries to improve their terms of trade when they purchase collectively rather than as individual countries. Thus, homogeneity in certain economic sectors provides a motive for integration. In fine, there are some reasons to believe that economic heterogeneity enhances unification and some evidence that similarity of economic production enhances it. Possibly both approaches are valid, though for different products or under different conditions. At this stage of our knowledge, it remains an open question as to whether this is indeed the case, and for what products and under what conditions homogeneity might be more predisposing to unification than heterogeneity, or vice versa.

The picture regarding differences in the national wealth or per capita income of integrating units is not much clearer. If we use an absolute scale, in which the integrating units are compared to all existing units, ranging from $10 per annum for Somalia to $2300 for the United States, we find that most unifications encompass countries that fall in the same general category of wealth.[14] The Benelux countries, for instance, all fall in the high category of $750 to $1250 annual per capita income. All LAFTA countries have average per capita incomes which are less than $600 per annum. if we take a closer look, however, we realize that there are important differences within each group. When compared on an absolute scale, LAFTA countries fall in the same general category, but when they are *compared to each other*, differences seem high. For example, the richest LAFTA country, Uruguay, has a national per capita income of $569,

[14] All figures are for the early sixties; the year varies according to data available. Figures concerning developing nations must be viewed as open to a considerable margin of error. All figures that follow are given in American currency.

while Peru, which is the least well off, has one of $140, or four times smaller. Thus if the absolute scale suggests that countries that are similar in their per capita income unite, a relative scale, using a member country as a gauge, suggests that countries that are quite different from this viewpoint may still develop effective unions. Actually in each nation there are large differences in per capita income; in the United States for instance, Delaware in 1960 had an annual per capita income of $3013, while that of Mississippi was only $1173.

While there are cases in which a union exists or progresses despite large internal differences, there is also considerable evidence that such differences in per capita income have been among the factors that hindered or undermined unions. The higher per capita income of Katanga contributed to its secessionist drive from the Republic of the Congo, and to richer Senegal's breaking its union with poorer Mali in the Federation of Mali.[15] Gabon, the richest of the former French Equatorial African overseas territories, initially refused to join even a Central African customs union.[16] The question that needs to be researched is not whether differences in wealth hinder unification, but under what conditions such differences do or do not hinder unification, and to what degree.

Homogeneity of background in ethnic origin, cultural tradition, language, and religion were once deemed essential for stable political unity. The Hapsburg empire, which included groups that varied greatly on these counts and which broke into more homogeneous national units, is often cited as a prime example of instability deriving from such diversity. Highly integrated Germany and Italy are composed predominantly of people who at the time of political unification's firm initiation had a comparatively high level of linguistic

[15] The differences in per capita income are not large, but other measures of economic strength show greater differences. The exports of Senegal, for 1958 and 1959, amounted to $31.9 million, while those of Sudan, for the same period, totaled $200,000. The infrastructure of Senegal is significantly stronger and promised a more rapid development for it than the much weaker one of Sudan could allow. See "From Mali to Mali," *The Economist,* December 3, 1960, vol. 197, p. 1040, and Mamadou Dia, *The African Nations and World Solidarity.* New York: Frederick A. Praeger, Inc., 1961, pp. 104–107.

[16] Rayford W. Logan, "Will African Federalism Work?" *Current History,* vol. 41 (1961), p. 203; Carroll Quigley, "French Tropical Africa," *Current History,* vol. 40 (1960), p. 85.

and religious homogeneity. Homogeneity of these elements is widely considered a prerequisite for national and supranational unification. Actually, however, a large number of nations, such as Switzerland and Canada, are highly divergent on all these counts. Nigeria contains 250 different tribes. When the Nigerian government issued pamphlets to explain its new constitution to its citizens, it had to publish them in 12 languages in addition to English. Many nation-unions are multilingual, including Benelux, and the East European Community union. Rupert Emerson, after reviewing the cultural composition of many nations, concluded: "The notion of a single national culture, shaping the community and embracing all its people, is an admirable one whose principal shortcoming is its remoteness from historical fact."[17]

In short, we find that quite a few successful unifications have been initiated, and political communities established, without cultural homogeneity. Moreover, one look at a map will suggest many instances in which cultural homogeneity existed for many generations in an area, and yet no political unification has taken place. Thus, cultural homogeneity is neither a prerequisite to unification nor a sufficient condition, though it might very well affect the probability that a union will evolve. Moreover, we see below that homogeneity is not a mere "given" or a cause, but must also be viewed as a property that is itself affected by unification; it is a consequence rather than a cause.

Of all the conditions prior to unification, the effects of homogeneity of political orientation and structure are least clear. With respect to foreign policy, we find unions that are homogeneous and unions that are quite diversified. On the one hand, we see unions such as the Warsaw Treaty Organization; and the European Economic Community, all of whose members participate in NATO. Resistance to the admission of neutrals—Sweden, Switzerland, Austria, and Finland—to full membership in the EEC illustrates some of the impeding effects of the diversity of foreign policy, in terms of bloc-orientations.

[17] Rupert Emerson, *From Empire to Nation*. Cambridge, Mass.: Harvard University Press, 1960, p. 149. See also Selig S. Harrison, "The Challenge to Indian Nationalism," *Foreign Affairs*, July, 1956, pp. 620ff.

On the other hand, the Scandinavian union includes NATO countries (Norway and Denmark) and a neutral one (Sweden) without undue strain. The British Commonwealth includes some NATO members (such as Canada), some countries are tied to the United States and the West by other military treaties (such as Australia), and some neutralist countries (such as Ghana). The question hence remains as to what importance there is in consensus on basic foreign policy orientation as a prerequisite for unification; and, in particular, are there clear limits beyond which dissension will break up a union?

Regarding internal political structures, the variance is even greater. On the one hand, there are homogeneous unions; all the members of the East European union, for instance, are Communist countries though there are significant differences in degree of de-Stalinization. On the other hand, NATO includes both firmly established democracies and Portugal. Democratic Costa Rica and authoritarian Nicaragua share the bonds of the Central American Common Market. Further, even with a federal union there may be large differences among unit (state) governments; in the United States, for example, one can point to the one-party system of many Southern states which diverges from the two-party system more common in the rest of the country.

Nonetheless, there are instances in which unification was impeded because of political heterogeneity. In the 1880s and nineties, the unification of Norway and Sweden was hindered because of political differences between the countries. Norway's government had a wider and more liberal base than that of Sweden, which was still controlled by conservative landed aristocracy.[18] Hence, the Norwegian liberals feared unification with Sweden in much the same manner as the British Labor party in 1962 feared unification with the EEC, in which the conservative components are stronger than they are in Britain.

Again the extent to which heterogeneity stands in the way of initiation of a union has to be empirically determined. Some degree of political heterogeneity can obviously be tolerated; a large degree might be disintegrative in effect. The British Commonwealth, de-

[18] Raymond E. Lindgren, *Norway-Sweden.* Princeton, N.J.: Princeton University Press, 1959, pp. 57ff.

spite its almost boundless tolerance for diversity could not house both white-racist South Africa and the new African states, once the race issue was made salient, and South Africa was under pressure to leave the Commonwealth in 1961. If there is a general "limit of tolerance" of unions, what it is has yet to be established.

Of special interest is the effect of cross-community cleavages. It is generally agreed that impediments to unification would be greatest when the various background factors are distributed in such a manner that division deriving from one background factor reinforces divisions deriving from other background factors. Thus in those Latin American countries where rich differ from poor in religion (the rich are Catholic and the poor non-Christian), in racial background (white versus Indians), in education, etc., the degree to which the society can be integrated is limited. On the other hand, it is held that even if heterogeneity is high with respect to many factors, if the various sectors of the population overlap with regard to these factors—for instance, if a significant proportion of workers vote Tory while a significant proportion of middle-class people vote Labor—societal cleavages would be less visible and the society's integration be higher.

The low level of class tension and conflict in the United States is often pointed to as evidence that the cross-cutting cleavages of class and ethnic differences helped integrate American society by reducing the divisive influence of each of these cleavages.[19] But, on the other hand, Kann shows that although the ethnic and cultural differences did not parallel the economic, social, and administrative divisions of the Hapsburg Empire, they were still among the central reasons for its disintegration.[20] Similar points have been made about other national independence movements; that is, they have been shown to be movements which seek to increase the parallels between cultural and ethnic groupings and political and economic boundaries. Thus, it is unclear just what direct effect the heterogeneity of background characteristics has on unification, and what effect heteroge-

[19] See, for instance, Robin M. Williams, Jr., in *American Society.* New York: Alfred A. Knopf, Inc., 1956, p. 531.

[20] Robert A. Kann, *The Habsburg Empire.* New York: Frederick A. Praeger, Inc., 1957, p. 66ff.

neous characteristics have on one another and thus indirectly on unification.

Heterogeneous units might initiate a union if the elites in power are "homogeneous." A unification drive might be initiated in several countries at an historical moment when "congenial" factions are in power simultaneously. But their domestic opponents may later come to power and undo the agreement or limit its expansion. For example, the Treaty of Rome was signed at a time when the internationalist and bourgeois Catholic Parties of Europe were simultaneously in power. The Protestants, Socialists, and right-wing nationalists in each country were critical or skeptical. (One reason, it seems, the United Kingdom found it difficult to join was that it had no internationalist-bourgeois Catholic Party.) The Gaullists opposed the Treaty of Rome (which was an M.R.P. [Mouvement Républicain Populaire] policy) and later opposed its further expansion. If the Socialists came to power in Germany, they would probably retard the implementation too. Even if the English Conservatives (the closest British analogue to the Catholic internationalist-bourgeois party) were successful in joining the Common Market, a subsequent Labor government would delay in expanding it.

Thus several heterogeneous countries can initiate a union if congenial factions are in power simultaneously. And perhaps the political union would remain in effect if these factions remained in power permanently or regained power frequently. But even if heterogeneity were much lower, unification would be less likely to be initiated if it so happened that the "uncongenial" political and social factions were in power simultaneously in the various countries.[21] (Note, though, that unification might be rushed when an elite is challenged in one unit and a "congenial" elite of another unit seeks to help it to hold onto its position. In April 1964, such an effort was made, when a merger between Zanzibar and Tanganyika was announced to strengthen the position of the moderate left President Abeid Amani Karume and his supporters in Zanzibar vis à vis what was reported as a pro-Chinese group headed by Abdul Rahman Mohammed.)

In sum, the statement that heterogeneity is inversely related to

[21] I am indebted for this point to William Glaser.

unification is much too simple to be tested, let alone to be held as valid. The effects of heterogeneity in each of the major social sectors (economic, cultural, political) are to be studied. Such a study will have to take into account differences in the scales used, and the stage of unification—initiation, termination, etc.—of the union under study. The role of homogeneity is to be examined in the preunification stage, to determine to what degree it is required as a *prerequisite*. A careful distinction is to be made between what is a necessary prerequisite and what is only an enhancing factor. Further, we would like to know if the need for homogeneity decreases or increases as unification progresses. The question is, therefore, not whether heterogeneity does or does not block unification, but what kinds and degrees of heterogeneity block or enhance unification—to what degree, at what stage of the process, and what effect one kind of heterogeneity has on the others.

THE ENVIRONMENT: ECOLOGICAL AND SOCIAL PROPERTIES

Environmental properties include ecological factors, such as the physical environment in which the union is initiated and by which it is surrounded; and social factors, the properties of nonmember units that affect unification.

Nonsocial (Ecological) Properties: The Effect of Discontiguous Territories

Many ecological factors affect the probability that a union will be initiated, including the morphology of the region, the distribution of natural resources within it, and the existence (or nonexistence) of a natural border that defines the area. In general, contiguous territory and a morphology that allows easy transportation and communication is believed to enhance unification. High mountain ranges, for example, are reported to have been an important barrier to unifications of Central America and South America; the recent development of a Pan American Highway is viewed as improving the chances that future unions will be more successful.[22]

[22] See Norman J. Padelford, "Cooperation in the Central American Region," *International Organization,* vol. 11 (1957), p. 50.

Ecological unity has often been considered so essential for political communities that there is a question as to whether a union of nonadjacent territories, that is, one in which the ecological base of the union is broken up by a "no-man's land" (such as seas) or by nonmember countries, can be successfully formed at all.

A discontiguous territory is an unsettling, tension-provoking factor even for national political communities. West Berlin and West Germany and West and East Pakistan are two well-known cases.[23] Another well-remembered instance was the separation of East Prussia from the rest of Germany by the Polish corridor. The separation of a small Israeli enclave on Mt. Scopus, in the Palestinian part of Jordan, is similarly a source of tension. Discontiguous territory seems to be one factor that inhibited the development of the EFTA, in which Austria and Switzerland share a trade area with Portugal, Britain, and the Scandinavian countries. Albania's low integration into the East European Communist union is in part explained by the lack of a shared border between Albania and other member countries. (Albania was more integrated into the union when Yugoslavia was also a member.) Mexico is the only member of the Latin American Free Trade Area who shares no borders with the others; it remains to be seen whether Mexico will be a viable member of LAFTA.[24] The nonadjacent Union of African States has so far acquired little sociopolitical reality. (Upper Volta interposes between the three members of the union: Ghana, Guinea, and Mali. If it would join the Union, it is believed that the situation would change radically in favor of the Union of African States.[25]) Contiguous empires such as the Chinese and tsarist ones were considerably more stable than the noncontiguous Spanish and British empires.[26]

It would be hasty, however, to conclude that political unification

[23] On the strain created by discontiguity in Pakistan see Charles Burton Marshall, "Reflections on a Revolution in Pakistan," *Foreign Affairs,* vol. 37 (1959), p. 253, and *New York Times,* February 18, 1962.

[24] Mexico accounts for only one percent of the trade within LAFTA, chiefly because of transportation difficulties. Walter J. Sedwitz, "A Common Market for Latin America?", *Current History,* vol. 43 (1962), p. 6.

[25] Erasmus H. Kloman, Jr., "African Unification Movements," *International Organization,* vol. 16 (1962), pp. 389–390.

[26] Quincy Wright, "Empires and World Governments Before 1918," *Current History,* vol. 39 (1960), p. 66.

is impossible without territorial unity. Japan is well integrated. So seem to be the Philippines. While the Union of Britain with Ireland was dissolved in 1922, Britain maintained its ties with North Ireland. Similarly, Canada's union with Newfoundland is viable. And the United States seems to have no difficulties in bridging the 2000 miles that separate Hawaii from the mainland.

The study of the effect of territorial contiguity on unification will have to proceed by examining the underlying sociological and political variables that are affected by lack of adjacency in order to determine, first, their specific effects and, second, whether those effects are entirely or predominantly negative; and then by studying what compensating mechanisms, if any, are used to reduce or overcome the disintegrating effects of discontiguity. The most often cited effect is the hindrance of transportation of goods and people, which in turn obstructs the integration of the societal units and cultural interaction by curbing commercial and interpersonal relations.

A second hindering effect of discontiguity is the limitations it sets on movement of military units. Nasser might have suppressed the 1961 Syrian secession, or it might not have occurred, if the Egyptian army had been free to interfere from its home bases, unhindered by the interposed states of Jordan and Israel. This seems also to account, in part, for the ability of small Albania to be the only pro-China country of the Eastern European Communist union.

Third, because of the long association with statehood and nationalism, territorial unity has become a symbol of political unity, and its lack has therefore become an expression and symbol of division, as is the case in the West Indies, where the islands, rather than their federation, are the major frame of political identification. It would be of interest to establish to what degree being on a separate island bolstered the distinct social identity of Iceland, Ceylon, New Zealand, Australia, and other island nations. To what degree the command over modern means of communication and transportation, which some of those countries are gradually acquiring, will allow them to facilitate the movement of troops and goods and to overcome differences in cultural tradition, language, and historical experiences created by the lack of such means in earlier generations is a question that has to be answered before the impact of the lack of adjacency on unification can be determined.

Finally, the fact that under some conditions geographical *dis*contiguity reduces the need for integration is to be further explored. Separation of groups that adhere to incompatible values—at least until nationwide education can build up shared values—seems to help preserve whatever unity exists in many a new nation. Developing communication at a more rapid pace than education might well increase the level of tension in such societies.

Social Properties: Enemies, Partners, and Diffusion

The threat of a common enemy is probably the condition most often credited with initiating the union of countries. Wheare, for instance, listed "a sense of military insecurity and the consequent need for common defense" as one of six factors present in every case in which the desire for federation has arisen.[27] Springer suggested that "how difficult it is for federal unity to be preserved, even if it is successfully initiated, without the sense of danger, is illustrated not only by the West Indian case but also by the examples of the other postwar federations that have been created out of former empires of European countries."[28] French West Africa and French Equatorial Africa are given as illustrations. But Deutsch and his associates have already pointed out that this is much less common than is believed, and that when a union is initiated to counter an enemy, it tends to disintegrate as the threat passes.[29] The question is why a defensive alliance sometimes does mature into a more encompassing and lasting union, while in other cases its life is as short, if not shorter, than that of the real or conceived threat. We return to this question when various sequences of unification are compared; suffice it to say here that the study of "initiation under threat" will have

[27] K. C. Wheare, *Federal Government.* London: Oxford University Press, 1946, p. 37.
[28] Hugh W. Springer, *Reflections on the Failure of the First West Indian Federation.* Cambridge, Mass.: Center for Educational Affairs, Harvard University, 1962, p. 51.
[29] Karl W. Deutsch *et al., Political Community and the North Atlantic Area.* Princeton, N.J.: Princeton University Press, 1957, pp. 44–46.

to take account of the predisposition toward unification of sectors *other* than the military, to determine the chances for such a union to succeed.

While the importance of common enemies may well be overemphasized, the desire to unite to offset the power of an overbearing member of one's own alliance is underplayed for obvious reasons. This seems to be a central factor in *accelerated subregional* unification. We find frequently that when a region is uniting, a subarea is uniting more rapidly than the rest, and that this subarea includes the weaker members of the region.[30] This holds for the Benelux countries in the EEC[31] and for the South in the United States.[32] But since in these cases stronger ties already existed among the subarea units than among the others before regional unification was initiated, the accelerating effects of the desire to countervail an overwhelming partner—West Germany and France in the EEC, the Northeast in the United States—have yet to be established. This would require demonstrating that such subareas continue to maintain a higher and more rapidly growing level of integration than the rest of the union, and that the more "overwhelming" the superior partner (or partners) are, the more integrated they become.

A third way in which a union may be affected by nonmember units is through diffusion or imitation, a process often studied by anthropologists but rarely by students of international relations. To put it more colloquially, there seems to be in international relations such a phenomenon as "fashion," which enhances the transfer of the institutions of one region to another. The Marshall Plan directly affected the formulation of the Molotov Plan; the formation of the

[30] Weaker in terms of general assets as compared to the leading member or members of the same union; the weaker countries try to countervail.

[31] See F. Gunther Eyck, *The Benelux Countries, An Historical Survey.* Princeton, N.J.: D. Van Nostrand Company, Inc., 1959, p. 87ff. In many areas, the Benelux countries are moving more rapidly toward economic unification than is the EEC as a whole. (The Benelux union was initiated before the EEC, but—it seems—its integration has been accelerated since it became a subunion of a more encompassing body.) See also Norman J. Padelford, "Regional Cooperation in the South Pacific," *International Organization,* vol. 13 (1959), pp. 380–393.

[32] W. J. Cash, *The Mind of the South.* New York: Vintage Books, 1960. For another case, see Arnold Rivkin, *Africa and the European Common Market.* Monograph Series in World Affairs, no. 2, University of Denver, 1963–1964.

Organization of European Economic Cooperation (OEEC), in Western Europe, under the initiative of the United States, affected the foundation of the Council for Mutual Economic Aid (CMEA) in Eastern Europe by the USSR. The European Free Trade Area (EFTA), created two years after the EEC, often imitated it. For instance, when the EEC accelerated reductions in customs for its members, the EFTA did the same. Even the rates of reduction were similar.[33] While the formation of economic unions in Latin America and Africa were discussed and planned before the development of the EEC, the particular treaties finally signed by LAFTA, and the *Conseil de l'Entente* were influenced by the text of the Treaty of Rome and the institutions created for its implementation.[34] None of these constitutes a case of pure diffusion but in each case desire to retaliate or to countervail the initial international treaty or organ played a central role in initiating the limitations. (The motive or motives should not be confused with the process by which the institutional patterns are borrowed and the aura of success—whether it be of friends or foes—enhances the process.)

While the present vogue is one of common markets, the earlier one was of regional commissions. The South Pacific Commission (established in 1947), for instance, "took its model" from the Caribbean Commission (established in 1946). An Economic Commission for Europe was founded in 1947, and one for Latin America in 1948.[35]

The question that arises whenever social patterns or political institutions (for example, the American Constitution) are transferred from one region to another, is: Are the conditions that allowed for

[33] See Miriam Camps, *Division in Europe*. Princeton, N.J.: Center of International Studies, Policy Memoranda, no. 21, p. 50.

[34] The Arab League was affected by the vogue to twice review the formation of an Arab Common market. *New York Times,* October 12, 1958; *Arab News and Views,* July 1, 1961, p. 1. For a recent report on the application of North American federal institutions to a South American country, see Leslie Lipson, "The Federal Principle and the Brazilian Reality," paper presented to the Sixth World Congress of the International Political Science Association, Geneva, September 21–25, 1964.

[35] This is not an instance of pure diffusion, since all commissions are U.N. organs; but without a "vogue"—based on diffusion—they would hardly be as acceptable as they were to the various countries represented. For another instance of diffusion, see Padelford, "Central American Cooperation," p. 43.

the functioning of the pattern in one region available or reproducible in the second region? When this is not the case, one of two things is bound to happen: (a) The imitation fails to be grafted because of different conditions and the new institutions are rejected. The vogue of unification, like other fashions, follows its own dynamics—a rapid rise in popularity is frequently succeeded by equally rapid extinction. Or, (b) the imported institutions survive, maintaining more or less the same formal structure as in the original region, but actually fulfilling different functions. For example, the introduction of EEC-type institutions in Central America serves, to a degree, to enhance industrialization—hardly a function they fulfill in Western Europe. Such unions—now formed in South America and Africa as well—are called, in deference to the source of the vogue, "custom unions," "common markets," or "free trade areas," while actually they are more partnerships-in-development. To what degree these unions are hampered by the use of instruments originally forged for different purposes, and to what degree the same international institutions can be used (after limited modifications) without negative repercussions to serve different functions—and which functions—is another question this paradigm raises but cannot answer.

System Properties

A process of increasing interunit bonds might start among units that had no previous relationship or that were not interdependent and did not constitute a system. All unification movements of which we are aware, however, were initiated among countries that were previously interdependent to some degree. At any rate, the study of the preunification stage is not complete unless the relationships among the potential participants in a union are investigated, even if the finding is that no such relationships existed. Both the preunification level of integration and its scope have to be assessed, and other relevant properties of the system have to be determined.[36] These properties will be remeasured when the unification process is terminated, and a comparison of the two sets of measures will inform us of the extent unification has advanced in a given period, under the impact of various unifying forces.

[36] See above, chap. 1, for a discussion of the concept of integration of systems.

Preunification Integration and Scope

Unification is a process in which the integration of a system is increased, a process that tends to be accompanied by expansion of the scope of the system in terms of the sectors that are controlled on a system rather than a unit level. (We assume here that the *initiation* of unification requires interdependence among the participating units, that is, they constitute a system. The process by which an unrelated aggregate of units becomes interdependent is too rudimentary and common to be included in the concept of unification, and is excluded here by definition.) This means that preunification integration and scope can be very low (sharing few international organizations), low (sharing membership in a bloc), or medium (as in empires), etc. The system is in a preunification state so long as both do not grow, whatever the level of integration happens to be (unless of course it is already maximal). Unification is a process, a change in the state of a system toward a higher level of integration, not a static feature of that system.

Shared Properties: The Example of Culture

The preunification system may have many shared properties; which one or ones we choose to study before and after unification depends on the specific problem at hand. We examine briefly the effect of culture[37] shared by the participants upon the initiation of unification.

According to a widely held opinion, shared culture is an essential property the system must have before it is "ripe" for unification. It is pointed out that under the impact of nationalism old political units (especially empires) broke up or were fused to form larger unions, such as Germany, Italy, in an effort to bring units that shared the same culture and political boundaries into balance. Deutsch, for instance, shows that sharing cultural symbols, ethnic origin, a language, a religion, a sense of identity, preceded the formation of a union in practically every case he studied.[38] Kann points to the pau-

[37] Culture is viewed in the broadest sense of the term, including religion, secular ideologies, language, arts, etc.
[38] Karl W. Deutsch, *Backgrounds for Community* (in progress).

city of the culture shared by a multination state, the Hapsburg empire, as partially accounting for its weakness and eventual disintegration.[39]

On the other hand, many political unions do not have most or all of these elements of shared culture. This holds true for national communities such as Canada, the Union of South Africa, Switzerland, Belgium, Nigeria, India, and for most of the multinational unions from Eastern European to the African and Malagasy Union.

One might view these two positions as completely contradictory and await additional findings and reexamination of earlier ones to determine which position is valid. It is possible, however, to view this contradiction as more apparent than real. Both of the following interpretations could resolve the contradiction, but which one, if either, does has to be determined empirically.

First, one might claim that most cultural values are politically irrelevant. Information can be exchanged, aesthetic values held in common, religious beliefs draw similar commitments—and the countries so disposed still may not share a sense of political identity, nor have the necessary foundation for a shared legitimate government. Russian scientists might subscribe to American journals, American scholars read Russian journals; Russians see *My Fair Lady* (and like it), Americans appreciate the Bolshoi Ballet, etc., yet the two countries might go to war the next day, let alone fail to form a union. After all, the West European societies were sharing culture and civilization during many hundreds of years and scores of brutal wars. This position suggests that sharing culture is not required for unification, nor does the lack of a shared culture prevent it; it simply has little effect on political unification.

True, there is a limited set of values and symbols directly related to unification, including legitimation of the new power center, a sense of identity, shared political rituals, and the like. But it is the emergence of these shared political values that the study of unification has to explain; their existence is part of our definition of integration. If we view the same factors as our dependent variable (integration) and as our independent one (culture) we are spinning tautologies.

[39] Kann, *The Habsburg Empire,* pp. 107–118.

Another possible way to resolve the apparent contradiction is to claim that unions whose members do not share a culture may be initiated but they will not develop successfully, at least not until their culture becomes shared. Thus, the Union of African States might well have little shared culture, and the British Commonwealth less and less as non-Western societies join it but the former has yet to become a sociopolitical reality, and the Commonwealth shows a parallel decrease of integration as the culture which is shared declines. Similarly, the integration of Nigeria or Thailand is neither high nor guaranteed; and as they have increased their level of integration they seem also to have increased their shared culture, though how much net progress was made on either score is debatable.[40]

This view suggests that shared culture is not a *pre*requisite for unification but a requirement that has to be fulfilled before the process can be advanced. No union, one might suggest, is highly integrated unless a shared culture has evolved.[41] This would also imply that while cultural exchange programs can hardly trigger a unification process when other factors are missing, once unification is progressing—let us say due to economic, military, or political factors—cultural interchange makes an independent contribution to unification in an "advanced" stage of the process (as compared to the initial). That is, the exchange acts as a *solidifier* rather than as a prerequisite or initiating factor.

It is important to point out in passing that there may well be other such solidifiers, that is factors that can operate effectively only in a later stage of a process. Joint scientific projects, international professional associations and conventions, increased tourism, international television networks, sister-cities movements, shared holidays, and regional universities may all be able to play a role in these unions in which they initially seemed "unnecessary" or impossible.

[40] For a discussion of the Thai attempts at integration see Michael Moerman, "Western Culture and the Thai Way of Life," *Asia,* vol. 1 (1964), pp. 41–47. On Nigeria see Kalu Ezera, "Federalism and the Quest for National Unity in Africa with Particular Reference to Nigeria," paper presented at the International Political Science Association Round Table on Federalism, Oxford, September 1963.

[41] Among the mechanisms used to build up a shared culture after initiation of unification is the sharing of a *second* language, as Russian is becoming in East Europe. The foundation of "supranational" educational institutions is another device.

THE UNIFICATION PROCESS: INTEGRATING POWER

Sociopolitical processes such as unification do not proceed in a trial and error fashion. Once initiated they tend to follow one of a limited number of patterns (which will be discussed in the subsequent section). Which pattern they follow is in part determined by the *kind* of integrating power that various elites exercise and that the evolving union commands. This raises the question of what kinds of integrating power are applied in the unification process and who is applying them.

A CLASSIFICATION OF POWER: A CONCEPTUAL DIGRESSION

To study the effect of integrating power[42] on the successful launching of unification endeavors requires a clear conception of the kinds of integrating powers that exist. The following threefold classification seems to be satisfactory; integrating power, we suggest, is either coercive (for example, military forces), or utilitarian (for example, economic sanctions),[43] or identitive (for example, propaganda).[44] The classification is exhaustive; each concrete power is either one of the three or is composed of their various combinations.[45] The classification covers both "real" (coercive and utilitar-

[42] For a definition of power, see chap. 1.

[43] "Utilitarian power" is preferred over "economic power" because it is a term that refers to administrative and technical assets as well as economic ones.

[44] In earlier publications we used the term *normative* to refer to the third kind of power since it is based on an appeal to the norms of the *subject,* as when a leader calls on his followers to follow him in the name of values to which they are committed. (Norms are specifications of values.) This use of the term raised some difficulties, since for some social scientists "normative" connotes value-judgments and oral prescriptions as against an empirical approach and neutral analysis. For others, it connotes legal norms to the exclusion of mores. To avoid unnecessary difficulties we use here "identitive" power, drawing on the fact that the power is based on the identification of the subject with norms, values, symbols over which the holder of power has control (e.g., only he can administer the sacrament), or on an identification with his personality that makes his approvals and disapprovals powerful.

[45] This classification is extensively discussed and applied in my *A Comparative Analysis of Complex Organizations.* New York: The Free Press of Glencoe, 1961, esp. chap. 1.

ian) and "ideal" (identitive) elements. It represent the three major sociological schools: the Italian school of Pareto and Mosca which was especially concerned with force; the economic-Marxist school; and the Weber-Durkheim tradition which emphasized sentiments and ideas.

In this study we use the threefold scheme to classify not only powers but also assets. Power is a relational property; it indicates that a unit can make some other unit or units—in the case of a system all the member units—follow its guidance. *Assets* are possessions that a unit or system has, regardless of those other units may have. Assets might be converted into power, as when a unit uses its economic assets to grant or withhold foreign aid in order to impose its wish on some other unit. On the other hand, a unit might consume these assets, accumulate them, or exchange them for others. All these actions would affect its power potential. (In the case of exchange, it is likely that a relationship will be produced that will have some power of its own in the sense that it will "pull" participants to stay within it in order not to lose the utilitarian advantage that the exchange—not any one of the participants—produces.)

This study suggests that it is fruitful to distinguish between three kinds of powers and assets. *Utilitarian* assets include economic possessions, technical and administrative capabilities, manpower, etc. Utilitarian power is generated when these assets of a unit are allocated or exchanged in such a fashion as to allow it to bring another unit to comply with norms it upholds, or with the system it upholds for its members.

Coercive assets are the weapons, installations, and manpower that the military, the police, or similar agencies command. The line between utilitarian and coercive assets is thin; civilians might be called to the flag and factories converted to military use. But as long as this conversion has not taken place, these will not be viewed as coercive assets. Coercive power (or force) results when coercive assets are used by one unit to impose its will or norms on the others or by the system to impose its norms on the member units. It is important to note here that coercion is used throughout this study to refer to the use of the means of violence, and not to pressure in a more generic sense, as this concept is sometimes used. Coercion here refers to the use of *force* to compel, and not to other means of enforcement.

The term *identitive* assets refers to the characteristics of a unit or units that might be used to build up an identitive power. These identitive potentials are usually values or symbols, built up by educational and religious institutions, national rituals, and other mechanisms. The larger the potential appeal of these values and symbols to other units, the larger the identitive assets of the unit under examination. The assets are transformed into power when a member unit or the system (through its representatives) succeeds in showing that a particular course of action it seeks other units or all member-units to follow is consistent with, or an expression of, these values and symbols that other units have come to be committed to.[46]

From the viewpoint of a unit subject to the application of power by either another member-unit or the system, the kind of power employed to attain compliance makes a considerable difference. The application of identitive power tends to be the least alienating (as when the United States succeeds in convincing a country that not trading with Cuba is in line with the values the particular country and the United States share); the application of force is the most alienating (as when the Marines take over). The exercise of utilitarian powers, such as cutting the sugar quota and/or foreign aid, are less alienating than the use of force, but considerably more than the use of identitive power.

International relations, in general, are characterized by the more frequent use of a coercion by one unit against another as compared to the interaction of other social units, and by the less frequent and less effective exercise of identitive power. Utilitarian power is frequently used in international as well as intranational relations. Unification processes are directed by all three kinds of power. Some unions are largely forced, as the Federation of Malaysia seems to be

[46] It is assumed for the purposes of this study—though it might well require exploration on some other occasion—that identification limited to a person, not fortified with an extension of such identification to values and symbols, is unstable and serves only as a limited and transient kind of power that can here be ignored. Charismatic power is typically a mixture of personal and normative (symbols and values) elements and is of course included in the concept of identitive power.

on important segments of the population of Sarawak and North Borneo, and the Federation of Rhodesia and Nyasaland was with regard to many Africans. Some are "encouraged" mainly by utilitarian means, as the European unification initially was in the OEEC. In order to receive American reconstruction funds under the Marshall Plan, a country had to commit itself to cooperate with other European countries.[47] Still other unions are initiated chiefly by an appeal to common values and by propaganda, as the United Arab Republic was. Some unifications are directed initially by a more balanced combination of various kinds of power: Prussia, for instance, used power of all three kinds—in good measure—to force, bribe, and persuade the German states to unite. Nor are all "subordinate" countries necessarily treated in the same way. Larger and more powerful Chile is more coddled and less pushed by the Latin American leaders, Argentina and Brazil, than small, weak, and highly dependent Paraguay.

EFFECTIVE COMPOSITIONS

Differences in Kind

The question of which composition of power is most effective for unification has not been answered. It is quite evident that different kinds of unions (such as military only or economic only) develop effectively when different kinds of power are used. The transition from stage to stage of unification of the same kind of union might well also require a change in the power applied to maximize the development of the union. Does one, perhaps, start best with coercion or does one best initially apply identitive power and resort to others only if that is not effective? What role does utilitarian power play in the growth of different kinds of unions?

One question deserves special attention in view of its political, ideological, and moral significance: Does the use of coercion in the initial stage of unification necessarily impede the long-run success

[47] Stephen S. Goodspeed, *The Nature and Function of International Organization*. New York: Oxford University Press, 1959, p. 569.

of that union?[48] If a positive answer to this question cannot generally be given, then the problem of the condition under which coercion is or is not detrimental must be raised. Is the extent of coercion used a major determinant, so that limited coercion, as used by Prussia to unify Germany, will not undermine the emerging union while extensive use of force, as in Rhodesia and Nyasaland from 1959 to 1962 will undermine it? Does extensive use of coercion become less ineffective when combined with extensive propaganda (identitive) efforts? Is there a "cut-off" point at which reliance on extensive coercion can be phased out? Can, for instance, the Soviet Union keep its Red Army out of Orthodox Communist Czechoslovakia without risking the loss of Czechoslovakia from the union? There could hardly be more significant questions to the architects of unions—or to those who wish to undermine them—but there are few systematic answers to them.

Differences in Quantities

Unification processes require changes in member-units and in the relations among them. Such changes tend to be resisted at least by some subunits[49] or by outsiders whose utilitarian interests and identitive commitments motivate them to support the maintenance of the status quo.[50] Hence, a comparison of the amounts of power supporting unification with the amounts of power wielded by resisting subunits or outsiders—that is, the drawing up of "balance sheets" and power inventories—is an essential part of the study of unification.

It is widely understood that power cannot be abstracted from its use. Power is a relational concept; a country has a power advantage over some countries and not over others; it has power for some pur-

---

[48] The answer depends in part on the criteria of success one chooses to use. A union can be *maintained,* at least in the short run, by extensive use of force. How *effective* it is, in terms of the level of integration attained, the scope of the unification, or resistance to external hostile powers, is a different question.

[49] A subunit is a segment of a member-unit (such as the agricultural subunit of West Germany, which is a member of the EEC). The three-level distinction—of system, unit (or member), and subunit—is necessary for the following analysis.

[50] On these "vested interests," see Talcott Parsons, *Essays in Sociological Theory.* New York: The Free Press of Glencoe, 1954, pp. 138–141 and pp. 315–318.

poses but not for others. But this point should not be overempha-sized. By listing the assets of a country, one can reach a quite helpful estimate of its power potential, both with regard to other countries and to various subject matters.[51] One cannot predict the outcome of each confrontation but one can form quite useful forecasts about the average outcome of a number of confrontations. For instance, few observers would hesitate to make such estimates of a number of military showdown between the United States and Mexico or the outcome of votes in the Warsaw Treaty Organization. This can be done because the assets of a country, including such items as its resolve and international "style,"[52] are its power-potentials: the more assets it has—all other things being equal, including assets of other units—the more power it will have.

We are also helped in estimating the power potential of a country by having some knowledge of the universal scale (or total range) of assets there are and the rules for conversion of assets into actual power. The knowledge of the universal scale and the position of a country on that scale enables us to forecast the likelihood of its encountering a power that will be superior (and hence neutralize its power). Knowledge of the "rules" of conversion[53] suggests that cer-tain assets are more helpful in some contexts than in others. Thus, countries that would hardly amount to much on the battlefield have the same full vote as the superpowers in the General Assembly of the United Nations. In this sense, with the same total amount of assets, they are more powerful in the United Nations than in the military field. Still, even here the *general* level of assets makes much difference; assets in one area tend to have an effect on power in another. Surely the United States and the USSR get their way more often in the United Nations than Iceland or Paraguay despite the fact that they all have an equal vote in the Assembly.

In short, it is true that the emphasis on power viewed in relation

[51] For such estimates, see Stephen B. Jones, "The Power Inventory and Na-tional Strategy," *World Politics,* vol. 6, no. 4 (1954), pp. 421–452; A. F. K. Organski, *World Politics.* New York: Alfred A. Knopf, Inc., 1962.

[52] On this concept see Stanley Hoffman, "Restraints and Choices in American Foreign Policy," *Daedalus,* vol. 91 (1962), pp. 680ff.

[53] That is, under what conditions, how many and which kind of assets are needed to generate a unit of power.

to a specific subject and a subject-matter serve as an important corrective to the earlier view, which tended to see power as an absolute characteristic. But one need not shift to the opposite extreme and state that one cannot tell whether a country is powerful until a context is specified. Some countries have considerably more *general* power-potential than others. The following discussion of the use of power to direct unification draws on this point.

Communication and Responsiveness

The communication capacity of a unit, as Deutsch pointed out extensively, is a major determining element in the unification process.[54] The effectiveness of the communication network of a unit or system affects the degree to which its assets can be converted into actual power. A military machine that commands superior weapons and manpower can be defeated by an inferior machine that has a more effective system of intelligence and internal communication. The ability of the central authority of an economic union to respond to losses by a member-unit that might drive that member out of the union is largely affected not only by the amount of utilitarian assets the central authority commands, but also by the timely reception of information about the location, spread, and intensity of the losses, and the alienation from the union they have produced.

Finally, Deutsch points to the need of the recipient of communication to be able to digest such information and respond properly.[55] Effective communication requires not only the transmission of information but also certain qualities and processes within the receiving units. Obviously if a decision-making unit is flooded (or "overloaded") with communications, is ideologically rigid, or for some other reason is not able to digest the communications received, the conversion of assets into powers, if not completely misdirected, will be as inadequate as if the unit had not received inadequate communication to begin with.

What is far from clear is the relative weight of the communication

[54] Deutsch *et al., Political Community,* pp. 12ff. See also Karl W. Deutsch, *Nationalism and Social Communication.* New York: John Wiley & Sons, Inc., 1953.
[55] *Nationalism and Social Communication,* pp. 96ff.

factor. Some authorities tend to see communication as a most central factor. Others stress much more the relative assets of a unit, viewing communication as one aspect of such assets, a condition that affects activization of the other assets but of little import in itself.[56] Moreover, the level of communication received and digested is itself largely affected by the power-backing a particular message has been given. A communication sent by an unknown economic expert would have quite a different impact from the same communication sent by the Farmers' Bureau. Our subsequent study provides some data to bear on this question of the relative role of communication in determining effective power configurations.

EFFECTIVE DISTRIBUTIONS

Whatever the kinds and amounts of power employed to initiate and bring about a union, the way this power is distributed among various units, that is, the relative power the units have, is of great consequence to the unification process. Two major dimensions have to be taken into account: (a) The degree of elitism, that is, the degree to which power is concentrated in the hands of one or a few units as against a more or less equal distribution among many,[57] and (b) the nature of the unit (or units) that has more power than others (if any), in terms of membership in the emerging union. Is the elite-unit (the power holder) a member or does it impose unification from the outside?

Degree of Elitism

Elite refers to a unit that devotes a comparatively high proportion of its assets to guiding a process and leading other units to support

[56] The dispute about the relative weight of power versus communication is one of the central issues in the human relations versus structural-functional dispute. For presentations of both sides see Amitai Etzioni (ed.), *Complex Organizations: A Sociological Reader.* New York: Holt, Rinehart and Winston, Inc., 1961, pp. 99–130.

[57] For a discussion of this subject in terms of differences of "sub-system dominance" see Morton A. Kaplan, *System and Process in International Politics.* New York: John Wiley & Sons, Inc., 1957, pp. 16–17 and Roger D. Masters, "A Multi-Bloc Model of the International System," *American Political Science Review,* vol. 55 (1961), p. 795.

it. It might be a person (for example, de Gaulle), a group of persons (for example, the British aristocracy), or a state (for example, the United States for the Western world). Regarding the last, a country is often referred to as the "leader" of a union or bloc; we prefer the term "elite" in this case because it is less anthropomorphic than "leader." When it is necessary to emphasize that we are concerned with a function, disregarding who or what is carrying it out, we use "elite-unit" rather than simply "elite." Elite-unit is preferred over "core area," used by Deutsch, because it might not be an area, but a social group. Unless otherwise specified, "elite" throughout this volume is used to refer to units that exercise political leadership, not leadership in economic, cultural or other matters.

The elite might be a member-unit in the system, as was Piedmont in the unification of Italy, an elite-unit *of* the system (or system-elite), as is the Federal Government of the United States, or a unit that is not a member of the system (external elite). We shall see that these are not mutually exclusive alternatives; an elite might be part external, part member, or even part member-unit and part system-unit. The latter occurs when a member-unit controls the system and uses this dominance in part to direct the system in accordance with its needs rather than merely with those of the unit. "Elitism" refers to the concentration of power; it becomes higher the more the system is controlled by one or a few units; it becomes lower the more evenly power is distributed among the member-units.

Many unification processes are carried out under the leadership of one elite. In most of the historical cases studied by Deutsch and his associates, one unit was by far superior to the others, in both its interest and its preparedness for unification, in terms of utilitarian assets as well as communicative capacities, and was thus able to initiate unification.[58] England played such a guiding role in its union with Wales and with Scotland; Britain also played this role in the formation of the EFTA (though it was formally initiated by Sweden); the USSR obviously has this elite position in Eastern Europe; Guatemala was the central force in first building and later disintegrating the central American Federation (1823–1839). In several other cases,

[58] Deutsch *et al., Political Community,* pp. 50ff.

two countries seem to hold an elite position; for instance, France and West Germany seem to be the major powers in the EEC.

In larger unions there is often a unit which plays the role of a lieutenant; it is not a first-rate power but is stronger than the smaller units. A lieutenant country is one whose power status is lower than that of the elite countries and higher than that of the followers. Italy has such a status in the EEC, Chile in LAFTA, Canada for a long period in the British Commonwealth. In view of the special role lieutenants play in other power structures,[59] it would be of great interest to investigate the possibility of their having a special role—not just a distinct power status—in international unions.

Other unification efforts, while not completely egalitarian, seem to come considerably closer to an even power distribution. The major participants of the Scandinavian union, Sweden, Norway, and Denmark, have similar power positions (though Sweden might be a little stronger than the others); the same is true for the members of the present Central American Union, and the two main members of Benelux. It seems safe though to generalize that egalitarian or near-egalitarian unions are considerably less numerous than elitist ones.

The most frequently found pattern is not necessarily the most effective one, though when a process is at least partially planned and effectiveness constantly assessed, frequency and effectiveness tend to be associated. The question is whether hegemony is a better way to unification than dual leadership, and dual leadership more effective than the absence of any clearly superior unit. Is hegemony the most effective power-distribution when the member-countries are quite willing to unify, or is it effective only when some or most potential participants are unwilling or at least reluctant to join a union or to stay in it?[60]

[59] James S. Coleman, Elihu Katz, and Herbert Menzel, "The Diffusion of an Innovation Among Physicians," *Sociometry* (1957), pp. 253–270, showed that new drugs are tried out in a community of medical doctors, not by the most prominent one or the least prominent one, but by some M.D.'s second in the prestige structure. Then, if a new drug proves successful, the leader adopts it, followed by the rest of the community. The lieutenants are thus used to trying out innovations; in this way innovations are made by the elite without directly endangering its leaders if they fail.

[60] The frequency of forced integrations as distinct from voluntary ones, has been pointed out by Crane Brinton, *From Many, One*. Cambridge, Mass.: Har-

A closely related question concerns the association between the configuration of powers applied and the power distribution. It would seem that when power is relatively concentrated in the hands of one or two units, coercion is more likely to be used; when it is fairly evenly distributed, identitive appeals are more common; and economic sanctions are frequently used in both elitist and comparatively egalitarian power distributions, but are more frequent in the elitist type. Whether this is really the case, and if these are the most effective combinations are open questions.

Degree of Internalization

The second dimension for an examination of the effect of various power distributions on unification is that of the membership status of the elite countries (in egalitarian unifications, all participants are members). Membership has to be viewed as a continuum; there are partial members in varying degrees, full-fledged members, and non-members. The United States, for instance, for many years has supported numerous unifications of non-Communist countries, participating in some (such as NATO), being an "informal member" in others (CENTO), and as a nonmember in still others (EEC). Britain is a member of the Commonwealth but not of the Federation of Nigeria, which it engineered and launched. France is a member of the EEC but not of the *Conseil de l'Entente,* although it has much influence over each one of the Entente's members (Ivory Coast, Upper Volta, Niger, and Dahomey) and their collective action.[61] The question is, what difference does the membership status of the elite-country make? Does effective leadership require membership? Are outside elites limited in the kind of power they can effectively exercise; in particular, is effective use of identitive power chiefly limited to member-elites? Do outside elites tend to be rejected after the initiation period and to be replaced by member-elites?

We refer to the process in which control of a system is taken over

vard University Press, 1948. See also Harold D. Lasswell, "The Interrelations of World Organization and Society," *Yale Law Journal,* vol. 55 (1946), pp. 889–909.

[61] See Immanuel Wallerstein, *Africa: The Politics of Independence.* New York: Vintage Books, 1961, pp. 108, 116.

by member-elites from external elite-units as *internalization,* since
control that was external to the system becomes internal. The term
is usually used by psychologists; its extension to social systems is
justified since analytical internalization means the same for both personality and social systems. In psychology it is used, as we do here
for social systems, to refer to the process by which standards of
behavior that were externally enforced become part of the person's
own system, that is, they become self-enforced, and by the same
token the person "grows" and becomes autonomous, that is, gains
self-control. In this sense, and in this sense only, one can speak about
parent social systems that guide the development of dependent ones,
gradually allowing them to increase their self-control until they mature and can function on their own. Differences in the pace at which
the dependent system seeks to build up its self-control and at which
the parent system will tolerate the process create strains both on the
interpersonal and intersocietal levels.[62] In short, the associations that
the term "internalization" evokes are quite appropriate for our study
of the development of unions, though as with all analogies their
assets are turned into liabilities if their limitations are not strictly
observed. Internalization is used here strictly to refer to the shift of
control from an external to an internal elite; no psychoanalytical
assumptions, for example, about national "superego" or "id," are
made.

An internal elite might increase its power, not at the cost of an
external one, but through a process in which control is transferred
from member-units to the elite of the evolving system, which might
be a member- or a system-elite. A system-elite is built up from the
powers given up by member units (for example, the formation of
supranational organs of the EEC); a member-elite is built up if these
powers are concentrated in the hands of one (or more) member-
unit(s).[63]

---

[62] On uneven pace of growth in self-control, see Amitai Etzioni, "The Epigenesis of Political Communities at the International Level," *American Journal of
Sociology,* vol. 68 (1963), pp. 407–421.
   [63] Ludwig Erhard's objection to the planning of the Economic Commission
of the EEC in 1962–1963 raises this distinction between system- and member-
elites: was it oriented against the very existence of a central unit (in favor of
laissez faire or of national controls coordinated through intergovernment chan-

An interesting phenomenon which deserves further exploration in this context is that some external elites, rather than allow their power of control to be "internalized," become themselves "internalized" to varying degrees in the process of unification.[64] The United States, for instance, had no intention of becoming involved in the Baghdad Pact when it was originally formed in 1955 (the pact became CENTO after Iraq's withdrawal in 1959); but in the late fifties there was a growing pressure on the United States to deepen its participation, a pressure which it only partially resisted. In 1960, the United States signed bilateral agreements with each of the members—a procedure frequently used to associate with a union without formally joining—which pledged it to take "appropriate action, including the use of armed forces" to help each country resist aggression. By 1961, the United States committed itself to appointing a permanent military staff commander for CENTO.[65] Similarly, France did not intend to become an informal leader of the *Entente* (Ivory Coast is the semiofficial, on-the-scene leader),[66] and even was ambivalent about its original formation. It is far from clear why this "drawing-in" process[67] occurs, why it remains "unanticipated," or why elite-countries become involved in more unions and to a larger degree than they had intended. No more is known about whether the internalization of elites makes them more responsive to nonelite members and to what degree, if any, such increased responsiveness enhances unification.

Theoretically, any point on the continuum of internalization of power (or elite-control) is as important as the next one; in practice there is at least one "qualitative jump." When a polity is recognized as "independent," it incurs a considerable increase in self-control;

---

nels), did he object to the excessive powers that felt the EEC organs were granted or had accumulated, or was he objecting to the disproportional influence France had over the Commission, and thus over the EEC?

[64] "Internalize" here refers to the process by which an outsider becomes a member of a union. Internalization of control refers to the transfer of power; internalization of a unit alludes to an extension of the bonds of membership.

[65] *New York Times,* April 29 and 30, 1961, and *The Reporter,* July 20, 1961.

[66] Immanuel Wallerstein, "Background to Paga, II," *West Africa,* August 5, 1961, p. 861.

[67] A stimulating discussion of this process will be found in Robert Endicott Osgood, *NATO: The Entangling Alliance.* Chicago: University of Chicago Press, 1962.

that is, an increase in the power of member- or system-elites vis-à-vis external ones occurs. This is the case because once recognized as a distinct entity the emerging polity is granted certain international privileges; it is referred to as an entity and the self-image of its members is validated by others.[68] It should be noted though that what seems like an arbitrary break from dependency to independence is almost invariably a gradual transition. There is as a rule a period of preparation with a gradual transfer of powers to the member-elites; and even the legal rights and international privileges are accumulated over a period of time rather than granted in one act. Thus, for instance, ambassadors are already accredited to the EEC though it still lacks most of the other marks of sovereignty. Full recognition of an international polity as independent does constitute a "jump" but a smaller one than it seems at first examination.

THE UNIFICATION PROCESS: INTEGRATED SECTORS

When the prerequisites are present and the integrating power is operative so that the level of integration of the system grows, its scope also tends to expand. That is, more and more sectors of the member-units are unified; and an increasing number of needs of the members are fulfilled through shared actions. In the following section, problems concerned with the sector in which unification is initiated are outlined first; then various explanations are suggested as to why it tends to expand its scope as the level of integration grows, and the directions in which the scope might continue to grow as unification advances further are proposed; finally, an exhaustive list of social sectors that can be shared is presented, and questions are raised concerning the order in which unification penetrates into these sectors.

[68] Friedrich points out that being recognized as a nation has an integrating effect on a country like India, which previously had few of the qualities of a nation. Carl J. Friedrich, "Nation-Building?" in Karl W. Deutsch and William J. Foltz (eds.), *Nation-Building*. New York: Atherton Press, 1963, p. 31.

THE FIRST STAGE: TAKE-OFF (A CONCEPTUAL DIGRESSION)

Until recently, most social scientists, when studying the beginning of a process or the formation of a polity, focused on the initiation period. The granting of a charter, the signing or ratification of a treaty, the founding convention, or similar events were considered the birthday of organizations, societies, and political movements. The concept of take-off, first used by students of aerodynamics, then economics, and recently introduced into political science by Deutsch and by Haas, calls attention to a second point in the "inauguration" of a process which is in many ways more important than its formal initiation.[69] Take-off occurs when a process has accumulated enough momentum to continue on its own, that is, without the support of nonmember units. This is not to suggest that the initiation point is irrelevant; the virtue of the concept of take-off is that it calls attention to the fact that for many processes the initiation stage and the take-off stage are not identical. To start an engine one needs an outside source of electrical energy (such as a battery). Once the engine has started, however, it is able to generate its own required electrical energy and no longer needs an outside initiating power. Economic development is often initiated by aid from developed nations, but it "takes off" only after the production capacity of a country has increased to the degree that it can answer current needs and still show a significant balance to be invested in the buildup of the means of production. In this way the basis for self-sustained growth is achieved.

Unification at the initiation stage is often dependent on external units or subunits; it has no momentum of its own. A significant change in the position of these units can bring the unification drive to an abrupt end. We know that at some advanced stage elements of a community-authority develop (for example, The High Authority of ECSC; the Economic Commission of the EEC), that the process

[69] W. W. Rostow, *The Stages of Economic Growth.* Cambridge, Eng.: At the University Press, 1960, chap. 4. Deutsch *et al., Political Community,* pp. 83–85. Ernst B. Haas, "Challenge of Regionalism," *International Organization,* vol. 12 (1958), pp. 440–458.

gains momentum (the EEC reduced tariffs ahead of schedule), and that unification seems to acquire power of its own, a power that counters attempts to halt the evolving union.[70] It is then that unification has "taken off."

Determinants of Take-off

What actually happens when unification takes off is far from clear. At least two changes in the nature of the process seem to occur that might account, at least in part, for the take-off phenomenon. One change is that the flow of people, goods, and communications across the national boundaries increases. Some such changes, though by no means all of them, require an increase in the amount of inter-unit decision-making. Increased *shared* activities—such as holding a common defense line—seem to increase the need for common decision-making even more than increases in interunit flow. Since the intergovernmental procedures are cumbersome for a large volume of decisions, such increases in flow and shared actions generate pressure to form a system-unit for decision-making, such as a "supranational" bureaucracy. This was the case in NATO (1951), the ECSC (1952), and the EEC (1958). The initial decision to form a system-elite tends to restrict the scope of decisions made by it (as was the case in the ECSC), or limit them to secondary matters, leaving major policy decisions to a superior intergovernmental Council of Ministers, whose workload is thus reduced (as is the case in NATO).[71] Once a supranational bureaucracy is formed, it tends, like other bureaucracies, to increase its functions, power, and legitimation and to resist attempts to reduce them. This is by no means always successful; an important subject for study is under what

[70] This would mean that it is now carried in part by mechanisms on the international level, not just by member-units—the nations—or by external powers. It is not implied that the union at this stage could repel all disintegrating threats, but that it would resist them on its own. The Economic Commission of the EEC played an independent role in bringing about a common agricultural policy of the EEC when the difficulties in forming one threatened the integration of this union.

[71] The relationship in the EEC is somewhat different. Formally the supranational bureaucracy only proposes, while the Council decides. See below, chap. 7.

conditions it is successful and under what circumstances it fails. But the endeavor of supranational authorities to increase their power is one major source propelling the process of unification toward a point at which it can continue to grow on its own.

Another factor accounting in part for take-off is *secondary priming;* that is, unification in one sector tends to trigger unification in others.[72] For instance, the opening of the trade barriers for steel and coal in six European countries, under the ECSC, created a need to remove preferences (which national railroads gave to coal and steel industries of their countries) in order to avoid indirect discrimination against imported products. Similarly, the action generated pressure to bring the working conditions in the coal mines and steel mills of the six countries closer to conformity in order to reduce differences in conditions under which the industries have to compete. It was also found wise to coordinate investment policies in these industries as well as policies concerning sources of energy other than coal. Thus the ECSC was one factor that led to the formation of a Western European atomic energy agency, Euratom.[73] Successful cooperation in these two important economic sectors was found difficult as long as the other sectors were segregated; thus the ECSC encouraged the formation of the Common Market. The extensive cooperation in economic matters required a joint economic policy, which in turn raised the question of forming a political basis to support such a policy, which generated pressure toward political unification; to date this has not gone much beyond setting up a European Parliament (which has mainly an advisory capacity), holding frequent meetings of the Foreign Ministers of the six countries, and creating a study group to examine plans for a European confederation or federation.[74] These economic and political unifications, in turn, have generated some

[72] See Rostow, *The Stages of Economic Growth,* p. 52, on "derived-growth sectors."

[73] William Diebold, Jr., "The Changed Economic Position of Western Europe," *International Organization,* vol. 14 (1960), pp. 12ff. See also his *The Schuman Plan.* New York: Frederick A. Praeger, Inc., 1959, esp. chaps. 8 and 13.

[74] On the political unification expected to be generated by the economic one, see Pierre Uri, "A French View of the Western Community" in C. Grove Haines (ed.), *European Integration.* Baltimore, Md.: The Johns Hopkins Press, 1957, pp. 81–92.

limited cultural cooperation, such as an exchange of teachers, some standardization of degrees to enhance students exchanges, and the formation of a few shared educational institutions.

The main point about this expansion of the original unification effort, or spill-over as Haas called it,[75] is that it is based on secondary priming. Unification in one sector (or subsector) triggers a similar process in others, rather than a thrust by any external force—hence the significance of the study of secondary priming for take-off. Once secondary priming sets in, unification continues even if the external powers that initiated the process have ceased to support it or are now trying to hinder its advance. How far secondary priming carries unification before it is exhausted is a question whose answer is as yet largely unknown.

In sum, the foundation of supranational bureaucracies and secondary priming accounts, at least in part, for the take-off of unification. This raises two questions: what patterns does unification follow once it has taken off and what is the optimal sector in which to initiate unification with a view to maximizing the extent to which integration will progress before it comes to a standstill.

The Take-off Sector

Unions may be initiated in many societal sectors including the military, economic, political, and educational sectors.[76] The question is, which one of these unifications provides the optimal base for take-off? Almost all possible sectors have been considered as optimal from this viewpoint by one authority or another. Deutsch points to the importance of the existence of a community of consent (or identitive union) at the first stage.[77] Kissinger sees in military alli-

[75] Haas provides an insightful analysis of this process in his *Uniting of Europe,* esp. chap. 8. The term secondary priming is preferred to spill-over as the latter term is used to refer to any secondary expansion including, for instance, an ecological one, while we seek to designate a specific kind of social expansion involved in unification, i.e., from one social sector to another, within one sector or from one subsector to another.

[76] Societal sector refers to all the social activities devoted to the service of one particular societal function. The adjective—economic, military, etc.—characterizes the function.

[77] Deutsch *et al., Political Community,* p. 71.

ances an effective way of binding nations together; he believes, for instance, that NATO could serve as an effective take-off base for unification of the 15 member countries.[78] Haas finds that economic unification (common markets) has the highest spill-over value, and therefore is obviously the best take-off base.[79] "Functional" organizations, increases in tourism, and cultural exchange have been viewed as effective ways to increase international integration and unification.[80] The effort to establish which sector (or sectors) is the optimal take-off base will have to draw on an analysis of the internal structure of the societies which participate in the unification process. Various societal sectors seem to differ in the degree to which they are interrelated. The more interrelated they are, obviously the more spill-over will occur. What is far from obvious is whether there is one sector that is the "most related" to the others, if it is the same in all societies, and which one it is.

EXPANSION OF A UNION'S SCOPE

A Stable Scope: Alternative Propositions

Once the first stage has been completed and a union has "taken off," the question arises as to how far unification has to proceed in order to form a stable union; are unification of all sectors and a high level of integration required, or will a lower level of integration and a less inclusive union be the most stable one; will it, that is, persist in time?

The highest degree of stability is reached, we suggest, only when a full-fledged political community is established; that is, when integration on all three dimensions (monopoly of violence, center of decision-making, and focus for identification) is high, and unification has penetrated all major societal sectors. Unification might stop short of high integration and full scope, and the resulting union

[78] Henry A. Kissinger, "For an Atlantic Confederacy," *The Reporter,* February 2, 1961, pp. 16–20. See also his *The Necessity for Choice.* New York: Harper & Row, Publishers, 1961, pp. 165–168.

[79] "International Integration: The European and the Universal Process," *International Organization,* vol. 15 (1961), pp. 374–378.

[80] For a review of this approach, see Goodspeed, *International Organization,* pp. 505–506.

might exist for a considerable period of time; moreover, high integration and full scope might be more difficult to attain and, hence, more risky to aim at than some less integrated and less encompassing form of unification. All that we hypothetically suggest is that, once attained and in the long run, unions that have become highly integrated and have a broad scope are more stable than those that are not so well integrated or inclusive.

A less maximalist view is represented by Deutsch and his associates. They found that the less integrated "pluralistic security communities" were more stable than the more integrated "amalgamated" ones. Of eight unions that failed, only one was "pluralistic" while seven were "amalgamated."[81] Since the Princeton authors have much data to support their position, it is incumbent on us to explain why we hold to the alternate proposition. The reason lies in the different conceptions of integration. Deutsch and his associates see a union as amalgamated (integrated in our terms)[82] once a common government has been established. The United States in 1789 became an amalgamated community; the Hapsburg Empire—and, for that matter, all empires by the definition introduced above—constituted amalgamated communities.[83] Sweden and Norway were amalgamated in 1814 because Norway was subordinated to a Swedish king.[84] From our viewpoint, these countries are only partially integrated; they lack at least one central element of integration, that of being the dominant focus of political identification of their citizens. Second, their scope is rather limited; the unions penetrated few of their societal sectors. Hence, in our terms, the unions Deutsch and his associates see as highly integrated are unions of medium integration and low or medium scope. We would concur that unions whose integration and scope are low are more stable than those whose integration and scope are medium (high, according to Deutsch); but this does not preclude the possibility that (by our definition)

[81] Deutsch et al., Political Community, p. 30.
[82] For other uses of integration, see Deutsch, pp. 5–7.
[83] For definition of empire, see supra, chap. 1. For discussion of empire as an amalgamated community, see Kann, The Habsburg Empire, passim.
[84] Raymond E. Lindgren, Norway-Sweden, pp. 9ff. Kann and Lindgren are two of the authors who participated in the formulation of the concepts reported by Deutsch et al., and who use these concepts in their volume.

highly integrated, broad-scope unions are the most stable of all. Because of these differences of definition, we feel that despite the weight of the evidence presented by Deutsch and his associate, both propositions—his and ours—should be held open till future research will decide which unions are more stable: those whose integration and scope are limited, or those in which these elements are high, to the degree that the unions have matured into political communities.[85]

We defined political communities above as systems which have reached a high level of integration on three dimensions (control, decision-making, identification). Since the discussion suggests that such integration tends to exist in unions that penetrate all the major societal sectors, that is, are wide in scope, the question arises as to what the full list of these sectors includes, so that we will be able to state when the unification is achieved or how far it has advanced toward completion. Following Talcott Parsons, we suggest that a full collectivity is one that solves autonomously its four basic functional problems;[86] *adapts* to its ecological and social environment, *allo-*

[85] The term union, as noted, is used throughout this volume to refer to international systems whose level and scope of integration is lower than that of fully integrated systems (referred to as political communities) yet higher than international systems whose level and scope of integration is low, such as most International Organizations. It is difficult at the present stage of our effort to specify at what stage a union's integration and scope achieves a level high enough to qualify as a community; or at what point its integration has regressed to the lower level of a mere international system. Both NATO and the British Commonwealth in 1964 were borderline cases, quite union-like in some spheres and less so in others. But the fact that some borderline cases cannot be readily placed (or have to be placed as borderline cases) does not invalidate this analytical scheme. Similarly, the objection that one cannot include "in one category" such different systems as the Nordic union, the Federation of the West Indies, and the unification of Germany, is not valid. First of all, they are not included in one category in the sense that although all are called unions, their level of integration is specified to indicate that they are low, medium, or highly integrated unions. Second, the boundaries of a category cannot be judged to be valid or false. Two considerations count: is the category used consistently and does it lead to fruitful insights, comparisons, and analyses. The following presentation of four case studies will provide an opportunity to evaluate our definitions from this viewpoint.

[86] A social sector, we have seen, encompasses all the activities devoted to the service of one particular social function. An analytical scheme of the functions served provides hence also an analytical scheme of sectors, though the two are not identical: one is a classification of needs, the other of answer to these needs. Sectors might be differentiated descriptively as economic, educational, military and the like, or analytically, as Parsons' scheme does. The relationship between

cates means and rewards among its subunits, *integrates* its subunits into one polity, and establishes as well as reinforces the *identitive* commitments of its members to a set of values. A union that has matured into a political community would tend to share and centrally regulate activities of all four types.

Sequences of Unification

Naturally the next question is, in what order, if any, are the various sectors unified? Do they have to be "assembled" in a specific order? If one is skipped, will this disintegrate the union, just retard it, or allow it to continue in a limping way until the missing link is added (though in the "wrong" order)? Here, more than with any of the other questions raised, we are in the realm of speculation rather than knowledge. Following the Parsonian model, one would expect the more successful—in terms of unification—sequence to be the one that starts with military or economic unification, and introduces political and identitive unification later.[87] It is of interest to note that the attempt to start European unification politically, by electing a European Parliament and government in the late 1940s and early fifties got virtually nowhere,[88] while the economic unification of the ECSC "spilled over" effectively into the EEC, which in turn generated pressures toward political unification. Seven attempts to federate Central America politically, undertaken over the last hundred years, have failed; very conscious of this factor, presently more successful efforts at unification stress economic integration. The two comparatively successful African interstate organizations, so far, are economic: the *Organisation Africaine et Malgache de Cooperation*

the descriptive and analytical classification of social sectors is a highly complex one, and as we shall see, need not be elaborated upon here.

[87] This point is considerably elaborated in the author's "The Epigenesis of Political Communities . . . ," pp. 416–417. While some political and identitive unification are involved in any military and economic unification, the latter two sectors can be unified to a considerable degree without political institutions (e.g. parliament, governments) and identitive institutions (e.g. churches, schools, mass media) being unified. To suggest that extensive economic unification requires political unification and hence that the two go hand in hand is to fall into the functionalistic trap which assumes that what is needed, will be.

[88] Goodspeed, *International Organization,* p. 591.

Economique and the East African Common Services Organization.[89] East European efforts at political unification under Communism have not succeeded; the measure of the success of efforts at economic unification—accelerated in the early 1960s—is hard to assess at this juncture, but it seems higher than the political one.

Deutsch and his associates offer an alternative hypothesis. Discussing the "assembly line of history," they state:

Generally speaking, we found that substantial rewards for cooperation or progress toward amalgamation had to be timed so as to come before the imposition of burdens resulting from such progress towards amalgamation (union). We found that, as with rewards before burdens, consent has to come before compliance if amalgamation is to have lasting success.[90]

If we may extend the right of interpretation to its limits, we would read the Princeton authors as suggesting, in Parsons' terms, that allocation (of rewards) ought to precede adaptation to the environment (burdens), and that identitive unification (consent) ought to come before political unification (compliance).

This of course does not exhaust the possible sequences; the four sectors might be assembled in 24 different ways, and of course other writers may find it fruitful to distinguish more than four sectors or four different ones. Moreover, we should be open to the possibility that there is, in fact, no one optimal sequence for unification but that each kind of union is "assembled" best in a different fashion. This brings us to the question: what kinds of unions are there?

THE TERMINATION STATE

A union "takes off" and "spills over" following one sequence or another, until it reaches a *termination* state. That is, for a period of

[89] Joseph S. Nye, Jr., "East African Economic Integration," *The Journal of Modern African Studies,* vol. 1 (1963), pp. 476–477. See also Carl G. Rosberg, Jr. with Aaron Segal, "An East African Federation," *International Conciliation,* no. 543, May 1963. See also Reginald H. Green, "Multipurpose Economic Institutions in Africa," *The Journal of Modern African Studies,* vol. 1 (1963), pp. 163–184.

[90] Deutsch *et al., Political Community,* p. 71.

time—before additional unification or regression sets in—the union's scope and level of integration remain basically unchanged.[91] Unions differ greatly in the levels of unification at which they stabilize, that is, stop increasing their integration and expanding their scope. These "termination" states provide a fruitful base for the classification of unions, not only because they provide a relatively fixed frame of reference (unlike the fluid state of the unions in other phases) but also because differences in termination states seem to correlate significantly with variables examined so far. In other words, unions that differ in the state at which they stabilize might differ also in the conditions under which they are initiated, in the forces that integrate them, in the sequence they develop, etc.[92]

LEVEL AND SCOPE

The state at which unification is terminated (or interrupted) can be measured in terms of the similarity of such a state to that of a political community. The preceding discussion suggests the following criteria:

(*a*) The level of integration, calculated on the basis of the degree of integration on each one of the three dimensions. Unions integrate gradually; hence, when unification stops, a union might be only partially integrated. Part of the means of violence, but not all, might be under the control of the new collectivity (as is the case in NATO); some but not all parts of the economy might be controlled by the community-authority (agriculture was largely exempted from the authority of the Economic Commission of the EEC until 1962); and identification with the new collectivity might be partial, in terms of both the percentage of the citizens whose identification has been transferred to the new polity and the intensity of the identification of those who did make the transfer.

(*b*) The number of sectors in which unification has taken place

[91] The length of the period is, like all such "cut-off" points, largely an arbitrary decision of the researcher, affected more by the scope of his study and the problem he is studying than by "reality."

[92] One reason such a relation is expected is that actors in earlier stages sometimes view the termination stage as the goal toward which their efforts are directed. This goal, in turn, affects the level and direction of their efforts.

and their nature in terms of the secondary-priming potential of these sectors. The higher the secondary-priming potential, the more likely the union is to resume its growth or to regress after a period of stabilization;[93] the lower this potential, the more likely the union is to continue in its "stable" state unless outside forces interfere.

(*c*) The degree of unification in each sector, for example, the ratio of international versus intranational trade.

It should be noted that even political communities whose level of integration and scope of unification is high may differ in the exact height of that integration and the breadth of that scope. While all political communities have, by definition, a center of decision-making, they differ in the scope of the decisions made by their governments. This distinction may be observed between communities with a federal government (high decision scope) and those with a unitary government (even higher decision scope). Actually, federal structures might themselves become more centralized (as has the United States over the last three decades) or less centralized (as the Soviet Union has become since 1957); and unitary governments may be either highly centralized (as is France) or comparatively less centralized (for example, Britain). Similar distinctions can be made on the other dimensions comparing high scopes to very high ones instead of just high to medium and low.

While above we advanced the hypothesis that highly integrated unions are more stable than those of medium or low integration, this does not necessarily hold for the most highly integrated unions. It is quite possible that a less maximally integrated structure will prove more stable, since it allows for more expression of unit loyalties and vested interests. But by the same token, a lower level of integration leaves more power in the units that might be used for secessionist purposes. An hypothesis suggests itself; namely, that the more integrated a community is (by other standards), the more unit autonomy it can tolerate.

[93] It should be noted that although in the examples of secondary-priming we have used until now, the interrelationship of sectors has resulted in the *extension* of unification from one sector to another, the process works in the same fashion for *de*-unification. De-unification in one sector might trigger de-unification in others, without any additional outside de-unification pressures, and the more closely related two sectors are, the more de-unification in one is likely to trigger de-unification in the other.

THE DOMINANT FUNCTION

Another major difference among various termination states is the dominant function that the new collectivity serves. This criterion not only differentiates unions (for example, military, economic, cultural unions), but also communities. It is true that a community encompasses all major societal sectors and in this sense serves all major functions; but communities can be characterized according to the function in which they invest more resources, manpower, energy, and which they value more highly as compared to other communities. While this predominant function changes over time, one can usually point to a particular function as dominating a given historical period. Thus it has been suggested that the United States, viewed as a community that emerged from earlier autonomous units, stressed adaptation in the industrialization period of 1875–1930; that concern with welfare and consumption took the place of the production emphasis after 1930; and that this was superseded in the late 1940s and early fifties by "other directedness"[94] and concern with ideological positions. At that same time, the Cold War with Communism intensified and the criticism of radicals at home reached a peak.[95] The return of an accent on adaptation marked 1958, as the Russian space probes and long-range missiles provided a strong environmental challenge to the United States. Unlike the earlier production concern, this one was focused on the means of violence rather than on consumption and on service to the national collectivity rather than directly to the individual. The scientist, the space-technologist, and to a degree the executive, rather than the entrepreneur or the merchant, were the new cultural heroes. Similar statements can be made about the changing

[94] This is, of course, the central thesis of David Riesman, Nathan Glazer, and Reuel Denney, *The Lonely Crowd.* Garden City, N.Y.: Doubleday & Company, Inc., 1953.

[95] Underlying this statement is the idea that the United States moved from the adaptive to the allocative, from a social integrative to an identitive integrative phase, over the last 75 years. It is derived from Talcott Parsons' treatment of the subject in his "A Revised Analytical Approach to the Theory of Social Stratification" in Reinhard Bendix and Seymour M. Lipset (eds.), *Class, Status, and Power.* New York: The Free Press of Glencoe, 1953, pp. 92–129. See also his " 'McCarthyism' and American Social Tension: A Sociologist's View," *Yale Review,* vol. 44 (1954), pp. 226–245.

focus of other unions. Yet many seem to have a "persistent" function that is stressed in the long run (though not necessarily "forever") despite short-run vicissitudes.

Before statements about the dominant function of a society or a larger political collectivity at a given period can be formed with proper precision and responsibility, much more theoretical work and empirical research are required. But it should be pointed out that it seems quite evident even now that the nature of the dominant function is an important variable for the study of unions and communities. For instance, we can already suggest that some functions—especially the political, social, and ideological ones—require higher integration and broader scope than others (for example, individual-oriented consumption). Hence, the level and scope at which the unification process is terminated and the nature of the function serviced collectively are crucial variables that both affect and are affected by the dominant function of the new unions and communities.[96]

---

[96] For an outstanding examination of the European scene from this viewpoint see George Lichtheim, "Post-Bourgeois Europe," *Commentary,* vol. 35 (1963), pp. 1–9.

Part Two

DISTRIBUTION AND CONFIGURATION
OF INTEGRATING POWERS:
A COMPARATIVE ANALYSIS

CHAPTER 3

Theoretical Framework

———•—•—•———

The paradigm of unification raises many researchable questions but answers none. We turn now to study four instances of unification in order to examine some of these matters in the light of empirical data, limiting our endeavor to explore a fraction of the questions raised in the preceding discussion.

Of the variables included in our paradigm, this study focuses on the effects of two sets of factors on the dynamics of unification—the effects of the distribution and composition of power. We seek to establish who is leading the unification movement (the distribution) and by what means (the composition); that is, which units command the integrating power and what kinds of power they exercise. More specifically, we would like to know if those unions in which power is concentrated in one or two units are more successful than those in which it is more evenly distributed. Under which conditions do external elites effectively guide unification and under which circumstances do they undermine it? What relative role does coercive, utilitarian, or identitive power play in unification? Which combinations are more effective? How important is communication between elite and nonelite units, and—elite-responsiveness to communications received, for successful unification?

Attempts to answer these questions are made with regard to both a stable and a changing state of integration, that is, from both a static and a dynamic viewpoint. We present in the remainder of this chapter a set of propositions about the effect of different power distributions and configurations on unification. The following four chapters hold some data bearing upon the propositions, each dealing with one case of unification or de-unification. The concluding chapter compares the four cases to each other and reexamines the propositions we have offered here.

INTEGRATING POWER: EFFECTIVE DISTRIBUTIONS

DEGREE OF ELITISM

Earlier studies of unification have reported varying degrees of elitism. In some cases, unification was guided by a small number of elite-units; in others, unions were formed without a concentration of integrating power in any one unit. In many of the historical cases studied, unification was found to be guided by one elite-unit, that had assets it was willing to invest in building up a union. Prussia's role in the unification of Germany is often alluded to as an example. In some other cases, two elite-units served as the unification leaders; for instance, Bern and an alliance of Uri, Schwyz, and Unterwalden constituted the "elites" of Swiss unification (in the pre-Reformation period).[1] It seems that three states, Massàchusetts, Pennsylvania, and Virginia, played a larger role than others in guiding the initial unification of the United States.[2] Haas, however, found no such elite-unit in the European Coal and Steel Community;[3] nor can one point to an elite-unit or units in the unification of Benelux.

The central question for us, however, is not what distributions are found, but which are most conducive to successful unification.[4] We expect to find that *unions that have fewer elite-units will tend to be more successful than unions that have a greater number.* In particu-

---

[1] Karl W. Deutsch, *et al., Political Community and the North Atlantic Area.* Princeton, N.J.: Princeton University Press, 1957, p. 38.

[2] See Allan Nevins, *The American States during and after the Revolution, 1775–1789.* New York: The Macmillan Company, 1924. For an interesting study based on content analysis, see Richard L. Merritt, *The Growth of American Community, 1735–1775.* New Haven: Yale University Press, to be published.

[3] Ernst B. Haas, "The Challenge of Regionalism," in Stanley Hoffmann, *Contemporary Theory in International Relations.* Englewood Cliffs, N.J.: Prentice-Hall, Inc., 1960, p. 230.

[4] See fn. 1, chap. 2, for definition of success or effectiveness.

lar, unions having one elite will be more successful than those having two, those with two more than those with three. It is difficult to imagine a union with more than three elites; we surely would expect such a union to be less successful than one that had fewer elites.

However, some unions are highly egalitarian in the sense that the distribution of power among the members is about equal, so that no one unit has a significant degree of power over the others, while as a group they hold power over any one deviant member—in short, the power rests in the system. For instance, trade among units that are in a similar stage of economic development and have a similar bargaining strength generates an integrating power that prompts units to stay in the system and penalizes those who are excluded or expelled. This power is generated by the exchanges *among* the members, not by the power of any *one* unit over the others. We expect *egalitarian unions,* whether they develop system-elites or not, *to be similar in their degree of success to monoelite unions.*

We expect a monoelite union to be more successful than any multielite pattern for the same reasons that students of corporations found a monocratic organization the most effective form of administration; that is, when there is only one elite-unit, it provides a clear center of policy formation, direction, and responsibility and a locus at which conflicts can be resolved. The increased strain in the Communist bloc since the rift between the Soviet Union and China illustrates the decline in directiveness that accompanies a shift from a mono- to a dual-elite international system.[5]

Among the multielite unions, we expect those with three or more elite-units to be less successful than those with two elites. As has often been pointed out, in a system with three or more members each participant is constantly confronted with the possibility that the two (or more) others will form a coalition against him.[6] During World

[5] For an elaboration of the effects of policentrism see Amitai Etzioni, *Winning Without War.* Garden City, N.J.: Doubleday & Company, Inc., 1964, chap. 2.

[6] Among sociologists, this point was stressed by Georg Simmel, in "The Number of Members as Determining the Sociological Form of the Group," *American Journal of Sociology,* vol. 8 (1902), p. 45. For relevant evidence see T. M. Mills, "Power Relations in Three-Person Groups," *American Sociological Review,* vol. 18 (1953), pp. 351–357; see also John W. Thibaut and Harold H. Kelley, *The Social Psychology of Groups.* New York: John Wiley & Sons, Inc., 1961, pp. 200–204.

War II there was a clear Anglo-American "coalition" against the third ally, Soviet Russia.[7] This general point applies particularly to elite-units that by definition have more power and whose maneuvers therefore tend to be more of greater consequence for the success of a union than those of lesser members.

It does not, however, follow that an egalitarian structure, that is, one in which all partners have similar power, is the least stable one. We would expect major decisions to be delayed for longer periods in egalitarian structures than in more "elitist" unions, but this very weakness may also be a source of strength. Once a decision is made, the members are more likely to feel committed to it, since they had more time to adjust to it and since it was more fully reviewed than would be the case in unions in which decisions are partially or wholly imposed from above, and at a comparatively rapid pace. Thus we expect *egalitarian unions to be less decisive than elitist unions, but more capable of generating commitment.* This proposition, much like the preceding one, has been supported indirectly in various experimental studies with small groups of students, kindergarten children, and factory hands.[8] This does not indicate a priori that it will hold true for relations among nations, but neither should the transferability of such findings be ruled out a priori. The validity of all these statements has to be examined in light of the empirical data to be presented below.

THE INTERNALIZATION OF ELITES

We saw above that leadership of a union is not limited to member-countries; many unions have, at least initially, external elites. We suggest two propositions with regard to such external elites: *as the level of integration and the scope of a union increase, the union will tend to internalize the functions performed as well as the authority held and the loyalists commanded by the external elite.* The external elite will either lose its position to some internal elite(s), or will gradually itself become a member of the union. In the last four dec-

---

[7] See, for instance, Lionel Gelber, *America in Britain's Place.* New York: Frederick A. Praeger, Inc., 1961, p. 40.

[8] Dorwin Cartwright and Alvin Zander (eds.), *Group Dynamics.* New York: Harper & Row, Publishers, 1953.

ades, there have been many instances of independence movements in which national elites took over the role of colonial elites as the unification of the national social groups progressed.

Second, *we expect the external elite to enhance the success of unification the more the direction of its application of power coincides with the power structure of the emerging union* and to hinder it the more the application of this power is counter to emerging structure. (The proposition assumes that the external elite is not powerful enough to change the power distribution among the member units to such a degree that it will "fit" the pattern of its intervention. Thus, for instance, if the external elite supports the weaker members of a union, this will hinder unification, assuming that the very intervention does not make them the stronger units.)

INTEGRATING POWER: EFFECTIVE COMPOSITIONS

DIFFERENCES IN KIND OF POWER

Unions differ significantly not only with respect to who has the power, but also with regard to the kinds of power applied. Which compositions are most effective? We expect that the *more identitive power the elites initiating and guiding unification command or the more the union-system generates, the more successful unification will be.*

Identitive power serves to build up and maintain the legitimation of the union and of unification efforts. The 1962 exchange of state visits between France and West Germany served to strengthen legitimation of the efforts to extend the scope of cooperation between the two countries to the political area. In a sense, de Gaulle was "campaigning" in Germany, and to a lesser degree Adenauer in France, to build up support for the Treaty of Cooperation, later ratified by the parliaments of the two countries. The European Parliament has some identitive power used to legitimize the EEC, especially its supranational elements. When identitive power is lacking, member-units are likely to become alienated from the union and/or its elites. Alienation may be expressed in many ways, from refusal to cooperate to secession. It particularly undermines the readiness of the members to make utilitarian contributions to the union or to other members unless those are fully and promptly reciprocated by utilitarian contributions from the union or other members to the particular unit.

We expect the *more utilitarian power the elites initiating and guiding unification command or the more the union-system builds up, the more successful unification will be.* Utilitarian power serves to build up and maintain the members' interests in the union and in further unification. Allocation of reconstruction or development funds through the union is one source of its utilitarian power. Interunit trade is another. When utilitarian power is lacking, the members are likely to reduce their utilitarian contributions to the union or to its elites and, when the opportunity arises, to shift to a more profitable union. Most of EFTA countries were quite willing in 1962 to drop out of their organization and to join the EEC when it became evident that the economic success of the EEC was greater than that of EFTA.

The relationship of coercive power (or force) to success of unifications is different from that of the other two powers. Many authorities view force as a basically disruptive power that needs to be suppressed rather than used. Actually, force is an essential element in the fabric of every fully integrated union. It has a deterring capacity when it is not used and a unifying function when used sparingly at critical moments. Many unifications, as they advance, reach a stage at which the other two integrating powers are temporarily lacking. It is at this stage, when members lose interest and belief in the union or fear that their ties to the union will become difficult to sever, that one or more units might withdraw or the union might be dissolved. The use of force at this stage to prevent secession may give the union the necessary time for the two other integrating powers to reexert themselves. It seems, for instance, that Hungary, which was held in the Communist bloc in 1956 by the use of force, was, by 1964, so reintegrated that little coercion or threat of coercion was needed to keep it in the union. Hence the use of force is often a prerequisite for the success or survival of a union. Unions that lack coercive power at the critical stage or that lack the resolve to use it disintegrate.[9]

While coercive power, unlike the other two integrating powers, plays a critical integrating role in the history of many a union, *it is not cumulative.* There seems to be a level beyond which the use of force defeats its purpose by generating such widespread and intensive alienation that it makes further unification less rather than more likely. Thus a union might exercise either too little or too much force.[10]

The similarity in the adjectives that characterize the kinds of integrating power and the dimensions by which the level of integration is determined (see Chapter 2) might suggest that propositions relating integrating powers to the level of integration achieved and maintained are tautological. Actually, the integrating powers are assets employed to bring about unification; the level of integration attained is a result of the exercise of these powers (as well as of other factors). The difference between integrating power and level of integration is hence the difference between cause and consequences.

To illustrate, let us assume that in an effort to unify two nations their school systems are merged so that similar curricula are taught in both systems; the same textbooks are used; students and faculty are free to transfer from the schools in one country to those in the other, etc. After several years of such a merger (all other things being equal) the young generation would probably have an increased sense of identification with the union of the two nations. The assets invested in the merger of the two school systems and emanating from their merger are an integrating power; the resulting changes in the identification of the students with the union is one measure of the

[9] This statement is derived from the two following ones: (a) that the tripartite scheme of coercive, utilitarian, and identitive powers is exhaustive; (b) that a critical stage is one in which the union lacks utilitarian and identitive integrating power.

[10] The terms used might leave the impression that there are accurate measurements of the force a country commands and that different levels of force can be compared on a fine scale. While the development of such a measure is not impossible, it is not required for the testing of the proposition advanced above. We can proceed by distinguishing among low, middle, and high level of usages of force.

increased integration attained. The two are thus clearly separable both analytically and descriptively despite the similarity in substance (in our example, both deal with "education").

As in other cause-and-effect relations, this is an analytical one. What is a consequence for one analytical step might be a cause for the next one. For instance, increasing the integration level of a system by investing funds in helping industries adjust to freer trade sees "increased trade" as a consequence and the investment of utilitarian assets as a "cause." But if we next examine the plans of a country to secede, the "increased trade" would be one cause countering its desire to leave the union under study, that is, it would be an integrating power.

DIFFERENCES IN COMMUNICATION AND RESPONSIVENESS

An adequate communications system requires both downward[11] communication (for example, government propaganda) and upward (for example, information about alienation among the population).[12] In addition to the mere transmission of both kinds of communication, the ability of the elite-units to digest communications received and to respond properly is required. In short, we expect a union to be *more successful the more effective its upward and downward communication channels are and the more responsive its elites are to the communication received.*

While we expect this relationship to hold for responsiveness in general, a very high responsiveness may have a negative effect on unification efforts, as the energies of the elites are likely to be preoccupied and their attempts to respond to the desires of all groups may prevent progress in any one direction. One might add that since most groups have a multitude of interests, which are not all compatible, there will be in most groups some interests that can be satisfied by

---

[11] Downward refers to communication flows from the elites to the member-units; upward—from members to elites.

[12] For the problems involved in measuring these communication flows, see Karl W. Deutsch, "Shifts in the Balance of Communication Flows: A Problem of Measurement in International Relations," *Public Opinion Quarterly,* vol. 20 (1956), pp. 143–160, esp. pp. 146–147.

de-unification and some by unification of the same activity. Hence it is impossible to be "completely" responsive to all groups; it would require unifying and de-unifying simultaneously. High responsiveness might therefore be associated with the most successful unification efforts; very high responsiveness would be excessive from this viewpoint; and complete responsiveness, a sheer impossibility.[13]

Largely, the question of which is more important, power or communication, is like the question of which is more important for shooting, the gun or the bullets.[14] Without communication power is aimless, and without power communication is without impact. The same is true for responsiveness; it bridges the communication received and the power applied. When the communication received is adequate and the necessary power available, the proper response is still needed to interpret the incoming communications and to issue the proper orders to the proper units. The efficacy of both gun and bullets is largely affected by the quality of the decisions made by the gunman.

But since the role of communication and responsiveness has been stressed frequently, we wish to emphasize that the action eventually taken depends not only on the qualities of the recipient of the communication, but also on the power of the sender. What is relevant is not only the communicative ability of the sender, how clearly he transmits his message, but also the degree of power with which he supports it. Hence the significance of political representation, a channel through which power-backed communications flow upward to the center of power and decision-making, as compared to other upward channels such as intelligence reports and public opinion polls where communication follows are not directly supported by

[13] For one of the best discussions of the effective balance between upward and downward communications, see William Kornhauser, *The Politics of Mass Society.* New York: The Free Press of Glencoe, 1959.

[14] Cf. Karl W. Deutsch's position on this matter. As rarely happens, his position is accurately telescoped into one paragraph on the jacket of his book, which states: "The theory that government is more a problem of steering than of power provides the basis of this new analytical framework for political study. It represents a significant contemporary shift in emphasis from the study of 'muscles'—arms, manpower, money—to the study of 'nerves,' the channels of communication by which the exercise of power is controlled." *The Nerves of Government.* London: The Free Press of Glencoe, 1963.

power. When the opportunities to communicate upward effectively are curtailed because of disproportional representation or are lost because representation is suspended, the ability of the power center to respond effectively is reduced.

It is true that a particularly alert and competent political leader, who has few blind spots on his radar screen, can use other modes of upward communication to gauge the power of various groups as communication about their needs and desires reach him. But most political leaders most of the time do not respond effectively unless these communications are backed up by power. Since the tendency is for governments that do not allow institutionalized representation to misjudge the distribution of power, they have a narrower political base than representative governments, and hence must spend both more coercive and identitive assets to maintain themselves in office than do representative governments. The same, we suspect, holds for the evolving government (or other authorities) of unions. Hence we expect *the stability of unions to be undermined and their growth curtailed when the pipelines of political representation are clogged or closed.*

Since at the early stages of unification integrating powers are comparatively weak and the rewards of controlling the system comparatively few, alienated units—especially if their influence on the decision-making center is lower than their self-assessed or actual power—will tend to break away rather than to try to take over the center of the union. We thus expect that *secession of alienated units will be much more common than revolutions in unions as compared to political communities,* that attempts at secessions will be more common than attempted revolutions, *and that the ratio will change in favor of revolutions as the process of unification increases the union's level of integration and scope.*

In sum, unification is more successful the greater the identitive and utilitarian power that the member-elites or system-elites command; to the degree that the union can be maintained by coercive power in its critical stages; and to the extent that those who control these kinds of power both send and receive adequate communications, are responsive to communication obtained, and provide for political representation of member units in rough proportion to their power.

SYMMETRIC AND ASYMMETRIC COMPOSITIONS

The relationships among members of a union can be fruitfully examined as exchanges in which assets that are an output of one unit are an input for one or more other units; that is, the outputs of one unit are exchanged for those of the others. Two key variables here are the rate of exchange and its substance.[14a] In completely egalitarian relationships the *rate of exchange* is one, that is, each unit is giving the same amount of assets it is receiving. In follower-elite relationships the rate of exchange is a ratio expressing the amount of power the elite has over the follower; the smaller the ratio and the less favorable the exchange is to the follower, the greater is the power of the elite. It is important to note that in interstate systems, as in interpersonal ones, there are clear limits to the degree to which power differentials can emerge. In the master-serf relationship, the master's power is limited because the serf might become so obstructionist that the cost of supervision would be unduly high; or the serf might prefer to die rather than to serve; or he might run away. Hence it "pays" the master to allow his serf a better rate of exchange by granting him enough food, rest, etc. for his work, to keep the costs of control down. The international parallels to these three states of relationship between the master and subject might be found in the relationship of the USSR to Finland (in 1939), to Hungary (in 1956), and to Yugoslavia (in 1948).

We reserve the team *egalitarian unions* for those in which the rate of exchange is close to one, and *elite-centered unions*[15] for those in which the ratio is a fraction. These terms refer to all assets ex-

[14a] Both sociology and the study of international relations have moved away from the use of these concepts, but there is a recent revival in their applications. See Karl W. Deutsch, "The Propensity to International Transactions," *Political Studies,* vol. VIII (1960), pp. 147–155; George C. Homans, *Social Behavior: Its Elementary Forms.* New York: Harcourt, Brace & World, Inc., 1961; Kenneth Boulding, *Conflict and Defense: A General Theory.* New York: Harper and Row, Publ., 1962, p. 193; and Peter Blau, *Exchange and Power in Social Life.* New York: John Wiley and Sons, 1964.

[15] The reference is to member- and not system-elites.

changed among the member units. (Performances that followers carry out in accordance with elite demands are classed as outputs of the followers and inputs of the elite.) We turn now to relate these two concepts to the question of the *substance of the exchange* in terms of the classification of integrating powers and assets introduced above.

An egalitarian-utilitarian relationship exists in international trade when the trading countries are in a similar stage of economic development and have similar bargaining power. An elite-centered relationship exists when the elite is exacting utilitarian assets from the followers (as in some colonial situations) or is contributing utilitarian assets to them in order to elicit certain performances from them (as when receiving foreign aid is conditioned by joining an alliance, changing the ownership of land or tax structure, etc.).[16]

Egalitarian-identitive relations exist when the units identify with each other, with the union as a collectivity, and with its system-elite, if there is such an elite (as when the member-states find that they share a common fate and destiny, a federal constitution in which they believe, and a federal government with which they identify). In elite-centered unions the identification is of followers with member-elites (as let us say of the old dominions with Britain in the Commonwealth. The attitude toward the crown is a typical expression of this identification.) It is crucial not to overlook the opposite flow of identitive assets; elites often identify with a union and gain gratification from their status as recognized leaders.[17] This is an output of the followers because, as we see below, the elite claim to leadership status and related gratifications is largely dependent on validation of this claim by the followers; if they do not recognize the elite as a leader, much of the leadership glory is lost.

[16] On this aspect of foreign aid see Hans Morgenthau, "A Political Theory of Foreign Aid," *American Political Science Review,* vol. 56 (1962), pp. 301–309.

[17] Without entering here into the complex problem of the use of psychological terms in discussing relationships among units other than personalities (especially among nations), we would like to explain the use of these terms in this study, in particular that of identitive gratification. We assume, but in the scope of this work do not document, that there are some mechanisms through which the psychological gratifications of the citizens affect the political action of a country. For instance, national prestige gained, let us say in the space race, is felt as a personal gratification by the citizens, which in turn affects their voting, which in turn affects the action of their government.

Coercion is rarely applied in egalitarian unions. It exists to the degree that the federal courts and police enforce union-wide norms. When the police enforce the norms of one part of the union on the others, that is, when the federal police or military force is more responsive to some units or subunits than to others, for instance to the white rather than to the African population in the former Federation of Rhodesia and Nyasaland, we have an elite-centered union.

The rate of exchange, which in nonegalitarian relationships favors by definition the more powerful unit, refers to the total assets exchanged, of all three kinds. The rate might be and often is different for the three kinds of exchanges, with frequently one unit being favored with utilitarian or coercive assets and the other with identitive ones. The relationships among big powers that provide military and economic aid in exchange for commitment to their bloc by previous nonaligned countries approximates this relationship (especially if little trade and no significant investments of the citizens of the big powers are involved).

The relationship between elites and followers might be *asymmetric* not only in the sense that the total amount of assets given and received by the various units would not be the same, but also in that the output of an elite will be more in terms of one kind of asset while its input will be more in another. The elite might "output" force (for example, military protection) and "input" utilitarian assets, which is a typical feudal relationship. The elite might provide utilitarian assets "in exchange" for follower identification and an affirmation of the elite's leadership status. (This means that the elite exchanges utilitarian assets for symbolic-identitive ones.) For example, the United States gave more per capital foreign aid than most of its allies; the Soviet Union gave more per capita foreign aid than any of its allies; Communist China has increased its aid program since it began to compete with Russia for the leadership of the Communist bloc; Britain gave more per capita aid to the less developed members of the Commonwealth than was given by any of the other developed members of the Commonwealth; France accelerated its foreign-aid program with its increased search for big-power status since 1958.

In the preceding sections of this theoretical discussion, each section led to the formulation of one or more propositions to be examined below in the light of the data. The analysis of exchange systems is at such a preliminary stage that forming specific propositions seems too arbitrary; we shall therefore approach the data regarding these matters with questions rather than propositions. As the study proceeds, we would like to be able to formulate some propositions about (a) which rates of exchange are more conducive to growth and stabilization of unification, and (b) what effects differences in the substance of assets exchanged in both symmetric and asymmetric exchanges have on the success of unification.

INTEGRATING POWER: A DYNAMIC PERSPECTIVE

UNIT PREPARATION AND POWER REQUIREMENTS

The success of unification is determined by the amounts and kinds of integrating power available as compared with that needed to introduce unification or to maintain a given level of integration and scope once it is achieved. *The amount of power needed to increase the level of integration and to extend the scope of a union is higher than that needed to maintain a given level of integration and scope,* all other things being equal.

We expect unification as a rule to require the application of power, since unification is a process of change in which the nature of the units participating, their relationship to each other and to their environment are altered. Increasing the level of integration requires three kinds of changes: the transfer of some of the regulation of utilitarian processes and the control of utilitarian structures from external- or member-units to the union; an increase in the union's control of means of violence and at the same time a decrease in the command by some other units of these means; and the shifting of loyalties from member-units or external-elites to the union. Each one of these changes is likely to undermine some vested interests, to contradict habits of action and thought, and to require some learning of new ones. Because all these changes are at least temporarily alienating, the use of integrating power is needed to legitimize the changes, to create new status symbols to replace outmoded ones, to compensate for losses suffered, and to support force to overcome the resistance of those who block the process.

While we have seen that many changes introduced as part of or because of unification are, at least temporarily, alienating, there are great differences in the degree and the spread of alienation generated. The most central factor affecting the resulting level of alienation seems to be the state of member-units at the time a unification effort is initiated. Unification, judged from this viewpoint, might be premature, mature, or overdue. *Premature* unification occurs when the population of the member-units have strong vested interests in the regulation of utilitarian processes on the unit rather than the system level, desire unit-control of coercive power, and strongly identify with the unit as compared with the system.[18] Unification initiated at this stage is usually imposed by an external elite or a few member-units or is formed because of some exterior reason, such as the threat of an enemy.

Mature unifications are those in which the level of vested interests in the unit is medium to low, in which there is no unit-control of coercion or only a limited one, and in which the population's identification with the units is weak and progressively weakening. An *overdue* unification is one in which there are widely felt needs for more interunit, union-wide regulation of utilitarian processes and control of the means of violence than is available and in which the population's identification with the system is higher than is needed for the existing level of integration.[19] The unification of such units is usually delayed by some external elite or by one or a few member-units. *Integrating power needed to maintain a unification effort,* once it is initiated, *tends to be greater for a premature unification effort than for a mature one, and even smaller for the maintenance of an overdue union* (at least in the initial stage).

The state of the member-units when the union is initiated has a considerable effect on the strategy most effective for the initiators

---

[18] Statements about felt needs, identification, interests, etc. refer to those segments of the population that are politically aware and effective.

[19] As reflected in the two other dimensions of actual control of means of violence and utilitarian processes.

and supporters of unification (as well as for those who oppose it). As unification progresses, alienation might mount either because it accumulates from the changes introduced successively, or because a specific change proved to be especially alienating. Occasionally, alienation reaches a level at which the unification effort or the union itself is endangered; that is, alienation approaches the level at which the integrating power will no longer be able to neutralize or counter-vail pressures to stop unification or to deunify. Those in control of the process—whether they are external elites, member-elites, or system-elites—must then choose between two strategies: to slow down or to accelerate unification. (We assume that it has been recognized that simply following a policy set at an earlier stage is no longer adequate.) The most effective strategy from the viewpoint of the needs of the unification process, would be to slow down unifica-tion, if in this way alienation can be reduced by spreading changes over a longer period of time (especially if the changes that have been delayed are not foreseen by the more alienated subunits), thus gain-ing more time for adjustment. For example: given enough time, a factory or a whole industry can reduce its labor force without firing anybody merely through attrition, by not replacing deceased person-nel and those who resign or quit. Acceleration is the best policy if the next stage of unification will create new integrating power strong enough to offset both the alienation that existed previously and that produced by the additional unification measures. The state of the member-units is a major factor in determining which one of these two strategies is the more effective. *We expect the acceleration strat-egy to be more successful when the level of alienation is still com-paratively low (as in mature and overdue unions),*[20] *and the deceleration strategy to be preferable when the level is compara-tively high (as in premature unions).* Whether one can hold constant other closely related variables in order to examine this hypothesis remains to be seen.

UNITS, SUBUNITS, AND REALLOCATION

One might expect that the changes produced by unification could be limited to the level of integration and scope of the union. In real-

[20] The general desirability of a unification program does not free its imple-mentation from generating alienation.

ity, unification invariably affects the power relationships among the units within the system and the subunits within each unit. For instance, a customs union between Australia and New Zealand has often been advocated, especially when the prospects of Britain joining the EEC seemed great: Britain's entry would have meant a loss of a market for both South Pacific countries, especially for New Zealand's farm products. Australia could have readily absorbed more of New Zealand's dairy products were it not for its own subsidized dairies which are not competitive with the New Zealand ones. "If a political settlement could be made with the Australian farm bloc which protests the subsidized Australian dairy industry, this form of economic alliance [between the two countries] would be possible almost overnight."[21]

While by no means the only factor, the different racial composition of Southern Rhodesia (in which the whites are comparatively more numerous), Northern Rhodesia, and Nyasaland (in which there are few permanent resident whites) was one major factor that led to the disbandment of the federation of these territories in 1963. The white population was using the federation to strengthen their status in Northern Rhodesia and Nyasaland.

To put it in more general terms, corresponding subunits within the various units are not in fact parallel in interest or in power. When, for instance, two countries enter a union, rarely if ever is the relative strength of the labor unions vis-à-vis management and government in one country the same as it is in the other. If we assume that unification leads to interunit (system) control of the economy, this control will reflect the general power relations in the system; for instance, when two countries unify, labor unions in the country in which they are stronger will suffer while those in the other one will benefit. That is one reason the British Labor Party objected to joining the more conservative EEC in 1962.[22]

The power relations among units and their subunits in a union

[21] Albert E. Norman, "Customs Union 'Down Under'?" *The Christian Science Monitor,* February 21, 1962.

[22] The actual resolution of the party refers to objections to joining on the terms then negotiated; but since Britain was expected to be required by the EEC to agree to even "worse" terms, in practice the Labor resolution amounted to an objection to entry.

are of course determined in a more complicated way than a simple averaging of those in the various member-units; but the tendency seems to be toward a "leveling of differences." It would follow that losses are greater the greater the difference in the relative power which corresponding subunits hold in their respective units in the preunification state. Hence unification requires overcoming not only the alienation and resistance of those whose interests and beliefs are affected by transferring powers from the unit to the system (for example, from states to the federation), but also the alienation and resistance resulting from the inevitable changes in power relations which unification brings about among the subunits of the unifying units.

The same point holds for the relations among the units themselves. Let us assume that five countries are voluntarily forming a union. At the time of the initiation of the unification effort there are certain power relations among them. These are almost without exception altered by the process of unification, mainly because as long as they were autonomous each unit had a roughly equal voice in matters conducted internationally (especially in matters on which votes are taken, as in various International Organizations) and each unit was more or less free not to participate if it felt participation to be against its interests. Once the union is established, however, a unit's influence over the union's course is more proportional to its real power as distinct from its formal voting rights; for instance smaller units tend to have much less influence than larger ones. (The reason a formal equality is tolerated in International Organizations but not in unions is that matters conducted jointly by unions are of much more vital interest to the participants than those conducted by International Organizations. The equality of votes that small and big states now have in the General Assembly of the United Nations is expected to be altered. We expect this to take place by taking out of the jurisdiction of the Assembly an increasing number of issues and turning them over to bodies in which different voting procedures prevail. The more significant the functions that the United Nations will actually fulfill, the less equal we expect the voting rights of states to be.) Moreover, the freedom not to participate is abolished, as was demonstrated in the American Civil War.

The differential effect of unification on various participating units is operative long before full unification is reached, as the following observation by Claude Jodin and Donald MacDonald about the evolution of Canadian-American ties suggests:

Both countries have benefited from the relatively close degree of economic interdependence. The facts on this point are so clear as to be indisputable. However, we think that it is appropriate to emphasize the fact that because the Canadian economy is substantially smaller than the American, a relatively high degree of economic interdependence can also have more serious effect on Canada than on the United States. A reduction of American imports from Canada, for example, would have a relatively greater over-all impact on the Canadian economy than would a similar reduction in Canadian imports from the United States. Also, certain American actions might prove to be a serious infringement on the sovereignty of the smaller Canadian economy, whereas similar actions on the part of Canada might have little, if any, effect on American sovereignty. Thus, the great difference in size of the two economies must always be taken into account in assessing the relative effects which one another's policies and actions have on the other.[23]

Hence the powers required for unification have to overcome not only the fears or resistance of subunits that are, or expect to be, losing power or assets from unification, but also those of units that themselves have similar fears. Thus, for instance, in the event of an American-Canadian unification, not only the French-Canadians or American conservatives would have to be mollified, but also the fears of Canada itself of being chronically outvoted once it is an integral part of a North American union.

While unification invariably affects the power relations among units and subunits participating in the process, it does not always favor the stronger over the weaker ones. Integrating power might be used to reallocate the assets of the union in favor of all or some of the weaker units or subunits to ensure their participation in the union, cooperation in a particular effort, etc.

In this matter, each union in effect must choose between two courses in building up integration. It might first reallocate assets to

[23] Canadian-American Committee, *The Perspective of Canadian-American Relations.* National Planning Association. U.S.A. and Private Planning Association of Canada, 1962, p. 6.

build up commitments of units and subunits that would otherwise refuse to participate or be obstructionist; or it might try to build up the system and its integrating power before reallocation is attempted, on the grounds that reallocation before integration might alienate those units (or subunits) that are deprived in the reallocation process to a degree that they might break away. More specifically, the question is often whether to invest scarce assets in building up the identitive power of the system (for example, in more downward communication) and the utilitarian benefits it generates without depriving any member unit or subunit (for example, by shifting the burden to later generations through bonds) or to reward the supporting subunits and punish the nonsupporting by taking from the latter and giving to the former (for example, by turning churches into party meeting halls). A combination of both lines may be attempted, but the question of relative emphasis cannot be avoided.

There are probably some conditions under which each strategy is the more effective one, but it seems that *for the initial stages of unification building up the union and its integrating power rather than reallocating tends to be the more effective course to follow.* Reallocation seems to impose higher strains than building up the system; therefore, unless the system is built up to a considerable degree, we expect it to be unable to contain the strains of reallocation among units or subunits.

In the general context of the question as to which sequence is more effective—stressing integration before reallocation, or vice versa—we might take special note of the conditions, if any, under which successful unification requires the application of coercive power. The formation of communities, national or international, is by no means as voluntary an effort as is often implied. Force is used both to remove externally imposed obstructions and to hold the units together until integrating power other than coercion grow stronger. In the early stages of the historical unification of the regions of France

the ringwall of the state cut them off, to some extent from the rest of the world; they were forced to work together and adapt to each other. They had time to gain a clear sense of identity, to smooth out some of their regional differences, and to become attached to their ruler and the institutions through which he rules. Where the framework of the state was strong enough and persistent enough, it even created a common nationalism out of very different linguistic and cultural groups. Languedoc was very like Catalnia and very unlike north France, yet it finally became thoroughly French.[24]

Coercive power is used not just to prevent secession but also to test and/or alter the power of one or more units or subunits that are resisting unification. In almost every unification there are one or more units or subunits for which the prospect of further unification is comparatively highly alienating; as unification progresses, the active resistance of such units increases. Even if there are constant efforts to make the union profitable for such units, or to appeal to their value commitments not to obstruct unification, or to threaten them with the use of force, often a point is reached at which—if unification is to be continued—the power of such an alienated unit "needs"[25] to be reduced or at least its weakness vis-à-vis the union has to be demonstrated in order to make it cooperate and in order to retain the cooperation of the other units. The union either has to show that it is stronger than the alienated unit and would therefore, if it desired, force it to comply (or that henceforth "voluntary" compliance could be enlisted) or it actually has to alter the units in such a way as to render its resistance ineffective. Since this test tends to require the use of coercive power and to occur in a limited period of time, we shall refer to it as the "coercive showdown." The American Civil War was of course a showdown between the industrial North and the agricultural South about the nature of the emerging federation, whose fuller integration was achieved only years after this showdown had taken place.[26] The Swiss after many generations of internal

[24] Joseph R. Strayer, "The Historical Experience in Europe," in Karl W. Deutsch and William J. Foltz (eds.), *Nation-Building*. New York: Atherton Press, 1963, p. 23.

[25] No moral judgment is implied. Such action is "needed" if the union is to prevent the alienated unit from seceding, taking over the system, and/or setting a precedent of noncompliance, all of which would curb further unification. Each of these consequences might be morally preferable to the use of force; the question here, however, is under which conditions the success of unification requires the use of force.

[26] Charlotte Muret, "The Swiss Pattern for a Federated Europe," in Edward Mead Earle (ed.), *Nationalism and Internationalism*. New York: Columbia Univ. Press, 1950, pp. 262ff.

armed conflicts had a last test of the power of the Catholic cantons in 1847 before the federation was formalized in 1848.[27] A similar test of power took place in the Congo in 1962 and 1963 between the central government and that of Katanga, and in Algeria in the months following its independence in 1962, between the Ben Bella forces and his opponents.

These instances suggest that a *coercive showdown during unification, if one occurs, is likely to come at a particular point in its life history.* We would expect it to come *after the external elites have withdrawn* (if there have been such) and *before the union's utilitarian and identitive systems and power are consolidated.*[28] Earlier, disunity is minimized and showdowns avoided because they might strengthen the control of the external elite and discredit the party that forces a showdown. On the other hand, delaying a showdown until the union's system and integrating powers are built up will tend to prevent an alienated unit from affecting the structure of the emerging union. The Congo had its coercive showdowns on the threshold of independence. The showdown in Switzerland came a year before the federation was formalized. The American showdown came "late" in terms of the number of years between the date that independence was gained and the emergence of the federation.

A METHODOLOGICAL NOTE

There probably will never be a science of international relations as there is one of physics or chemistry, if for no other reason than that experiments are practically impossible and the number of cases is too small to allow for a rigorous statistical analysis. Moreover, each unification is unique in the sense that any particular *constellation* of factors is most unlikely to have been or to be repeated. By studying *factors* the reappear in different combinations and in differ-

---

[27] Muret, p. 275.

[28] Additional coercive showdowns might be "necessary" if new deviant units emerge that are powerful enough to resist the other integrating powers. This is especially likely to occur when the system deteriorates after a period of high integration or if the first showdown was not decisive. The history of France seems to illustrate both possibilities.

ent environmental contexts, one can expect to gain some insights into the dynamics of a particular unification from an analytical study of others. Some uniformities might even suggest themselves; that is, certain relations among factors might reappear in different instances of political unification. Whether these uniformities would hold in cases other than those studied is an open question.[29] At the present stage of our knowledge, such transferability of a finding should not be assumed but should be retested for each case. Still, the virtue of formulating a uniformity is that when confronted with a new case we do not have to start from scratch; we may use the uniformity as a proposition with which to begin our study.

The understanding of each unification process requires a knowledge of the particular region in which it takes place; its history, sociology, ecology, etc. No two unions are alike. Studying other unions cannot and is not meant to replace the need to explore a given union if we seek to understand its dynamics. Hopefully, though, in conducting such a new study we shall be helped by insight gained from the exploration of other efforts at unification. How much can be gained in this way and how much is "unique" to each union is a question that will have to be explored practically by studying unions in both ways, rather than decreeing a priori that one method of research is superior to the other.

We hope in a later publication to report on other cases; in this first report four cases are analyzed: The European Economic Community (EEC), the Nordic Council, the United Arab Republic (UAR), and the Federation of the West Indies. These cases differ on many counts. Some include highly industrialized, modern societies; others are composed of underdeveloped, traditional societies. Some are unions of old established nations; others have only recently gained their independence. The four cases studied are, however, contemporary

---

[29] The difference between a uniformity and a generalization ought to be stressed. A statement of *uniformity* suggests that for all the cases examined, a certain relationship reappears. No claim is made that this relationship will reappear in other than the cases studied. A *generalization,* on the other hand, assumes, until proven otherwise, that a statement supported by a study of a sample is valid for the whole population of such cases. For a study of uniformities concerning the dynamics of four revolutions, see Crane Brinton, *The Anatomy of Revolution.* Englewood Cliffs, N.J.: Prentice-Hall, Inc., 1952.

ones; by drawing all of our material from one historical period we exclude one large set of factors—those unique to other periods—thus making comparisons of those included somewhat more incisive. The contemporary period was selected because an extensive study of earlier cases has already been conducted by Karl Deutsch and his associates,[30] because no encompassing comparative study of contemporary unions exists, and because the study of contemporary unifications and de-unifications has a direct bearing on present international problems.

The particular four cases analyzed were selected in part because there is available a relative wealth of source material about them, our effort being one of secondary analysis; in part because they vary greatly with regard to the independent variables to be studied; and, finally, because they allow us to study the dependent variable, the level and scope of integration, from a dynamic perspective. The dynamic analysis is possible because all four unions changed during the period studied: the Federation of the West Indies and the United Arab Republic disintegrated; the integration-level of the Nordic Council and the European Economic Community rose. The integration of no contemporary union has fallen lower than that of the West Indies or has reached a higher level than that of the EEC. Thus, the full range of levels of contemporary integration is represented as well as both increases and decreases in this central variable.

There are, as the paradigm presented in Part One shows, many factors that affect unification. The following examination of four cases focuses on two major sets of factors, namely the distribution and the composition of integrating power as they affect the success of unification. Other factors are discussed only to the degree required for the understanding of the propositions we shall explore. At the end of this chapter may be found a summary of these 17 propositions. The cases themselves are not studied in an exhaustive way, and no attempt is made to provide a comprehensive history or sociology of these unions. We are more interested in particular relationships than in particular unions; we wish, for instance, to understand the effect of the delay of reallocation of assets among participants

---

[30] Deutsch *et al., Political Community.*

on the unification of the Nordic area and of the European Economic Community as contrasted with the effect of early reallocation on the de-unification of the united Arab Republic and of the Federation of the West Indies, rather than to describe these four unions from every possible aspect. Understanding the particular relationships requires some general analysis of the nature of the unions we deal with and some discussion of specific factors other than those on which the study focuses, since they significantly affect the relationship studied. But while we deal to some degree with the unions as such, this is only as "background" to our study; we direct our attention primarily to particular factors.

To avoid having to go through each case 17 times, once for each proposition, we shall examine the propositions in groups, starting with those concerned with the distribution of power in the union (that is, among members), and that between members and external elites. We then turn to explore the composition-propositions, that deal with the difference in kinds of power employed, and close with an examination of the dynamics of these relationships.

Only part of the sources used are primary. Those include a few interviews with leaders of the West Indies and the EEC and with citizens of countries of the four unions. Some use has been made of local newspapers (for example, Jamaica's *Gleaner*), documents, and statistics (such as those published by the Caribbean Commission). Lacking the much larger resources a primary study would have required, the rest of the material had to be drawn from secondary sources. The various sources available are rather uneven, as is reflected in our case reports. There is an abundance of material, growing by the day, on the EEC, and a great paucity on the other three cases. Being unable to conduct field research, we had to make do with documents, statistics, interviews, and secondary articles, to the degree that such were available.

This volume closes with a comparative examination of the four cases along the lines suggested by the preceding theoretical discussion. The value of comparative analysis has been often stated. We, too, found that it assisted us in curbing ethnocentric statements, and served to illustrate the large variety of possible combinations in which the factors under study might appear.

SUMMARY

The purpose of this study is to determine under what conditions unification efforts succeed or fail. We do not sit in judgment; personally we may wish well to one union and shed few tears over the loss of another. But whatever our sentiments, we wish to better understand what makes some unions flourish and others flounder. This general question can be studied from many perspectives; here the focus of the query is: who is guiding unification, using what kinds of power, to what effect. Realizing that unification is a process of change, we naturally wish to know who is motivated to introduce the change and what instruments he is using to do so. Since unification rarely takes place in a vacuum, the enhancing or curbing effect of units that do not participate in a particular union but have power over it—that is, the external elites—has to be taken into account. Shifting our attention from the outside to the inside, the question of the effect of various distributions of power among the members is raised.

Both insiders and outsiders use a variety of combinations of three basic kinds of power: coercive, utilitarian, and identitive. The differential effects of various compositions of this integrating power on the success of unification is a question that is raised again and again throughout this study. Each and all of these powers might be a potential rather than an effective instrument without three facilitating factors: "adequate" communication (upward and downward), representation (upward), and responsiveness (downward). But what is adequate is a question that remains to be answered empirically. When integrating power is ineffective, that is, it does not suffice or is not adequately activated, alienated units may seek either to alter the structure of a union or to secede. We wonder if we are correct in suggesting that the tendency is to secede from rather than to attempt to take over the union, and if so why this is the case.

Finally, since we are dealing with a process and not with an existing, established structure, it is of particular importance to study all these questions in a dynamic perspective. The distribution of powers at the time of initiation of a unification effort is likely to be altered later; and the *kinds* of power available or used almost invariably changes over time. But in what direction power distributions and compositions change and to what effect remains to be seen.

This raises the problems of the strategy of unification. Since the changes that inevitably accompany unifications are likely to alter power relations among the member units and among subunits, every union faces the question of how quickly to proceed with unification and, once faced with mounting alienation, whether to accelerate or to decelerate. In particular, it must decide to what degree, if any, to use force to keep the parts together until their sociopolitical "glue" has a chance to dry.

All these questions are explored in four contexts: in the Nordic light, under the Caribbean sunshine, in the fog of Western Europe, and in the haze of the Middle East.

SUMMARY OF SEVENTEEN PROPOSITIONS
TO BE EXPLORED

INTEGRATING POWER: EFFECTIVE DISTRIBUTION
Degree of Elitism
1. Unions that have fewer elite-units will tend to be more
   successful than unions that have more. In particular,
   unions having one elite will be more successful than those
   having two, and those with two more than those with three.
2. Egalitarian unions, whether they develop system-elites or
   not, tend to be similar in their degree of success to monoelite unions.
3. Egalitarian unions tend to be less decisive than elitist
   unions, but more capable of generating commitments.
The Internalization of Elites
4. The external elite tends to enhance the success of unification the more the direction of its application of power coincides with the power structure of the emerging union, and
   to hinder it the more the application of this power is countered to the emerging structure.
5. As the level of integration and the scope of a union increase, the union tends to internalize the functions performed, as well as the authority held and the loyalties
   commanded by the external elite.
INTEGRATING POWER: EFFECTIVE COMPOSITION
Differences in Kind of Power
6. The more identitive power the elites initiating and guiding
   unification command or the union-system builds up, the
   more successful unification tends to be.
7. The more utilitarian power the elites initiating and guiding
   unification command or the union-system builds up, the
   more successful unification tends to be.
8. The relation between the application of coercive power
   and the success of unification is curvilinear. (That is, in
   contrast to the two other kinds of power, the higher appli-

cation of force, above a given level, is expected to produce less, not more, unification, all other things being equal).

Differences in Communication and Responsiveness

9. A union is more successful the more effective its upward and downward *communication* channels are and the more *responsive* its power elites are to the communication received.

10. The stability of a union is undermined and its growth curtailed when the avenues of *political representation* are clogged or closed. (Note: political representation is viewed as a central avenue of power-backed communication.)

11. *Secession* of alienated units will be much more common than revolution in unions as compared to political communities.

12. The ratio will change in favor of revolutions as the process of unification increases the level of integration and scope of the unions.

Symmetric and Asymmetric Compositions

(These are "sensitizing questions," not propositions)

The relationships of differences in *rates of exchange* to the level integration and scope are to be explored.

The relationship of differences in the *substance of exchange* to the level integration and scope are to be explored.

INTEGRATING POWER: A DYNAMIC PERSPECTIVE

Unit-Preparation and Power Requirements

13. The amount of power needed to *increase* the level of integration and to extend the scope of a union tends to be higher than that needed to *maintain* a given level of integration and scope.

Mature Unions

14. Integrating power needed tends to be greater to maintain a *premature* unification effort than a *mature* one; and even smaller, at least in the initial stage, to maintain an *overdue* one.

15. *Acceleration* strategy tends to be more successful in the

mature and overdue unions and *deceleration* strategy in the premature unions.

Subunits and Unification

16. For the initial stages of unification, *building up* the union, *rather than reallocation* among units or subunits, tends to be more effective.

17. The *coercive showdown* of a union tends to come at a particular point in its life history: (a) as the power of external elite declines, (b) before the union's utilitarian and identitive systems and power are built up, or (c) after they have weakened.

CHAPTER 4

A Union That Failed: The United Arab Republic (1958–1961)*

When the United Arab Republic was formed early in 1958, many factors appeared to be working in its favor. Syria and Egypt seemed quite similar; both populations were Arabic-speaking, predominately Moslem, and identified with Arab nationalism; both states were members of the Arab League, republics, and neutralist in their foreign policy. Initially the union commanded considerable enthusiasm; it was to be the first stage in the formation of an all-encompassing Arab nation. Actually, as we shall see, the background conditions were less favorable than they seemed. The union was born prematurely and the integrating power was in constant decline, especially in the last year of the union. Strenuous efforts to bring Syria under Egyptian control and to radically change its social and economic structure combined to alienate practically all the politically effective groups in Syria, including the army, landlords, socialists, and business circles. When the showdown came, Egypt's force was not deployed to suppress the secession, for President Gamal Abdel Nasser decided to let the phoenix of Arab unity return to ashes peacefully, in order not to prejudice its expected resurrection. Thus, while the United Arab Republic was born free from the distorting interference of external elites and was led by one vigorous elite-unit, it collapsed three and one half years after it was established.

* I am indebted to Professor Maan Z. Madina for the transliteration of the Arab names.

AN INEFFECTIVE DISTRIBUTION

A RELUCTANT ELITE

By 1958, Arab unity was a popular and established cause that had evolved over many years. The aspiration for unity can be traced back at least to the awakening of Arab consciousness late in the 19th century.[1] Pan-Arabism, though limited in scope, was encouraged by the British during World War I, in their fight against the retreating Ottoman empire. The idea of Arab unity gained greater popularity in Syria after 1949, when the Palestine debacle suggested that national goals could not effectively be pursued by each Arab state independently. Unity was a central theme in the ideology of the powerful *Baath,* a leftist now-Communist party that preferred union with leftist Egypt to union with conservative Iraq, which was led into the Western-oriented Baghdad pact by the government of Nuri al-Sa'id. While a declaration that Syria was part of one Arab nation was included in her 1950 constitution, Egypt had its period of intensified isolationism and "Egypt first" policy between 1952 and 1955, when Nasser was preoccupied with domestic developments. It was only in 1955 that Nasser's international ambitions were aroused, supported by a rapid succession of major developments in the Middle East that built up the stature of the Egyptian president. The Baghdad Pact with "imperialist Britain" marked Iraq, the other major contender for Arab leadership, as "reactionary." Egypt's favorable reception in the conference of neutral nations in Bandung raised the spector of a third force, the Afro-Asian bloc, led by Tito, Nehru, and Nasser. The Soviet-Egyptian arms deal, Russian aid for the construction of the High Dam at Aswan, the nationalization of the Suez Canal, and the support of the United States and the USSR in halting the Sinai campaign against Egypt all built up Nasser's prestige. It was at this juncture that the flag of Arab unity was raised in Egypt, the flag of one nation from the "Persian Gulf to the Atlantic Ocean." The Arab

[1] George Antonius, *The Arab Awakening: The Story of the Arab National Movement.* London: Hamilton, 1945.

nation was to be one of three concentric circles; the other two would be the Islamic and the African groups, all of which would converge in Cairo.[2]

The first efforts at Arab unification were made through the Arab League formed in 1945. In April 1950, after the demoralizing results of the Palestine war, the members of the league signed a pact that was to lead to military and economic unification of the member countries.[3] But by 1955, little economic, military, or political unification was evident. Splits in the Arab world deepened, especially between the authoritarian monarchies committed to the West (including at that time Iraq, Jordan, Yemen, and Saudi Arabia) and the neutralist, at that time pro-Soviet, republics of Syria and Egypt. The increasing ambitions of Egypt, the mounting tensions between Syria and Iraq, Egypt's fear of being isolated from other Arab countries following the Baghdad pact,[4] and the growing exasperation with the failure of the league's multilateral unification plans, led Egypt and Syria to initiate bilateral steps toward unification in 1955. Nasser, an astute politician, chose the gradualist approach of sector-integration, leading toward, rather than trying to jump into a political community.

The first formal unification step was taken on October 20, 1955, less than eight months after the signing of the Baghdad Pact. A mutual defense pact was concluded between Egypt and Syria containing many of the same clauses as the league pact, including a call for mutual assistance in case of attack as well as the establishment of a joint command. But, unlike the league's pact, this one was soon partially implemented. A joint commander-in-chief was appointed on November 8, 1955. While the Syrian army did not come to

[2] G. Nasser, *The Philosophy of the Revolution.* Buffalo, N.Y.: Smith, Keynes, and Marshall, 1959, pp. 74–77.

[3] "Convention for Facilitating Trade Exchanges Regulating Trade between States of the Arab League," *Basic Documents of the League of Arab States.* New York: Arab Information Center, 1955, pp. 29–38.

[4] An important factor that led Egypt to initiate closer links with Syria was Nasser's fear of being isolated from other Arab states. This became openly manifested after the hastily concluded Baghdad Pact which was considered as "a danger against the national safety of Egypt." See 'Abd al-Mun'im Shumays, *al-Thawra al-Arabiyya al-Kubra,* Cairo, 1963, p. 540.

Egypt's defense during the Sinai campaign in November 1956,[5] Egypt used Syrian airports to disperse its fighter planes under attack by Israel, France, and Britain. The next use of the military provisions of the treaty came on October 15, 1957; two Egyptian battalions landed in Latakia, Syria, as tensions mounted on the Syrian-Turkish border over Alexandretta. They were sent to Aleppo, closer to the Turkish border and center of Syrian opposition to the influential *Baath,* which at that time favored unification with Egypt. This was, by and large, the extent to which cooperation between the two military establishments had grown before 1958.

But unification measures were not limited to the military sector. On September 2, 1956, an agreement was reached enabling the formation of joint Syrian-Egyptian corporations. On September 3, 1957, a treaty was signed declaring a full "economic union" of the two countries, and a committee was appointed to make specific recommendations to implement the treaty. In November of that year, another agreement was concluded to ease the transfer of capital between the two countries. An Arab Cultural Unity agreement was ratified on March 15, 1957, aiming at cultural cooperation and the unification of educational methods through the exchange of teachers and students, joint conferences, coordination of sport and art events, and the like.

That all this was aimed at evolving a broad union rather than limiting the cooperation to a few sectors is evident in a resolution unanimously approved by the Syrian Parliament on July 5, 1956, setting up a committee to negotiate the formation of a federal union with Egypt. This resolution was passed within two weeks after the ratification of a new Egyptian constitution, Article I of which declared that the Egyptian people were "a part of the Arab nation."[6]

It appears that Nasser intended to let the union grow gradually by signing new treaties and allowing them to be implemented during

---

[5] According to one Syrian source, Syria did live up to its obligations; it "marched fifteen kilometers into Israel and stopped only when Nasser cabled he could not afford another front" (private communication). According to Israeli sources, no Syrian advance was made.

[6] 1959 Constitution, *Révue Egyptienne de Droit International* (Le Caire), vol. 7, no. 1 (1956), p. 151–152. See also "Background to Unity," *Middle East Journal,* vol. 12 (1958), p. 57.

the designated period. But his hand was forced. To understand how this came about, a flashback is necessary.

Since 1949, Syria had experienced an active political life, which became particularly hectic after the ousting of dictator Adib al-Shishakli in 1954. Among the contenders for control of the country were the army and the conservatives (various business groups and landlords), the Communists and, since 1954, the Arab Socialist Renaissance party (*Hizb al-Baath al-Arabi al-Ishtiraki*), popularly referred to as the *Baath*. Its program called for Arab unity, socialism, and democracy.[7] As Nasser's thinking developed more in the direction of Arab unity and socialism, his affinity with the *Baath* grew.

Baath had never been more than a minority party that held 20 seats in a 142-man parliament, but its influence grew rapidly, as it allied itself with army officers and intimidated the conservative majority with a series of political trials.[8] In 1955, Colonel Adnan Malki, assistant chief-of-staff of the Syrian army and a key *Baath* man, was assassinated by a member of the extreme right-wing Syrian National Socialist party. The act triggered a successful purge of the right wing from the army.[9] Still, the *Baath* could not advance its socialist program, nor was its growth secure in the face of the merchant-landlord opposition. Union with Egypt was expected to advance Arab unity and the socialist cause, as well as the *Baath*'s power.

In 1958 a Communist "scare" was partly generic and partly worked up to bring the conservatives to support a union with Egypt. One observer described the situation in the following terms:

Syria had been in a state of strong ferment for many months, and the country was ruled by a coalition of *Baath* National Socialists and Communist elements, including pro-Soviet politicians such as Khalid Al-Azm. *Baath* had come to regard itself as the leading force in the country, and the Communists as a small and uninfluential sect. It must have been a shock when they realized last winter that Communist party membership was more nu-

[7] See Jacques Rastier, "A la Recherche du socialisme syrien," *Orient,* vol. 1 (1957), pp. 175–177. See also Michel 'Aflaq, *Fi Sabil al-Ba'ath,* Beirut, 1959. And the constitution of the *Baath.*

[8] See George Lenczowski, "Syria: A Crisis in Arab Unity," *Current History,* vol. 42 (1962), p. 202.

[9] Manfred Halpern, *The Politics of Social Change in the Middle East and North Africa.* Princeton, N.J.: Princeton University Press, 1963, pp. 267–268.

merous than their own, and that Communist influence in the army and other key positions was almost equal to their own.[10] There should have been a series of by-elections, but *Baath* could not afford to have them in these circumstances. And thus, in mid-January 1958, they suddenly advanced the slogan of "union now."[11]

Other observers minimized the role of the Communist "scare," pointing to the fact that there was no active resistance to the union with Egypt, a resistance one would expect if the Communists were powerful, not to mention ready to take over, and that at this point Soviet efforts to penetrate the Middle East were not tied to the use of local Communists, as the contradiction of the great Soviet-Egyptian accord with the jailing of Communists in Egypt showed.[12] These observers put more stress on *Baath*'s fear of conservative Syrian efforts for union with Iraq as the precipitant cause. In fact, union with Iraq was favored by the conservative groups, especially the "right wing" Nationalists, led by Sabri al-Asali.[13]

In any event, in January 1958, a delegation of army officers and politicians, mainly of the *Baath* party, called upon Nasser to request immediate initiation of a union of the two countries. Nasser was reluctant to proceed, though he could hardly flatly refuse his allies in Syria and renounce his recently built-up unity propaganda. More-over, the offer to serve him Syria on "a silver platter" whet his ambition. Cautiously, Nasser set two conditions, which he hoped would make the Syrians reconsider their unification plan and, if ac-cepted, make the union less brittle. He demanded that all political parties be abolished in Syria and that the union take the form of a

[10] General Afif al-Bizi, who became commander-in-chief (and chief-of-staff) of the Syrian Army in August 1957 was widely believed to be a member of the Syrian Communist Party; the same holds for Lt. Col. Mohammed Jarrah who became at the same time, Assistant Chief of the Gendarmerie (Author's com-ment).

[11] Walter Z. Laqueur, "The Prospects of Arab Unity," *Midstream,* vol. 4 (1958), p. 19.

[12] S. H. Longrigg, "New Groupings among the Arab States," *International Affairs,* vol. 34 (1958), p. 309; P. Seale, "United Arab Republic and The Iraqi Challenge," *World Today,* vol. 16 (1960), pp. 296–305.

[13] Fayer A. Sayegh, *Arab Unity.* New York: Devin-Adair Co., 1958, p. 186. See also Patrick Seale, "The Break-up of the United Arab Republic," *World Today,* vol. 17 (1961), pp. 471–479, and Frederick Harbison, "Two Centers of Arab Power," *Foreign Affairs,* vol. 37 (1959), pp. 678–680.

unitary state, not a federation. When his demands were accepted, the union was established on February 1, 1958.

Thus, while there were several background conditions favoring unification, some ideological and some administrative, the immediate unification attempt was precipitated by transient motives before sector-unification had progressed enough to provide a solid basis for unification. Most of the treaties signed between 1955 and 1958, especially those pertaining to economic and cultural measures, were by February 1958 little more than paper links. In this sense the union was premature; that is, a large amount of integrating power was to be required to hold the parts together. The need for this integrating power was further accentuated by the formation of a union, whose institutional structure was broad in scope, between two societies with a variety of differences—differences that at first did not seem important.

DIFFERENCES BETWEEN ELITE AND SUBJECT

By 1958, the left-wing revolution in Egypt was well established. Many landlords, most aristocracy, and non-Moslem businessmen were uprooted or learned to remain politically passive; religious authorities cooperated or were suppressed; Communists were jailed and their organization destroyed.[14] Nasser, the sole ruler of the country, advanced several social reforms and maintained a high level of popularity among the peasants, urban masses, workers, and intellectuals, as well as an effective control of the army.[15]

Syria, on the other hand, had in 1958 a multiparty system: landlords, merchants, religious authorities, tribal chiefs, and labor unions were organized and active. While the army was the most powerful group, it limited its role to the frequent unseating of one political clique and the seating of another, and—with one exception—had not

[14] On the attitude of the regime to religious leaders, see P. J. Vatikiotis, "Dilemmas of Political Leadership in the Arab Middle East: The Case of the U.A.R.," *International Affairs,* vol. 37 (1961), pp. 190–194.

[15] See Tom Little, *Egypt.* New York: Frederick A. Praeger, Inc., 1958; Jean and Simone Lacouture, *Egypt in Transition.* London: Methuen & Co., Ltd., 1958; Keith Wheelock, *Nasser's New Egypt.* New York: Frederick A. Praeger, Inc., 1960; and Nadav Safran, *Egypt in Search of Political Community.* Cambridge, Mass.: Harvard University Press, 1961. Parts 4 and 5.

tried to run the country and directly control its civilian political life. Compared to Nasser's monocentric socialism, Syria was a pluralistic society in which free enterprise still was predominant.[16]

There were similar differences in economic need and perspective. Both countries were underdeveloped and seeking to develop; both were agricultural countries, whose main export was cotton; both were receiving in that period substantial Soviet foreign aid to help finance their development. But a closer exploration suggests some rather important economic differences and problems. The per capita income in Syria was almost twice as high as in Egypt ($204 per annun in Syria compared to $109 in Egypt. Figures are in American currency). The population of both countries was very much conscious of these differences.[17] Egypt was highly overpopulated; only about 13,000 square miles of its land were habitable; population density in the habitable parts of the country was one of the highest in the world—1400 per square mile, compared to 763 in Belgium, which is by European standards densely populated. Syria was not plagued by population pressures. At the same time in 1958, Egypt was in the midst of an industrialization drive; that of Syria was fluttering. The fact that both countries produced the same major export crop made their economies more competitive than supplementary.

We expect elite-units (if there are any) to have to make utilitarian sacrifices necessary to pay for unification, both to partially compensate the other member-units for their adjustment pains and to pay in part for the shared institutions. From this viewpoint, the UAR was born deformed; Egypt had the elite-status and ambition, but Syria had the "surplus" resources. While Egypt has 0.25 *feddan* arable land per capita, there are 2.9 in Syria (1 feddan = 1.04 acres.)[18] For countries that live on agriculture, this is a major difference.

Nor were the two cultures as similar as is often suggested. The

[16] William Henry Chamberlain, "Egypt-Syria Split," *Wall Street Journal*, October 5, 1961.

[17] Daniel Lerner with the collaboration of Lucille W. Pevsner, *The passing of Traditional Society.* New York: The Free Press of Glencoe, 1958, p. 302. See also Halford L. Hoskins, "Operation Bootstrap in the United Arab Republic," *Current History*, vol. 38 (1960), pp. 268–269.

[18] See Nevill Barbour, "Impressions of the United Arab Republic," *International Affairs*, vol. 36 (1960), p. 27.

Syrians had a different ethnic origin; the spoken dialects of Arabic in the two countries were dissimilar; Syria experienced French, Egypt, British rule. The non-Sunni minorities were bigger and in 1958 played a more important role in Syria than in Egypt, including Alawis, Druzes, Greek Orthodox, and Armenians, each numbering more than 100,000. One observer stated: "Syria was not Egypt, either in ethos, spirit, trade pattern, standard of living, individual temperament, food, dress, or any of those intimate life habits which make people distinct."[19] Even their attitude to Pan-Arabism was different: Syria had been the hub of Arabic activity for many years; Egypt joined the movement late and was quite ambivalent about it. Most directly relevant to the development of the union was the difference in attitude toward authority. Egypt has a long tradition of subjugation to authority that some students suggest goes far back to its early history and derives from its "hydraulic" nature, that is, its economic need to maintain a centralized irrigation system. Syria, on the other hand, has a long "individualistic" legacy bordering on turmoil.

Differences in the conception of the institutional expression to be given to the union were quite important. The Syrians expected a loose federation, in which matters of defense and foreign policy would be decided jointly and other matters would be controlled autonomously by each country, with some degree of union-wide coordination.[20] After all, the two countries had no shared border, were separated by Israel and Jordan, had no major air or naval fleets; and Egypt had only one major, overcrowded harbor. While the conservative groups were tired of political instability (Syria had witnessed six military coups since independence in 1945) and welcomed a decline in political activity, they expected business to continue as usual, without any or at least with less political interference.

[19] P. J. Vatikiotis, *The Egyptian Army in Politics.* Bloomington, Ind.: Indiana University Press, 1961, p. 167. See also Charles Issawi, "Economic and Social Foundations of Democracy in the Middle East," *International Affairs,* vol. 32 (1956), pp. 40 ff.

[20] Ragaei El Mallakh, "Economic Integration in the United Arab Republic: A Study in Resources Development," *Land Economics,* vol. 3 (1960), pp. 252–265. The resolution, passed by the Syrian parliament in November 1957, calling on its government to open immediate negotiation with Egypt, names federation and not the formation of a unitary state as the purpose of such negotiations.

One observer, returning from a trip to Syria in March 1958, reported:

A prominent banker in Damascus told me: "So long as it's only politics that's involved, the new setup is fne. We must be careful not to attempt any brusque changes in the economies of our countries. After all, the Egyptians are not very intelligent in these matters. Their economy must be run by the central government; ours flourishes under private management. If we do not try to change things too fast, the new Union may work out." An important merchant said: "We could do with a little less politics in Syria for a while. Maybe now the students will go to their classes at the University occasionally and normal commerce will become possible." [21]

Some Syrians even felt that they would be on the top. The *New York Times* man in Damascus, Foster Hailey, reported that "the Syrians believe themselves smarter and more energetic than their Southern cousins. It would be only a matter of time, many are reported to say privately, until the Syrians would achieve political and economic dominance." [22]

Egypt's concept of the union, however, was one of a unitary state. The Arab world had known its share of leagues that accomplished little and alliances and federations that had lasted short periods (that of Iraq and Jordan, for instance, formed shortly after the UAR, lasted only five months, from February 14 to July 14, 1958). Nasser felt a loose federation would not do if the UAR was to appeal to the imagination of the Arabs and serve as the basis of a larger union that would last longer and accomplish more than those of the past. (Egyptian writers, under Nasser, had pointed out that federation was alien to Arab tradition.[23]) Hence the UAR was born with a considerable lack of convergence of expectations of the very nature of the union, thus further increasing the need for integrating power, a need already high because of the differences between the member-units and the premature initiation.

Taking into account the differences in economic, political, and

[21] C. Gallagher, "The United Arab Republic Today . . . Egypt and the Arab World," *American University Field Service-North African Survey,* vol. 7 (1960), p. 12.

[22] *New York Times,* January 22, 1958.

[23] See Muhammad al-Tammawi, *al-Tatawwur al-Siyasi li al-Mujtama' al-Arabi (The Political Evolution of Arab Society).* Cairo, 1961, p. 341.

cultural characteristics, the differences in expectations of the union, and the relative paucity of resources in the elite-unit, this unification effort could have succeeded only if there had been a large amount of integrating power. Actually, it was never high and continually declined.

THE CHANGING POWER OF INTEGRATION: AN HISTORICAL PERSPECTIVE

The decline of integrating power took place concomitantly on several fronts. While the utilitarian power was exhausted, the identitive power was also reduced; this in turn was accompanied by a closing of the channels of communication and representation, insufficient responsiveness, and a shift in strategy that triggered the final crisis, one that the limited coercive power applied could not avert. Since developments on all these fronts were highly interrelated, a brief outline of the sociopolitical history of the UAR is necessary before we can provide a commentary relating these developments to the analytical perspectives of this study.

The success or failure of the UAR was to be determined by Egypt's ability to build up the ties of the Northern region (as Syria was called) to the Southern one. While Nasser's policy throughout was one of amalgamation rather than federation, implementation of his objective was carried out in a variety of ways and means. At first, there was some reliance on the Syrians, especially the leftist *Baath.* Then, a more direct rule by Egypt was combined with an effort to win the support of the alienated conservative majority in Syria.[24] In the third period, intensive Egyptianization, especially through direct rule from Cairo, was combined with economic regimentation and a socialist drive. None of the three methods worked; oscillation among them proved fatal.

---

[24] The conservative majority refers here to the majority of politically powerful groups. It is impossible to determine if the politically inactive groups were conservative or not; it seems best to exclude them from such calculations. The majority of the student and intellectual groups was on the left side, but their political influence was smaller than their number would indicate.

INDIRECT RULE (FEBRUARY 1, 1958– JULY 8, 1959)

The efforts to achieve legitimation of the union and to increase identification with the UAR were particularly great in the early months. Nasser and Shukri al-Kuwatli, the Syrian premier, interrupted their conference at Koubba Palace, where they were working out the details of the unity proclamation, to attend prayers at the Great Al-Azhar Mosque, where they heard the value of unity preached; the service was broadcast throughout Egypt. A plebiscite was held on February 21, approving the union and electing Nasser as the first president of the UAR. (The questions put before the people in the plebiscite were, "Do you favor union between Syria and Egypt?" and "Do you favor Nasser as the first president of the United Arab Republic?") The vote was 99.9 percent in favor of the union in Egypt; 1,312,759 people in Syria were reported to vote for the merger, 39 to vote "no." Shukri al-Kuwatli was given the title of the "first citizen of the United Arab Republic."

The February proclamation said: "Finally Arab unity was to be realized." The Syrian premier and Egypt's president declared that the unity of Syria and Egypt "aims at the unification of all the Arab peoples." The Syrian premier added that the UAR was "the first step on the path to entire Arab unity."[25] Nasser, not to be outdone, stated that "Today we live a new and glorious dawn for the dawn of our unity is here at last."[26] The high emotional commitments invested in such symbols as *ittihad* (union) and *wihdah* (unity) were tied to the new political structure. The founding of the union aroused a wave of enthusiasm across Arab capitals in the Middle East and great hopes for Arab unity were engendered by the founding of the UAR; at least reports to this effect were extensively fed to the citizens by the government information services.

The invitation to other Arab countries to join and the expressed hope for greater unity soon bore fruit when, five weeks after the foundation of the UAR, Yemen—whose Iman was seeking to coun-

[25] *New York Herald Tribune,* February 2, 1958.
[26] Press release of the former Egyptian delegation to the United Nations, February 6, 1958.

tervail British pressure—joined in a loose federation with Egypt and Syria. (The three countries together were referred to as the United Arab States.[27]) According to one source, Lebanon was expected to join next. Attempts were made to encourage Iraq and Jordan to join by appealing to the *Baath* elements and other pro-Nasser groups in these countries. The prospects of Arab unity seemed more real than ever before.

An additional effort at building up the legitimation of the union was taken on March 5 when a provisional constitution was proclaimed. It promised everything from democracy and social justice to the rule of law and the protection of private property.

In outlining the Union's government, much attention was paid to placating potential Syrian apprehension and providing a façade of equality. Two regional executive councils were set up, one for Egypt and one for Syria. The council to govern Syria was composed entirely of Syrians. Moreover, of the union's four vice presidents, two were Syrian. A National Assembly with legislative power was promised to be set up later, much to the relief of Syrian politicians, who faced unemployment since Nasser had demanded the abolition of parties early in 1958. (Actually, as parties were disbanded in Syria, the parliament building in Damascus was used to house the Ministry for Agrarian Reform.)

Behind this extensive effort to strengthen the acceptance of the union was the political reality: Most important decisions were in Nasser's hands. Still, Syria was directly ruled largely by Syrians, especially by the *Baath*, whose number-one political leader, Akram Hurani, became a vice president of the UAR. *Baath* members also held key ministries in the executive council of the Northern region (as Syria was now called). A second channel of control, the Syrian security organization (*Deuxième Bureau*), was headed by a Syrian, Colonel Abd al-Hamid Sarraj, whom Nasser made minister of the interior. The Egyptians were playing their role largely behind the scenes, planting their men in all key military and some key administrative posts. To justify their positions in Syria, a system of exchanges was created whereby for every Egyptian officer appointed

---

[27] The relationship to Yemen will not be further discussed here.

to a Syrian army post, a Syrian officer was given a post in the Egyptian army. Few Egyptians held publicly known high-ranking posts in Syria at this stage, and those who did were usually well known and liked in Syria, like Abu-al-Nour, who was an Egyptian military attaché in Syria before the union and now as deputy commander of the Syrian Army. The Syrian chief-of-staff of the Army, Major General Afif Bizri, however, was deposed, as his post became unnecessary with the unification of the Syrian and Egyptian army into the one of the UAR. And the Syrian police were taken over by Egyptian officers.[28]

But all these subtleties were largely lost on the Syrians. The conservatives awakened from the Communist scare only as the socialist nature of the Union became more and more evident, especially as the *Baath* began a vigorous drive for agrarian reform. Some 35,000 acres of land were confiscated within less than six months. This, it was learned, was only the beginning: During his visit to Syria in October of 1958, Nasser promised to introduce the same program of land reform that he had in Egypt.[29] More than a loss of property was involved; the Syrian agrarian reform drive was highly vindictive, as the *Baath* used it to settle personal and political grudges, in particular with the conservatives.

At the same time, the authoritarian nature of the government and the first signs of Egyptianization began to worry the Syrian conservative groups. During a weekend visit to Syria, Nasser dissolved the municipal councils (following the earlier abolition of political parties); terminated the special legal status the tribal sheiks had enjoyed since time immemorial; announced (with no explanations) that one of the two Syrian vice presidents had been dropped from the UAR government, and that the power of the union's cabinet over the regional councils had been strengthened, that is, Syrian autonomy had been reduced.

All this increased Syrian alienation, which was at this stage directed largely neither at Nasser nor at the idea of Arab unity, but at the *Baath,* which was blamed for having brought Syria into its de-

[28] Woodrow Wyatt, "Is Nasser's Star Rising or Setting?" *New York Times Magazine,* May 11, 1958, p. 22.
[29] *The Economist,* October 18, 1958, p. 210.

pendent state and whose members were the direct rulers, ruthlessly carrying out their reform measures. Nasser's popularity hardly suffered, in part as a result of a clever maneuver on his side (he rarely showed up in Syria, and his orders were carried out by others), and, in part, of a general tendency to deflect alienation from autocrats to their underlings.[30] The mounting resentment toward the *Baath* fully expressed itself in the July 1959 elections that marked the first major turning point in the short life of the UAR.[31]

"RIGHT DEVIATION" AND INCREASED EGYPTIAN RULE (JULY 8, 1959–JULY 1, 1960)

On July 8, 1959, elections to local councils of the National Union took place. The National Union was formed in Egypt by the government to provide an outlet for the politically active, as the only non-state political organ allowed by the regime; it was, however, organized and controlled by the government itself. Roughly it was to serve the state the way a company-union serves the corporation. The National Union was expected to provide a ladder of local and regional committees to guide the masses—"freed" from the prerevolutionary parties, municipalities, and landlords—to support the work of the revolution.[32] It had a measure of success in Egypt, and now the first tier—local committees—was to be introduced into Syria. The old politicians could run for election, but not under party labels. Despite the lack of labels, the sharp decline in the support of *Baath* was very evident in the severe loss its leaders suffered in the election.[33] Its candidates polled only about 3 percent of the vote and won only 250 of the 9485 seats contested.[34]

[30] See the author's *A Comparative Analysis*, pp. 215–216.

[31] For a fine analysis of the first period see Simon Jargy, "Le Declin d'un Parti," *Orient*, vol. 3 (1959), pp. 21–39. See also his "La Syrie province de la R.A.U.," *Orient*, vol. 2 (1958), pp. 17–32.

[32] By far the best analysis of the National Union will be found in Vatikiotis, *The Egyptian Army*, pp. 51 ff. For an Egyptian viewpoint, see Mohammed Hasanayn Haykal, "The National Union," *al-Ahram*, July 21, 1961.

[33] *The Economist*, July 18, 1959, pp. 163–164.

[34] H. B. Sharabi, *Governments and Politics of the Middle East in the Twentieth Century.* Princeton, N.J.: D. Van Nostrand Company, Inc., 1962, p. 133. See also Harry B. Ellis, "UAR Booster Party Somersaults in Syria," *The Christian Science Monitor*, August 10, 1959.

Nasser took this as a sign that *Baath* has outlived its usefulness. He never liked sharing with it the control of Syria, since he was suspicious of any autonomous center of power and of the ideological appeal of *Baath*'s democratic brand of socialism and its Syrian-nationalist view of Pan-Arabism. Following the elections, Nasser undertook his first major "surgery" on the Northern region. He "allowed" all but one junior *Baath* minister to resign from his government, including the one remaining vice president, Akram Hurani.[35] In October 1959, he appointed his most trusted Junta member, the Egyptian chief-of-staff, Field Marshal Abd al-Hakim Amer, to be proconsul of Syrian, with unlimited authority, reporting directly to him.[36] The only important Syrian figure to survive this round of Egyptianization was Sarraj, the head of the internal security machine, whose tough methods were of service to Nasser and who was hated enough in Syria to be unable to build up a wide following of his own. He had a following among leaders of some labor unions who owed him their position, and among one faction of army officers. On the street, his popularity was that of an admired roughneck, who stood up to King Ibn Saud (who Sarraj claimed gave him a $20 million check to assassinate Nasser), but he was not a charismatic leader.[37]

Field Marshal Amer took two major steps after he gained control. To further mollify the conservative majority, he slowed down considerably the agrarian reform by enforcing a decree that the state be regarded as the successor to landlords whose lands had been requisitioned, taking over their outstanding bank debts. In effect, this meant that the state was compensating the landlords for the land it took away from them,[38] a measure to which the *Baath* objected. Also, the "resignation" of the *Baath* ministers suggested to the merchant and landlord that other steps toward socialism would not be taken too hastily.[39]

Second, Amer began organizing the local political committies of

---

[35] *The Economist,* January 2, 1960.
[36] Maurice Harari, *Government and Politics of the Middle East.* Englewood Cliffs, N.J.: Prentice-Hall, Inc., 1962, p. 77.
[37] Private communication with Mr. George Hagger.
[38] *Middle-East Newsletter,* January 22, 1960, p. 3.
[39] *Al-Hayat,* September 6, 1959.

the Syrian branch of the National Union. On December 30, 1959, Amer announced the formation of a special advisory committee to assist him in the formation of the National Union. In line with his "rightist" policy, none of the five members was a member of the *Baath*.[40] As a further conciliatory move, Amer, who recognized the differences between the two economies, recommended that efforts to amalgamate the two should be slowed down.[41]

Quick to win friends, the field marshal won a modicum of success in Syria, reflected in the facts both that many Syrians turned to him for help and that the number of complaints received by his office fell from 3000 a day to 500 four months after his arrival in Syria. But the major direction in which the economy and administration of the UAR were guided, for reasons to be discussed below, not only nullified his successes but aggravated the strains on the union. There was no particular turning point at which the "right deviation," as Amer's policy seemed in retrospect, was terminated. But as of mid-1960, at a gradually accelerating pace, efforts were made to socialize the economy of Syria, to wear down conservative groups rather than win their support, and to concentrate practically all the power and control in Egypt. Actually while Amer was pacifying the conservatives in Syria, Cairo was initiating the shift to the left.

RADICALIZATION AND EGYPTIANIZATION (JULY 1, 1960–SEPTEMBER 27, 1961)

From 1958 to 1961, Syria experienced three years of drought. Compared to a wheat crop of 1.354 million tons in 1957, that of 1960 was only 553,000 tons, and the production of barley fell, in the same period, from 721,000 tons to a meager 157,000.[42] This turned Syria, which consumes about 750,000 tons of wheat a year, from an exporter to an importer of wheat and barley. For the first time in Syria's history, it had to draw on the United States, in November 1959, for wheat and animal feed to satisfy its minimal needs. Syria's general export trade was halved, and only 30 percent of its textile

[40] For *Baath* expectations, frustrated by these moves, see Arnold Mattinger, "Syrian Politics Now," *Swiss Review of World Affairs,* vol. 9 (1959), pp. 22–23.
[41] *The Times* (of London), May 26, 1960.
[42] *The Economist,* October 22, 1960, p. 354.

production capacity was used.[43] Despite the fact that the Soviet Union financed a large part of the development projects in Syria in that period, Egypt had to sacrifice its own scarce resources to finance both the union's administrative machinery and to cover deficits in Syria's budget. In February 1961, the sum transferred from Egypt's account to that of Syria (the two regions had separate currencies, central bank accounts and budgets) amounted to £2 million.[44] According to one source, this was just the last payment in a long sequence; Egypt provided Syria over three years with $40 million to $50 million,[45] and Egypt paid 75 percent of the special joint UAR budget that covered matters of common concern to the two regions, including defense, foreign affairs, the presidency, and the National Assembly. But these Egyptian contributions did not produce economic stability or please the Syrians. The friction between the UAR and Iraq and Saudi-Arabia heavily curtailed Syrian exports to these countries, created wide unemployment, and affected its important transit trade with these countries. Syrians became increasingly worried by repeated rumors of plans for Syrian-Egyptian population "exchanges," which Syrians construed to mean plans to transfer peasants from overpopulated Egypt to Syria.[46] At the same time, fear of Nasser's socialism mounted.

In response to all this, the flight of capital from Syria reached a peak. In 1958 and early 1959, on the order of $120 million was illegally transferred from Syria to Lebanese and European banks.[47] The value of the Syrian lira sank on the Lebanese exchange by nearly 20 percent.[48] It was valued about 10 to 13 percent less than the Lebanese lira in the years preceding the union; in February 1961 it was valued about 30 percent less. Because of the drought, the crisis of confidence, and—as we shall see in detail below—the trade pattern Egypt imposed, the trade deficits of Syria increased sharply in each year of the UAR. These were, in millions of Syrian lira, a low 68.1

[43] *The Economist,* February 18, 1961, p. 648.
[44] *The Economist,* February 18, 1961, p. 648.
[45] *New York Times,* March 6, 1961.
[46] See, for instance, *Rose-al-Yesef,* August 28, 1961.
[47] Sharabi, *Governments and Politics,* p. 132.
[48] Claire Sterling, "Syria Secedes from Nasser's Empire," *The Reporter,* October 26, 1961, p. 30.

in the pre-UAR days of 1957; a jump to 254.1 in 1959, and a rise to 415.5 for 1960. Gold and foreign currency reserves of Syria declined by 22 percent from U.S. $62 million by the end of 1957 (eve of the formation of the UAR) to $48 million by January 1961. The Syrian national debt had almost doubled in terms of percentage of the national income; it was 13 percent in 1957, 25 percent in 1960. Not all of this can be "blamed" on the drought; the Syrian income per capita fell from 592 Syrian lira in 1957 to 466 in 1960, a decline of 21 percent which brought it below the 1955 level, also a year of heavy drought.

It would be a mistake to suggest that the economic effects of unification were all on the loss side. Under Egyptian prodding and with the help of Egyptian personnel, a master development plan was drawn up in Syria. Plans for the building of a large dam on the Euphrates were completed and foreign credits assured. The building of a 110,000 ton fertilizer plant in Homs was initiated. Several road constructions were undertaken.[49] Water wells were dug, a refinery constructed, swamps were drained in the valley of Ghab, and work on a railroad line, Lataqia-Haleb-Qamishli, was initiated. But practically all of these were long-run projects and their potential yield could not ameliorate the immediate crisis. Moreover, most of them were initiated under the 1957 Soviet aid agreement and little credit for this potential contribution to Syria was attributed to Egypt.

One of the few short-run achievements of unification was a partial customs union introduced in September 1958.[50] Trade among the two countries increased rapidly (see Table 1), but the flow of goods from Syria to Egypt soon surpassed that of goods from Egypt to Syria.

Egypt, we have noticed, was an elite with more will than resources. It could have contributed to Syria's government expenditure for a while longer (though one observer, analyzing its resources, predicted in 1958 that its ability to do so would be exhausted by 1961).[51] But the specter of Syria, with its considerably higher stan-

[49] The United Arab Republic *Achievements and Future Development Plans.* Cairo: UAR Information Department, 1960; Dragan Stojiljkovic, "Significant Measures for the Development of the UAR," *Review of International Affairs,* vol. 11 (1960), pp. 8–9.

[50] Mallakh, "Economic Integration," p. 253.

[51] *The Times* (of London), February 12, 1958.

Table 1 EXPORT-IMPORT IN THE UAR

Year	Syrian exports to Egyptian region	Syrian imports from Egyptian region
	(in millions of Syrian lira)	
1958	16.50	25.50
1959	68.50	42.00
1960	61.00	55.00

dard of living and an unregulated economy, freely consuming what by the austere Egyptian standard were luxury items, annoyed the Egyptians endlessly. They were paying their affluent junior partner, from their poor resources, or foreign aid that they could use, in order to set the pattern for a greater Arab union under Egyptian leadership. But as early as the fall of 1959 and increasingly in 1960, reports of ill will and alienation spread from Syria throughout the Arab world. One Egyptian officer put it: "Syria is a loss to us; we have to support it and we get nothing out of it." Nasser, who held back his ire for the first two years, finally expressed his dissatisfaction in the third one. In a Damascus speech, following the third anniversary day of the UAR (on February 22), he asked the people

whether they wanted their country's wealth, particularly foreign exchange, spent on "perfumes and refrigerators (in Beirut)" or on industrial plants to provide jobs for workers.

In another speech, President Nasser noted pointedly that during the last three years of severe drought in Syria, the Egyptian Region had provided $40,000,000 to $50,000,000 to help Syria. He said he felt this had been "somewhat unjust, because the free economy, or economic anarchy, prevailing here (Syria) was allowing hard currency to find its way abroad."

"This meant," President Nasser added, "that on transferring foreign currency from Cairo to Damascus this currency was free to proceed to Beirut or Paris or some other capital."[52]

When the Amer mission curbed the Syrian complaints but failed to stop them, Nasser launched a triple drive: (1) to extend the Egyptianization of the control of Syria; (2) to introduce state controls to the previously comparatively free Syrian economy in order to bring its

[52] *New York Times,* March 6, 1961.

economy in line with the socialist Egyptian one, in order to accelerate the implementation of his UAR-wide economic plan, and in order
to halt further flight of capital; and (3) to reduce indulgence by introducing into Syria austerity measures already in effect in Egypt, as
well as some new ones. Many of the new decrees, which theoretically were for both regions, were in fact applicable only or particularly to Syria.

One of the first steps toward curbing Syria's "indulgence" was
taken on April 18, 1960, when the import of luxury items to Syria
was forbidden, including that of cars (other than buses), washing
machines, heaters, and refrigerators. On August 3, an annual tax of
50 lira was imposed on TV sets, which were more common in Syria
than in Egypt. But these and similar acts were just forerunners of the
major change that was introduced on February 5, 1961 when the free
trade in foreign currency was stopped, and thus the export and import business came under government control.

But not all the measures were aimed at controlling the Syrian
economy in general or preventing the flight of capital in particular.
Several measures aimed at helping "the masses of peasants and
workers" against the merchants and landlords, while still other measures had both "austerity" and "socialist" goals. As early as April
25, 1960, a minimum wage and a minimum salary were decreed. On
July 5, 1960, a price list of drugs was published, and the profit margin of importers and chemists was set, only to be further reduced by
a decree on August 14, 1960. On December 5, 1960, merchants were
warned not to "juggle" the price of coffee and tea which had become
scarce. On February 9, 1961, the export of lamb was forbidden since
the price of meat was rising. On March 3, 1961, banks were "Arab-
ized," and the state was granted 35 percent of their stock and a seat
on their boards of directors. In the same period, the state opened its
own bank and an import-export agency. On July 20, all major banks
and insurance companies in the UAR were nationalized (both more
prevalent in Syria than Egypt); the work week was cut to 42 hours;
a progressive income tax was introduced; no salary might exceed
5000 lira per annum, and any income above 6000 lira was to be
taxed 100 percent. (The only 6000 lira salary in the UAR was to be
allowed to Nasser himself.) Industries were ordered to share profits

with workers by granting them 25 percent of the net income; worker's representatives were ordered on all corporate boards.[53] A Government Cotton Committee was set up to control export of this important product, and exporters were required to turn over half of their capital to the government in exchange for bonds. On July 10, 1961, the only private shipping line in the UAR was nationalized; later in the same month the timber, transport, metal, cement, and chemical industries were nationalized. On August 9, the government of the UAR issued a release stating that 90 percent of all major business establishments had been nationalized. The work day was reduced to seven hours a day. Land reform was again pushed with much vigor, with Nasser himself traveling across Syria handing out land to the peasants.

In the face of all this, the conservative groups could not but feel that the economic basis was systematically and rapidly being eroded. It was a long way from their looking forward to the union as the "rest" from politics, or from the short period of romance with Amer.

With the regimentation of the economy and the radicalization came an increased transfer of control from Syrian hands to Egyptian ones, and from Syria to Egypt. On August 3, 1961, less than two months before the secession of Syria, the regional cabinets were dissolved and power was concentrated in one union cabinet, whose seat was in Egypt, although it was to meet four months a year in Syria.

At the same time, Egyptian control of the Syrian army was extended. Earlier, Syrian officers had been transferred to Egypt and Egyptian officers to Syria. But while the Syrian officers were given high-sounding titles, the Egyptians first took over strategic intelligence posts and then many command positions.[54] At this stage, the pace of transfers to Egypt was increased, and many Syrian officers were pensioned or given civilian posts in the foreign ministry. As an additional precaution, large amounts of ammunition were transferred to Egypt.

While Syrian control of the army declined, the Syrians paid more

---

[53] See *al-Ahram,* August 11, 1961 and August 23, 1961. For a discussion of the background to the introduction of these measures see Malcolm H. Kerr, "The Emergence of a Socialist Ideology in Egypt," *The Middle East Journal,* vol. 16 (1962), pp. 127–130.

[54] Seale, "Break-up of the United Arab Republic," pp. 472–473.

for it, both compared to preunion days and compared to what Egypt was paying. The Syrian expenditure toward maintaining the military forces was £14 million for 1957–1958, 23.9 for 1956/1960, and 26.1 for 1961/1962. In terms of the percentage of the total Syrian budget, military expenditure increased during the union years from 38.5 percent (1957/1958) to 47.2 percent (1961/1962). Egyptian expenditure, in the same years, was 25.5 percent and 27.1 percent, respectively. In terms of per capita expenditure, the Egyptian's ranged between £3.0 to 3.9 in these years, while the Syrian's started at 3.3 but grew to 5.9. That is to say, Syrian payments increased 66 percent during the less than four Union years.

The final break came when the effective pro-Nasser but Syrian-led and staffed internal security organization was inactivated. Nasser relied for more than three years on the much feared, Syrian superpoliceman, Sarraj. He had been the head of the Syrian internal security organization for five years and minister of the interior for the Northern region since the founding of the UAR in 1958. In 1959, he became the secretary-general of the National Union in Syria, working hard to gain political support for the union. He was assisted by six loyal officers, five of whom graduated with him from the military academy in Homs in 1947 and all of whom fought together in Palestine. In September 1960, Sarraj became the chairman of the executive council of the Northern region and, in 1961, one of the vice presidents of the Republic.

In fact, Sarraj was Nasser's most steadfast supporter in Syria. But as tensions mounted, Nasser felt he could not trust even Sarraj. When Sarraj quarrelled with Amer over authority in Syria, Nasser ordered Sarraj to run his organization from Cairo and sent Amer once more to Syria, this time to uproot Sarraj's men and influence. While Sarraj retained the title of Minister of the Interior, his security machinery was turned over—by Amer—to the office of the president. In August 1961, Sarraj moved to Egypt, but when he found that he was in effect stripped of power, he resigned on September 26, and left for Syria. This weakening of the internal security organization gave the Syrian army an impetus to try to regain its former position. A group of seven officers having the rank of colonel and major, all members of prominent Damascus families, started planning a coup in January 1961.[55] The coup followed a familiar pattern.

A tank column is sent on the capital shortly before dawn from Qatana, a camp twenty miles away; small detachments of two or three vehicles filter through the sleeping city arresting half a dozen key men and occupying the radio station, the central telephone exchange, the headquarters of the army, police, and gendarmerie, the airport and the prison at Mezze. The populace hears the news at breakfast time.[56]

On September 28, 1961, this exercise was once again completed in Syria.

The officers, calling themselves the Supreme Arab Revolutionary Command, announced that they were in control of the country and that they were restoring "freedom and dignity" to the people of Syria. Amer was flown home to Egypt. There was no armed resistance by Syrians to the secessionist army, only small-scale protests of student groups. The 15,000 Egyptian troops in Syria did not fight. Nasser, who first thought that the rebellion was local, dropped about 120 paratroopers at Lataqia, in northern Syria. A few were killed, most were captured without resistance. Egyptian naval units that sailed from Egypt toward Syria were recalled in mid-sea. The Egyptian units in Syria seem to have received no firing order from Cairo. Sending troops by land was not possible because of interposing Israel and Jordan. By September 29, 1961, the secessionist government was firmly established as the government in Syria. Nasser chose not to try to preserve the union by bloodshed, now required to regain control of Syria. He preferred to leave the way open for future unification attempts with Syria and other countries by not impressing into their collective memories a harsh military reprisal. As Nasser stated: "Unity cannot be protected by military force."[57] Nasser did not oppose the recognition of Syria's new government by other countries or its readmission to the Arab League and the United Nations. He retained the title United Arab Republic in anticipation of new unification efforts.

[55] *New York Times,* October 16, 1961.
[56] Seale, "Break-up," p. 471.
[57] *U.S. News and World Report,* October 9, 1961.

The ease with which the coup was carried out shows how little the union was grafted onto Syrian society; in September 1961, there was no one politically effective group, and probably no ineffective one in favor of the union.[58] This does not negate the facts that the idea of unification is still close to the heart of many Syrian intellectuals and leaders and that Nasser has retained a considerable following in Syria. This particular union, not the idea of unity, lost support.

After the official dissolution of the union, the steps taken by the military regime and its landlord and merchant-class allies, reflected the alienating aspects of Egyptian rule. Objecting to extensive Egyptian domination, the new government shipped home Egyptian officers, teachers, administrators, and agents and returned the command of the Syrian army to Syrians. Opposing the state control of the economy, it restored the largely private enterprise economy Syria had before the union. Representing a coalition of the military with the conservative majority, it abolished most nationalization measures and halted the agrarian reform. Objecting to direct military control of civilian life, it restored party politics and a civilian premier. But after returning to the barracks with much fanfare to leave the government to the civilians, the military officers did not hesitate to go back to the nearby capital whenever, in their judgment, the civilian politicians veered too far off the course set by them.

INTEGRATING POWER IN AN ANALYTICAL PERSPECTIVE

The integrating power needed to maintain a premature union, especially in view of the differences between Syria and Egypt, was large. This was barely available at the outset; soon the integrating power derived from transient causes was lost and the more permanent sources exhausted. It is important to state again that particular union, not unity, lost support. Having described these developments chronologically, we turn in this section to review briefly, from a

[58] In part, the lack of resistance to the secessionist forces is also to be attributed to the surprise of their move and the rapidity with which it was completed.

more analytical perspective, the "ups-and-downs" of each kind of integrating power.

The identitive power of the union was never high; Syrian conservatives initially supported unification as the lesser of two evils, preferring it to rule by local Communists. But as the radical and authoritarian nature of the UAR became evident, the conservative majority became highly alienated. The *Baath* initially supported unification despite its misgivings over Nasser's version of Pan-Arabism and nondemocratic socialism. But as its leaders were removed from office, as Amer introduced his "right deviation," and as the authoritarian nature of the regime became evident, the *Baathists* became highly disillusioned. Most Syrian politicians and intellectuals, being accustomed to multiparty political life within the limits imposed by the army, resented the increasing role of the secret police, the suspension of political life, and the authoritarian regime represented by Sarraj and his men, as well as the Amer and his machine.

Syrians in general expected a federation, not an amalgamation; they were embittered by the Egyptian monopolization of control. In the first period, and to a considerable degree in the second one, the major targets of alienation were still local—the *Baath* and Sarraj. But in the third period, as the role and nature of Egyptian rule became more evident, alienation focused directly on Nasser and the UAR. Hence the union's identitive power became exhausted.[59]

The unitarian ties of the union were never large. The two economies, as has been pointed out, were not complementary but competitive in their major crops (cotton, sugar) and industries (textiles), though it was not impossible to adjust them from this viewpoint.[60] The discontiguous territory, the lack of major naval or air fleets, and the limited port facilities in Egypt did not help the evolution of utilitarian ties. Development projects, many of which were supported by the Soviet Union in a premerger 1957 treaty with Syria, and others initiated by Egypt, were slow to show their benefits. Trade be-

[59] For an inter-Arab discussion of the reasons for the Egyptian-Syrian union failure, see *Muhadar Muhadathat al-Wihdah*. These minutes of the April 1963 Egypt-Syria-Iraq unity meeting remained secret until the second *Baathist* defection, after which they were published in Egypt.

[60] Some interesting suggestions for such an adjustment were made by Mallakh, "Economic Integration."

tween the countries increased but could hardly offset losses of trade with Iraq and Saudi Arabia. The harsh economic effects of the three-year drought (1958 through 1960), the flight of capital generated by efforts to amalgamate two economies built on different principles and to imprint a socialist mold were aggravated by the sour orientation of the officials of the poor elite-country to their comparatively well-off subject. By September 1961, unemployment was widespread; the value of the Syrian lira fell; Egypt cut its contributions; and its nationalization and austerity drive alienated all the economic interest groups in Syria. Thus, from Syria's viewpoint, by 1961 the union had no more utilitarian appeal than it had identitive power.

With identitive and utilitarian power decreasing rapidly, the union might have been maintained by coercive power, at least for a transitional period. At first glance, it seems that force was not introduced until late in September 1961, when it was too weakly deployed to prevent a secession and when Nasser decided not to apply it in an attempt to restore the union. Actually though, coercive power was used all the time, and the final break occurred when it too declined, bringing the total of integrating power close to zero.

The three years of "preparation" that preceded the foundation of the UAR were in fact marked by the increasing use of force to weaken resistance to unification in Syria. One observer recorded that in the period

A series of equations was established; a true patriot must be an Arab nationalist; an Arab nationalist must believe in and work for, the unity of the "Arab nation"; those who oppose the principle of Arab unity are traitors to the Arab cause. . . . Once the equation of opposition to unity with treason was established, it was not too difficult for the *Baath* to attack its actual or potential adversaries. A victim of attack could be accused with relative impunity of all sorts of crimes in the Arab political vocabulary. He could be called an imperialist stooge, a feudal reactionary, a Zionist agent. . . . A series of political trials between 1955 and 1957 based, first, on the murder of a popular officer, Colonel Adnan Malki, and then on the alleged discovery of the Iraqi and American plots to overthrow Syria's government, further enhanced the power of the *Baath* and its military allies.[61]

Thus selective terror and political trials were two, though by no means the only factors to encourage the conservatives to submit themselves to the Egyptian-dominated union.

[61] Lenczowski, "Syria," p. 202.

Once the UAR was established, Nasser did not hesitate to draw on Sarraj's *Deuxième Bureau,* and the latter's spectacular career reflected the increased need for his secret police services. As one group after another was alienated, as the National Union designed to absorb alienation did not take root in Syria, and as the effects of Amer's revisions were nullified, reliance on the security forces increased. In the last period, when radicalization and Egyptianization reduced identitive and utilitarian powers to the breaking point, Sarraj's men remained the only Syrian power loyal to Nasser, and he became the head of the Syrian regional government and a vice president of the republic. He also held several key economic posts. As far as Syria had a ruler of its own, it was the authoritarian rule of Sarraj, the superpoliceman. It was only when Sarraj was stripped of power that the sudden weakening in the coercive control of Syria brought the total of integrating power below the level that could sustain the UAR.

The army of a developing nation should never be viewed as merely a foreign policy weapon. Nine times out of ten, it has a police function. Very much aware of this fact, Nasser was quick to reduce the power of the Syrian army and its independence and to deploy 15,000 Egyptian troops in Syria. When the showdown came, neither move turned out to be adequate: the Egyptian force was not large enough to prevent a secession attempt; much of it was stationed next to the Israeli border, and some next to the Turkish one; reinforcements could not readily be sent; the Egyptian units were indifferent to Syrian secession,[62] and Nasser wanted to avoid major bloodshed. The question that comes to mind is why was the European force in Syria neither large enough nor alerted? More generally, why did Nasser and his men allow the integrating power to fall that low? Why did he not follow a strategy more in line with the power structure in Syria and in the union? The answer lies in part in the background factors. It is quite possible that, given the differences between the countries, the discontiguous territory, the three-year drought in Syria, and Egypt's paucity, no amount of power that could be effec-

---

[62] Private communication with Mr. George Hagger. According to one source, the Egyptian officers did not fight for the union because at this stage they were happy to be freed from it.

tively mustered could make the UAR a success. In part, though, the fate of the union was determined by the nature of the communication system and the strategy followed; because of their distorting effect, the union was strained and the available powers partially misused.

COMMUNICATION, REPRESENTATION, AND RESPONSIVENESS

The overall communication and representation structure of the UAR was quite unsatisfactory and hence directly contributed to its disintegration. Upward communication was more limited than downward, but the latter was not too effective either. Responsiveness, as compared to communication, was high, but not high by absolute standards. The UAR deteriorated on all three fronts during most of the period, especially as of mid-1960.

Abolition of political parties was one of the conditions Nasser set for Syria before the union was proclaimed and was one of the first steps he took after it was established. The *Baath*, however, remained an effective upward political channel until the July 1959 elections and the Amer revision. After that time practically no upward non-governmental representation existed other than that provided by the National Union. But the National Union was much more a downward channel of communications and manipulation that was to absorb, rather than transmit, upward communication. It was successful to a degree in Egypt, a country that passed from one kind of authoritarian regime under King Farouk to another under Nasser without the benefit of free-wheeling political experience.[63] For the Syrians, after years of intensive political life under a multiparty system, the National Union seemed a crude façade, an outright manipulation, an insult to their political sophistication, and an organization controlled by a coalition of Egyptians (Amer) and the Syrian secret police (Sarraj). Thus, in Syria, the National Union had little upward and little downward communication value. Various propaganda efforts were more effective, especially radio campaigns, and even more successful were Nasser's annual visits to Syria on Union Day. On the anniversary days of the UAR Nasser stomped the country, making ideological

[63] See Vatikiotis, "The Egyptian Army."

speeches, distributing land to peasants, listening to complaints, holding hands with Syrian politicians (the Arab equivalent of kissing babies). These ceremonies were particularly effective in the first two years of the UAR. The 1961 visit, during which impetus was given to the radicalization and Egyptianization drive and in which Nasser publicly censored the Syrians for their "indulgence," surely had less unification value.

The value of downward communication declined over the years as it became less and less trusted and as rumors replaced government sources as a major supplier of information. As the law first set up regional councils only for those to be abolished, the maturity dates of bonds issued in compensation for the land expropriated were delayed from 30 to 40 years, and the amount of interest paid was greatly slashed, declining from 3 percent to 1 percent by September 1958;[64] and since the 200 feddan first promised were, on July 25, 1961, reduced to 100 feddan, including installments due to beneficiaries through previous legislation, a growing crisis of confidence was generated. When the July 1961 nationalization drive was initiated, even small owners, who actually had nothing to fear, worried about the fate of their property and joined the ranks of the opponents of the regime. Although Syrians were worried about rumors of Egyptian plans for using Syrian lands for colonization purposes for its population surplus, these rumors were neither confirmed nor effectively squelched.

The ability of various social groups to communicate upward to the center of decision-making through representation was sharply curtailed when the political parties were abolished with the initiation of the union. In the following years, the remaining channels of representation were gradually closed. The Syrian ministries were merged with the Egyptian ones in the same year in a way that increased Egyptian control and reduced Syria's ability to effect UAR decision-making. Further reduction in Syrian representation came as the regional councils were abolished on August 16, 1961, though the temporary UAR constitution stated that each region would have an autonomous council of its own; almost all the remaining regional decision-making power was transferred to the central UAR cabinet.

[64] Issawi, "Foundations of Democracy," pp. 60–61.

The new government had seven vice presidents, five Egyptians and two Syrians, and 36 ministers, 14 of whom were Syrians. In practice, however, most decisions were made by Nasser and his trusted "inner" cabinet that included no Syrians. Especially important were the five Egyptian vice presidents, all of whom were members of the original revolutionary junta. Among them, Amer was the most responsive to Syrian needs, as reflected, for example, in his suggestion to slow down the unification of the two economies; however, forces beyond his control soon pushed through a policy that neutralized the effects of his effort. Thus, while he was in touch with and aware of Syria's needs, his influence on policy was, in the long run, not great enough to make policy responsive to these needs.

The two Syrian vice presidents were Sarraj and Kahhala. The increasing role of Sarraj in controlling Syria reflected not only the increasing reliance on force, but the increased closing of upward representation. Sarraj did not represent, nor was he in close touch with, most Syrian groups; his method was intimidation.[65] Nureddin Kahhala was a small-time bureaucrat, trained in the United States in engineering, with no political capability or function.

As of early September 1961, the UAR government moved further to dismember the Syrian polity and reduce its chances of political expression. It divided the northern region of the UAR into several districts that were to be directly controlled from Cairo.

There was a continuous upward flow of intelligence information about Syria. Egyptian officers took over intelligence positions in the Syrian army in 1958, even before they took over command positions; this provided an additional source of power, since much of the intelligence collected was internal. But intelligence reports are often slanted to please the "client"; even if they contain wholly valid information, they have no power-backing, the way the communication of representatives has in a democratic system. Thus, UAR intelligence information could flow upward, but it could not exert pressure for particular responses to change policy in line with the demands and power of the various politically effective groups. Nasser, there-

[65] "Sarraj was good at catching the regime's enemies but not at encouraging its friends. A police chief cannot easily turn statesman overnight." Seale, "Break-up," p. 476.

fore, most certainly knew that the conservative majority in Syria was disaffected and that the *Baath* was bitterly disappointed, but was he aware of the extent and intensity of these feelings? It seems they were not presented in a way that forced Nasser's attention to the extent of alienation and the necessity for more appropriate responses.

The responsiveness of the UAR suffered, like the whole communication structure, from the general authoritarian nature of the regime and the difference between Egyptian and Syrian society and culture. Nasser and his select group of trusted men made all the important and many not so important decisions. This created considerable congestion at the decision-making center. Since all the decision-makers were Egyptians, some lack of understanding of the Syrian situation was unavoidable. For instance, Nasser's decision to implement in Syria the same laws of agrarian reform introduced in Egypt did not take into account the greater availability of land in Syria, the differences in irrigation systems and climate, and the fact that the state in Syria owned large amounts of land that could be allocated before the estates of landlords were confiscated. Late in April 1958, a delegation of Syrian farmers came to Cairo to protest the announced intention to extend to Syria the benefits of the protection of the Farmer Law. Its most unacceptable clause limited land holding by any one family to 200 acres. That, the peasants felt, might be needed in land-hungry Egypt, but not in Syria.

STRATEGY: OSCILLATION AND ACCELERATION

Nasser's policy toward Syria had a dominant theme, but it was far from consistent. While it was largely oriented toward gaining control and accelerating social change, the balance swung from time to time to a more responsive position. As a consequence, Nasser's policy fell between two chairs, and the one it tried to sit on most of the time was not necessarily the right one.

Regarding the question of federation versus a unitary state, the real question was not constitutional, that is, what legal structure to give the UAR. The USSR is a federation and Britain a unitary state, and yet pluralism can express itself much more readily in Britain than in the USSR. The real question was how much autonomy to grant Syria in the control of its domestic affairs. In principle, Nasser decided to award little such freedom and later to reduce it even further. In hindsight, it is easy to state that this was a mistaken policy. But we must note that much weaker but also less demanding (in terms of the integrating power needed) structures, such as federations (for example, the 1958 Iraq-Jordan one) and alliances among Arab states (for example, the Arab League), did not last longer or amount to more than the UAR. Hence, the impression one gains from examining the history of the UAR, that a genuine federation would have been more likely to last than the centralization of power imposed by Nasser, cannot be documented and must be held with much reservation.

Theoretically, Nasser could have started with a centralized unitary state and, as he became aware of the disintegrative pressures in Syria, he might have given them some legitimate outlet by shifting to a decentralized, federal structure.[66] But Nasser's response was the opposite. After a brief attempt at giving Syria some self-rule, the UAR moved toward more Egyptian control and more Syrian subjugation, undermining consistently all centers of independent Syrian power, beginning with the political parties, the army, and the tribes, turning to the *Baath,* then to the landlords and business groups, and closing with the internal security organization. Thus, the decline of the administration of Syria by Syrians paralleled the erosion of autonomous nongovernmental bodies.

The increased Egyptian subjugation of Syria was accompanied by efforts to change the social structure of Syria, to shift the balance of power of the various groups vis-à-vis each other (while cutting the power of all of them vis-à-vis the Egyptian controlled state and its political arm, the National Union). This policy was less consistently pursued than that of subjugation, though it was fairly dominant most of the time. In general, Nasser favored radicalization; that is, after he developed the taste for socialism relatively late in his career, he based his Egyptian regime more and more on peasants, workers, intellectuals, and mobs (the four typical mainstays of leftist revolutionaries) in addition to the army, and less and less on the traditional

[66] Seale, "Break-up," p. 476.

and modern conservative groups: landlords, merchants, exporters-importers, manufacturers, and the like.

Nasser started by allowing his Syrian ally, the *Baath,* to have a field-day with Syria's landlords and business classes. When their complaints mounted, he—through Amer—decelerated several revisions, playing up to the conservative majority—or, as he later put it, "appeasing Syrian reactionaries."[67] But despite the relative success of this policy in Syria, his revolutionary ambitions in Egypt, his attempt to appear at the forefront of "progressive" forces in the Middle East as part of his nonaligned African and Arab stance next to Tito and Nkrumah, his reaction to Syria's "indulgence" and "ungratefulness," and his desire to enhance Egyptian control by undermining the bases of Syrian independent power, all caused him to reinitiate, with new vigor, the radicalization drive. Thus, in retrospect, radicalization was the major theme; the "go-slow" revisionist approach, a deviation.

The combination of Syrian subjugation and radicalization—in short the acceleration strategy—proved disastrous to the UAR because it *alienated the major power groups in Syria without breaking their power.* The army was the key group. Nasser did not take any drastic measures, like merging the Syrian and Egyptian units, disbanding the Syrian army, or transferring most of the Syrian army to various Egyptian posts. After all, Syria was a partner to a union whose position was supposed to set an attractive example to get other Arab republics into the union, and not a country that lost a war against Egypt. He limited himself to gradually weakening the Syrian army, under thinly veiled pretexts. One of the most often repeated was the "professionalization" of the Syrian army. The effective curbing of political factions in the army and its association with various political civilian groups was supposed to improve the army's quality. But since little else was done in this direction at the same time, the conclusion seems warranted that the aim of this drive was first of all to remove the major tool of political power from the Syrian groups, which regularly measured their power by appeals to the army. This maneuver gave substance to the 1958 agreement to disband and ban

[67] *New York Times,* October 17, 1961.

Syrian parties; but whatever improvement this would bring to the army (which was meanwhile gradually dismantled) was clearly of little genuine interest. This policy sufficed to alienate utterly the Syrian officers, but it did not suffice to render them harmless. Similarly, Nasser's agrarian policy was not radical enough and consistent enough to please the leftist intellectuals, the *Baath* party, and probably the many peasants who did not benefit from it because of its slow pace,[68] but it succeeded in driving the fear of socialism and economic loss into the heart of every landlord. The agrarian reform was declared in Syria in September 1958. It was to affect 30 million *dunum* of land (a Syrian *dunum* is equal to a quarter of an acre), about half of which was governmental and half was in private hands. At that time, 3240 landlords, about 1 percent of the local owners, owned 38 percent of the arable land in Syria. Three years later, only 1.8 million *dunum* were handed out to 8000 families, and about 7 percent of the families benefited from the program. Also, the land plots given were smaller than promised, about 50 *dunum* arable land or 250 *dunum* nonarable land, instead of 80 or 300 respectively. The initiation of the reform, however, was enough to make most of the landlords abandon long-run investments in land improvement or agricultural equipment, little of which were provided by the government. Credit for agriculture, provided by the Agricultural Board, was practically not expanded: 59 million Syrian lira in 1957, 61 in 1958, 54 in 1959, and 62 in 1960. Nationalization was extensively introduced in July and August of 1961, when the UAR was in effect about to fall apart, but the business groups were under fire as of April 1960, haunted by measures that worried and alienated them but did not neutralize their power. As the makeup of the first Syrian Cabinet after the secession indicated, it was these groups, triggering the army, that finally ended the UAR.[69]

Theoretically, Nasser could have worked consistently with the conservative majority, though his debts to the *Baath,* his position in Egypt, and his international ambitions made this course unattractive. The other alternative was a ruthless, Soviet-style revolution, uproot-

[68] *Rose-al-Yusil,* July 31, 1961.
[69] Erskine B. Childers, "The Lessons of Syria," *The Spectator,* May 18, 1962, p. 641.

ing the landlords and merchant classes supported in 1958 by the *Baath*, giving the peasants land on a large scale to win their unwavering support to the regime and nationalizing the industries and controlling business immediately. This was an approach difficult to assume toward a country that was a partner of a union rather than an occupied country, but in line with the leftist *Baath* approach and certainly Nasser's newly founded nondemocratic socialist creed. Such an approach would still have been a gamble because the power of the conservative groups was difficult to undermine in view of the social composition of the Syrian army (which despite its temporary coalition with the *Baath* largely recruited its officers from "prominent" families). The support of the peasants and workers without that of the army, as we shall see, would have been of little value. Nasser, who never turned to large-scale violence though he did not shun small-scale force, did not take this gamble. He initially let the *Baath* turn the socialist revolution into a private and party vendetta, thus losing much of the legitimating appeal the revolution might have had; then he let Amer try a revisionist approach which Nasser should have realized would be contrary to his other plans; and finally shifted back to a radical but not violent, Soviet-style undercutting of the economic basis of the conservative groups.

The net effect of Nasser's strategy was to alienate at one time the socialists and intellectuals, at another the conservatives, and always and increasingly the army. The peasants and workers could hardly come to his rescue, nor were they particularly helped by the eventual radicalization. As political groups, illiterate, lacking in organizational skill, dispersed in many villages and generally absent from the urban centers, they were ineffective.[70] As Syrian nationalists, their status deprivations were similar to those experienced by other groups as Egyptianization became more and more evident. Because of the economic crisis, many workers were unemployed, and peasants received lower prices (in real income terms) than before the establishment of the UAR.

REALLOCATION

The UAR's attempts to reallocate assets among *sub*units in the Northern region had a de-unifying effect on its ties with the Southern

[70] Vatikiotis, "The Egyptian Army," p. 116.

region (Egypt); parallel attempts to reallocate assets between the two regions themselves were similarly de-unifying. The basic pattern of the Egyptian design for the economic relationship between the two regions of the UAR was for Syria to be the agricultural hinterland for the accelerated industrialization of Egypt, Syria providing food supplies to Egypt and Egypt using Syria as an outlet for its comparatively expensive and low quality industrial products. As the details of this master plan became known to the Syrians, they became a major disillusioning factor in the union.

There were several ways in which the Egyptian design expressed itself and became known to the Syrians. One was the master development plan, more commonly referred to as the Five-Year Plan (1960–1965).[71] It called for increased investment, by sectors, in the two regions (see Table 2).

In addition to the obviously higher percentage of investment in agriculture and irrigation in Syria and in industry in Egypt, one must take into account that most of the investment in the development of Syrian transportation was aimed at making the exportable agricultural products cheaper, while investments in Egyptian transportation were to be tied to industrial development (transportation of raw material to industry and of products from industry to internal and export markets). Thus, investments in Syrian agriculture amounted to 51 to 61 percent of the total investment planned (depending on whether one charged half or all of the transportation investment toward agri-

Table 2 FIVE-YEAR PLAN

Sector	Egypt	Syria
	(percentage of investment)	
Irrigation	9.8	30.5
Agriculture	13.3	9.9
Industry (including electricity)	34.1	18.7
Transportation	16.0	19.7
Services	26.8	21.2
	100.00	100.00

[71] On the Syrian side of this plan, see Mashru 'Khitat al-tanmiya al-igtisadiyya wa-l-ijtima 'iyya li-l-sahawat al-Khams (Damascus, July, 1960).

culture), while the Egyptian one amounted to about 25 percent. Investment in industry, by the same criteria, was about 19 percent in Syria and 46 percent or higher for Egypt.

While industry contributed only 21 percent of the Egyptian national income at the beginning of the development plan in 1960, it was expected to grow to provide 30 percent, an increase of 9 percent in the five-year period. Syrian industry provided at the beginning of the same period 11.4 percent of the Syrian national income; at the end of the period it was to provide, according to the Cairo planners, 12.7 percent or an increase of only 1.3 percent.

The same tendency to prefer Egyptian industrialization is revealed if investment plans are broken into sectors (see Table 3).

In interpreting these figures, informed Syrians could not fail to take into account that the Syrian chemical industry was largely to serve agriculture (through production of fertilizers and pesticides), while the item that headed the Egyptian set of priorities was basic industry (the metal industry at 25.8 percent), which has a low priority (6.1 percent) in the Syrian plan. The textile industry, which both regions were highly competitive, drew almost 7 percent of the Egyptian investment, but none was planned for Syria.

We cannot examine here the claim that Syria's natural advantages lie in agriculture and Egypt's in industry, and hence the planned division of labor would have benefited both regions of the UAR. The politically important fact is that Syria was not consulted about its willingness to serve as the agricultural hinterland of Egypt, nor were

Table 3 INDUSTRIAL INVESTMENT PLAN

Branch	Egypt	Syria
	(percentage of investment)	
Oil	15.6	41.5
Electricity	17.6	12.4
Natural resources	9.1	5.9
Metal industry	25.8	6.1
Chemical industry	11.5	25.8
Textile industry	6.9	
Food industry	6.3	7.5
Miscellaneous	6.5	0.8

the Syrians unaware of the widely held belief that agricultural countries lose out in terms of per capital income in such divisions of labor. It is usually colonial powers that are charged with the plans to keep a country as a "backward" agricultural one, while they seek to provide the industrial goods.

A Syrian seeking to justify the Egyptian plan could have pointed to the fact that while the plan aimed the Syrian economy in a direction many Syrians would consider undesirable, at least the plan provided an impetus for development which was lacking in the years preceding the establishment of the UAR. But then there were some other important aspects of the Five-Year Plan that even such a Syrian would find unattractive. For instance, the plan called for increasing the employment opportunities in the two regions, but in a quite unequal manner, as shown in Table 4.

The plan obviously aimed at increasing employment as compared with population growth in one region but not in the other. In Syria there would hardly be a change in the employment opportunities, as the growth of employment would just about keep pace with the growth of the population; while in Egypt a net improvement of 5.3 percent was planned.

Finally, the UAR master-plan was to affect the foreign trade of the two regions and their trade with each other. A study of the trade pattern planned reveals once more that the agricultural role designed for Syria was one major way in which Egypt was to affect the reallocation of assets between the two regions. As far as the nature of the

Table 4 EMPLOYMENT OPPORTUNITIES IN THE UAR

	SYRIA			EGYPT		
	Base year 1959/ 1960	5 years later 1964/ 1965	Percent-age of increase	Base year 1959/ 1960	5 years later 1964/ 1965	Percent-age of increase
Population (in millions)	4.5	5.1	12.5	25.4	28.4	11.8
Labor force (in millions)	1.5	1.7	12.4	5.9	7.0	17.1

products to be traded was concerned, the Syrian export to Egypt, by 1965, was to be composed 84 percent of agricultural products and only 12 percent of industrial ones, while the Egyptian exports to Syria were to be 77 percent industrial and 19 percent agricultural. At the same time, the Syrian trade was to become much more Egypt-oriented—26 percent of the total Syrian exports were to go to Egypt (as compared to 1.6 percent in 1958), while the respective figures for Egyptian exports to Syria were 9 percent (as compared to 3.6 percent in 1958).

What would this change in the direction of the Syrian trade have meant for Syria? First of all, it would have deprived Syria of an important segment of her foreign currency earning, which is gained from exports to countries other than Egypt; it would allow Egypt to save foreign currency by buying its food products with local currency and at lower than world market prices (for reasons discussed below) while Syria, lacking foreign currency, would have to buy Egyptian industrial products that were 20 to 50 percent above world market price and lower in quality.

At the same time, by deflecting Syrian exports to Egypt, Egypt could export her products—such as cotton, textiles—to the international market, replacing Syria's exports. This was more than a plan: Syria, which exported textiles at the rate of 49 million Syrian lira in 1957, exported 15 percent less in 1959 (41 million lira), and textiles was its number-one export item. Syria's other industrial exports—chemicals, metals, and glassware—also fell in this period from 12 million lira in 1957 to 8 in 1959. The Syrian products had become noncompetitive in the world market, as Syria was forced to buy expensive Egyptian raw materials. Specifically, while Egypt's trade with Arab countries other than Syria increased, Syria's trade with these countries fell from 157 million Syrian lira in 1957, by 20 percent, to 125 million in 1960.

The high price Syria paid for Egyptian imports and the low price Egyptians paid for Syrian exports were all affected by a set government exchange rate—43 percent higher than that in the free market—which the UAR introduced between the currency of the two countries. That is, in February 1958 the free-market exchange rate was 6.2 Syrian lira for one Egyptian one; the rate set by the Cairo government was 8.9 Syrian lira for one Egyptian lira.

In short, Nasser did not accelerate sufficient change to undermine the groups committed to the status quo and to win the support of those committed to social change; he did not decelerate enough to capture the support of the status quo groups, but enough to disappoint those who favored change. His oscillation cost him the support of both sides. His attempt to affect the allocation of assets between the two regions by his Five-Year Plan, trade pattern, and financial arrangements generated an economic crisis in Syria and alienated most of the politically active groups. The army, itself aware of his unsure hand, was controlled enough to be alienated but not enough to be neutralized. Drawing on widespread alienation among the civilians, it administered the last stroke; the ease with which the UAR tumbled reflected the thinness of the political basis of this particular union. But what actually tumbled was the institutional structure, while the building stones of union—to the degree they were ever available—remained basically intact.

CHAPTER 5

A Union That Failed: The Federation of the West Indies (1958–1962)

————————•◆•◆•————————

The short history of the Federation of the West Indies is one of a unification drive initiated by a power external to the region. Attempting to make the idea of federation more acceptable to a greater number of islands in the region, the planners reduced again and again the scope of the proposed federation. This not only curtailed the integrating power needed for the initiation of the federation; it also did not leave the new federation with a broad enough basis to grow, to extend its scope and level of integration, or to serve important interests of its members, especially the more powerful ones. When the federation came into active conflict with the interests of the leading members, long before it developed the ideological, economic, or military power necessary to counter secessionist attempts, the union was dissolved. Thus was terminated the life of an institutional structure that never had a realistic sociopolitical basis. In other words, as little federation as there was, it was more than the West Indies union was willing and able to carry.

AN INEFFECTIVE DISTRIBUTION OF POWER

An Imported Federation

The Federation of the West Indies, formally established on January 3, 1958, was initiated and supported by a country that never became or intended to become a member—the United Kingdom. Its collapse became in effect inevitable on September 19, 1961, the day on which Jamaica voted to secede.[1] The federation failed, in part, because most of the West Indians who supported it did so mainly for exterior and transient reasons as a "convenient way to nationhood" and, in part, because the governmental structure established by the federal constitution was not congruent with the actual power relations among the member-units. This lack of congruity is best understood in the perspective of earlier efforts at federation.

By the end of World War II, Britain had decided to favor a federation of all her Caribbean possessions. In this effort, London seems to have been motivated by four factors. Among the islanders, sentiment for independence had been slowly growing.[2] The increase of this desire was paralleled by a world reaction against colonialism and by the development in Britain, especially as a result of the policy of the Labor party,[3] of a climate of opinion favorable to the claims of the colonies for independence.[4] While the United Kingdom was quite anxious to rid herself of the burdens of this colonial administration,[5] it felt an obligation to provide for the welfare of the islands and was determined to oversee their progress toward stable self-government within the Commonwealth. The London government at the time found it inconceivable that these colonies, especially the smaller ones, could separately attain economic self-sufficiency. A 1947 British report on the Caribbean emphasized, "it is clearly impossible in the modern world for the present separate communities [in the West Indies], small and isolated as most of them are, to achieve and maintain full self-government on their own."[6] Though Britain had been considering some form of unification among the islands for many years, at this stage it made federation a prerequisite

[1] *The Economist,* September 23, 1961, p. 1142.

[2] *West Indian Economist,* July 1958, p. 17.

[3] Morley Ayearst, *The British West Indies: The Search for Self-government.* New York: New York University Pres, 1960, p. 33.

[4] Ronald V. Sires, "Government in the British West Indies: An Historical Outline," *Social and Economic Studies,* vol. 6 (1957), p. 124.

[5] *West Indian Economist,* July 1959, p. 13.

[6] *Closer Association of the British West Indian Colonies.* Command paper No. 7120 (1947), quoted by Douglas G. Anglin, "The Political Development of the West Indies," in David Lowenthal (ed.) *The West Indies Federation: Perspectives on a New Nation.* American Geographical Society Research Series no. 23. New York: Columbia University Press, 1961, pp. 38–39.

for independence, though no explicit and formal commitment to tie the two was made.

For more than three-quarters of a century, Britain had favored federation among her Caribbean possessions. In 1871, it sponsored the formation of a federation of the Leeward Islands (including Antigua, St. Kitts, Nevis and Anguilla, Montserrat, Dominica, and the British Virgin Islands). But there was a great deal of dissatisfaction with the federation.[7] Dominica withdrew in 1940,[8] and in 1956, with the approach of independence, the entire federation was dismantled.[9] When, in 1875, Britain tried to unite Barbados with the Windward Islands (then consisting of Grenada, St. Vincent, St. Lucia, and Tobago), the Barbadians rioted in protest; they feared that a union with the poorer Windwards would increase their economic burdens and would lead to a loss of autonomy by the imposition of a non–self-governing Crown Colony system. Barbados had a fully elected representative assembly, but under federation this would have been abolished.[10]

Federation remained a goal, though often an inactive one of British Caribbean policy, as the Colonial Secretary indicated in 1905.[11] In 1929, for example, Britain supported a suggestion of the "unofficial" members of the Legislature and Executive Councils of Antigua for a federation of the islands of the eastern Caribbean from St. Kitts to Trinidad.[12] An administrative union of the Leewards and Windwards was proposed by the West Indian Sugar Commission in

[7] While this administrative structure is commonly referred to as a federation, it was more a partially unified colonial administration of earlier less related colonial units.

[8] *Europa Year Book 1962,* vol. 2, p. 267.

[9] David Lowenthal, "The West Indies Chooses a Capital," *Geographical Review,* vol. 48 (1958), p. 341.

[10] For a report on this effort, see Bruce Hamilton, *Barbados and the Confederation Question* (1871–1855). London: Crown Agents for Overseas Governments & Administrations, 1956.

[11] Jesse Harris Proctor, Jr., "The Functional Approach to Political Union: Lessons from the Effort to Federate the British Caribbean Territories," *International Organizations,* vol. 10 (1956), p. 36.

[12] The "unofficial" members of the Executive or Legislative Council were those members who did not hold any governmental office such as colonial secretary, financial secretary, or attorney-general by virtue of which they would be entitled to positions on the councils. Their inclusion was at the discretion of the governor.

1930.[13] A commission was appointed to study the matter and its report issued in 1933 favored a common governor for the Leewards, Windwards, and Trinidad, with the retention of considerable autonomy by the individual islands. This was to have been a step toward a wider federation,[14] but support for even such a limited federation was insufficient. The plans aborted because the islands feared that federation would bring increased administrative costs and because Trinidad objected to any union with the poorer and smaller islands.[15]

The idea of a West Indian federation was not, however, given up by Britain and it gained a measure of following among some of the politically conscious West Indians, as the Moyne Commission discovered in 1938–1939.[16] The Commission recommended that federation be retained as the ultimate goal of British Caribbean policy and suggested that the Leeward Federation, at that time still in existence, be broadened to include the Windwards. This suggestion, however, was never implemented because of disagreements among the islands, which this time focused on questions regarding customs duties.

In part pursuing its policy of federation and in part as a matter of administrative expediency, Britain sought to build up inter-island ties and organizations. In 1919, a West Indian Court of Appeals was created by the United Kingdom. The Imperial College of Tropical Agriculture was established under Royal Charter at Trinidad in 1924,[17] and in 1934 a West Indian Trade Commissioner to Canada, who represented the islands as a group, was appointed. In 1940, following the Moyne Commission report, the United Kingdom set up the Colonial Development and Welfare Organization, which advised on the expenditure of development funds contributed by Britain to the West Indies and made attempts at social reforms and economic development in the region.[18]

[13] *Report of the West Indian Sugar Commission,* Cmd. 31517 (1930).
[14] *West Indies Report of the Closer Union Commission.* Cmd. 4383 (1933).
[15] Ayearst, *The British West Indies,* p. 228.
[16] *West Indian Royal Commission Report, 1938–1939.* Cmd. 6607 (1945).
[17] The I.C.T.A. was originally not very "regional." It had but a few West Indian researchers and served for training of colonial officers for other regions as well. It has, however, become more "regional" over the last two decades.
[18] Proctor, "Functional Approach," p. 37.

A joint attempt at regional cooperation was made by Britain and the United States (later joined by France and the Netherlands) with the establishment of a Caribbean omission in March 1942, which served to coordinate their policies toward the Caribbean region. This was followed in January 1944 by the instituting of a series of West Indian conferences which, under the Caribbean Commission's auspices, were held at two- or three-year intervals to discuss and debate Caribbean-wide issues. The conferences tended to follow British suggestions. But the time the 1958 federation was born, this "functional" step-by-step approach had made very little progress, never reaching the take-off point. The total number of regional organizations operating by 1958 was small and their significance for the islands' interests and values was very low. At the same time, the island administrative structures and polities—as distinct from the regional ones—did increase significantly, mainly because of the growing demand for self-government.

Agitation for self-government had begun in the 1920s largely through the work of a cultivated group of persons on each island,[19] who had been educated either in England or in the West Indian secondary schools, which are largely modeled on Great Britain's and which therefore reflect a strong British influence.[20] Initially, the bulk of the population showed little interest in self-government. But this apathy was modified by the great depression of the thirties, which severely affected the already depressed island economies. The islanders began to hold the colonial governments and the dependent character of their colonial status responsible for their impoverished economic state. Strikes and riots directed against the governments broke out at different times in Jamaica, British Guinea, St. Vincent, Trinidad, and Barbados in the period from 1934 to 1938.[21] Nationhood and an extension of political rights were seen as necessary requisites for solving the islands' economic problems.[22] At this time,

[19] For an account of island activity in the pursuit of self-government, see Ayearst, *The British West Indies,* pp. 33 ff and pp. 68–98. See esp. p. 33.

[20] Lambros Comitas, "Metropolitan Influences in the Caribbean: The West Indies," *Social and Cultural Pluralism in the Caribbean, Annals of the New York Academy of Sciences,* vol. 83 (1960), pp. 813–814.

[21] Ayearst, *The British West Indies,* pp. 34–40; Sires, "Government in the British West Indies," p. 124; and Comitas, "Metropolitan Influences," p. 811.

[22] *West Indian Economist,* July 1958, p. 17.

the more important political parties and trade unions were formed; all were island-based and not regional. These included Jamaica's People's National party, founded in 1938 with the avowed objective of achieving Jamaican independence,[23] and the Progressive League, established in Barbados in the same year, whose goal was the extension of the franchise and which developed into the Barbados Labor party.[24] In general, the successful West Indian political party was built upon an appeal to island ideals: greater self-government for each colony and more rapid advance toward independence.[25]

Britain responded in part to the demands for self-government, by urging consideration of federation upon the governments of its Caribbean possessions as a *prelude* to independence. If the indigenous drive for independence could be channeled to support the drive for federation, which was largely imported, the Federation of the West Indies—it seemed—had a chance. However, contrary to the plan, the following years witnessed a continuous decline in the number of British possessions accepting this condition, as one after the other withdrew from the negotiations leading toward the formation of the federation. The Bahamas rejected the British federal plan, advanced in 1945, out of hand; they did not consider themselves part of the Caribbean.[26] The proposal was revived when Britain convened a conference at Montego Bay, Jamaica, in September of 1947. Here the Jamaicans offered strong resistance to the idea of unification with the less developed islands. Bustameste of Jamaica characterized the proposed federation as a "pooling of poverty."[27] While the smaller islands were more pro-federation than the larger ones,[28] they had some reservations as well. In particular, they feared domination by the larger islands.

The 1947 Conference, however, accepted the desirability of a loose federation on the Australian model and it established a Stand-

---

[23] Sires, "Government in the British West Indies," p. 125.

[24] Ayearst, *The British West Indies*, p. 89.

[25] Morley Ayearst, "A Nation: Some Characteristics of West Indian Political parties," *Social and Economic Studies*, vol. 3 (1954), p. 189.

[26] Annette Baker Fox, *Freedom and Welfare in the Caribbean.* New York: Harcourt, Brace and Company, Inc., 1949, pp. 173ff.

[27] *West Indian Economist*, July 1958, p. 17.

[28] Lloyd Braithwaite, "Progress Toward Federation, 1938–1956," *Social and Economic Studies*, vol. 6 (1957), p. 148.

ing Closer Association Committee composed of delegates from the colonial legislatures, whose task was the consideration of some of the problems of federation: fiscal tariff policies, unification of currency, and the outline of a federal constitution.[29] This time British Guiana led the opposition; it objected to federation in principle, for reasons of domestic politics that need not be explored here. Also, British Guiana, which is not an island but part of the mainland, was oriented to the realization of what it considered to be its "continental destiny."

The Standing Closer Association Committee began its deliberations in November of 1948 and issued its report, the Rance Report, in October 1949. This report called for a weak federation with very limited central authority. It also provided for the continuation of British influence. The executive power of the federation was to be exercised by a Council of State consisting of fourteen members, eight of whom were to be chosen by the British Prime Minister and six to be selected at the discretion of the Crown-appointed governor-general. The governor-general also held reserved powers over defense, matters of financial stability, and internal safety.[30] The envisaged federation would have been a Crown colony of an advanced type; nevertheless, for Jamaica the proposed federation represented a step backward, for it offered less autonomy than Jamaica had already achieved in its relations with Britain.[31] Other "territories" were even less favorably disposed: British Guiana, British Honduras, and the British Virgin Islands, from then on ceased to participate officially in negotiations toward federation.

In April 1953, the British Colonial Office convened another conference of West Indian leaders—this time in London. Its task was the consideration of the Rance Report. The resistance of many of the islands to federation was still high; hence, the already limited power of the federal government was here once more reduced. At Jamaica's insistence, the union's federal government was to be prevented from

---

[29] *Conference on the Closer Association of the British West Indies Colonies. Montego Bay.* Part I. Cmd. 7291 (1948).

[30] *Report of the British Caribbean Standing Closer Association Committee, 1948–1949.* Col. No. 255, 1950.

[31] Wendell Bell, "Attitudes of Jamaican Elites Toward the West Indies Federation," in *Social and Cultural Pluralism in the Caribbean,* p. 866.

collecting income taxes for the first five years of its existence and
was thereby made dependent upon contributions by the islands for
its financial support. Similarly, though free movement of persons
among the islands was stipulated in the preamble to the constitution,
mechanisms for implementing this principle were not established
because of Trinidad's opposition. This issue was never resolved.
Trinidad feared the immigration of unemployed West Indians from
nearby islands, whose admission, under current arrangements, could
be controlled at its discretion. This power it was unwilling to surrender. The diluted constitutional proposals of the 1953 London Conference were accepted by the island legislatures, with only minor
qualifications.[32]

Efforts at extending the scope of the federation were launched
at a new London conference in 1956. Here the British linkage of
independence to federation was made more explicit: no single territory, it was said, could hope for Dominion status.[33] This threat appears to have been directed primarily toward Jamaica, who felt itself
capable of striking out on its own both economically and politically.
Actually, Jamaica did not doubt that Britain would sooner or later
grant it independence; for Jamaica, adherence to federation meant
the difference between delayed and rapid achievement of nationhood.[34] Hence, no wonder, the new British pressure was to little
avail, as the results of the 1956 conference showed. The major issue
of this conference, the establishment of a customs union, was not
resolved. This time Jamaica and Trinidad were at the head of the
opposition, with the former committed to a protectionist policy and
the latter to free trade. Jamaica agreed to accept the customs union
in principle only on condition that implementation be postponed.
Thus, the effort to extend the scope of federation failed.

Nor did these conferences provide any sense of assurance that
federation would entail the rapid independence which at least the
larger islands seemed to desire. It has been pointed out that one of
the most significant features of the 1956 London conference was the
"dependent" character of the emerging federation; this was reflected

---

[32] Ayearst, *The British West Indies,* pp. 233–234.
[33] Ayearst, *The British West Indies,* p. 235.
[34] Bell, "Attitudes of Jamaican Elites," p. 866.

in the islands' demands for an increased financial subsidy from the United Kingdom and in the fact that the commissioner, who was to oversee the foundation of the federal governmental organization, and the chairmen of all the prefederal commissions, on which the work of the Conference was based, were all British.[35]

Finally, on August 2, 1956, more than 3000 miles away in London, Parliament passed an act empowering the establishment of the Federation of the West Indies by an order-in-council which was ratified in July 1957. A British governor-general was appointed by the Crown in October 1957. It was he, who, upon arrival in the West Indies' capital in January 1958, set a date for the first federal elections, which were held in March 1958. (The legal termination of the Federation of the West Indies also took place in London, on May 31, 1962.)

Various authorities on the West Indies differ in the stress they put on the role Britain played in engineering the federation. West Indians tend to emphasize it; British writers tend to minimize it.[36] The evidence seems to us to support the West Indian position to the degree that it holds that Britain played a major role in constructing the federation in a way that was not in line with the sociopolitical reality of the region—a reality that the London government could not change to conform to the federal design. Nor did Britain provide the mass education necessary to make the federation, and the closely related idea of a West Indian nationland, really acceptable in the region. A West Indian interviewed on this point made the following comment: "People going abroad—particularly students—got a feeling of nationalism and were in the vanguard. They saw themselves as great citizens, not members of colonies. But the idea had not caught on with the masses." Another one said: "It was a federation of politicians rather than people," and still another observed: "the Federation remained academic."[37] While British writers tend, correctly in our

[35] Braithwaite, "Progress Toward Federation," p. 159.
[36] See "Failure of a Federation," *Round Table,* vol. 52 (1962), pp. 273–278 for a British viewpoint. Cf. Jesse Harris Proctor, Jr., "Britain's Pro-Federation Policy in the Caribbean: An Inquiry into Motivation," *The Canadian Journal of Economics & Political Science,* vol. 22 (1956), p. 319.
[37] W. J. F. Kontak, "Some Important Caribbean Questions," 1963, Stencil, pp. 4, 2, and 21 respectively.

judgment, to object to viewing the federation as having been forced on the West Indians, this does not mean that Britain was not the major driving force behind its initiation and establishment. Britain did not impose federation; it just promoted it.

To make the federation more acceptable, Britain did delay its initiation again and again to allow time for more indigenous support to accumulate,[38] and the federation was not launched until its constitution was approved by all the legislature of the islands that were to participate. Other islands, as we have seen, chose not to participate and were not forced to do so. Moreover, quite a few distinguished West Indian intellectuals and leaders came over the years to favor the federation, including Marryshow, Merivale, de Vertinil, Salmon, Murray, Rippon, and Sir Norman Lamont.

In what sense was this then a British federation? The idea was largely British; it was promoted by the Colonial Office and was "sold" mainly to a thin layer of West Indians.

Few of these people [West Indians] thought of themselves as West Indians. Each little island was schizophrenic, one small but powerful section speaking of England as "home" and regarding the rest of the population as "they." The people who met to talk about the federation were, for the most part, officials; sincere, devoted but certainly not representative of something that has yet to be created—West Indian sentiment. . . . When the Colonial Office set up within itself a West Indian department to deal with these territories it was in fact "imposing from above a supervising unity in the government of the region."[39]

Many of the local supporters of the federation were rather ambivalent about it as reflected in the fact that some shifted rather readily to an antifederation position when this seemed opportune (as did, for instance, Bustamente, the leader of the Jamaica Labor party). Others (such as Norman Manley, the leader of the People's National party), who did not cease to favor federation, fought for the reduction of its scope though this endangered its very existence. Most supporters of federation (including Dr. Eric Williams, Trinidad's

[38] Proctor, "Britain's Pro-Federation Policy," p. 327.
[39] *The Gleaner,* December 7, 1958. See also P. M. Sherlock, Vice-Chancellor of the University College of the West Indies, "Story of Federation," *Sunday Guardian* (Port of Spain), April 20, 1958.

Premier, and Norman Manley) held such conflicting conceptions of
what the federation was to be, that it is obvious that any consensus
for federation did not constitute agreement about its scope or purposes or powers.

Above all, the federation established in the West Indies followed
the pattern Britain believed best; it was not the kind of federation
that might have evolved in the region without outside interference.
This holds not only for the slanting of the federal structure in favor
of the small islands, but also in terms of the so-called "Colonial
limitations," the residue of British control left in the West Indian
Constitution. How acceptable those limitations were can be readily
judged from the fact that the very first meeting of the West Indian
Federal Parliament occupied itself with demands to revise the constitution to remove the powers reserved to the Queen-in-Council, as
well as the powers left in the hands of the British governor-general,
for instance his powers regarding the appointments of senators and
his status as the president of the Council of State. True, these powers
were reserved only for a transition period, but the West Indians, more
committed to independence than federation, desired that they be removed at the earliest possible day. If the British felt they had gained
acceptance for the federation as such, a Canadian publication pointed
out: "For two decades many West Indians considered the basic purpose of federation was to provide a 'convenient path to nationhood.' "[40]

The fact that the Federation of the West Indies was largely initiated and advanced by an external elite, with ambivalent indigenous
support, meant that a high level of integrating power was needed to
maintain it. This power was not available. Hence the initiators of the
federation were under continuous pressure to reduce its scope in
order to adjust it to the low amount of supporting power available.
This reduction was never sufficient; since the integrating power
available was so low, it probably was unable to sustain any federal
institutional structure, however limited in scope. The demands put
on the power that was to uphold the federal structure were further

[40] Elisabeth Wallace, "The West Indies: Improbable Federation?", *The Canadian Journal of Economics and Political Science,* vol. 27 (1961), p. 452.

increased by the introduction of a structure that did not fit the socio-political reality of the region.

AN UNEVEN INTERNALIZATION

While Britain planned to withhold full independence until the federation was to be firmly founded, it did gradually increase the self-government rights of the islands in the years that preceded the establishment of the federation. This "internalization" of the British power of control by the members of the region was effected in a way that worked against the federation policy Britain was pursuing at the same time. The rate at which self-government was granted varied from island to island with the larger islands obtaining greater autonomy at an earlier date. Universal adult suffrage was introduced into Jamaica in 1944, into Trinidad in 1946, into Barbados in 1949, and into the Leewards and Windwards in 1951. In 1953, a ministerial form of government was established in Jamaica. But not until 1956 were ministerial systems established in each of the Leewards and Windwards (with the exception of Dominica). Finally, full internal self-government was achieved by Jamaica in 1959, and by Trinidad in 1961, while full internal self-government has not yet been attained by the Leewards or the Windwards. The fact that the islands acquired self-government at an uneven pace was one factor that hindered the evolution of the union Britain favored, since the more autonomous units were reluctant to federate with the less autonomous ones (see above).

Further, as the first federal elections revealed, Britain also introduced into the federation a governmental structure that was not in line with the actual distribution of power among the islands. To document this point, a brief description of the islands is necessary. The federation was composed of two larger and eight small islands. The two larger islands are Jamaica and Trinidad. The eight small islands are Antigua, St. Kitts-Nevis-Anguilla,[40a] and Montserrat—usually grouped as the Leeward Islands; Dominica, St. Lucia, St. Vincent and Grenada—which constitute the Windward Islands; and Barba-

[40a] The three islands, St. Kitts, Nevis, and Anguilla, constitute a single unit—the Colony of St. Christopher, Nevis, and Anguilla.

dos. Of their total area, Jamaica, with an area of 4411 square miles, contains over half the population concentrated in one unit. Trinidad has more than a quarter of the population. This means that together these two islands account for almost 80 percent of the total population. In contrast, tiny Montserrat contains .03 percent of the federation's area and .41 percent of the population. (For a comparison of the areas and populations of the islands, see Table 5.) Politically the two larger islands were more autonomous than the other eight; economically they were more developed and their per capita income about twice as high as the average of the other islands. (See below for a discussion of these differences.)

The United Kingdom, feeling responsible for the fate of the small islands in a union with the larger ones and finding greater support for her policies among the small islands,[41] supported a federal constitution that favored the small islands considerably over the larger ones. As one might expect, this alienated Jamaica and Trinidad.

Table 5 AREA AND POPULATION OF THE ISLANDS OF THE FEDERATION OF THE WEST INDIES, 1960

Island	Area (sq. mi.)	Percent of total area	Population	Percent of total population
Jamaica	4,411	57.60	1,613,148	51.70
Trinidad-Tobago	1,980	25.80	825,957	26.50
Barbados	166	2.20	232,085	7.40
Grenada	133	1.70	88,677	2.80
St. Vincent	150.3	2.00	80,042	2.60
St. Lucia	238	3.10	94,718	3.00
Dominica	289.5	3.80	59,124	1.90
Antigua	108	1.40	54,354	1.70
St. Kitts-Nevis-Anguilla	155	2.00	56,644	1.80
Montserrat	32.5	0.03	12,157	0.40
TOTAL	7,663.3	99.63	3,116,906	99.80

Source: *Statesman's Year Book, 1962–1963*

[41] Edwin Chin Shong, "The Politics of Trinidad and Tobago," unpublished paper, n.p.

One source of discord was the allocation of seats in the federal legislature. In the discussions leading to the formation of the federation, the assumption was that representation would be proportional to population. This formula, however, was varied to avoid a situation in which the two larger islands might dominate the government.[42] The distribution of seats in the House of Representatives was such that Jamaica, which contained more than half the federation's population and contributed 43 percent of the funds of the federal government, was given 17 of the 45 seats, or less than 39 percent of the representation; and Trinidad, which contributed 39 percent of the federal revenue, was entitled to only 10 seats, or 22 percent of the representation. In the Senate each island was allotted two senators, with the exception of tiny Montserrat which had one. Under this arrangement, Jamaica and Trinidad each controlled only about 10 percent of the senatorial representation.[43] The two larger islands were, and felt themselves to be, highly underrepresented, though Jamaica was more distressed as it feared an "eastern" coalition of Trinidad and the Little Eight, all in the eastern region of the federation, against itself.

A second source of dissatisfaction to Jamaica and Trinidad was that under the terms of the federation's constitution, an individual could not hold office in the federal and island legislatures concurrently.[44] In practice, this meant that the most powerful men in the islands, who had some regional *charisma,* such as Normal Manley and Alexander Bustamente of Jamaica and Eric Williams of Trinidad, were excluded from federal office unless they were willing to resign their positions in the island governments, which were the very positions on which their power and prestige rested, and accept offices comparatively lacking in power in a weak federation. It had been widely expected that Manley would be the federation's first Prime Minister and Williams its second.[45] Such an arrangement, had it not in effect been precluded by the provisions of the Constitution,

[42] *West Indian Economist,* September 1958, p. 7.
[43] Ayearst, *The British West Indies,* pp. 237–240; Anglin, "The Political Development of the West Indies," pp. 51–52.
[44] Anglin, "Political Development," p. 51; Braithwaite, "Progress Toward Federation," p. 154.
[45] Private communication with Mr. Noel Brown of Jamaica.

would have granted alternately to Jamaica and Trinidad the leadership of the federation, thereby increasing their commitments to it. This might have contained the rivalry of the two larger islands for control of the federation.

The larger islands were further alienated from the federation by the success in the first federal election in 1958 of the Federal Labor party, which did not receive a majority of the votes in either Jamaica or Trinidad.[46] Not only were the opponents of the victorious party, who were largely concentrated in Jamaica and Trinidad, disappointed in the outcome of the election, but even the Federal labor party's supporters in the two larger islands were alienated when neither Manley nor Williams became Prime Minister. The Prime Minister chosen, Sir Grantley Adams, was from one of the small islands, Barbados.

It has been argued that under the conditions, Adams, who agreed to run only after Manley's and Williams' refusal, was the best possible compromise available, as neither of the two major islands would have been willingly led by a leader from the other. Moreover, if Manley, Bustamente, and Williams, the three charismatic leaders of the region, were not available, Adams was the next most influential figure. Also, the fact that he was vice president of the party of which Manley was the president would assure Manley the real power—control of the federation. In addition, it would keep the way to the premiership of the federation open for Manley, if he desired to step in after the federation began to succeed, and his vigorous opponent, Bustamente, who endangered Manley's position in Jamaica, was somehow neutralized. But it turned out in fact that the selection of Adams left both major islands uncommitted to the federal leadership; he had all too little *charisma;* he first resented and then rebelled against Manley's control, while Bustamente—far from fading out— won in his desire to take Jamaica out of the federation and put Manley out of office. To add to the sense of alienation of the larger islands, eight of the eleven ministerial posts in the federal government were given to representatives of the small islands. And these eight included all the key portfolios.

[46] Anglin, "Political Development," pp. 47–48.

In short, the structure of the federal government did not parallel the actual power relations of the emerging union. Jamaica and Trinidad, the largest and least economically dependent of the islands, which were expected to make the greatest contributions to and sacrifice for the federation, were placed in subordinate positions. Under these circumstances, that the federal government structure was not consonant with actual power relations, the initiation of a union required a comparatively high level of integrating power; this was not available.

INADEQUATE INTEGRATING POWER

Utilitarian Power: Little and Decreasing

The utilitarian ties of the ten islands were always small, providing for a few integrative rewards to participants or penalties to secessionists; with segregated administrative structures, weak economic-political ties, a meager federal budget, extremely small federal trade, and a sugar subsidy not tied to federation, the islands were much more ten utilitarian units than one. Differences in utilitarian assets among the islands, large to begin with, grew over the years. All these points deserve some elaboration.

The Federation of the West Indies as established following the agreements reached at the London conference of 1956, was highly limited in scope and level of integration. Each island retained its own separate political and administrative structure. The exclusive powers of the federal government were restricted primarily to the field of external relations and encompassed such areas as control of foreign currency exchange, defense, foreign relations, interisland and international communications. Such patently federal concerns as the University College of the West Indies, the West India Regiment, and the Federal Public Services were also included. In addition to these matters, included in a federal "exclusive list," some items, such as civil aviation, currency, and customs, were included in a "concurrent list." On these matters the federation and the territorial legislatures were to have jurisdiction concurrently, but in the case of conflict federal law was to prevail. "In practice, the territorial governments interpreted 'concurrent' as meaning 'with their concurrence,' and they were in a position to call the tune."[47] All powers not specified as exclusively federal or concurrent were reserved to the territories.[48] Explicitly exempted from federal control (at least for the first five years of the federation's existence) were such areas as income and profits taxes, interisland migration, and the formation of a customs union. There was no federal police and no federal currency. (In 1951, the eastern Caribbean territories, including British Guiana, unified their currencies, but Jamaica and British Honduras refused to join them.)[49] As Wallace pointed out, "the political framework of The West Indies resembled the American Articles of Confederation . . . far more closely than that of a genuinely federal state."[50] Norman Manley, Jamaica's Prime Minister and for years a firm supporter of the federation, called it "the most improbable federation ever conceived."[51] "The Constitution," exploded the Trinidad *Nation,* "is an abortion. Its budget is a mockery . . . God knows the Emperor Valley Zoo would be a more viable independent state."[52]

The meager administrative structure of the federation was foreshadowed in the administration of the islands during the prefederal period. On the surface, the political structures of the federated islands appear similar. In each there was a governor or administrator, an executive council, and a legislature. All the islands had been exposed to British rule for more than a century (though Trinidad was exposed for a shorter period than the others). But the British rule was not as homogeneous as it might seem at first glance, and the system of administration did not tend toward unification. Each island was administered as a separate unit directly tied to the Colonial Of-

[47] Charles H. Archibald, "The Failure of the West Indies Federation," *World Today,* vol. 18 (1962), pp. 233–242. Quoted from p. 238.
[48] *West Indian (Federation) Order-in-Council, 1957* (Third Schedule), Parts I and II.
[49] Anglin, "Political Development," p. 56.
[50] Wallace, "The West Indies," p. 444.
[51] "The West Indies, p. 444.
[52] *The Nation* (Trinidad), September 16, 1959. Quoted in David Lowenthal, "Levels of West Indian Government," *Social and Economic Studies,* vol. 11 (1962), p. 372.

fice in London, and British aid, up to the time of federation, was as a rule given to each island individually. It has been pointed out that the administrative structure of new states strongly reflects the structure existing in the colonial period. That is, territories jointly administered by colonial powers tend to form a single state, while those administered separately tend to maintain their district structures after independence. The West Indies conformed to this pattern.

The weakness of the utilitarian structure of the federation is also reflected in the paucity of its finances, which prevented the government from expanding its activities and helped perpetuate the low level of administrative ties. Under the constitution, a ceiling of BWI $9.12 million (U.S. $5.32 million) was placed upon federal income.[53] Anything in excess of this would have to be channeled to the member units. The inadequacy of this sum can be seen in the following comparison: in 1959, the federal government's ordinary expenses amounted to approximately U.S. $6 million of which 30 percent was disbursed for the maintenance of the University College of the West Indies; in the same year, Trinidad's governmental expenditures alone were U.S. $65 million. Moreover, the federal government was not granted the right to tax incomes and profits for the first five years of its life. It was largely dependent upon contributions from the islands. About BWI $3 million were gained from issuing currency while the total assessments of all the islands produced, during the life of the federation, a minuscule annual income of BWI $9 million.[54]

Even if the governmental administrative and political structures were divisively distributed among the islands, nevertheless a measure of unity could have been provided by voluntary associations, if those were regional rather than island-bound. In effect, there were few effective federation-wide economic and political associations. Labor unions in the West Indies are island-based. The only labor federation is the Caribbean Congress of Labor, which was both very loosely organized and not coextensive with the federated islands; labor unions on other islands, such as Bermuda, are also included. Fears of competition deterred union members from offering support to the federation and led them to agitate against the growth of re-

[53] BWI $1.00 = U.S. $.59.
[54] Anglin, "Political Development," p. 58.

gional ties. Labor leaders in Trinidad and Jamaica feared the influx of lower-paid workers from the smaller islands, an occurrence that the Little Eight expected under federation.[55] Thus, not only were there no effective interisland union ties before federation, but federation further contributed to the lack of labor solidarity.

The federation's political parties were weak confederations of strong island units. No federation-wide parties were formed until the islands were faced with the prospects of a federal election in 1958. The parties that were then organized were alliances of existing island parties.[56] The West Indian Federal Labor party (WIFLP), led by Norman Manley, was a confederation of the following island parties: Jamaica's Peoples' National party, the Barbados Labor party, the Antigua Labor party, the St. Kitts' Workers league, the Grenada Labor party, the St. Lucia Labor party, and the Montserrat Trades and Labor union. Trinidad's peoples' National Movement was even more loosely associated with the WIFLP.

The leaders of the federal parties, Norman Manley and Alexander Bustamente, were primarily oriented to island politics as is evident in their unwillingness to resign their island offices in order to seek federal office; they preferred to maintain their positions in Jamaica, as did Eric Williams in Trinidad. Further, as soon as the elections were over, the party alliances began to fall apart. Bustamente, head of the Democratic Labor party, quarreled openly with Albert Gomes, a leader of the Trinidad branch of the party.[57] Norman Manley, though head of the Federal Labor party, withdrew his support of Grantley Adams, the federation's Prime Minister and chief elected official of the Federal Labor party.[58]

The weakness of federal administrative and political structure, of interisland labor and political associations, and, in short, of all utilitarian structures, was fully paralleled by the limited interisland exchange system.[59] The island economies are based predominantly on

[55] Private communication from Mr. Noel Brown of Jamaica.
[56] Anglin, "Political Development," pp. 46–49.
[57] Anglin, "Political Development," p. 48.
[58] *Economist,* January 16, 1960.
[59] J. C. King, "Note on Interregional Trade," *Social and Economic Studies,* vol. 7 (1958), p. 136.

agriculture, and production, such as of sugar or spices, is mainly for export. The major markets for West Indian products are to be found in the United Kingdom, the United States, and Canada. In 1958, for example, the islands comprising the federation sent two thirds of their exports to the United Kingdom, the United States, and Canada; only 7 percent of the export trade was interisland.[60] In 1960, interisland trade—declining rather than increasing—constituted only 2 percent of the federation's total trade.[61] Moreover, at the insistence of Jamaica, which had a strongly protectionist trade policy, no customs union was formed. While the effects of such a customs union would have been limited, in view of the small volume of interisland trade,[62] still even this did not materialize.

The island's major crop is sugar, which is exported mainly to Britain. Expansion of sugar exports was not to be expected, since sugar can be grown almost everywhere in the world.[63] Further, West Indian sugar cannot compete on the world market and is heavily subsidized by London. Under the Commonwealth Sugar Agreement of 1951, Britain annually buys the largest part of the West Indies sugar crop at prices well above the world market. In 1962, Britain paid more than twice the world price. Most of the remainder of the sugar crop is purchased by Canada, which also pays an above-the-market price.[64] This serves to tie the West Indies closer, not to one another, but to Britain and Canada. In short, the weak utilitarian ties among the islands imposed but a thinly shared superstructure on deep differences in utilitarian structures and assets, differences that were large and grew larger till they became so great that the federation could no longer contain them.

[60] "Federation of the West Indies: Its Economic and Financial Significance," *Round Table,* vol. 50 (1960), p. 149.

[61] *New York Times,* March 5, 1961.

[62] For a discussion of the anticipated effects of customs unions, see A. D. Knox, "Trade and Customs Union in the West Indies," in G. E. Comper (ed.), *The Economy of the West Indies.* Kingston, Jamaica: Institute of Social and Economic Research, University College of the West Indies, 1960, pp. 255 ff.

[63] E. F. Nash, "The Problem of Overseas Markets," *Social and Economic Studies,* vol. 7 (1958), p. 130.

[64] *Trinidad and Tobago: The Making of a Nation.* British Information Services Pamphlet I.D. 1356, July 1962, p. 25.

Utilitarian Differences: Large and Increasing

In general, the islands are poor. The per capita income in 1957 averaged BWI $490 for the region. But differences among the islands were great. In the same year, per capita income was BWI $612 in Trinidad and BWI $510 in Jamaica, while the average of the remaining islands was only BWI $283. Together Jamaica and Trinidad account for 85 percent of the total national income of the British West Indies islands. (Table 7 summarizes the statistics on national income for 1957.)

At the same time, there were great and growing differences in the *composition* of the economy of the ten islands, the de-unifying effect of which will become evident below. While agriculture is significant in all the islands, it has never played an equally important role in their economies. In Jamaica and Trinidad, agriculture has been steadily declining in significance and is being replaced by mineral products—oil and bauxite, respectively. In 1957, for instance, income from agricultural products constituted less than 14 percent of the Gross Domestic Product of either Trinidad or Jamaica, while agricultural production accounted for 34.3 percent and 49.4 percent of the Gross Domestic Product of Barbados and Montserrat, respectively. (For comparable figures for the other islands, see Table 6.) Trinidad has large deposits of oil (it is the second largest producer of oil in the Commonwealth)[65] and Jamaica is the world's largest supplier of bauxite.[66] As a result, the economies of the small islands, dependent as they are upon agricultural exports, are much less stable than the economies of Trinidad and Jamaica. The small islands are especially vulnerable to fluctuating prices in the world market whereas the demand for bauxite and oil is more steady.[67] A partnership between the larger and the small islands was thus one of comparatively well-off islands with poverty-stricken ones, of islands with a steady income with those that had no assurance about their next year's income.

[65] *The West Indies and Caribbean Year Book, 1962,* p. 292.
[66] *The West Indies and Caribbean Year Book, 1962,* p. 185. See also H. W. Springer, "The West Indies Emergent: Problems and Prospects," in Lowenthal (ed.), *The West Indies Federation,* p. 8.
[67] Springer, "The West Indies Emergent," pp. 8–10.

Table 6 AGRICULTURAL INCOME AS PERCENT OF THE GROSS
DOMESTIC PRODUCT OF THE ISLANDS OF THE FEDERATION
OF THE WEST INDIES, 1957

Island	Percentage
Jamaica	13.8
Trinidad	13.7
Barbados	34.3
Grenada, St. Vincent, St. Lucia and Dominica–Windward Islands	42.6
Antigua	30.4
St. Kitts, Nevis, Anguilla	42.6
Montserrat	49.4

Source: *National Income Statistics: The West Indies.* Trinidad: Federal Statistical
Office, 1960, p. 16.

The islands also differed greatly in government revenues, import, and export. Jamaica's governmental revenue in 1954 was almost 170 times as large as that of tiny Montserrat and about 7 times
as large as that of Barbados.[68] Trinidad's exports were almost 17
times as large as Barbados' and over 1000 times as large as Montserrat's in 1960.[69] Only the larger islands and Barbados regularly
balanced their budgets; most of the Little Eight usually did not.
They habitually received grants and loans from Britain to cover the
deficits. In 1957, those amounted to about £2 million above and
beyond the 3 millions granted from the Colonial Development and
Welfare Fund. The poorer island feared the larger ones would not
want to be saddled with this burden; the bigger ones were not
claiming they would. Their orientation was expressed by a Jamaican journalist, not particularly favorable to the federation, who
noted that the small islands seek to be "supported in a style they
are not accustomed to."[70]

Not only were there important differences among the islands with

[68] *The West Indies and Caribbean Year Book, 1962, passim.*
[69] *The International Year Book and Statesman's Who's Who, 1962, passim.*
[70] Thomas Wright in the *Daily Gleaner,* June 8, 1961. Quoted in Wallace,
"The West Indies," p. 455.

Table 7 NATIONAL INCOME AND PER CAPITA INCOME FOR THE
ISLANDS OF THE FEDERATION OF THE WEST INDIES, 1957

| | National income for 1957 | | |
Territory	Total (in millions of BWI $)	Per-capita (in BWI $)	Percent of total West Indian income
Jamaica	821.8	510	54.5
Trinidad	471.5	612	31.3
Barbados	100.0	431	6.6
Grenada, St. Lucia, St. Vincent and Dominica (Windwards)	79.7	244	5.3
Antigua	15.9	284	1.1
St. Kitts, Nevis, Anguilla	15.0	261	1.0
Montserrat	2.8	195	0.3
FEDERATION TOTAL:	1,506.7	491	100.0

Source: *National Income Statistics, The West Indies,* p. 21 and David Lowenthal
(ed.), *the West Indies Federation: Perspectives on a New Nation.* American
Geographical Society Research Series no. 23. New York: Columbia University
Press, 1961, p. 99.

respect to economic assets, but these differences were increased considerably rather than decreased during the period immediately preceding and following federation. In 1950, for example, Jamaica's
"national" income was five times as large as that of Barbados and
nine times as large as that of the Windwards. By the end of 1957,
the difference grew still larger: Jamaica's "national" income was
over eight times as great as Barbados' and more than ten times as
great as the Windwards'.[71]

Similar increases in divergence can be seen in per capita income.
In 1951, Trinidad's per capita income was BWI $396, and Jamaica's
was BWI $257. By 1957, Trinidad's per capita income had increased
by BWI $216, or almost 55 percent, and Jamaica's per capita income
had grown to BWI $510, which represented an increase of almost

[71] *National Income Statistics, The West Indies.* Trinidad: Federal Statistical
Office, 1960.

100 percent. The per capita income of Barbados, the island closest in income and growth to the two larger ones, increased by slightly less than 25 percent to BWI $431.[72]

At the same time, the rate of growth in the other small islands, where there was any growth at all, was much lower than that of Jamaica and Trinidad. Such growth as did occur was the result of higher prices for primary products and increased financial assistance from Britain, and not due to genuine and lasting development. When grants-in-aid are excluded, Montserrat, Nevis, and Anguilla manifested no increase in their Gross Domestic Product in the federal period. St. Kitts' economy was stagnant. Dominica, Grenada, and St. Vincent showed small increases. Only Antigua's growth was on a par with that of Trinidad and Jamaica. But it must be noted that Antigua's economy before expansion was at a near-starvation level and its growth was based mainly on tourism.[73] Thus, in the federal period, the economic gap between the larger and small islands tended to widen.[74]

Besides the growing differences in assets and prospects, another major economic process pulled the larger and small islands apart. While in the past the islands were not trading much with each other, they were at least largely trading with the same outsider—Britain— and hence might have found joint interests in negotiation with her over terms of trade or organizing trade facilities. Whatever such interests existed diminished in the years immediately preceding and following federation, as the economies of Jamaica and Trinidad were oriented more toward the United States and less toward the United Kingdom. Agriculture remained predominant in Barbados, the Leewards, and the Windwards. But the two larger islands were engaged in administering extensive industrialization drives in the last decade, and the shift in their economies from agriculture to industry was sharp and reoriented their trade.

[72] *National Income Statistics, The West Indies*, p. 21.

[73] "Actually or potentially then, all these economies, with the possible exception of Antigua, are stagnating economies, i.e., economies in which real growth may be non-existent and in which income must decline relatively to the larger territories and to the world as a whole if general economic expansion continues." Carleen O'Loughlin, "Economic Problems of the Smaller West Indies Islands," *Social and Economic Studies*, vol. 11 (1962), p. 45.

[74] *National Income Statistics, The West Indies*, p. 8.

The industrial expansion of Jamaica was greatly accelerated from 1952 on by the commercial mining of bauxite. This involved a reorientation toward North America, as the initial development of the bauxite industry was the work of two American companies and one Canadian firm.[75] The influence of the bauxite industry on the Jamaican economy grew rapidly; by 1954, bauxite mining accounted for 4.0 percent of the Gross Domestic Product (at factor cost). By 1960, the contribution of the bauxite mining to the Jamaican economy more than doubled; it accounted for 9.3 percent of the Gross Domestic Product.[76] In 1950, Jamaica's exports consisted almost entirely of agricultural products.[77] By 1957, bauxite products constituted 44 percent of the total value of Jamaica's exports[78] and, by 1960, half of all Jamaica's exports were made up of bauxite and alumina.[79] The influence of this development was considerably larger than that of British economic aid.

The growing ties to the United States and the declining ones to Britain and the Commonwealth were reflected not only in the growing importance of American investments but also in Jamaica's patterns of trade. Between 1955 and 1957, its imports from the sterling countries decreased from 51 to 47 percent, while its imports from the dollar area in the same years increased from 36 to 54 percent.[80] In 1952, the United Kingdom took 68.5 percent of Jamaica's exports where the United States bought 14.8 percent of her exports. By 1959, Britain's share of Jamaica's exports had been just about halved, while that of the United States had nearly doubled. (Table 8 traces these changes in Jamaica's export markets.) Much of this shift reflects the growth of the importance of bauxite in the Jamaican economy. Almost all of the bauxite exported is sold to the United States.[81]

[75] *Jamaica: The Making of a Nation.* British Information Services Pamphlet I.D. 1403, April 1962, p. 20.
[76] *Economic Survey: Jamaica 1960.* Kingston, Jamaica: The Central Planning Unit, 1961, p. 6.
[77] *Jamaica: The Making of a Nation,* p. 16.
[78] *Jamaica: Report for the Year 1957.* London: Her Majesty's Stationery Office, 1960, p. 5.
[79] *Economic Survey: Jamaica 1960,* p. 26.
[80] *West Indian Economist,* July 1958, p. 16.
[81] *Economic Survey: Jamaica 1960,* p. 25.

Table 8 PERCENTAGE OF JAMAICAN EXPORTS PURCHASED BY THE
UNITED KINGDOM AND THE UNITED STATES ANNUALLY, 1952–1959

Country	1952	1953	1954	1955	1956	1957	1958	1959
United Kingdom	68.5	58.7	54.3	51.0	48.2	35.5	38.1	34.5
United States	14.8	17.6	17.5	20.1	26.2	20.6	30.1	25.4

Sources: *Colonial Reports: Jamaica 1954.* London: Her Majesty's Stationery
Office, 1956, p. 40; *Jamaica: Report for the Year 1957.* London: Her Majesty's
Stationery Office, 1960, p. 98; and *Handbook of Jamaica: 1960.* Kingston,
Jamaica: The Government Printing Office, 1960, p. 290.

The decline of Jamaica's reliance on Great Britain as a source of
investment and as a market represented a decrease in Britain's power
over Jamaica at the very time that Britain was encouraging the formation of the federation. Further, the expansion of Jamaica's economy notably increased its independence vis-à-vis Britain, and
because of the nature and direction of this freedom, it did nothing to
encourage closer ties to the other islands of the federation. In fact,
industrialization may have made Jamaica's ties to the other major
island, Trinidad, even more tenuous.

Since 1954, both Jamaica and Trinidad have established cement
industries in competition with one another.[82] And, in 1958, Jamaica
announced plans to found an oil refinery to be supplied by crude oil
from Venezuela.[83] This proposal was strongly protested by Trinidad's prime minister, Eric Williams, who saw in it a threat to his
island's major industry.[84] At the very least, the completion of such a
project would mean the elimination of gasoline imports from Trinidad, which in turn would further reduce the already extremely limited interisland ties.

Trinidad, like Jamaica, has become less dependent on British aid
and investment over the years, though its dependence was never so
great as Jamaica's. In general, Trinidad's postwar expansion was

[82] *Jamaica: The Making of a Nation,* p. 21, and *Trinidad and Tobago: The
Making of a Nation,* p. 31.
[83] *West Indian Economist,* August 1958, pp. 17–22.
[84] *West Indian Economist,* September 1958, pp. 10–11.

largely financed from local resources and loans,[85] while Jamaica's postwar growth was more dependent on Colonial Development and Welfare grants.[86]

The mainstay of Trinidad's economy is petroleum;[87] it both produces its own oil and imports crude oil mostly from Venezuela for refining. Crude oil accounts for nearly half of Trinidad's exports. Between 1954 and 1960 the value of Trinidad's petroleum output more than doubled, while the importance of agriculture sharply declined; and it is in this area that Trinidad's dependence on Great Britain was greatest. Trinidad's major crop is sugar and its major customer is Great Britain who, as we saw, pays preferential prices for West Indian sugar. In 1954, agriculture was still responsible for almost one fifth of the Gross Domestic Product (at factor cost); in 1960, this proportion had declined to 13 percent. In 1960, sugar accounted for only 8 percent of Trinidad's exports, while petroleum products constituted over 80 percent of the exports.[88]

Moreover, Trinidad has access to American financial assistance, which the other islands do not. The United States maintains a naval base at Chaguaramas, Trinidad. The Trinidad government actively sought to increase American payments for this privilege; their demands in 1962 amounted to U.S. $500 million.[89] While no one expected the United States to pay that much, the expectation of increased payments reduced Trinidad's commitment to the federation by raising its fears that as a member it would have to share some of these new funds with the other islands. (Following independence, the United States promised to build a road from Port of Spain to the United States base and pledged $30 million over a five-year period for development projects.) Foreign aid or investments, available to one unit of an evolving union but not to others, have in general a de-unifying effect.

The dependence of the West Indies on Great Britain was also

[85] *Trinidad and Tobago: The Making of a Nation,* p. 18.
[86] *Jamaica: The Making of a Nation,* p. 12.
[87] *Trinidad and Tobago: The Making of a Nation,* p. 22.
[88] "The Trinidad Scene: A Prosperous Approach to Independence," *Financial Times,* June 29, 1962.
[89] *New York Times,* September 9, 1962.

affected by the cutting of trade ties between Cuba and the United States. In 1960, the United States decided to stop importing sugar from Cuba and opened its market to West Indian sugar which it bought at prices even higher than those set by the Commonwealth Sugar Agreements.[90] The major beneficiaries of the American policy were Jamaica and Trinidad, who were allocated the largest quotas, though all the islands shared to some extent in the unexpected advantage.

The growth of tourism in the islands since World War II has similarly bound some of them closer to the United States, but not to each other, and it removed some of them from Britain's pressure to unify. In 1960, the value of the tourist industry to Jamaica was U.S. $38 million,[91] to Trinidad, U.S. $10.6 million,[92] and to Barbados, U.S. $5.16 million.[93] Of the small islands, Antigua was the only one to attract a large number of tourists.[94] Since the larger islands in general attract an increasingly disproportionate amount of tourist income, the development of tourism made the larger islands still less interested in federation and served to orient them outwards—to the sources of tourists, especially the United States. Again their dependence on Britain was reduced.

While Britain's utilitarian power was shrinking, it was far from losing all its impact. The United Kingdom made capital aid grants, and it was its policy to withhold such assistance from any island that seceded.[95] The effectiveness of such a deprivation or threat of deprivation varied according to the island. Though Jamaica received 26 percent of all British grants made in the years 1951–1960 to the units of the federation, such grants, in 1959, constituted only 4.5 percent of its government revenues. Trinidad, in the ten-year period, was allotted 7 percent of the grants, but these in 1959 accounted for only 0.4 percent of its governmental revenue. Tiny Montserrat in the corresponding time period was given only 5 percent of the British

[90] *Trinidad and Tobago: The Making of a Nation*, p. 32.
[91] *Jamaica: The Making of a Nation*, p. 22.
[92] *Trinidad and Tobago: The Making of a Nation*, p. 32.
[93] *Barbados: An Economic Survey.* London: Barclay's Bank DCO, 1962, p. 13.
[94] *The West Indies and Caribbean Year Book, 1962*, p. 379.
[95] *Time*, April 20, 1962.

grants, but in 1959 such grants constituted almost 71 percent of its total governmental budget.[96] Thus, the actual use of such utilitarian power by Britain—or the threat to employ it—would have had the greatest effect on the small islands, which were already more loyal to the federation, but little effect on the major ones, which broke up the federation.

In sum, the utilitarian power of the external elite declined with and during federation because the dependence of the islands, in particular the larger ones, continued to decrease, and the larger islands were drawn increasingly into the American economic orbit. Moreover, in addition to large differences in the per capita income of the ten islands, the successful development drives of the comparatively affluent ones further differentiated them from the eight stagnated poor ones. Thus, increasing economic differences further strained and reduced the very limited utilitarian basis of the federation.

Low and Declining Identitive Power

With declining utilitarian integrating power, the federation might have been preserved had there been a strong sense of identification with it. This, however, was lacking. Where, before federation, there had developed some sense of West Indian identity, its strength was not sufficient to establish its priority over island loyalties. Each island continued to be conscious of its uniqueness and individuality. As David Lowenthal points out, "for West Indians . . . the island is in most contexts the most compelling area symbol. A man who says 'I am a Jamaican,' or 'I am a Barbadian,' is very likely expressing the broadest allegiance he knows."[97] One West Indian, stated to an interviewer: "There is no oneness; there is a tradition of separateness."[98] It has been remarked sarcastically that the West Indian nation exists only when the West Indian team plays cricket against an

[96] Lowenthal, "The Social Background of West Indian Federation," in *The West Indies Federation,* p. 98.

[97] Lowenthal, "The Range and Variation of Caribbean Society," in *West Indies Federation: Social and Cultural Pluralism in the Caribbean,* p. 787. See also Vera Rubin, "Colonialism, Nationalism and Parochialism in the West Indies," paper presented at A.A.A.S. Symposium on the Development of New Nations, December 29, 1960.

[98] Kontak, "Some Important Caribbean Questions," p. 2.

outside team. Too much of the West Indian identification was with negative "countersymbols" especially complaints about the Colonial Office. Such symbols when not backed up by a wide front of positive ones provide an unsatisfactory, often transient, basis for a union. Developments under federation led to its further reduction. There was some attachment to the concept of West Indian nationality, especially among the educated middle classes. To some extent this derived from a kinship that educated West Indians felt for one another, generated by their common education in British or British-modeled schools. An educated Jamaican may feel more at home with an educated Barbadian than with an uneducated person from his home island. Education in Britain seems to be important here, for many West Indian leaders became aware, for the first time, of their common identity as a result of their experiences in England where to be a "West Indian" rather than a "St. Kittian" or even a "Barbadian" had more prestige. To be an islander, even a Jamaican or a Trinidadian, had the connotation of backwardness and provincialism; to be associated with the West Indian nation identified them with a larger unity and a movement that had appeal and status in Britain. Similarly, artists, writers, sculptors, many of whom have studied and lived in Britain, have engendered some sense of common background by their use of West Indian themes and traditions in their work.[99] The audience for West Indian literary and artistic productions is, however, limited primarily to the small group of educated persons.[100] These middle-class, educated groups, which included politicians, intellectuals, teachers, and administrators, provided the strongest supporters of federation.

Working-class people felt some sense of identity with one another which cut across islands, but this was limited by a number of factors. Prominent among these was the fear of Jamaicans and Trinidadians of competition from lower-paid labor from the small islands. Moreover, working-class identifications were more encompassing than those engendered by the ten federation islands that extended throughout the Caribbean. Hence, working-class ties could not serve as a basis for a particular, West Indian identity.

[99] Springer, "West Indies Emergent," p. 3.
[100] Remy Bastien, "The Intellectual and the Plural Society," in *Social and Cultural Pluralism in the Caribbean, p. 901.*

Another factor that limited the development of a West Indian nationalism was strong ethnic differentiations and identifications.[101] These were especially important in accounting for the separatist feelings and secession of Trinidad. Relations between the East Indians and Negroes in Trinidad are tense and the former greatly fear a federation dominated by the latter.

The East Indians, who form almost half of the population of British Guiana and are the second largest racial group in Trinidad view federation with suspicion. In Trinidad, particularly, they are becoming increasingly race conscious. They see the possibility of being swamped in a predominantly African domination.[102]

Actually, while the East Indians constitute only 35 percent of the population of Trinidad, they have a higher birth rate than the other groups and were expected to gain a majority in the island within ten years. There are almost no East Indians in the other federation islands. Federation, which was expected to bring about freedom of movement of the population, would not only have doomed them to the status of a permanent minority in a Negro federation, but would also have largely reduced the East Indians' chances for majority status in Trinidad.[103] From the start, East Indians opposed the federation and were influential in Trinidad's decision to withdraw.

Their representative, Ranjit Kumar, objected to "any immediate moves for federation";[104] East Indian delegates to Caribbean conferences tended to take an independence first, federation later position.[105] When the proposals of the 1953 London conference were submitted to the Trinidad legislature, the East Indian members were the major opposition; they cast four of the six negative votes and were responsible for all the abstentions.[106]

Language has both unifying and disunifying effects in the West

[101] Kontak, "Some Important Caribbean Questions."
[102] *The Times* (of London) April 13, 1950.
[103] Jesse Harris Proctor, Jr., "East Indians and the Federation of the British West Indies," *India Quarterly,* vol. 17 (1961), pp. 370–395.
[104] Trinidad and Tobago Legislative Council Debates, January 3, 1947, p. 41.
[105] Trinidad and Tobago Legislative Council Debates, January 3, 1947, p. 37.
[106] Ayearst, *The West Indies Federation,* p. 234.

Indies. English is the language of educated people throughout the islands and serves to tie them together. But each English-speaking island has its own Creole dialect which presents problems of communication to residents of other English-speaking islands. Moreover, French patois is predominant in Dominica and St. Lucia and is spoken to some extent on Grenada and Trinidad, but it is hardly understood on the other islands.[107]

The federation was initiated with rather limited identitive power in its support; the experience of federation, far from building up this power, actually further undermined it. The scope of the federation was so limited, the authority of the federal government so low, its budget so minuscule, its functions so restrictive, that for most people most of the time there was no experience of federation at all. Annual debates in the parliament on the work conducted by the federation in the previous year served only to emphasize the paucity of its accomplishments. In this way, the initial lack of power sufficient to form a solid basis for federal work created the impression of an ineffectual union, thus further undermining the federation. The fact that the most well-known charismatic figures in Jamaica did not share the federal leadership, for reasons that have been discussed, served to emphasize even more that island politics not the federation, were the real framework. "Unable to promise either bread or circuses, it has naturally had difficulty in attracting able public men, securing wide popular support, and creating a focus for new loyalties."[108] All this came into sharp relief when the continued participation of Jamaica in the federation was put before the voters in 1961. It highlighted both the fear of economic deprivations expected to result from continued membership and the lack of commitment to the West Indian nation.

The use of coercive power by the British or by the federal government to prevent or reverse the secession of Jamaica and Trinidad was never even contemplated. The federation had practically no coercive force of its own. The West India Regiment was largely a ceremonial unit that served to greet visiting dignitaries and parade

[107] Lowenthal, "The West Indies Chooses a Capital," *Geographical Review*, p. 340.
[108] Wallace, "The West Indies: Improbable Federation?" p. 448.

on festive occasions, not to counter secessions. There was no federal police and the federation had no control over the island police forces. Britain, for reasons that need not be discussed here, did not use the coercive power available to her as she did in 1963 in support of Malaysia.

In sum, there was little utilitarian and little identitive power to hold either Jamaica or Trinidad in the federation. Participation in the federation, as these islands saw it, could only lead to major losses, such as those involved in slowing down their development drives and sharing their assets with much poorer islands. There was little reason for them to seek to control the federation and change its allocative processes in their favor, since extremely few assets were allocated by these processes anyhow. To put it strongly, even if all the federal assets could have been channeled to the two larger islands, which surely neither Britain nor the small islands would have tolerated, there was little in these assets to tie the larger islands to the federation. There was, so to speak, no federal pattern they desired; they first curtailed the federal scope, but the more it was reduced, the more the remaining meager scope was felt unnecessary. They chose to secede. When secession came, the West Indies did not have the coercive power to prevent or delay secession till the other kinds of integrating power could be developed.

THE EFFECT OF A DISCONTIGUOUS ECOLOGY

If one were to explain the whole development of the Federation of the West Indies by ecological factors, it is surprising how far one might go. The main point is that the process of "breaking away" from the union began at its territorial "edges," not at the center. The first British Caribbean possession to refuse to join the federation was the Bahamas, located in the northwest corner of the proposed federation. Secondly, British Guiana indicated her disapproval of the idea of federation. In this she was followed by British Honduras and the British Virgin Islands on the northwestern edge. The next island to secede was Jamaica, which was the most westerly of the island territories, about 1000 miles away from the eastern islands. Trinidad, last to secede, is at the southeast "end" of the federation. Barbados is the most eastern island, but it is in the middle of the Windward group on the north-south axis and is considerably closer to the second of the smaller island groups, the Leewards, than to either Jamaica or Trinidad. It serves presently as the center of the remaining Little Eight.

The ecological secession pattern might be explained by the possibility that the territories at the fringes of the federation might have fewer opportunities than the islands in the middle for contact with other member-units in terms of commerce, tourism, and administration. While the preceding analysis has suggested that many factors, other than the ecological, account for the secession pattern there can be little doubt that the lack of contact and of communication facilities to span the sea stretches that separate the members of the federation from one another was a divisive factor.

The poor communication conditions prevailing among the islands until World War II seem to have limited interaction among them and contributed to the development of separate identities and economies. Jamaica, in particular, was separated from the others; the distance amounts to about a thousand miles. There was no regular communication link between Jamaica and any of the other islands till after World War II. It was considered a major achievement of a leader of the West Indian movement, Albert Marryshow from Grenada, to have included in his travels of the Caribbean between the wars that faraway place, Jamaica. The islands' contacts with London were much more frequent than their contacts with one another. Hence the bishops of the Province of the West Indies found it more convenient to meet their archbishop in London than on one of the islands in the region.[109] In the mid-twenties, mail from one island to another would often go through New York or London. Even now, communications and transportation difficulties and high rates set limits on interisland contacts of social, administrative, and economic natures. "Air fares are much too expensive to have encouraged meaningful ties among the islands. Even commercial sea shipment from Jamaica to Barbados costs almost as much as one from the West Indies to London . . .

[109] Springer, "West Indies Emergent Problems," p. 47, fn. 2.

Only two per cent of the islands' trade is within the Federation."[110]
It is still cheaper to fly from Jamaica to New York than to Trinidad,
still cheaper to go by boat from St. Lucia to London than to Kingston.[111] In short, the major de-unifying effect of the ecology is that,
by limiting communication, it seems to curb utilitarian and identitive
ties. To what degree this is due to the ecology and to what degree to
the state of underdevelopment, which prevents large investments in
communication facilities, is a question we return to below in a comparative context.

An Unresponsive Federal Government

Ultimately, the federation was dismantled by the two better-off,
more powerful islands. The prospects of having to share their assets
with the other eight islands led them to secede. It is important,
though, to realize that the economic differences do not in themselves
account for the secession. We do not suggest that richer units never
share their assets with poorer ones. In every welfare state the richer
classes pay more taxes than the poorer ones and gain a smaller proportion of the services the state renders; that is, the state utilitarian
system is used to reallocate the national wealth in favor of the poorer
classes. But this is the case largely after the lower classes have entered into and are accepted as members of the national society. When
this is not the case, as it is not in many underdeveloped countries,
such voluntary reallocation among classes within the nation-state
does not occur. The same holds for relations among territorial units.
When the citizens of such units identify intensely with one regional
union, territorial reallocation of wealth frequently occurs. The citizens of New York State, for example, pay more federal taxes and
receive fewer federal services than those of West Virginia. Such
identitive commitment to the federation did not, however, exist on
the part of Jamaica and Trinidad.

The attachment of the larger islands was further threatened by
the way in which Colonial Development and Welfare (CDW) funds,
contributed by Britain, were to be allocated under federation. Be-

---

[110] *New York Times,* March 5, 1961.
[111] Wallace, "The West Indies," p. 457.

tween 1959 and 1964, the federation was to be granted £9 million in CDW funds. Previously, each island received these funds directly from Britain. Now they were to be channeled to the federation and allocated by the federal government. The proposed allocation is presented in Table 9. By this means, under federation, the bulk of CDW grants were to be given to the small islands and to the federal government and not to the larger islands. Especially important is the fact that Jamaica and Trinidad would each receive much less than they were accustomed to under the system of direct aid from Britain. For the five-year period 1955–1960, Jamaica had been allotted £3 million; under federation, Jamaica's allotment was to be reduced to £400,000 for a comparable five-year period. Similarly, Trinidad during 1955–1960 was scheduled to receive £350,000; under the system of federal allocation, her five-year share was to be reduced to £100,000. This attempt at reallocation of the islands' income raised the objections of both Trinidad and Jamaica, whose commitment to the Federation of the West Indies was still quite weak.

Table 9 PROPOSED ALLOCATION OF COLONIAL DEVELOPMENT
AND WELFARE FUNDS BY THE FEDERATION OF THE WEST INDIES
FOR THE YEARS 1959–1964
(amounts in £)

3,240,000	Federal government
1,000,000	Dominica
900,000	St. Kitts
900,000	St. Lucia
680,000	Antigua
540,000	Grenada
540,000	St. Vincent
200,000	Montserrat
500,000	Barbados
250,000	Jamaica
150,000	Jamaica's dependencies
100,000	Trinidad

Source: *West Indian Economist,* January, 1960, pp. 10–11.

There is another way in which such reallocation might, in effect, come about. In many unions there are one or more elite-units who contribute more in utilitarian assets to the other units than they receive. In the case of such asymmetry, what occurs is an "exchange" of utilitarian assets for the symbolic gratification of leadership in the union. But Jamaica and Trinidad, as we have seen, were excluded from federal leadership: they were underrepresented in the House of Representatives; they held none of the major cabinet posts; and the federation premiership was held by a man from Barbados.

A good illustration of how—and by whom—both of the larger islands were kept from gaining at least the symbolic gratification of federal leadership is found in the selection of the federal capital. In 1949, the Standing Closer Association Committee recommended Trinidad as the site of the capital. However, at the 1953 London conference, Trinidad was rejected, largely at Jamaica's insistence, and Grenada was chosen. (Having two major contenders for the leader's title tended, in general, to deprive both.) But because of severe hurricane damage, Grenada proved unsuitable, and in 1956, an all-British Site Commission issued a set of recommendations for the location of the capital. The very small islands were ruled out because of difficulties of access and lack of facilities. The Site Commission suggested Barbados, Jamaica, and Trinidad in that order, indicating a strong preference for Barbados and denigrating Trinidad because of the "corruption" of its public life. Jamaica was considered undesirable because of its "aloofness," both spatial and psychological, from the eastern Caribbean. Further, the Site Commission feared that if either Jamaica or Trinidad became the capital, it would dominate the federation.[112] Both the larger islands, however, felt that the commission's evaluation offended their nationalist sentiments and revealed a strong British preference: it was suggested that Barbados was chosen because it was the most "British" of the islands, as it had an uninterrupted history as a British possession and was most amenable to British influence. West Indians described Barbados as "the funnel through which British flavoring

---

[112] Lowenthal, "The West Indies Chooses a Capital," pp. 346–347.

could be dripped into the federal cake." As a reaction, the islands chose Trinidad as their capital.[113] This, however, did not serve to strengthen Jamaica's commitment to the federation; she felt that this choice gave Trinidad an opportunity to control the government that Jamaica could not match.

If genuine sharing of the leadership of the federation between the two rival major islands was impossible, a clear leadership by one was probably the next best thing—in the sense of providing a leader who had the assets and the will to lead. But, aside from Jamaica's objections and rivalry, Trinidad was not awarded such a status, by either Britain or the Little Eight. The mere location of the capital at Port of Spain, Trinidad, in the face of the continued disproportional control of the federation by Britain and the small islands (especially Barbados), failed to rouse a sense of leadership in Trinidad. Also, though much closer to the small islands than Jamaica, Trinidad is even closer to the South American mainland.

The crisis that triggered Jamaica's secession was one in which the struggle over federal leadership was coupled with another attempt at interisland reallocation of wealth. In May 1959, federal Prime Minister Adams (a small islander) announced, to the consternation and dismay of the Jamaicans, that in 1963 federal income taxes would be levied retroactive to 1958. Jamaica was most opposed to such a move, since as the largest island with a per capita income about twice as high as that of the average island it would have been assessed the largest proportion of taxes. Her leaders protested that even under current arrangement Jamaica was not getting a fair return on her contributions and she would not consider an increase. The rallying cry of Jamaica's opposition to federation became "Jamaica must lead or leave." Even Manley of Jamaica, a supporter of federation and leader of the party in control of the federal government, began to waiver in his support; he threatened secession from the federation unless Jamaica's interests were given more consideration.[114]

The conflict over reallocation through taxes fed into an older one, of leadership and federal representation. In an effort to deal with Jamaica's dissatisfaction, a new Constitutional convention was con-

---

[113] Braithwaite, "Progress Toward Federation," pp. 161–162.
[114] *The West Indian Economist,* October 1959, p. 19.

vened at Jamaica in October, 1959. There, Jamaica demanded that representation in the House of Representatives be apportioned on the basis of population. His would have given Jamaica a majority of seats in the House, with Trinidad in second place, and would have made the government much more responsive to the interests of the larger islands. With control of the House, Jamaica could prevent the implementation of unacceptable measures, such as a customs union, freedom of movement, and high federal taxation. But here the rivalry between the two major islands reenters: Trinidad was opposed to granting Jamaica so much power; she demanded representation on the basis of per capita contributions, which in her case were twice as large as Jamaica's. The convention broke down without any agreement having been reached,[115] leaving the government in the hands of the small islanders and with the prospects of its being made more responsive to the larger islands in the future rather slim. Still trying to bring about a change in the structure of representation, the Prime Minister of Jamaica again threatened in January 1960 to take Jamaica out of the federation.[116]

Manley based his effort to keep Jamaica in the federation, which he personally favored, upon increasing Jamaica's ability to mold the federation so that its scope would remain limited mainly to the performance of certain external functions.[117] For this, Jamaica needed control of the House of Representatives. Unable to gain such control, Jamaica increased its pressure by threatening to secede; to make the threat more credible, Manley announced in June 1960 that Jamaica would hold a referendum on adherence to federation the following year.[118]

Meanwhile, a new constitutional convention was scheduled for June 1961 in London. In anticipation of this convention, a conference was held at Port of Spain, Trinidad, in May 1961. At this conference, Jamaica and Trinidad reached an agreement concerning the federation. Under the terms of the agreement, Jamaica's representation in the House of Representatives would be increased, though she

[115] *The Economist,* October 24, 1959, p. 323.
[116] *The Economist,* January 16, 1960, p. 194.
[117] *The Economist,* January 1960, p. 194.
[118] *The Economist,* June 11, 1960, p. 1081.

did not achieve the majority she sought. The establishment of a customs union and implementation of the principle of free movement were to be delayed for nine years, with the expectation that they might be postponed indefinitely in following review-conferences. Finally, the islands were to be given veto rights over any proposal for direct federal taxation. Thus, Jamaica could hope to block any attempt at reallocation which it did not approve. Accordingly, the revision of the federal constitution proposed at the 1961 London conference was to further reduce its limited scope. The federal responsibility, at least initially, was to be restricted largely to the maintenance of two battalions of troops, a post office, and the university. Its annual revenue was to be limited to £6.5 million,[119] which is a small amount even by West Indian standards.

Thus, even before secession, Jamaica and Trinidad had succeeded in reducing the federation to a bare minimum. However, support for even such a truncated federation was lacking. The question of support soon came to a test, as a referendum, earlier used as an instrument of interisland politics by Manley, now had to be faced on his island, Jamaica. In a hard-fought campaign, Manley supported the federation, promising Jamaican leadership and pointing to concessions made to it at the Trinidad conference. Sir Alexander Bustamente, his cousin and bitter opponent, aroused the fears of the masses, who were uncommitted to the idea of federation, by stressing losses the federation would inflict on the island. In September 1961, the people of Jamaica voted to secede.[120] Three months later, Trinidad (and neighboring Tobago) dropped out of the federation. Finally, on May 31, 1962, the date set for independence, Britain formally dissolved the Federation of the West Indies.[121]

How unresponsive the governmental structure of the West Indian federation was to the interests of the two large islands and how little room was left for their leadership aspirations to be gratified is evi-

[119] *The Economist,* June 3, 1961, pp. 978–979.
[120] Out of an electorate of 775,000, 61.1 percent voted: 256,261 (54.1 percent) for secession; 217,319 (45.9 percent) against it.
[121] The setting of the date was reported in the *New York Times,* February 7, 1962. The event itself was not so recognized.

dent in the above account. The British attempts to protect the interests of the small islands and the rivalry between the two major ones
had effectively deprived both Jamaica and Trinidad of the symbolic
gratifications of leadership. Had Jamaica and Trinidad been persuaded to remain within the federation, it might have proved viable;
but the large islands would have been faced with the continuing prospect of a struggle, both with the small islands and with each other,
over control of the federation. The only federation they seemed to
be able to tolerate was one so limited in scope and power as to be
ineffectual. The danger that it might not remain so sufficed—when
exploited in intraisland politics—to terminate even this thin bond.
Jamaica opted-out first; this left Trinidad with the alternatives of
remaining in the federation and bearing alone the union's major economic burdens or withdrawing.[122] Trinidad, influenced by the strong
East Indian minority, also decided on the latter course of action. It
invited the eight islands to join with it in a unitary state, but they
preferred poverty to loss of identity in a state that would have been
dominated by Trinidadians. Hence, as Eric Williams himself put it,
"one from ten leaves nought."

Subunits and the Federation

The federation was to affect not only the relations among the
islands but also among various subdivisions of their populations and
in a way that proved to be one more factor contributing to its failure.
The islands, with all due respect to the differences among them, have
in general the typical social structure of underdeveloped countries.
There is a small layer of relatively affluent educated citizens and a
comparatively large segment of the population that is illiterate and
poor, especially the peasants and the workers. The initiation of urban
development, especially in the larger islands, typically created in the
cities a proletariat of unemployed masses and slum dwellers, who
are released from the traditional bonds of the countryside but are not

[122] On Trinidad's fear of economic burdens in "carrying" the small islands,
see "Nine Islands Seek a Happy Union," *The Times* (of London), January 18,
1962.

yet absorbed into the modernized part of the society. These "masses," even more than the villagers and regularly employed workers, are given to charismatic movements and demagogic appeals. Ideologically the lower classes, in general, and the proletariat, in particular, are open to radical leftist appeals.

One effect of the federation was to strengthen the hand of the more conservative, educated, well-off, middle-class groups on the islands. As long as Britain ruled the islands, these groups could expect that by maintaining law and order Britain would in effect guard them against violence and anarchy as well as the more radical forms of mass-based social change movements. The middle-class groups, in particular on the larger islands, feared for their fate after independence; by uniting with their equal numbers on other islands and by controlling the federal authorities, they hoped to safeguard their position on their particular islands. This is not to suggest that only affluent, conservative, or right-wing groups favored federation. Many of the moderate left groups, the Labor parties and unions on most of the islands, favored federation, in part for the same reasons as the conservatives: they feared anarchy and the extreme left and saw in federation a hedge against both. Moreover, with the prime ministers of the larger islands and of the federation belonging to the Labor ranks, as in many other underdeveloped countries, labor—especially in its interest in law and order—was very much part of the island "establishments." Moreover, as in Britain, intellectuals played a significant role in the West Indian labor movement, and these, with few exceptions, favored West Indian nationhood.

This kind of attempt to use the Federation of the West Indies to strengthen the groups in power against those favoring radical social change (or groups at least potentially recruitable by those who favor it), required either the use of force to suppress antifederalist groups or a "selling" of the federation idea to the "masses" on the basis of national values and symbols. Suppression of opposition was ruled out by the democratic institutions the islands proudly inherited from Britain; elections were free and the opposition could organize itself and advance its cause, even by making demagogic appeals to the masses (such as those provided by Bustamente, though neither he nor his party represented the radical left). Hence, the success of the federation depended to a great extent on the success of national education to make the use of demagoguery against it ineffective.

Such an education did not take place, in part because the roots were lacking; much of the "West Indian" appeal was associated with the values and tastes the educated elite acquired under British influence, experiences the "masses" did not share. Hence an appeal to their "West Indian" sentiments was largely an appeal to values to which they were not committed. (Not that all the members of the elite favored the federation even at its inception. Of 232 Jamaican elite members studied in 1958, 51 percent said Jamaica had more to lose than to gain from being part of the federation;[123] 41 percent took the opposite view.) Second, the federal government, which was poor in budget, initiative, and charismatic leadership, did not engage in a wide education drive to gain support.

One observer summarized the situation as follows:

What, in fact, has happened is that natural parochialism has been reinforced by (1) the failure of both West Indian political groups deliberately to educate their island electorate on the meaning of Federation, and (2) the tendency ever since Montego Bay to encourage a narrow official view about public relations.

There has been no planned education of the masses . . . Public apathy will not be overcome until that neglect is rectified and until, in turn, the West Indian worker and peasant is persuaded that the federal venture . . . is not merely a venture that will more immediately benefit the middle class elements of the federal membership.[124]

Thus, lacking any firmer emotional basis, the federation depended for its mass support on the mass appeal of a small number of charismatic leaders. In Trinidad, where Eric Williams favored the federation, the population continued to support it without serious challenge (other than from the East Indian quarter), until Williams—after Jamaica seceded—decided that Trinidad ought to withdraw, too. But even Williams was not acting in a vacuum, as is illustrated by the

[123] Bell, "Attitudes of Jamaican Elites," p. 864.
[124] Gordon Lewis, Professor of Political Science, University of Puerto Rico, *The Sunday Guardian* (Port of Spain) supplement in honor of the West Indies federation, April 20, 1958, p. 30.

following example: although he favored a strong rather than a weak federal authority, he insisted in the 1961 London conference that freedom of movement be kept out of the federal constitution.[125] This was in part because he feared massive immigration from the smaller islands to Trinidad and in part in response to East Indian fears that immigration would increase the Negro control of the island. After all, Williams, though fresh from a victorious election, had to maintain his popular support. What might have happened to him had he continued to support the federation unequivocally was shown by what happened to Manley in Jamaica.

Manley, the charismatic leader of the region, favored the federation. He ran his 1959 election campaign on this theme and won handsomely. But Manley's deep association with the floundering federation led his opponent, the third charismatic leader of the area, Sir Alexander Bustamente, to build his future opposition on the antifederation theme. Sir Alexander, in a highly demagogic campaign leading to the 1962 elections,[126] called anyone who supported the federation a "traitor."[127] He was fanning the fear of economic deprivation among the masses of Jamaica, when a change in British policy played into his hand. Jamaica already had a large number of unemployed, about 100,000 men,[128] and the fear—though probably unjustified—of immigration of unemployed workers from the smaller islands to Jamaica was rampant. Jamaica is overpopulated and reduces its labor force problems by emigration to Britain. But as restriction of West Indian immigration to Britain was then being discussed, Sir Alexander could raise the specter that emigration from the island would be sharply curtailed as the influx of immigrants to it mounted. The problem was compounded by already increasing unemployment. (In 1960, the population increased by about 40,000 and the labor force by 24,000; jobs in industry—the main growing sector as sugar workers were replaced by mechanization—increased only by 2700.)[129]

Manley declared a referendum for 1961 apparently for bargaining

[125] *Public Opinion,* June 17, 1961.
[126] Archibald, "Failure of the West Indies Federation," p. 235.
[127] *Daily Gleaner,* January 23, 1961.
[128] *Daily Gleaner,* July 2, 1962.
[129] *The Gleaner,* June 6, 1961.

purposes with the other islands. He announced that the referendum would take place only after all the sessions of the constitutional review conference had been concluded, "so that the people will know what federation they are voting about." His tactics initially paid off, as the Little Eight supported his position in London,[130] turning down all 24 items of constitutional revision favored by Trinidad; the British government also delayed further discussion of restriction on immigration from Jamaica till after the referendum. Still, as Bustamente's campaign mounted, Manley had to campaign on his success in reducing the scope and level of integration of the federation—already dangerously thin—in the hope of winning the referendum.

With Jamaica and Trinidad leaving the federation, the remaining islands were being guided by Britain toward an east Caribbean federation under the leadership of Barbados. Barbados is the largest of the small islands, containing 235,000 of the remaining 725,000 population of the islands. Barbados is more centrally located relative to the small islands than either Jamaica or Trinidad. Further, Barbados is a major port for interisland trade and therefore would welcome increased ties among the islands.[131] Finally, a Barbadian, Sir Grantley Adams, was prime minister of the Federation of the West Indies, and Barbados is viewed as an uncontested leader by the other small islands.

Thus, the much smaller Barbados seems a more "natural" leader of a West Indian unification, since she has positive utilitarian interests in the remaining union, no ethnic barriers, and since there is no competition over leadership. Such a union has the full support of Britain. One of the links joining the eight islands is the hope for renewed ties with the larger islands, and possibly even with mainland British Guiana,[132] if not in federation, perhaps in some looser form of association.[133] The federation that failed never had much of a so-

[130] "Failure of a Federation," *Round Table,* vol. 52 (1962), p. 277.
[131] Lowenthal, "The Social Background of West Indies Federation," p. 69.
[132] Trinidad in 1963 favored the inclusion of British, Dutch, and French West Indies in one trade association. *New York Times,* July 23, 1963.
[133] Barbados, however, is ambivalent about such an association as it fears the industrial competition of Trinidad. *New York Times,* July 26, 1963.

ciopolitical basis; it was an administrative structure without a union to support it. Efforts to increase unification not only failed, but because of developments in the major islands, the federation experience resulted in some reduction of whatever ties existed among the islands before it was attempted.

CHAPTER 6

A Stable Union: The Nordic Associational Web (1953–1964)[1]

———————◆·◆··◆———————

In the 75 years preceding the foundation of the Nordic Council in 1953, relations among the member countries of the Nordic union[2]—Denmark, Finland, Iceland, Norway, and Sweden—were marked by frequent consultations and by numerous attempts to coordinate policies and programs in such fields as social welfare, health services, education, legislation, finance, trade, and transportation and communication.[3] In some instances, contacts among the governments involved the mere exchange of views; in others, parallel programs were established as, for example, when similar laws were passed;[4] and in still other cases, joint ventures were undertaken, such as a currency union among Norway, Sweden, and Denmark, which existed from 1875 until the outbreak of World War I.[5] Supplementing the formal governmental contacts were informal ones, including a network of

[1] We focus here on the period since the formation of the Nordic Council in 1953. In line with our emphasis on contemporary unions, earlier developments of the Nordic union are examined only insofar as they affect the union in the period under consideration.

[2] "Nordic" refers to the five member countries of the Nordic Council; "Scandinavian" to the four member countries other than Finland. See Paul Dolan, "The Nordic Council," *Western Political Quarterly,* vol. 12 (1959), p. 511, fn. 1.

[3] For a review of these efforts, see Frantz Wendt, *The Nordic Council and Cooperation in Scandinavia.* Copenhagen: Munksgaard, 1959, chaps. 1–8, pp. 9–100.

[4] Ivar Strahl, "Scandinavian Cooperation in the Field of Legislation," in *Scandinavia Past and Present,* vol. 3, *Five Modern Democracies.* Copenhagen: Arnkrone, 1959, p. 115.

[5] Wendt, *The Nordic Council,* p. 30.

communication among business circles, private citizens, and interest groups in the various Nordic countries.

The Nordic Council was founded to extend the area of consultation and cooperation among the governments and to coordinate many of the already existing cooperative programs, whether governmental or nongovernmental. In the decade that has followed the foundation of the council, the Nordic union has been able to maintain and to increase somewhat its level of integration and its scope. Basically, however, it is a stable rather than a steadily growing union. Its integrating power is not high, and unification has not penetrated into high spill-over sectors.

DISTRIBUTION OF POWER

Egalitarianism and Indecisiveness

Relations among the members of the Nordic union are characterized by a high degree of egalitarianism; no single country or coalition of countries is clearly dominant in the area. This has not always been the case. Historically, Denmark and Sweden have been dominant, with Norway, Iceland, and Finland in varying positions of subordination. There have been many changes in the power constellations of the region that need not be reviewed here. What is relevant to our discussion is the fact that since the end of the Napoleonic wars Sweden has been the most powerful Nordic nation. In 1814, Denmark's position was weakened by the cession of Norway to Sweden. The Swedish rule of Norway was very limited, as Norway retained almost complete autonomy in internal affairs. Still, the Swedish rule generated much hostility among the Norwegians. A struggle for independence followed and, in 1905, Norway achieved sovereignty over all her affairs.[6] Norway's independence removed a major barrier to increased cooperation between the two countries by eliminating an important source of conflict and alienation.[7]

[6] For a discussion of this period see Raymond Lindgren, *Norway-Sweden.* Princeton, N.J.: Princeton University Press, 1959.
[7] *Norway-Sweden,* p. 234.

A similar change took place in the relations between Denmark and Iceland. Though Iceland achieved independence in December 1918, she remained associated with Denmark by accepting the latter's king and being represented by the Danish foreign service until 1944. Removal of the last vestiges of an earlier subordinate status reduced animosities between the two countries and opened the way to Iceland's fuller participation in Nordic cooperation.[8]

Finland gained her independence from Russia in 1917, but a measure of intra-Nordic antagonism evolved in the conflict between Finland and Sweden over the Swedish-speaking but Finnish-controlled Åland Islands. The status of these islands was settled in 1922 by a decision of the World Court which recommended that they remain under Finland's protection but be granted extensive self-government rights.[9] Thus, another source of tension was removed from the area. The period following the settlement of the Åland Islands dispute was characterized by Finland's increasing participation in Nordic affairs.[10]

The emergence of the subordinated Nordic countries as independent units helped create conditions under which their voluntary participation in a Nordic union could be forwarded. First of all, active opposition to the previously enforced attempts at increased integration was dissipated. Further, the removal of a source of conflict that served to divide the countries—Finland and Norway from Sweden and Iceland from Denmark—reduced the sense of alienation that the subordinated countries felt toward their superior neighbors and paved the way for the development of positive sentiments. In other words, an increase in egalitarianism was conducive to greater commitment to the union.[11]

[8] Donald E. Nuechterlein, *Iceland—Reluctant Ally.* Ithaca, N.Y.: Cornell University Press, 1961, pp. 3–5.
[9] Eino Jutikkala, "Between the World Wars," in Urho Toivola (ed.), *Introduction to Finland—1960.* P92000: Werner Söderström Osakeyhtiö, 1960, p. 47.
[10] Raymond E. Lindgren, "International Cooperation in Scandinavia," *The Year Book of World Affairs,* vol. 13 (1959), p. 96.
[11] The efforts of the subordinate countries to establish their uniqueness vis-à-vis the dominant ones by an appeal to history had the unanticipated consequence of furthering Nordic solidarity by focusing attention on experiences in the past that were shared by the Nordic countries. Thus, the 19th-century romantic movement, which began as an affirmation of differences among the Nordic countries, ended by stressing their commonality.

Nonetheless, there remained important differences among the Nordic countries. In terms of population, national assets, per capita income and military capability, Sweden is clearly the most powerful Nordic nation. In 1961, Sweden's population was almost as large as that of Norway and Denmark combined. In 1960, the market value of her Gross National Product was nearly twice that of the second richest Nordic country, Denmark, and about 50 times that of Iceland. Sweden's per capita income in the same year exceeded Norway's by 25 percent and Finland's by over 50 percent. (For comparative statistics relating to population and income for all five countries, see Table 10.) Of the Nordic countries, Sweden alone is believed capable of producing nuclear weapons.[12] But these advantages have had little effect on those matters that are jointly carried out in the union. While Sweden has initiated more programs that would increase unification than any other Nordic country, these programs were often not implemented.[12a] Sweden's greater assets provided her with one of the requirements for leadership in the union, but it appears that she lacked the will or skill to push through her programs in the face of opposition or lack of interest on the part of the other Nordic countries. In the late 1930s,

Table 10 POPULATION (1961) AND GNP AND PER CAPITA GNP AT MARKET PRICE OF THE NORDIC COUNTRIES (1960)

Country	Population (1961)[a]	GNP at market cost (1960)—in million U.S. $[b]	Per capita GNP at market cost (1960)—in U.S. $[b]
Denmark	4,565,500	$ 5,964.0	$1,302
Finland	4,446,222	4,829.0	1,085
Iceland	177,292	234.6	1,371
Norway	3,956,211	4,481.0	1,251
Sweden	7,495,129	12,179.0	1,628

Source: a—*Europe Year Book, 1962,* vol. 1, *passim.*
          b—*Yearbook of Nordic Statistics,* 1962, Table 63, p. 42, and Table 65, p. 43.

[12] Herbert Tingsten, "Issues in Swedish Foreign Policy," *Foreign Affairs,* vol. 37 (1959), p. 481.
[12a] The Danes have probably written more unification programs, but political initiative seems to have been more often Swedish.

Sweden proposed the creation of a Nordic federation to be based upon a dynastic union.[13] This was not accepted by the countries toward which it was directed.[14]

Again, in 1949, after the Communist *coup d'état* in Czechoslovakia, Sweden proposed a Nordic defense alliance based upon the principle of nonalignment with either East or West.[15] Nonalignment, of course, was consonant with Sweden's traditional policy of neutrality in foreign affairs. But beyond this, Sweden insisted upon nonalignment because it wished to ensure Finland's adherence to the alliance, and this it knew to be possible only if the alliance were neutral.[16] But once more Sweden's proposal was not accepted. Norway and Denmark, for reasons explored below, abandoned negotiations for a Nordic alliance and joined NATO instead. In the 1950s, Sweden was the most consistent supporter of a proposed Nordic common market.[17] But despite its backing the scheme foundered. Thus the "inequality" in Nordic initiative did not matter much, as initiative did not generate fellowship or mature into leadership.

Denmark has been second to Sweden in efforts to promote Nordic cooperation. It was under Danish initiative that the Scandinavian Interparliamentary Union was founded in 1907[18] to provide opportunities for contact and unofficial consultation among delegates from the various Nordic parliaments. It was at the 28th meeting of this organization in Stockholm in 1951 that the Danish prime minister, Hans Hedtoft, suggested that consultations among the parliamentarians be established on a regular basis.[19] This suggestion led to the formation two years later of the Nordic Council itself, whose struc-

[13] To symbolize the Nordic union, a picture is often used of the first meeting of the kings of Denmark, Norway, and Sweden held at Malmö, Sweden, in December 1914, at the instigation of the Swedish monarch, Gustav V.

[14] Dolan, "The Nordic Council," pp. 512–513.

[15] Helge Jung, "Sweden's Armed Forces Through the Ages," in *Scandinavia Past and Present*, p. 136.

[16] "Sweden's Armed Forces," p. 137.

[17] Dolan, "The Nordic Council," p. 525.

[18] Stanley V. Anderson, *The Nordic Council*. Unpublished Ph.D. dissertation. Berkeley, Calif.: University of California, 1962, p. 21.

[19] Nils Herlitz, "The Nordic Council," in *Scandinavia Past and Present*, p. 43.

ture and competence very closely resembled those of a Nordic consultative body proposed by the Danish government in October of 1938; at that time, however, sufficient support could not be generated among the other Nordic countries.[20]

Further, the organization and deliberations of the Nordic Council itself reflect Sweden and Denmark's greater initiative in trying to forward the union. The tasks which would have been allocated to an inter-Nordic bureaucracy, had it existed, are divided between Sweden and Denmark.[21] Sweden's secretariat handles all the legal questions arising under the council, while the Danish secretariat is responsible for the council's public relations. The Swedish and Danish secretariats supervise all interim committee staff personnel, and the council's only permanent committee secretaries are located in Stockholm and Copenhagen. Between the two, Sweden has a slight edge over Denmark as reflected in the fact that Sweden's secretary-general has been chosen to represent the council at several international conferences. Moreover, the council's editorial and publishing activities are located in Stockholm where the council's annual reports are prepared and where the editorial offices of the official journal, *Nordik Kontakt,* are located. Further, in the case of matters submitted for council consideration, the Swedish government and Swedish representatives (as individuals) were more active than the government and delegates of any of the other countries, and more proposals were submitted in Swedish than in any other language. (In part, this latter factor reflects the use of Swedish in council deliberations by Finland's representatives.) Proposals by Danish delegates ranked second. Together, Sweden and Denmark have dominated council activities. The vast majority of joint proposals by delegates from different countries were submitted by Swedish and Danish parliamentarians. In the first eight sessions of the Nordic Council, 109 proposals were sponsored by delegates from two or more countries; 79 of these instances involved delegates from Sweden and Denmark.[22]

Although Sweden and Denmark have been comparatively more

[20] Wendt, *The Nordic Council,* pp. 102–103.
[21] Anderson, *The Nordic Council,* p. 104.
[22] Anderson, *The Nordic Council,* pp. 96–97, 102–105, and 181–187.

active in council affairs than the other member countries, the structure and methods of procedure of the council nevertheless ensure a high degree of equality in the relations of the members vis-à-vis one another.[23] Representation in the Nordic Council is of two kinds: ministerial and parliamentary. Each country may send as many of its cabinet ministers as it chooses to council sessions. But while ministerial representatives may submit proposals to the council for consideration, they cannot vote on proposals or serve on any of the council committees. Thus differences in the number of ministerial delegates sent to council sessions can at most have an indirect effect on the essentially egalitarian relations of the member units.

Parliamentary representatives form the core of the Nordic Council. Despite wide divergence in population, each of the four major members, Denmark, Finland, Norway, and Sweden, is entitled to the same number of parliamentary representatives—16. Only tiny Iceland has fewer representatives—5. Meetings of the Nordic Council are held each year in a different member country on a rotating basis. The council has no permanent secretariat of its own. Each national delegation has its secretariat, and the secretariat of the host country acts as general secretariat for the session.

The chief of the host delegation acts as president of the council and the leaders of the other four delegations are designated vice presidents. Together these five officers constitute the presidium, whose function it is to oversee the council's work until the next session. To this end, the presidium ordinarily meets four or five times a year to consider how the various governments have acted with respect to council recommendations, to plan the next session of the council, etc. The president of the presidium is again the leader of the host delegation. The designation of a special position as president of the council and of the presidium does not confer on the leader of the host delegation or his country any additional power; his status is that of *primes inter pares.*

[23] The following description of the structure of the Nordic Council is based upon Nordisk Rad, *Statute of the Nordic Council Recommended to the Governments by the Council at the 5th Session at Helsinki in February 1957;* Nordisk Rad, *Rules of Procedure for the Nordic Council* (adopted February 22, 1957); Anderson, *The Nordic Council;* Dolan, "The Nordic Council," pp. 514–517; and Wendt, *The Nordic Council,* pp. 108–115.

Each country and each delegate is free to submit matters for consideration by the council. Delegates may, however, vote only on matters directly involving their countries. Thus, in the matter of a proposed bridge linking Denmark and Sweden, only the parliamentary representatives from these two countries were entitled to vote.[24] Further, once a council recommendation is made, since it is only advisory, each government is free to accept or reject it. These procedures were introduced to insure that no country's sovereign rights would be infringed upon with council sanction by any other country or by any coalition of countries. Thus if any one country or group of countries should come to dominate the council—which is most unlikely—it would hardly matter in terms of control of the region.

The method of voting in council proceedings similarly serves to protect the egalitarian relations of the member countries. Formally, decisions of the council and its committees are carried by majority vote, and delegates vote as individuals and not by country. In practice, however, decisions require unanimity or near unanimity, and solidarity among the members of each delegation is high, so that individual votes ordinarily reflect national policy.

Of 172 recommendations sent in the first eight years of its existence by the Nordic Council to the governments of its member countries, all but 24 were passed by the council without opposition. In only nine instances were negative votes cast; in the other 15 cases, opposition was limited to abstentions by delegates. No negative votes were cast at all during the 1953, 1955, and 1957 sessions, and in 1955 only two abstentions were recorded. (Where significant numbers of delegates did abstain, the dispute almost always revolved about matters of the council's competence or procedure rather than about substantive issues.[25])

The emphasis on unanimity and solidarity has important consequences for the scope and decisiveness of the Nordic union. It means that the Nordic Council functions primarily as a vehicle for the manifestation of an already existing consensus. The council provides little opportunity for the expression of dissent or for the resolution of differences. Generally, only those matters on which the representa-

---

[24] Anderson, *The Nordic Council,* p. 289.
[25] Anderson, *The Nordic Council,* pp. 293–295.

tives of *all* nations are agreed ever reach the council floor. Such unanimity is often achieved in committee by the watering down of proposals to the lowest common denominator. Where unanimity on the substance of a proposal cannot be reached, the delegates may decide (unanimously to be sure) that the council should take no action on the issue. This was the procedure followed when unanimity could not be achieved in committee on a Norwegian proposal for a uniform law for the protection of animals.[26] In other instances in which division among the members appeared, a decision was avoided by referring the matter to a subcommittee for further study. Action on an issue was thus postponed for weeks, months, or even years. And in the end the matter might still not be resolved. The negotiations toward a Nordic common market, of importance in themselves, provide a fine illustration of this pattern.[27]

The first steps toward a Nordic common market were taken in 1948 when the governments of Denmark, Norway, Iceland, and Sweden set up a Joint Scandinavian Committee for Economic Cooperation to examine the feasibility of a customs union. The committee issued its report in 1950. The report, though acknowledging the value of a customs union, did not recommend its establishment because of Norwegian opposition. The committee, however, did agree to continue its investigations into the possibility of abolishing existing tariffs on specific categories of goods.[28] The committee was still engaged in this talk when the Nordic Council held its first session in Copenhagen in February 1953. The Nordic Council then took over sponsorship of the committee, which was rechristened the Nordic Economic Committee; at that time it requested that the report already in progress be readied for the council's 1954 session. At that session, the Nordic Council adopted a modified version of the committee's recommendations for a common market, which were then accepted by the member governments. A conference was called for October 1954, at Harpsund, Sweden, at which the governments of

[26] Anderson, *The Nordic Council,* p. 276.

[27] Unless otherwise noted, the following account of negotiations toward a Nordic Common Market is based upon Dolan, "The Nordic Council," and Wendt, *The Nordic Council,* pp. 165–232.

[28] John H. Wuorinen, "Scandinavia Looks at European Unity," *Current History,* vol. 42 (1962), p. 161.

Denmark, Sweden, and Norway formed a number of committees, among them the Scandinavian Economic Cooperation Committee, to investigate the implementation of a common market as recommended. In January 1956, the committee presented a provisional report to the Nordic Council, though it had completed only about half its work. The council, at its 1956 session, took no action on the report and instructed the committee to try to complete its work by the summer of 1957.

At the next council session at Helsinki in 1957, because of developments in the EEC, no action was taken on a Nordic common market. The council contented itself with a statement expressing satisfaction that the Nordic Economic Cooperation Committee's report would be ready by July 1, 1957.

The committee's report was published on October 21, 1957, and a meeting of government officials was held at Hindes, Sweden, in November 1957 to consider it. It was agreed that no action should be taken on the committee's proposals until the outcome of the negotiations toward a European free trade area became known. The countries recommended that further study of the Nordic common market be undertaken under the Economic Cooperation Committee's auspices. And, in 1958, the committee presented a supplementary report that called for an increase in the items to be included in the Nordic common market. The sixth session of the Nordic Council, held at Oslo in November 1958, did not discuss the committee's proposals directly. It merely recommended that the Nordic governments enter into negotiations regarding economic cooperation in order to prepare concrete proposals to be presented to the Nordic parliaments when the time was "ripe." Thus, negotiations were transferred to a governmental level. A meeting of prime ministers was held at Oslo in January 1959; again, the prime ministers recommended further study of the matter. Another conference of the Nordic Economic Cooperation Committee was held at Helsinki in May 1959, at which the items to be covered by a Nordic common market were extended, but still further negotiations were deemed necessary.[29] By July 15, 1959, Denmark announced her decision to join in the establishment of a

[29] *American Scandinavian Review,* vol. 47 (1959), p. 83.

seven-nation European Free Trade Association (the Outer Seven). Norway and Sweden soon followed. With this, plans for a purely Nordic common market collapsed.[30] Eleven years of study, consultation, and negotiation had produced little but thick volumes of reports.

This indecisiveness becomes more evident when one contrasts it with the speed with which negotiations for a European common market were conducted. The work on the Treaty of Rome, on which the EEC is based, began in June 1955. The treaty was completed by March 25, 1957, and in the same year it was ratified by the members' parliaments. On January 1, 1958, it went into effect.

Even where positive action has been taken by the Nordic Council on a proposal, implementation does not necessarily ensue, for the recommendation must be accepted by the governments of the member countries; and this has by no means always been secured. After considerable deliberation and negotiation, the council succeeded in arriving at a definition of drunken driving acceptable to all the delegations; nevertheless, when the matter was submitted to the governments, Denmark refused to ratify it.[31] Though Sweden and Norway had signed an agreement in March 1956 for joint construction and operation of a connecting highway between their central border districts,[32] Sweden in the same year rejected a council resolution calling for uniformity in travel practice: the Swedes refused to drive on the right side of the road as is the custom in the other Nordic countries.[33] It was not until 1963 that the Swedish Parliament agreed to the proposed change which, however, will not be implemented until 1967.[34] While it is of next to no practical importance, for the completeness of the record it should be noted that Icelanders expect to continue to drive on the left side of the road even after that date.

Concern with equality informs other shared Nordic organs with similar consequences for the scope and decisiveness of the union.

---

[30] Arthur Montgomery, "From a Northern Customs Union to EFTA," *Scandinavian Economic History Review,* vol. 8 (1960), pp. 65–67.

[31] Wendt, *The Nordic Council,* p. 158.

[32] *American Scandinavian Review,* vol. 44 (1956), p. 181.

[33] *American Scandinavian Review,* vol. 44 (1956), p. 88.

[34] *New York Times,* May 13, 1963.

For example, both the Nordic Cultural Commission [35] and the Norden Association (a nongovernmental organization whose stated goal is the advancement of Nordic cooperation)[36] have structures like that of the Nordic Council; there is no central secretariat—only five national sections, with control equally divided among the countries. The efforts of these organizations are likewise largely limited to areas whose spill-over potential is low and in which cooperation among the Nordic countries is of long duration, such as education, science, and the arts. These organizations have sponsored conferences of groups such as teachers, artists, journalists, and scientists. As in the case of the Nordic Council, their deliberations are often marked by delay and inconclusiveness. For instance, in 1947, the Nordic Cultural Commission took under consideration a proposal for cooperation in the field of oceanography. This matter was studied and discussed for seven years before being dropped by the commission.[37]

The highly egalitarian nature of the Nordic union and its concern with unanimity as the basis of decision, although it is not conducive to action, is helpful in maintaining commitment. Since consideration of a question or proposal can be prevented by any country in a committee, the council's deliberations are limited to matters all members are willing to discuss. Thus, Finland can adhere to the Nordic Council because of her ability to veto or withdraw should the council ever take up matters of military policy or become involved in the East-West struggle.[38] Further, as each government is free to reject those recommendations it feels are not consonant with its national interest, discussion, decision, and implementation in the Nordic union are under the control of the individual countries. This arrangement has less potential for generating alienation among the members: since positive action requires unanimity or near-

[35] On the Nordic Cultural Commission, see Nils Andrén, "The Nordic Cultural Commission, 1947–1957," *The Norseman,* vol. 15 (1957), pp. 375–382, and Gunnar Christie Wasberg, "The Nordic Cultural Commission," *American Scandinavian Review,* vol. 49 (1961), pp. 169–173.

[36] For a somewhat optimistic account of the achievements of the Nordic Association, see Frantz W. Wendt, "The Norden Association," *American Scandinavian Review,* vol. 44 (1956), pp. 245–249.

[37] Andrén, "The Nordic Cultural Commission," p. 377.

[38] Wendt, *The Nordic Council,* p. 105.

unanimity, the Nordic Council does not undertake discussions or pass resolutions objectionable to any member. What may be alienating in some instances is the lack of action. For example, dissatisfaction with the length and indecisiveness of the Nordic common market negotiations, which was due in large part to Norway's opposition, led Denmark and Sweden to consider the establishment of a common market without Norway and outside the framework of the Nordic Council.[39] But by and large the Nordic union is just a noninspiring, indecisive, high consensus-commanding, egalitarian endeavor.

THE EFFECT OF EXTERNAL SYSTEMS AND PLURAL MEMBERSHIPS

The Nordic countries are involved in several multinational systems, but they are not always members of the same ones. These external systems and their major members are often more powerful than the Nordic countries taken jointly or separately. Developments in these systems—whether in the direction of increasing or decreasing integration—are often more important for Nordic integration than developments in the Nordic union itself. Sometimes the effect of external systems is to push the Nordic countries closer together; sometimes the effect is to pull them apart.

The high point of Nordic economic cooperation came during World War I, especially in the years 1917–1918. German submarine warfare and the Entente blockade seriously affected shipping to and from the Nordic countries and made them more dependent on one another. In response to these conditions, a program of intra-Scandinavian exchange was set up, under which Denmark supplied Norway and Sweden with agricultural products and received in return supplies of metal and wood from Sweden and fish and fertilizer from Norway. During this period, intra-Scandinavian trade rose from a prewar level of 12 to 13 percent of the total foreign trade of the Nordic countries to 30 percent.[40] After the war, when

[39] "A Common Market," *The Norseman,* vol. 13 (1955), p. 377.
[40] Eli F. Heckscher, Kurt Bergendahl, Wilhelm Keilhan, Einar Cohn, and Thorstein Thorsteinsson, *Sweden, Norway, Denmark and Iceland in the World War.* New Haven, Conn.: Yale University Press, 1930, pp. 101–103.

the external pressure was removed, the Nordic exchange arrangements fell into disuse and the regions trade returned to the prewar level.[41]

While developments in external systems during World War I encouraged integration among the Nordic countries, World War II found the Nordic countries pulled in divergent directions because of the influence of non-Nordic systems. Initially, the Nordic countries were united in a policy of neutrality. The first split in their position came in April 1939, when Denmark signed a nonaggression pact with Germany. To gain Denmark's acquiescence to the agreement, Germany had threatened it with economic and military sanctions. Denmark was immediately vulnerable to the Nazis' military power: its armed forces were weak, and it is contiguous with Germany.[42] Despite the treaty, however, Denmark was invaded and occupied by the Nazis within a year. Norway was also attacked the same day Denmark was, but the fate of the two countries was different. While there was little Danish resistance to the German occupation forces, Norway put up an heroic fight. The reasons for the difference in resistance are many; the Danes had long expected a Nazi occupation and had surrendered in spirit before the Nazi invasion started; the Norwegians did not expect the German troops to cross the water, as Britain "ruled the waves." Also, as the Danes have pointed out, the mountainous Norwegian terrain lends itself more to guerilla warfare than the flat Danish land. It also seems that though both countries were pro-British, the Norwegians were more so than the Danes.

Whatever the reasons, the result was a quite different occupation experience for the two countries; Denmark was maintained by the Nazis as a "müster" (model) protectorate, which until August 1943 was ruled by its own government and allowed to maintain a Danish police and army. Late in 1943, the Germans instituted direct rule in Denmark and disbanded its forces, because sabotage in the railroads in the Danish peninsula had increased and the Danish forces had proved ineffective in preventing it. Norway, on the other hand, was subjected from the start to the full measure of Nazi rule, draw-

[41] Wendt, *The Nordic Council,* p. 28.
[42] *The New International Year Book 1939,* pp. 194–195.

ing relief only from a few Norwegian collaborators. All this had an impact on the postwar period; the Norwegian economy was much more damaged than that of Denmark (the Germans practiced a scorched-earth policy in the northern part of Norway).[43]

Sweden, on the other hand, was able to maintain its neutrality. It allowed German troops and war material frequent transit through her territory to Norway,[44] it refused Norway's government-in-exile permission to establish itself in Stockholm.[45]

Finland cooperated with Nazi Germany; it willingly joined the Third Reich in the latter's military moves against its arch enemy, Russia.[46] (The Finns prefer to refer to their "co-belligerent" status with Germany.) Russia, it must be recalled, had attacked Finland shortly before and annexed small parts of Finland's territory when a Finnish-Soviet peace was concluded. Finland claimed it joined with Germany to restore this territory. Iceland, on the other hand, was solidly in the Allied orbit. Early in the war, it was occupied by the British when a German attack was feared, and Iceland's participation in the Allied camp was thus ensured.[47]

As we see, the Nordic countries were pulled in different directions during World War II. Two of them—Denmark and Norway—were forced into the Nazi orbit, though the resistance of the latter was greater; one—Finland—actively allied herself with the Third Reich; Sweden remained neutral; and Iceland cooperated with the Allies.

These divergences had important consequences for the growth of Nordic integration during the postwar period. The intensification of the Cold War in 1947 and the establishment of a Communist government in Czechoslovakia in 1948 raised anew the problem of defense in the Nordic countries. Initially, the effect of these extraregional events was to provide an impetus toward increased intraregional co-

[43] Karen Larsen, *History of Norway.* Princeton, N.J.: Princeton University Press, 1948, pp. 534–565, and private communication with Gunnar Leistkow.

[44] Tingsten, "Swedish Foreign Policy," p. 474.

[45] Private communication with a Norwegian diplomat.

[46] Cf. G. A. Gripenberg, "Finnish Neutrality," in *Introduction to Finland—1960*, pp. 57–58.

[47] Gunnar Leistikow, "Iceland Between East and West," *American Scandinavian Review,* vol. 43 (1955), p. 347.

operation. In 1948, Sweden proposed that the Nordic countries form a defense alliance that would not align itself with either of the major blocs.[48] Compared to the other Nordic countries, Sweden's military position was strong, but Norway and Denmark's military establishments had been severely damaged during the war and they could not rearm without outside help, which Sweden, it seemed, was unable to supply.[49] In addition, many people in Danish and Norwegian official circles felt a need for greater security than a purely Nordic arrangement could provide and they were willing to mesh their countries' defenses with that of Western Europe.[50] Norway and Denmark's unfortunate experiences with neutrality during World War II had caused some to question that policy, though there remained considerable opposition in both countries to participation in the Atlantic alliance which the United States was then organizing.[51] Norway and Denmark were torn between joining the Swedish-suggested defense union and NATO. Denmark tried to secure American arms for the proposed Nordic alliance outside NATO, but when the United States refused its request (following the Vandenberg Resolution), Denmark felt compelled to join NATO; in this it was followed reluctantly by Norway[52] and Iceland.[53] Ultimately, the fate of the Nordic defense was thus decided in Washington.

The division of the Nordic countries with respect to defense arrangements has had a retarding effect on the growth of other aspects of the Nordic union; as a result, the possibilities for joint action and coordination in military matters and in matters of foreign policy, both areas of much potential spill-over, were severely limited.[54]

[48] Arne Ording, "Norway in World Affairs," *American Scandinavian Review,* vol. 43 (1955), pp. 144–145.

[49] Joe R. Wilkinson, "Denmark and NATO: The Problem of a Small State in a Collective Security System," *International Organization,* vol. 10 (1956), p. 390.

[50] Reider Omang, "Fifty Years of Norwegian Foreign Policy," *The Norseman,* vol. 13 (1955), p. 159.

[51] Ording, "Norway," p. 147.

[52] Nils Örvik, *Trends in Norwegian Foreign Policy.* Oslo, Norway: Norwegian Institute of International Affairs, 1962, p. 25; "Denmark and NATO," p. 399.

[53] Nuechterlein, *Iceland,* pp. 75ff.

[54] Bjarne Gran, "Norway and Northern Cooperation," *The Norseman,* vol. 12 (1954), pp. 230–231.

These matters are as a rule not even discussed in the deliberations of the Nordic Council.[55]

The relationship between Finland and the USSR provides another powerful illustration of the ability of an external power to retard Nordic integration. Following the settlement of the Finnish-Russian conflict in 1940, Finland proposed a defense alliance with Sweden and Norway, but the Russians announced that they would consider such a move a violation of their recently concluded peace treaty with Finland, and so the plan was abandoned forthwith.[56] Again, in 1948, when Sweden proposed the Nordic defense union, Finland, because of Russia's opposition, did not participate in the negotiations.[57] Instead it signed a treaty of "friendship, cooperation and mutual assistance" with Russia.[58] When the Nordic Council was formed in 1953, Finland did not become a member. But with the general thaw in interbloc relations in 1955 and after first carefully exploring Russia's reaction, Finland decided to apply for membership in 1956; it participated for the first time in the council's deliberations in 1957.[59] But its participation was hedged with restrictions; in order to placate her powerful Russian neighbor, Finland, before accepting membership, announced that if the Nordic Council ever took up questions of military policy or became involved in matters relating to conflicts of interest between East and West, its representatives would not enter into the discussion.[60]

When Norway, Sweden, and Denmark joined the OEEC in 1949 and EFTA in 1960, Finland was again inhibited from participating. It was not until February 1961 that Finland was able to arrange an associate membership in EFTA.[61] With the decision of Sweden, Norway, and Denmark to apply for affiliation with the EEC, Finland's relations with the other Nordic countries were once again threatened;

[55] Lyman B. Burbank, "Scandinavian Integration and Western Defense," *Foreign Affairs,* vol. 35 (1956), p. 145.
[56] "Finland," *The New International Year Book, 1940.* New York: Funk & Wagnalls Company, 1941, p. 266.
[57] Dolan, "The Nordic Council," p. 513.
[58] Gripenberg, "Finnish Neutrality," pp. 61–64.
[59] Dolan, "The Nordic Council," pp. 511–512.
[60] Anderson, *The Nordic Council,* pp. 55–56.
[61] *New York Times,* February 16, 1961.

Russia's opposition to the EEC, at that time, was so great that it would not approve of Finland's association with the Common Market countries.[62] The other Nordic countries' concern about Finland's place in the periphery of the Soviet orbit led them to consider the formation of a Nordic common market (in addition to their EEC association) primarily to provide an economic link between Finland and Western Europe.[63] In short, Finland's participation in the various Nordic military and economic arrangements has been prevented or delayed by the influence of an outside power.

The delay in and ultimate collapse of plans for a Nordic common market provide another instance of the far-reaching effects of external systems and consequent developments on Nordic integration. In 1948, the United States, through the agency of the Marshall Plan, embarked on a program of extensive financial aid to promote the economic recovery and reconstruction of postwar Europe in such a way as to encourage the development of enterprises in areas where they could be most efficiently carried on. To function well, such an arrangement required the lowering of trade barriers, and it was in the pursuit of this goal that negotiations toward a Nordic common market were begun in 1948.[64] The Nordic common market, as envisaged, would have been absorbed ultimately into a larger European free trade area.[65] But no such market was ever created. The trade ties of all the Scandinavian countries are stronger with their non-Nordic European neighbors than they are with one another. The Scandinavians hence preferred to participate in efforts to establish a 17-nation European free trade area rather than attempt to create a market of their own. When this effort failed in 1959, due to factors over which the Nordic countries had no control, Denmark, Norway, and Sweden in order to protect their non-Nordic European interests decided to join with Portugal, Austria, Switzerland, and the United Kingdom in the formation of a seven-nation European Free Trade Association

[62] Wuorinen, "Scandinavia Looks at European Unity," p. 164.

[63] This matter was discussed at the fifth Nordic Council session at Helsinki, February 1–15, 1957.

[64] F. V. Meyer, *The European Free Trade Association.* New York: Frederick A. Praeger, Inc., 1960, p. 1.

[65] Montgomery, "From a Northern Customs Union," p. 65.

(EFTA). With this, efforts toward a Nordic common market were dropped: neither Switzerland nor Britain would consent to regional subgroupings within EFTA.[66]

The initial effect of this decision was to divide Finland from its European Nordic neighbors, for Russian pressure delayed its entry into EFTA. Finally, in March of 1961, it was able to arrange, with Russian approbation, an associate membership.[67]

This Nordic coordination of economic policy and membership in economic unions did not last long. When the United Kingdom in 1961 decided to seek EEC membership, Denmark applied unilaterally for membership in the EEC; Norway (whose trade ties to Britain are considerable) decided later to follow suit.[68] Sweden was even more hesitant about EEC affiliation. It worried about compromising its nonalliance policy, its economic interests in Finland, which could not be expected to become an EEC member, and its sentimental commitment not to leave Finland alone. When finally Sweden, too, applied for admission, it was as an associate rather than as a full member.[69] Finland, because of Soviet opposition to the EEC, did not feel free to join its Nordic neighbors and apply for membership in the EEC.[70]

Once again the Nordic countries find themselves divided in economic policy. The fact that this difference in policy did not, by 1964, lead to dismemberment of EFTA was due more to de Gaulle's veto of British membership in the EEC than to any Nordic integrating processes. In matters of foreign affairs and military security, the Nordic countries were and are divided: Denmark, Norway, and Iceland are members of the Atlantic Alliance; Sweden remains neutral; and Finland (albeit reluctantly) finds itself subject to Soviet influence. Attempts to promote integration of the Nordic economies by means of a customs union failed, largely because of policies made

[66] "From a Northern Customs Union," p. 72. See also Arthur Montgomery, "The Swedish Economy in the 1950's," *Scandinavian Economic History Review,* vol. 10 (1960), pp. 230ff.

[67] Wuorinen, "Scandinavia Looks at European Unity," pp. 163ff.

[68] *American Scandinavian Review,* vol. 49 (1961), p. 425; *New York Times,* May 3, 1962.

[69] *New York Times,* May 9, 1963.

[70] Wuorinen, "Scandinavia Looks at European Unity," p. 164.

by external powers, notably Great Britain. And, for the same reasons, the Nordic countries find themselves currently disunited in economic policy.

COMPOSITION OF POWER

Low Utilitarian Power

Trade relations are a most significant factor in the national economies of the Nordic countries. In 1960, the value of the export-import sector of the Danish economy was equal to 55.2 percent of the Gross National Product at market price. The corresponding figures for the other Nordic countries in the same year are as follows: Finland—42.4 percent; Iceland—50.6 percent; Norway—52.2 percent; and Sweden—44.8 percent.[71] By contrast, in the case of the United States, the value of foreign trade equals 5.0 percent of the GNP market price.[72] The bulk of Nordic trade is with non-Nordic countries: only about 12 to 14 percent of the area's trade is intra-Nordic.[73] Thus, the utilitarian powers of the union insofar as they derive from trade relations are comparatively low.

In the case of Denmark, sales to the other Nordic countries accounted for 14.6 percent of its total export. West Germany alone purchased 19.0 percent of its export, while the EEC countries as a whole absorbed almost one third. The United Kingdom is Denmark's second largest single customer; in 1960, it took about 14 percent of Denmark's export.[74] The non-Nordic members of EFTA accounted for over 27 percent of Denmark's export.

The export situations of Norway and Sweden are similar to that of Denmark. The proportion of their exports going to other Nordic countries was comparatively low: in 1960, it was 20.2 percent for

[71] These figures are derived from the *Yearbook of Nordic Statistics 1962,* Table 37 on p. 28 and Table 65 on p. 42.

[72] Gunnar Jahn, "Short Survey of the Norwegian Economy," in *Scandinavia Past and Present,* p. 482.

[73] Lindgren, "International Cooperation in Scandinavia," p. 111.

[74] Per B. Johansen, "The Importance of Foreign Trade: Denmark as a Trading Partner," *Danish Foreign Office Journal,* Special Issue for the XVIIIth Congress of the ICC 1961, p. 14.

Norway and 19.8 percent for Sweden. In both instances, the United Kingdom and West Germany constituted their largest single markets. The EEC countries absorbed over one quarter of Norway's exports and almost one third of Sweden's. The corresponding figures for the non-Nordic EFTA members are 25.0 percent and 18.7 percent. The Icelandic pattern follows that of the three larger Nordic countries with one exception: Iceland's second largest customer is the USSR.

Finland is least dependent on Nordic markets: less than 10 percent of its export is purchased by other Nordic countries. Like Iceland, its major markets are to be found in the United Kingdom and the USSR, which together accounted for almost 40 percent of its exports in 1960. Though Russia's share of Finland's export was less than 15 percent, Finland's reliance on Russia is greater than this figure would indicate; Russia buys from Finland such high cost articles as engineering tools, in whose manufacture Finland has a large investment but which it cannot produce cheaply enough to compete on the world market.[75]

The differentials between Nordic and non-Nordic markets are in general not large. But they are important from the point of view of this discussion, for they demonstrate that the utilitarian attractiveness of non-Nordic countries to the Nordic countries, insofar as it is based on trade ties, is as great as or greater than that of the Nordic union.

Further, it appears that the possibilities for increasing the utilitarian attractiveness of the Nordic union to its members are rather limited. This is partly due to the similar nature of their economies. For instance, wood and wood products and their export are important factors in the economies of Finland, Norway, and Sweden, and these countries are thus to some extent competitors for the same markets. Again, the bulk of Denmark's agricultural exports consist of dairy, poultry, and pork products,[76] and it seems unlikely that it can expand its Nordic markets for these items, for Norway and Sweden also have significant surpluses in these products.[77] Fish and fish products are

[75] Montgomery, "From a Northern Customs Union," p. 63.

[76] P. Nyboe Andersen, "Denmark's Foreign Trade," in *Scandinavia Past and Present*, pp. 737–738.

[77] Frank Meissner, "Scandinavian Customs Union," *The Norseman*, vol. 12 (1954), p. 253.

the major element in the Icelandic economy: they account for over 95 percent of Iceland's exports. The Nordic countries are unlikely to increase their fish imports from Iceland because they either have sufficient fish for their needs or, as in the case of Norway and Denmark, produce an exportable surplus.[78]

Further, significant increases of trade ties among the Nordic countries through the establishment of a common market seem unlikely. Agricultural and industrial production enjoy considerable advantages in some Nordic countries because of soil and climatic conditions, natural resources, etc. It is widely believed that the corresponding economic sectors in the relatively less favored countries would be severely damaged by the initiation of a common market. In the period under study, both Norway and Sweden feared for their agricultural producers, should Denmark, whose agriculture is more productive and efficient, have free access to their markets. Norway in particular feared that further weakening of its agricultural sector would result in the depopulation of many of its rural districts, and therefore was most insistent about the exclusion of agricultural products from the proposed common market. Such a policy of course limited Denmark's interest in the Nordic common market, for agricultural products constitute over half of its exports. Moreover, had the Nordic common market come into existence, Denmark would have been expected to open its markets to industrial products from the other Nordic countries.[79] Iceland, because of the exclusion of food products, did not even participate in the common market negotiations since, as we have seen, virtually all of its export falls in this category. Further, both Iceland and Norway, whose industries are small and highly protected by the government, were afraid of the swamping of their markets by the industrial products of the other Nordic countries, especially Sweden.

The Nordic area is one of those to which a simple theory of the "relative advantages" of free trace seems not to apply. For Norway, a key country in the region, saw Denmark as a country that has a

[78] Wendt, *The Nordic Council,* pp. 229–230; and Andersen, "Denmark's Foreign Trade," p. 737.
[79] Kay Heckscher, "Denmark's Dilemma," *Contemporary Review,* vol. 192 (1957), pp. 193–194.

"relative advantage" over Norway in agriculture and Sweden as one with a similar advantage in industry. Should Norway open its doors to free trade, major dislocations were expected in both of its major economic sectors. The fate of Southern Italy in the unification of Italy, and of the South in the unification of the United States, seemed to suggest that such regional weakness might remain, that a region entering weak into a process of unification might stay weak. This general and basic problem was reflected in a more technical and immediate one. Norway imposed high duties on many imports into its market, including those of other Nordic countries,[80] while about 80 percent of its products entered Sweden and Denmark duty-free.[81] Hence, Norway would have to practice more "give" and less "take" if it were to enter a Nordic common market without major guarantees of assistance for its development, in the hope of bringing its economy to a par with that of other Nordic economies. (First, Norway's smaller enterprises would have to be consolidated. In 1957, Norway had 20,000 industrial undertakings employing a total of 330,000 people, while Sweden employed 686,000 in 17,000 enterprises.) No capital was available to pay for this giant task. Hence the regional utilitarian exchange system remained limited.

The preceding argument was often advanced by those who objected to the extension of Nordic utilitarian bonds. Those who favored such extension could argue that when Norway finally reduced its tariff barriers in the early 1960s, though not as a partner of a Nordic union but as a member of EFTA, no such dislocations occurred. It is, however, too early to judge which side is right for several reasons. The Norwegian economy might well have been overprotected and only its ability to withstand fuller reduction of tariff barriers than those achieved to date (about 50 percent) would serve as a test; second, barriers on trade other than tariffs, which Norway used for protection, have not yet been significantly affected. Also, agricultural products were not included in EFTA. To date, total trade in the area, measured as a percentage of the total foreign trade, has increased by only a few points. While Norway's exports grew in

[80] Lindgren, "International Cooperation in Scandinavia," p. 111.
[81] Dolan, "The Nordic Council," p. 524.

1963 by 8 percent, its import growth was larger. Hence, the question, to what extent can the Nordic utilitarian exchange system be significantly intensified without causing major dislocations, remains unanswered in general and regarding Norway in particular.

Similarly, the Nordic utilitarian-administrative system, though it has grown in the past decade, still remains rather limited in effectiveness and scope. Few shared institutions have emerged, and those which have (such as the Nordic Council and the Nordic Cultural Commission) are usually organized along national lines. No supranational organs have been established; there is not even a Nordic bureaucracy to service the various commissions and committees that have been formed or to act as a center of regional communication.

Contacts among the Nordic governments are frequent and occur at many levels. Much of the intergovernmental communication is informal. An official of one government may contact an official of another government without going through diplomatic channels, as is the usual procedure in communications between governments. Though personal communication was a common practice before the formation of the Nordic Council, as a result of a council recommendation the practice has been extended so that almost all contacts between national administrations and even local authorities are direct.[82] This process is of course expedited by the ease of telephone communication and transportation among the countries. The Nordic Council and the Nordic Cultural Commission, with their annual sessions and reports and with their numerous committees and commissions, have increased the opportunities for consultation and have extended the network of formal regional communication to include parliamentarians as well as government officials.

In addition, there has been a considerable increase in the number of joint meetings held by Nordic cabinet ministers. The foreign ministers ordinarily confer twice yearly; the ministers of social justice, once a year; and the ministers of social welfare and of education, biennially.[83] At the United Nations[84] and in other international orga-

[82] Wendt, *The Nordic Council,* p. 139.
[83] Anderson, *The Nordic Council,* pp. 7–10.
[84] Tormod Petter Svennevig, "The Scandinavian Bloc in the United Nations and its New Outlook," *The Norseman,* vol. 13 (1955), pp. 145–153.

nizations, such as the OEEC, the Council of Europe, and the Inter-governmental Committee for European Migration[85] there is frequent consultation among the Nordic delegations. These consultations have resulted in the formation of a consensus in many matters of social policy,[86] but they have been comparatively less successful when foreign policy matters are concerned. A study of voting patterns in the General Assembly of the United Nations in the late forties and early fifties showed that the Nordic countries manifested unanimity with respect to 19 out of 39 issues or only about 50 percent of the time.[87] A later study shows that overall identical votes were 68.4 percent, though members tended to abstain in order to avoid having to vote against each other. The study shows that the Nordic group was most divided on procedural issues, which include the question of the admission of Communist China to the United Nations, next on matters concerning the development of international law, and least on questions of human rights.[88]

The various programs and associations that have grown out of the numerous consultations and frequent communication among the Nordic countries have had a minimal spill-over effect in expanding the scope or increasing the level of integration of the union. In 1958, the Nordic countries formed a passport union so that non-Nordic citizens travelling anywhere in the Nordic area need have their passports checked only once—at the point of entry into the region.[89] Norway and Sweden have unified customs procedures along their long common frontier.[90] In some instances, the Nordic countries have cooperated in the establishment of diplomatic missions, especially

[85] Lindgren, "International Cooperation in Scandinavia," pp. 100–105; Halvard Lange, "Scandinavian Cooperation in International Affairs," *International Affairs,* vol. 30 (1954), p. 286.

[86] Kaare Salvesen, "Cooperation in Social Affairs Between the Northern Countries of Europe," *International Labour Review,* vol. 73 (1956), pp. 350–352.

[87] Svennevig, "The Scandinavian Bloc," p. 147. On this matter, see especially M. Margaret Ball, "Bloc Voting in the General Assembly," *International Organization,* vol. 5 (1951), pp. 14ff.

[88] Thomas Hovet, Jr., *Bloc Politics in the United Nations.* Cambridge, Mass.: Harvard University Press, 1960, p. 75.

[89] Halvard Lange, *The Nordic Council: A Political Assessment,* Royal Norwegian Ministry of Foreign Affairs: 1959, mimeo, p. 5.

[90] Lindgren, "International Cooperation in Scandinavia," p. 102.

in the new nations. For example, Denmark was the only Nordic country to establish an embassy in Accra where it acts on behalf of all the Nordic Council members. Sweden plays a similar role in Monrovia.[91] But the total list of such items of regional unification measures is not long; the items are "light-weight" in terms of their sociopolitical significance and they have not accumulated to provide the basis of a unification take-off.

Since 1954, the Nordic countries, with the exception of Iceland, have formed a common labor market: citizens of one country are free to work in any of the other countries without securing work permits. Government assistance in the form of job information and contacts is provided for workers seeking employment outside their countries. It was anticipated that this program would promote the unification of the Nordic economies by a partial redistribution of the labor force among the countries of the region.[92] But the expected results have not been achieved. The number of emigrant workers is small—about 110,000 out of a total population of over 20 million,[93] and the labor exchange affected mainly two countries: Sweden and Finland. In 1960, about 70 percent of the Scandinavians working in countries other than the land of their birth worked in Sweden. Of the 81,200 Nordic aliens working in Sweden, 51,388, or over 60 percent, were Finns.[94]

Several joint business enterprises have been undertaken by the Nordic countries. In 1960 a hydroelectric power plant that exports one half of its output to Stockholm,[95] was opened at Nea in Norway. Further, Norway, Sweden, and Denmark have established a joint airline, SAS, which is administered in such a way as to divide control equally among the three countries. Its board of directors has six rep-

[91] Anderson, *The Nordic Council,* p. 13.
[92] Bertil, Olsson, "The Common Employment market for the Nordic Countries," *International Labour Review,* vol. 68 (1953), p. 366.
[93] *American Scandinavian Review,* vol. 47 (1959), p. 392.
[94] *Yearbook of Nordic Statistics,* p. 48. It is somewhat doubtful whether this movement of workers resulted from the 1954 agreement, since Nordic citizens have been able to work in Sweden without permits since 1943. See *American Scandinavian Review,* vol. 47 (1959), p. 392. Moreover, it appears that the number of such workers has declined, for in 1957 there were 86,000 Finns, Norwegians, and Danes employed in Sweden. *Idem.*
[95] *American Scandinavian Review,* vol. 48 (1960), p. 403.

resentatives from each country, and the chairmanship rotates from country to country on an annual basis. Similar principles are followed in the selection of the executive committee and in the nomination of the top-management officials—the president and three executive vice presidents.[96] But again, these are exceptions to the rule, which is one of national, not regional, companies.

Nordic banks have regional ties that allow for money deposited in one country to be routinely withdrawn in another, a policy that was initiated by governmental postal savings banks and spread to private banks. Publishing houses have affiliates in other Nordic countries. But similar ties exist among banks, publishers, etc. in countries that do not form a regional or any other union. While these contacts are more institutionalized in the Nordic area than, let us say, between the United States and the United Kingdom, the difference is rather small and its importance for further unification, even smaller.[97]

In 1955, the Nordic countries signed an agreement by which all Nordic citizens resident in any particular Nordic country were guaranteed all the social benefits to which the citizens of that country were entitled. This means that a Finnish citizen living in Sweden is entitled to the same social benefits such as workmen's compensation, health insurance, and old age pensions as a Swedish citizen. But each country's welfare programs remain independent of the others; there is no common social policy and no movement toward the establishment of any supranational body to establish policy and implement a regional welfare program.[98]

In summary: the utilitarian power of the Nordic union was not high and did not grow appreciably during the period under consideration. The trade ties linking Nordic countries to non-Nordic countries are more important than those that bind the Nordic countries together. Though contacts and communications among the Nordic countries are frequent, few joint structures have been formed and those that were established were concentrated in areas of low poten-

[96] H. Throne-Holst, "Scandinavian Airlines System," in *Scandinavia Past and Present,* pp. 373–378, and Robert A. Nelson, "Scandinavian Airlines System: Cooperation in the Air," *Journal of Air Law and Commerce,* vol. 10 (1953), pp. 178–196.

[97] Lange, "The Nordic Council," pp. 7–8.

[98] Salvesen, "Cooperation in Social Affairs," pp. 342ff., 356–357.

tial spill-over, such as science and education. Little has been accomplished by way of increasing the economic integration of the union: attempts to form a Nordic common market failed and the Nordic common labor market did not affect to any significant degree the distribution of the labor force in the Nordic countries. No joint military organizations have been established, and in the political realm, despite much consultation and discussion, no center of communication and coordination was established in the period under study. Contacts were intermittent; there was little provision for continuing formal contact among the governments. Even the Nordic Council meets for only a brief period annually (usually seven to ten days. In 1963 it was decided to reduce this period to five days per year). The council has no permanent secretariat and, in a sense, is organized anew each year. The intergovernmental committees and organs have remained consultative and advisory. The Nordic union has evolved no mechanisms for compelling discussion, for making decisions, or for enforcing resolutions—even those voluntarily and unanimously arrived at.

UNFOCUSED IDENTITIVE POWER

There exists among the citizens of the Nordic countries an awareness of a common Nordic identity and a sense of Nordic solidarity. Scandinavians tend to refer to other Scandinavians not as foreigners, though they might designate them as Danes, Swedes, or Norwegians. Citizens from all the Nordic countries are proud that two of their number have been chosen to serve as secretary general of the United Nations.[99] Indeed, in various international organizations, delegates from the Nordic countries identify themselves and are identified by others as a unit for certain purposes. There is always one Nordic member on the governing board of the International Labor Organization who is considered to represent all Nordic interests, and similar practices are followed by the World Health Organization and various other organs of the United Nations.[100] When a Nordic delegate is

[99] Norman J. Padelford, *Scandinavian Views of the United Nations.* Cambridge, Mass.: Center for International Relations, Massachusetts Institute of Technology, 1958, mimeo, pp. 1–3.
[100] Salvesen, "Cooperation in Social Affairs," p. 350 and 351.

elected to office in the United Nations, the reports of the election usually assert explicitly that he was selected as the (unofficial) representative of all the Nordic states.[101] The Nordic countries, their citizens stress, are all small and relatively lacking in power when compared to such giants as the United States, the USSR, West Germany, and the United Kingdom. Collaboration makes it possible for them to speak with a greater impact in international affairs than if each one were acting on its own.[102] Cooperation in diplomatic as well as other matters among the Nordic countries is believed to be almost automatic—the result of shared values and common interests. The Nordic countries are frequently thought to constitute a natural area for collaboration because of similarities in historical background, language, religion, political and legal systems, economic level, and international status. In short, there is a consciousness and even an ideology of regional cooperation. Moreover, deliberate efforts are made to increase cooperation.

The intensification of the sense of Nordic solidarity and the expansion of the areas of Nordic cooperation are objects of direct concern to various voluntary associations in all the Nordic countries. During an 18-month period from 1957 to 1958, *Nordisk tidskrift,* the official publication of the Nordic Association, carried notices of 77 meetings that were directed toward increased Nordic cooperation.[103] This was an average of over four such meetings per month. The platforms of the major political parties of Norway, Denmark, and Sweden all pledge to work for an increase in Nordic collaboration.[104] Further, there exists in all five Nordic countries an association with quasi-governmental status whose avowed purpose is the encouragement of Nordic cooperation—the Norden Association.[105]

The Norden Association has a total membership of over 120,000, and its activities extend into a number of areas, including education,

[101] Svennevig, "The Scandinavian Bloc," p. 147.

[102] Helge Seip, "The Pursuit of the Possible in Scandinavian Cooperation," *The Norseman,* vol. 14 (1956), p. 146.

[103] Lindgren, "International Cooperation in Scandinavia," p. 98.

[104] Walter H. Mallory (ed.). *Political Handbook of the World 1960.* New York: Council on Foreign Relations, Inc., 1961, pp. 55–56 (Denmark); p. 150 (Norway); and pp. 181–182 (Sweden).

[105] See Wendt, "The Norden Association."

the arts, the sciences, and politics. The Norden Association publishes periodicals and books and sponsors lectures about the Nordic countries to expand its members' familiarity with the other countries in the region. Under its aegis, a program has been undertaken for revising history textbooks so that each country's past role, especially in Nordic conflicts, may be more accurately presented.[106] The real concern is of course not historical revision per se but reduction of Nordic antagonisms. The Norden Association has also set up a Language Board in the hope of retarding divergences among the Nordic languages; it administers several programs for increasing contacts among citizens of the several Nordic countries; it arranges student and teacher exchanges and visits between families of similar background and position in different countries in the area. In the cultural field, a number of joint institutions have been established, including a Nordic Institute for Theoretical Nuclear Physics at Copenhagen and a Nordic college for journalists at the University of Århus in Denmark.[107] Television programs are produced cooperatively. Publishing firms have close affiliations.

All these similarities, activities, and contacts seem to be of limited value in significantly deepening or expanding the scope of the Nordic union. There are several reasons that account for this limitation. Contacts between the various countries seem primarily to involve educated elitist groups, such as teachers, lawyers, jurists, scientists, and labor union leaders. Further, the sense of affinity encouraged by such contacts and by the broad network of Nordic cooperation is not tied to support for any shared institutions, to say nothing of supranational organs: it is what psychologists call a "nonspecified" sentiment. The educational systems of the five countries as well as their cultural institutions, from museums to libraries, have a national and not a regional structure. Even the Norden Association, whose aim is regional unification, is organized along national lines; it is five separate organizations; delegates from these national organizations meet together to harmonize activities, but there is no regional headquar-

[106] Haakon Vigander, *Mutual Revision of History Textbooks in the Nordic Countries.* Paris: UNESCO, 1950.

[107] Private communication with a Norwegian diplomat. On this point, see Max Sørensen, "Le Conseil Nordique," *Révue Générale de Droit International Public,* 58 (1955). Third Series, vol. 26, No. 1, pp. 64–69.

ters. In this, it is very much like the Nordic Cultural Commission and the Nordic Council itself.

The ideology of cooperation seems to be stronger than the actual measure of cooperation. Thus, while Scandinavians tend to insist, somewhat defensively, that they cooperate so effectively that no regional institutions are required and that their mode of voluntary cooperation is superior to that of a regional superstate, a point to which we shall return below, it is of interest to note here that the historical consciousness of the various Nordic nations hold memories that agitate against regional bodies, whether or not these are needed for effective cooperation. Foremost among these memories are the histories of the various unions that the area knew in the past. Those include the Kalmar Union (1389–1523), which in its original form encompassed the subgroupings Sweden-Finland (until 1809), Denmark-Norway (1375–1814), and the Union of Norway and Sweden (1814–1903). Such unions have left a legacy of antagonism that is still a salient factor in relations within the Nordic union.[108] The various efforts at achieving independence have given rise to rather strong feelings of national consciousness, feelings superseding any sense of Nordic identity. As Professor John H. Wuorinen has pointed out, the individual Norwegian, Swede, Dane, or Finn feels rather deeply "that the people whose language he speaks, whose past he shares and whose ways of thinking are much like his, are *his* people and stand apart from others in culture, traditions, language, and mores in general."[109] In addition, a mild apprehension of Swedish predominance has some effect on the actions and decisions of Norway, and to a lesser extent Denmark, with respect to the Nordic union.[110]

Norwegian and Danish opposition to the Swedish-proposed defense alliance of 1948—though it was determined by other causes—also reflected an uneasiness over an alliance in which Sweden would

[108] John H. Wuorinen, "Scandinavia and the Rise of Modern National Consciousness," in Edward Mead Earle (ed.), *Nationalism and Internationalism: Essays Inscribed to Carlton J. H. Hayes.* New York: Columbia University Press, 1950, p. 461.

[109] "Scandinavia and the Rise of Modern National Consciousness," p. 462.

[110] Burbank, "Scandinavian Integration," pp. 146–147 and Padelford, "Regional Cooperation in Scandinavia," p. 598.

be the dominant member; it would supply the bulk of the arms, and the commander-in-chief of the joint Nordic forces would in all probability be a Swede.[111] Further, in the matter of the Nordic common market, Norway's hesitance can in part be traced to its apprehension of Swedish influence. Norway was concerned that the implementation of a common market or customs union would require some sort of supranational agency, possibly dominated by Sweden, to coordinate programs and to enforce rulings. This development, Norway felt, would compromise its independent status.[112] This was also one reason it opposed the establishment of a Nordic bureaucracy in connection with the Nordic Council.[113]

In intra-Nordic business arrangements, some antipathy toward Sweden is also occasionally expressed. Both Danes and Norwegians complain about Swedish preeminence in the operation of their joint airline, SAS, whose initials a Norwegian jokingly alleged stand for "Svensk Alt Sammer" or Altogether Swedish.[114] (Sweden has a larger investment in SAS than the other countries; SAS headquarters are in Stockholm and its president, Curt Nicolin, is a Swede.) Norwegians and Danes were astounded to find out that of the ten largest corporations in Scandinavia, nine are Swedish, as are most of two hundred-odd corporations whose 1963 turnover was higher than 100 million kroner ($19 million).

Despite Norway's great need for outside capital to develop her resources and build up her industry, there is great reluctance to accept investments from Sweden. Norwegian business circles were opposed to the Nea power-plant arrangement whereby Norway produced hydroelectric power for Swedish consumption; cheap and plentiful water power is seen as Norway's major asset, and there is strong objection to sharing it with Sweden.[115] A proposal for the development of Norwegian copper deposits by a Swedish company was firmly rejected in Norway; the enterprise was viewed as an attempt at Swedish "infiltration" of Norwegian industry. This attitude prevailed despite the fact that Norway would have controlled 40 per-

[111] Private communication with a Norwegian diplomat.
[112] Dolan, "The Nordic Council," pp. 524–525.
[113] Anderson, *The Nordic Council*, pp. 59ff.
[114] Private communication with a Norwegian diplomat.
[115] "Will Norway Export Power?", *The Norseman*, vol. 12 (1954), pp. 78–79.

cent of the company and despite the fact that without Swedish capital Norway could not hope to develop the area under consideration.[116]

Six centuries of Swedish domination of Finland have left a residue of antipathy toward Sweden on the part of Finland, though probably in the prenationalist period little awareness of Finnish separation existed and the main manifestation of tension was between Finns and the Swedish aristocracy in Finland, rather than between the two countries. There is also some ill feeling between Danes and Norwegians deriving from the long association of the two countries: for over 400 years the Danish language and Danish culture were dominant among Norway's urban, educated, and official classes, and Norway's attempt to create a distinct nationality involved the reduction of these Danish influences.[117] For their part, Swedes feel themselves superior to the other Nordic countries, less superior to the Danes, more to the Norwegians; the Swedes see themselves as more sophisticated and cosmopolitan and their country as having greater stature in international affairs.[118]

One interesting indication of the limited scope of Scandinavian cooperation may be seen in the fact that while authors who write about this cooperation are abundant with superlatives, an examination of publications dealing with various general problems of the Nordic countries—such as the *Norseman* or the *Scandinavian Times* (for English-reading publics) as well as publications in the Scandinavian languages—rarely mention a Scandinavian country besides the one being examined, when questions other than cooperation are discussed. That is, one gains the impression that cooperation is not a major dimension of most domestic matters and hence unless such international matters as trade or diplomacy are examined, the problems of each country can be treated independently. When parallel areas in the other countries of the region are mentioned, they are presented as points of interest and comparison; they are not treated as part of the same problematic area, one to be faced regionally.

[116] Burbank, "Scandinavian Integration," pp. 146–147; "Swedish Mining Plans," *The Norseman,* vol. 11 (1953), pp. 307–308.
[117] Wuorinen in "Scandinavia and the Rise of Modern National Consciousness," pp. 463–464.
[118] Private communication with a Norwegian sociologist.

Moreover, surprisingly little space is devoted to the reporting and analysis of regional cooperation. There is considerably more belief in Nordic similarities and cooperation than there is in one Nordic reality. From time to time, an occurrence brings this fact to the consciousness of the people of the region. In 1964, a book by an American psychiatrist, Dr. Herbert Hendin, entitled *Suicide and Scandinavia,* created a lively public debate. One of the points emphasized was that Denmark, Norway, and Sweden "are essentially a homogeneous area, all welfare states, sharing such relevant factors as religion and climate—yet while Denmark and Sweden (and Finland) have some of the world's highest suicide rates, Norway has one of the lowest." The book was viewed by Scandinavians, however, as "above all a healthy reminder that the three peoples are really far more different than their ways of life would indicate."[119]

The same point is illustrated by the development of Nordic languages. Basically the Scandinavian languages are very similar to each other, and from this viewpoint the region has fewer communication problems than most.[120] Citizens of the three countries who come into regular contact are largely accustomed to each other's languages. The proceedings of the Nordic Council and of various regional associations are carried on in all three languages without translations. According to one interviewee, the differences are as small as those between the English spoken by an American and that of an Australian. He said, "they are limited largely to those of pronunciation and some grammar." Other observers recognize slightly greater differences. Gunnar Leistikow stated that, "Danes, Norwegians, and Swedes can become accustomed to the sound of each other's languages within a few weeks."[121] David Philip stated that "the educated citizen of one of the three countries can quite easily *read* books written in one of the two languages of the other countries, and even follow *fairly* easily a conversation or a lecture in one

[119] Both quotations are from the *Scandinavian Times,* May–June 1964, No. 3, p. 200.

[120] *The Scandinavian Year Book for 1953,* p. 24.

[121] "Cooperation Between the Scandinavian Countries," in Henning Friis (ed.), *Scandinavia Between the East and the West.* Ithaca, N.Y.: Cornell University Press: 1950, p. 309.

of the other Scandinavian languages."[122] The *Scandinavian Times* was less charitable:

It was a season, then, for rediscovery of the Scandinavian community. Even language barriers—caused chiefly by laziness, for Danish, Norwegian and Swedish are essentially alike—seemed to fall. At the Stockholm festivities, Danes and Swedes conversed merrily—in English.[123]

Among the three Scandinavian countries, the Norwegians are slightly favored, as they understand Swedish and Danish more readily than the speakers of these two languages understand each other.[124] The two other Nordic languages are more dissimilar. No Scandinavian who is not trained in either Icelandic or Finnish will understand these languages, nor do the citizens of these countries understand another Scandinavian language unless they have studied it. Icelandic is most akin to the "Old Norse," as the early pronunciation and vocabulary of a language once widely spoken in the region is designated.[125] While the Scandinavian countries assimilated large influxes, first of German, then of Latin and French, the Icelanders absorbed few new words and those only by translating them into their own linguistic tradition.

While Icelandic roots at least rest on the same lingual foundation as the three Scandinavian languages, those of Finnish have a quite different tradition. Finnish is not a Scandinavian language but is part of the Finnish-Ugrian group (as is Hungarian); it is akin to Estonian and to some Russian languages. An untutored Scandinavian can understand part of Icelandic, but little Finnish. These language barriers, however, pose few problems for Nordic communication. Most Icelanders speak some Danish (which is the first foreign language taught in their schools), and many Finns speak Swedish.

Nevertheless, over the years the Nordic languages have grown farther apart. The various national independence movements of the 19th century were especially important in increasing linguistic dif-

---

[122] David Philip, "The Originality of Scandinavian Culture," *The Norseman*, vol. 13 (1955), p. 79. Italics provided.

[123] *Scandinavian Times*, No. 2 (March–April 1964), p. 10.

[124] Lindgren, *Norway-Sweden*, p. 276.

[125] "Iceland," *The Encyclopedia Americana*, vol. 14, pp. 637–638.

ferences. Norway made a conscious effort to reduce the Danish elements in its language. More recent changes in the Norwegian vocabulary were, in general, not paralleled by similar changes in the Danish one; also, a reform of orthography made Norwegian written as it is pronounced, while Danish orthography still follows historical traditions. At the same time, the Finns were making efforts to reduce the amount of Swedish spoken in their country, and Icelandic textbooks, which used to be in Danish, are being replaced by texts written in English, which is gaining as the second language of the island.[126]

Some measures have been introduced to reduce the existing differences among Scandinavian languages and to prevent the development of new ones through the agency of the Language Boards established in each country of the region under the auspices of the Norden Association. (Danish upper-case nouns, for example, have been changed to lower-case, in keeping with Swedish and Norwegian traditions.) But the success of such measures has so far been rather limited.

The question arises under what "regional" conditions, if any, the differences among the languages would decline. While there is no conclusive study of the subject, the history of European nationalism seems to suggest that, in the case of languages as similar to each other as the Scandinavian languages are, the various dialects and local tongues combine elements when the educational systems of various localities "merge" (students and above all teachers are ecologically mobile), and when careers, in general, are pursued in one social structure that brings together people from a variety of localities and imposes on them basically uniform language requirements. All these conditions are lacking in Scandinavia, as educational systems and social structures are fundamentally not regional but national. We, of course, do not imply that a region-state should be formed in order to reduce minor differences in language; but should a region-state be created or approximated for other reasons, we would expect Scandinavian languages gradually to merge. This, in our judgment, should not be expected to take place in the present

---

[126] Gunnar Myrdal, "Psychological Impediments to Effective International Cooperation," *Journal of Social Issues,* supplement no. 6, 1952.

union, even if tourism among the countries should be doubled and other interpersonal contacts tripled.

In sum: the great similarities in cultural, social, and ethnic background and the many historical bonds do not in themselves a union make. Their effect on the relations among the countries in a region depend on what is made of them. Large cleavages can be minimized, as were those between the United States and the USSR during World War II, and smaller differences can be emphasized, as are historical ones in the area under study. The Nordic countries have built out of a common past a set of separate units that may even be said to have a national consciousness of its own. While the last few decades of cooperation have reemphasized the shared heritage of the past and the affinity of the present, *the balance between regional sentiment and national sentiments still favors the national ones.* The fact that there are no effective regional institutions and symbols as there are national ones (the kings, the parliaments, the constitutions, supreme courts, etc.) both expresses and reinforces the superiority of national over regional identification. History is thus used to justify separateness and a rather jealous preservation of national sovereignty. Hence a broader and deeper regional integration, at least one that is more institutionalized and has its own symbolic power and unifying drive, is not present. (All Scandinavians interviewed said it is "impossible.")

While there are many shared values, mores, sentiments, and ideas in the Nordic area—the first among them being a consciousness of shared identitive assets—they are not related to a network of Nordic institutions and symbols. They are not used to establish one, nor are they significantly deepened or extended by such institutions and symbols. The role regional institutions could play in bringing about a shift to the priority of regional bonds over national ones— especially since identitive similarities (not to be confused with identitive bonds) are at so high a level—deserves some additional elucidation.

HARMONIZATION VERSUS INTEGRATION

There is no region in Europe and few exist in the world where culture, tradition, language, ethnic origin, political structure, and religion—all "background" and identitive elements—are as similar as they are in the Nordic region. Nevertheless, a United States of Scandinavia, or other forms of a regional political community, are not developing and seem unlikely to develop. The mere existence of homogeneity can provide only a convenient backdrop; it is not in itself a source of a drive toward greater integration. But since attempts have been made to expand and significantly deepen Nordic integration—attempts that, if successful, would probably have led toward a regional political community—the question of why these failed must be answered. Our answer here is in conflict with the position held by many of the citizens of the region.

The Scandinavian position is essentially that harmonization of the activities of the five national states is both the highest level of cooperation the region is capable of supporting *and* is a superior form of cooperation to that of a regional superstate. There can be little argument with the first statement. In one form it is tautological, as the inability to form a political community is derived from the fact that none has been formed so far. Surely no one would argue that a political community has been formed or that signs indicate one is about to be formed.

Interpreted differently, this statement is taken to suggest that no political community could be achieved even if greater and different kinds of efforts to bring about such a community were made. This might be a valid observation: as suggested above, the Nordic countries are a group of small powers caught in the political and economic orbits of a number of big powers; they are not free to set the level of regional integration they desire. In a sense, each is more integrated into a non-Nordic system than into the Nordic one, at least as far as power considerations go. In the view of the member countries (with the exception of Finland), the level of integration of the Nordic region is not forcibly held down, but is a voluntary Scandinavian decision to keep integration at a relatively low level in order to avoid certain "costs": risking a showdown with the USSR (Finland's concern); giving offense to Britain (Norway's concern); or moving away from the continent (Denmark's concern). But the costs seem to be of such magnitude that—unless they change considerably because of some changes in extra-Nordic systems—they make a Nordic political community rather difficult to create.

The fact that the Nordic countries are highly democratic further strengthens our statement. Less democratic governments could ignore the economic plight and psychological deprivations that large segments of their populations might suffer, especially in the short run, if they would actively pursue political unification. A Scandinavian government that would follow such a course would in all likelihood be replaced by a government more responsive to the people. The people seem to be unwilling to make any major sacrifices for so abstract a goal as political unification, especially since present systems seem to work well; hence it is felt that there is little need for greater integration.

Actually, each country is quite jealous of its national sovereignty, and the regional mode of cooperation is highly responsive to these jealousies. Little attempt is made to use regional institutions to advance regional sentiments. The fact that the Nordic Council did not establish a permanent secretariat is an illustration of the union's high responsiveness to its individual members' desires; no such organ was set up largely because of their apprehension that the council would thereby become to some degree independent of the constituent members and therefore less responsive to national pressures.[127] Further, part of the opposition to the Nordic common market was based on a belief that the imposition of common tariffs would require some form of supranational enforcing agency endowed with the power to apply sanctions to the member-states.[128]

Thus the Nordic regional system is highly responsive to its component units: it maintains without any modification the level of integration of which the member nations approve; it does not act as an independent lever to bring about a higher level of integration. Hence we conclude that from the viewpoint of unification, the Nordic structure is clearly not merely a highly responsive, but an overresponsive structure: it limits the development of regional foci of identification and of a center of allocative processes, not just to the level the region would tolerate, which is both prudent and in the long run inevitable;

[127] Anderson, *The Nordic Council,* pp. 59ff.
[128] Dolan, "The Nordic Council," pp. 524–525.

it also acts as a reflecting mirror instead of as an active agent. No wonder this is a stable but scarcely growing union! The Nordic countries seem to prefer the losses involved in maintaining full sovereignty over whatever gains delegating some powers to a regional body might entail.

The prevailing Scandinavian attitude toward supranationalism is illustrated in the following: During the negotiations over a Nordic common market, when a minority report to the Nordic Council meeting charged that the establishment of a common market would lead to wider and possibly supranational unification, the majority did not extol the virtues of this kind of union but chose to deny that it had this potential or that any such aim could be pursued by the respective governments:

The assertion that a common market of the scope provisionally envisaged should lead to an economic union and further, to a political union with supranational bodies and major losses of competence for national political authorities is mistaken, improbable and contrary to the wishes of the three governments.[129]

Supranationalism is clearly a political liability. But the fact that it is unpopular or that there is no *felt* need for it cannot in itself be taken as evidence that no need would be served by greater integration or that increased integration through intraregional efforts— difficult to envision as it is—is impossible. People in general tend to accept "satisfying" rather than optimal solutions.[130] Since there is no war and none seems imminent, a state of affluence prevails, wide-ranging welfare-state services are available, and next to no unemployment exists, the citizens are, in general, somewhat apathetic and express few felt needs. "Because everything is all right, things work well, nobody feels a need for federation," said an interviewee. "Unification is exceedingly little discussed," said another. At least theoretically, much economic benefit could derive from an economic Nordic union, increased security from a non-aligned Nordic camp, and higher status from a regional union, and still the people would be unaware of these benefits until they came about.

[129] Anderson, *The Nordic Council*, p. 206.
[130] On this tendency see James March and Herbert Simon, *Organizations*. New York: Wiley & Sons, 1958, p. 141.

Moreover, a felt need is often greatest after the opportunity to act has been forfeited, that is, after a crisis has already occurred. Thus the Scandinavians very much felt the need for a union when they faced the pressures of Nazi Germany, but creating one on short order was then impractical. The same is true for periods when the USSR suddenly increases its pressure on Finland. Finally, the felt need of a population is determined at least in part by its leadership. Hence the question arises why the Scandinavian leadership sees the present mode of regionalism as not just the only possible one, but also a superior one.

The idea that harmonization of national states renders a more effective mode of cooperation than a unified political community is the one most open to question. This statement seems to be an ideology that attempts to "explain" the somewhat embarrassing facts that despite all the identitive ties, differences in utilitarian interests prevented the development of Nordic common market, and deep differences in the conception of national security and experience prevented the foundation of a Nordic defense union—organizations that, respectively, could have been the economic and military foundations of a Nordic political community. On strictly methodological grounds, one ought always to suspect statements that imply that an existing arrangement is not only the best possible one, but also one that maximizes a whole set of values. And this is what most Scandinavian spokesmen, both experts and laymen, suggest.

More specifically, it is claimed that the Nordic countries' system of cooperation, in which national units harmonize their activities but do not surrender control over any of these activities to a regional body, allows them to act jointly and voluntarily at the same time. To the degree that similarities of interests and outlook exist, they are reflected in informal consultations, a tradition of compromise, and a genuine desire to cooperate, as well in a few institutional links of the consultive kind. Such bodies as the Nordic Council and regular meetings of ministers provide the opportunity to work out a coordinated course of action. To the degree that no such consensus exists or can be formed, the system allows each country to pursue its own course. "We have all the advantages of federation, without the disadvantages," stated one interviewee, an official of the Swedish government. The argument both in tone and in substance is quite similar to the "freedom in unity" used to support the similarly informal consultative, voluntary (but also not quite effective or extensive) cooperation of the British Commonwealth. In a typical release, the Danish Information Office pointed out that:

It is characteristic of Nordic cooperative endeavors that they avoid all political abstractions and all speculations regarding final goals. Rather, they aim at the solving of concrete, practical problems, advancing step by step and accepting gladly every conquest, no matter how small.[131]

When one then points out that the Nordic countries cooperate only on matters that have no great importance, such as some *marginal* educational, cultural, scientific, and welfare matters, and that they do not form a united regional body in matters of defense, foreign policy, or economics, one gets the response that because of international factors (such as Soviet influence over Finland) and matters of an economic nature (such as real and assumed weaknesses of the Norwegian economy), no higher level of integration could be attained, whatever the institutional arrangement. The level of integration that can be attained through harmonization has reached the point of declining marginal utility and little progress can be expected unless a new unifying factor is introduced (or unless progress is generated by extraregional processes or powers).

A third, and strong, possibility is that, because the Nordic countries are comparatively close to each other in terms of background, values, and sentiments, the establishment of a set of regional institutions could serve to overcome other unfavorable factors and unfreeze the unification process. Such institutions could provide a strong focus of regional action and loyalties, which might tip the scales to overcome the nationalist suspicions and feelings of superiority that now stand in the way of more effective and more extensive regional cooperation. (If the countries were farther apart, a mere institutional change would be less likely to provide such a focus.) It is precisely because of basic similarities of values and interests that a regional decision-making body and civil service could be highly successful.

[131] Danish Foreign Office Periodical, March 2, 1956.

No proof can be given for our proposition that if the Nordic area were to command a set of supranational institutions, a considerably higher level of integration could be attained. It might even be suggested that if such institutions did exist, this in itself would imply that a major barrier to the advancement of unification, the strong adherence to national sovereignty, had already somehow been weakened. But let us assume that such an institutional structure has come into being without any significant changes in any other circumstances, through one of those accidents with which history abounds. What effects might such an institutional structure have?

First of all, it would provide a set of regional symbols to focus identification, to promote regionalism over nationalism. Till now, nations have effectively monopolized the conditions Durkheim stated as needed for a society: "to worship" itself. Each Scandinavian country has all the marks of sovereignty from a king to a parliament. Identification with the region, on the other hand, is a highly intellectual and abstract matter, with few permanent symbols. The sporadic, short, and dull sessions of the Nordic Council, which hardly command enthusiasm, symbolize harmonization, not regional integration.

Secondly, Nordic institutions would provide a focal point around which transnational interest groups, parties, and labor unions could direct their efforts in order to create regional cleavages (for example, Nordic labor versus management) that cut across national ones. Thirdly, they would provide a "neutral" regional civil service committed to the welfare of the region and not to any particular segment of it, capable of working out compromises that would not require one nation to make concessions to another but that would require all of them to make some concessions to the community-at-large.

The Scandinavians claim that no regional decision-making institutions are needed, because the national ones, anxious to cooperate, are acting as if such institutions did exist. For instance, in the area of legislation, one Danish official pointed out:

This considerable uniformity in Scandinavian legislation is brought about by appointing inter-Scandinavian expert committees who prepare the texts of bills which the individual governments then submit to their legislatures for discussion and adoption. Thus, by enacting identical laws in the parliaments of the various countries common legislation is, in fact, achieved even though no Scandinavian parliament exists to legislate for the entire territory.[132]

But this line of analysis takes an extremely passive view of the role of institutions in the growth of a community. It suggests that to the degree that a consensus exists it can be expressed, and to the degree it does not none should be forced. But there is a third possibility, that of creating a new, additional consensus through give-and-take in regional bodies; this is easier to come by when the participants realize that a consensus must be reached or no action will be taken, a pressure that commonly operates in national parliaments. Leaving it up to the national legislatures to volunteer regionalism without such pressure tends, as we have seen, to sharply limit the areas in which consensus is reached. While many identical laws are passed by the parliaments of the various countries, their number hides the fact that policy on crucial matters is not agreed upon and cooperation on others is slow and cumbersome.

While it is difficult to see at this point any social movement—surely not any provided by the timid Norden Association—that would lead to the formation of an effective regional institutional structure, extraregional processes might provide an even more "congenial" background for Nordic unification. The lower the Cold War tensions, the closer the United States and the USSR move toward general accommodations, and especially to the degree that European tensions are diffused, the easier it will become for the Nordic NATO countries and the non-NATO ones to move toward a higher level of regional integration. Similarly, the development of the EEC will have considerable effect on the Nordic community. The EEC provides an example of a unification process that is partially supranational; the more successful it is, the more likely imitations in other regions will follow. Also, the more successful the EEC turns out to be in forming a political union of its own, which omits Nordic countries, the more likely they are to seek their own political unification. After all, EFTA itself was born as a response to the EEC. Similarly,

[132] Strahl, p. 114.

if the EEC were to fail or regress to become just a much larger free trade area (including both the present EEC and EFTA countries), there still would be room, though not much motivation, for the accelerated unification of subareas, as for instance the Benelux union. The most divisive effects on the Nordic region will be generated as long as some Nordic countries continue to expect to become members of the EEC while others expect to stay out, as seems to be the case at the present time.

In sum: The Nordic area is not, as it is often put, one of a high predisposition toward unification because of the great similarity of identitive assets of member countries and the ideology of cooperation they share. These are offset by extraregional factors, commitments to national sovereignty, and lack of leadership. An effective regional institutional structure could have tipped the scale, but one has not been created.

CHAPTER 7

A Growing Union: The European Economic Community (1958–1964)

———————•◦•———————

The European Economic Community (EEC) is not only maintaining its levels of integration and scope; during the period analyzed here its unification was advanced. Much of the success of the EEC is due to the fact that the institutional structure initially introduced demanded the backing of only a comparatively limited amount of integrating power; its development relied instead on the availability of an increasing amount and variety of such power, an effective system of communication and representation, and the implementation of a gradualist strategy. The very success of the EEC, however, has created forces that threaten its future development.

INTEGRATING POWER: AN EFFECTIVE DISTRIBUTION[1]

A discussion of the EEC must distinguish what the Community is at present from what it might later become. To mention but a few of the possible directions the EEC might follow, it could develop

---

[1] Because of the extensive treatment the EEC has received in both the professional and the lay press, the basic facts about its development are fairly well known. For this reason the present discussion devotes less space to factual representation and hence more to analysis than those of other cases. It was also considered unnecessary to maintain even a semblance of chronological order in the presentation.

229

into a single economic unit, a confederation, or a United States of Europe. At the end of 1963, it was still chiefly a customs union, in which 60 percent of the tariffs among the members had been removed and tariffs levied on nonmembers had been harmonized to about two thirds of the planned level.[2] In the period between January 1, 1958, when the Treaty of Rome came into effect and the end of 1963, trade among the six member-countries had increased by 85 percent and their total Gross National Products by 33 percent.[3] Though confronted with a major crisis following the French vote against the admission of Britain to the EEC, the Community not only survived, but turned to expand its scope by steps aimed at harmonizing the economic, fiscal, and monetary policies of the members. The EEC is thus by far the most successful union of those examined here. What kind of leadership directed this successful effort? Was there any one unit that, more than others, controlled the formation and development of the EEC? Does any one unit make disproportionate contributions to the Community, or, conversely, is there one that derives a disproportionate share of assets from the EEC? Two kinds of units will be examined with these questions in mind: the member countries as potential internal elites, and the United States as an external elite.

Two Political Elites in an Egalitarian Economic Union

Of central importance is the fact that the main utilitarian benefits that the members of this union enjoy are not derived from any one member, nor are they drawn from the contributions of any one elite. Rather they are generated by exchanges among the members, by increased intercountry trade. (At least, this is what the members believe.) Equality of benefits is approximately matched by that of contributions; all member-countries made some sacrifices to bring the

---

[2] On January 1, 1961, there was a 30 percent reduction of the difference between national tariffs and the target tariffs of the EEC. The target tariffs, however, were not based (as originally planned) on some average of the national levels, but on a level 20 percent lower. The second reduction, of another 30 percent, took place on July 1, 1963.

[3] *The Wall Street Journal,* January 24, 1963, and the EEC information service.

union about, but none, it seems, made significantly more than the others.

It has long been accepted that increased international trade is beneficial to all participants; but it does not follow that they benefit to the same degree, even if they are in a similar stage of economic development. A highly detailed study of the various members of the Community would probably show some differences of gains among them; however, there is no feeling in the EEC that one country consistently made more significant gains from the formation of the union than did the others. The same holds in relation to the sacrifices made in order to bring the union about. Protection has been reduced for inefficient coal mines in Belgium, small farmers in West Germany, the motor industry in Italy, textile manufacturers in France, and so forth; but there is no evidence that any member made significantly disproportionate sacrifices. Nor is there any feeling among the Six that this was or is the case. From this viewpoint, the union is highly egalitarian.

In the few cases in which one country or sector was thought to suffer disproportionately from the transition process, the Community either allowed a delay in the reduction of tariffs or in the elimination of other protectionist devices, or the member was otherwise compensated through available funds. Thus, for instance, Italian shipbuilders and French producers of paper pulp continued to receive various forms of state aid to facilitate their modernization and hence their adjustment to new market conditions.

Typical of an egalitarian union, the control of the EEC is to a large degree in the hands of a system-elite and not under the control of a member-elite. The system-elites are organs established under the Treaty of Rome, including the Economic Commission, the Council of Ministers, and the Court of Justice. Unlike most international organs, those of the EEC have some supranational authority and, even more, supranational power. They are staffed and controlled by all member countries and do not serve as an indirect means for an elite-member to exercise undue influence.

The Economic Commission, the executive body of the EEC, draws about one quarter of its staff from Germany, France, Italy, and Benelux. The members of the staff are each pledged to serve the

Community rather than their national states. In general, such formal pledges may not assure system- rather than unit-orientation; in the commission, however, the staff has developed a genuine spirit of international civil service and a "European" enthusiasm. "By no means all of the commission employees, even of the upper ranks, are dedicated 'Europeans' . . . Still, the spirit of 'Europeanism' prevails, and those employees who do not share it keep their reservations to themselves."[4] This spirit is reinforced by Community life in a suburb of Brussels, Uccle, where many of the staff live and where they have their own school and shopping center, diplomatic immunity, and prestigious "European" license plates. Their relationships with the Brussels society are indifferent, which further orients them toward each other and enhances the "European" spirit.[5] Thus, not only formally, but also in practice, the commission is a system-elite, above and distinguishable from any one member.

The Economic Commission, though, is not the ultimate authority of the EEC. It is subordinate to the Council of Ministers, in which the governments of the member countries are represented, usually by their foreign ministers. It is in this organ that an elite-country might seek to exert special power over the system; but the Council of Ministers itself—with some notable exceptions—tends to act like a system-elite. It is an organ through which the Six seek to harmonize their interests and in which EEC interests per se are actively taken into account. In the negotiations, the spirit is one of cooperation rather than of exclusive focus on the furtherance of respective national interests. This is apparent in the reluctance of council members to be the last to hold out against a resolution and deadlock the Community; France's veto of British membership is a rare exception, not the rule. It is also reflected in the efforts of the ministers of foreign affairs, the regular members of the council, to urge their less "European"-oriented colleagues (such as the ministers in charge of economic matters, transportation, energy, or agriculture) to make

---

[4] John Brooks, "The Common Market—II," *The New Yorker,* September 29, 1962, p. 62.

[5] The significance of such Community correlates to organizational life for the reinforcing of organizational norms is explored in the author's *A Comparative Analysis of Complex Organizations.* New York: The Free Press of Glencoe, 1961, chap. 5.

concessions in order to reach a consensus. Even when the ministers act solely as representatives of their respective states, and when such representation runs counter to Community needs and trends, no one country regularly prevails. On several occasions the more powerful members (by extra-Community standards) have had to give in to other members. Thus, for instance, in 1961 France finally agreed to a 20 percent reduction of external tariffs and Germany to the acceleration of integration, though initially both were quite strongly opposed to these steps. In short, the Council of Ministers at best acts to express Community needs; at worst, as an intergovernmental unit in which no single country has a decisive elite position.

The relationship between the Economic Commission and the Council of Ministers also reflects the system orientation. According to the Treaty of Rome, the supranational commission was to initiate and formulate proposals, which were to be presented to the council for approval. In practice, the two have grown together and their functions have become somewhat mixed. The commission not only presents proposals but consults with the national governments and interest groups, maintains continuous close contact with the national permanent representatives in Brussels, and confers with the large body of experts, both those of the EEC and those attached to national delegations, that has formed in Brussels. Moreover, the commission sits in council meetings, acting as if it were a seventh member, one especially concerned with Community interests. In this way, the commission has more power than the makers of the treaty envisioned. Critics in the European Parliamentary Assembly, which is much more "European," that is, system-oriented, than the national governments, have attacked the commission for being coopted by the council and the national delegations of representatives and experts. But while it is true that the commission does consult and consider national positions (a point to which we return below), a detailed analysis of several critical decisions reached by EEC organs shows that the opposite is happening. The commission often "coopts" the national delegations, and in a sense the Council of Ministers, to its supranational Community spirit and orientation, rather than the reverse.[6]

[6] Leon N. Lindberg, "Political Dynamics of European Economic Integration," unpublished Ph.D. dissertation, University of California, Berkeley, 1962.

The Court of Justice has not had an opportunity to function extensively, but its structure is clearly as system-oriented as that of the other organs, if not more so. Its seven judges are chosen from among persons of high reputation and unquestioned impartiality. They are appointed for periods of six years by the governments acting in common agreement.[7]

Although the above description reflects fairly strong system-elites that do not discriminate among members, this generally valid picture of a highly egalitarian union must be qualified. To begin with, the six member countries do not have the same number of votes in the council. The actual voting arrangements are rather complex; there are five different voting procedures. But the main pattern, both in terms of frequency and significance of issues covered, is that of a qualified majority. Here, Germany, France, and Italy have four votes each, the Netherlands and Belgium two each, and Luxembourg one. The majority required is 12 votes out of 17. To preclude a big-power combination against the smaller states, the vote has to be either by consensus of four countries or in support of the commission proposal. Until recently, the significance of this difference was limited, since voting was almost always unanimous; it does, however, indicate some recognition of power differences among the members. Moreover, whatever the formal structure may be, the members cannot but be conscious of the differences in their international status and economic power. This is one of the reasons the Benelux countries continue with their own accelerated unification; as long as they act together, they feel that there is a better chance to be heard. This is also one reason why they are favorable toward Britain's joining the EEC. The Benelux states feel that Britain would support them on many issues and that British membership would tend to counterbalance either France or Germany as well as a French-German axis.

Thus far neither France nor Germany has used its greater weight to effect the EEC exchange and allocative processes; in utilitarian matters their power remains largely latent. In other spheres, however, the power of these two elite-countries is more evident. France blocked British membership in the EEC in January 1963 against the

[7] EEC Treaty, Article 138.

desires of the other five members. In 1960 and again in 1961, France in effect vetoed proposals for increased supranational unification, preferring instead an intergovernmental confederal structure.[8] When the resistance of the smaller members to the French proposals proved too strong, France in 1962 initiated measures that were intended to bring about the less central type of political union it prefers with Germany alone. These steps provided for the regular meeting of heads of state and foreign ministers to formulate joint positions in various international matters, to plan intergovernmental coordination of cultural matters, and to allow assignment of armed forces units to commands of the other country.[9] It is to be noted, however, that though other EEC members might later participate in these French-German programs, by the end of 1963 France was unable to gain acceptance of its position on such matters by the other members. (The smaller countries feared being outweighed in a tighter union led by France and Germany and favored British membership both was a counterbalance and as an assurance of a more pro-American line which they tend to favor.) With the replacement of Adenauer by Erhard in October 1963, a German government less receptive to French leadership came into office; the drive for political union of the two states, never very strong, slowed down considerably, showing once more that no one country can regularly and continuously lead the way in the EEC.

With regard to the relationship between these two more powerful members of the EEC, France has an edge in the Community over West Germany. This expresses itself more in intellectual initiative and leadership than in strict power terms. The title "father of the EEC" is usually reserved for Jean Monnet, a Frenchman, who recruited a high proportion of the first half of the Economic Commission from the Quai d'Orsay. While both Adenauer and de Gasperi made significant contributions to the advancement of European unification, the unofficial title of the European Coal and Steel Community (which served as the take-off base of the EEC) is the Schuman

[8] See Roy Pryce, *The Political Future of the European Community.* London: John Marshband, Ltd., 1962, p. 42.

[9] *New York Times,* November 11, 1962. These programs have since been embodied in the French–German Treaty of Cooperation signed on January 22, 1963 by Chancellor Adenauer and President de Gaulle.

Plan, named after the French Foreign Minister at that time, Robert Schuman. Another Frenchman, Robert Marjolin, chaired the study group that outlined the Action Program, a major policy document specifying plans for further economic unification in the post-1962 period (discussed below). When Ludwig Erhard, then Germany's Economic Minister, criticized the plan, he stated that he saw French handwriting in it.

While Germany does not match French leadership, it is clearly the second most powerful member of the EEC, significantly above not just any one of the others, but all of them put together. When France was blocked, it was usually because Germany supported the positions of some or all of the other members; and, when the French position prevailed, it was often only after it had been adjusted to take German preferences into account. Adenauer is believed to have indicated his willingness to go along with a French veto of British membership in the EEC; he neither liked nor trusted the British, at least since the days they unseated him from his post as the mayor of Cologne in 1945.[10]

As of late 1963, the leadership edge of France was declining. With the accession of the Erhard government, Germany's passivity was replaced by a more active and "flexible" policy, and a more pro-British one. Above all, Germany responded to United States advances that offered to strengthen the hand of the Germans in retaliation for de Gaulle's reduced commitments to the American-led NATO alliance. While there was no open German-French struggle over leadership by 1964, the lack of clear definition of a superior elite caused some loss in directiveness and a slowdown in unification, especially of new sectors. De Gaulle had to threaten that "perhaps the Common Market will disappear"[11] before the crisis generated by German objections to the EEC-outlined (and French-favored) common agricultural policy was overcome. Little progress was made in the unification of military and foreign policy matters once Erhard attained power. In the event of the sudden departure of de Gaulle, while Germany at the same time continued to be led by

[10] *New York Times,* December 9, 1963. See also George Lichtheim, *The New Europe,* New York: Frederick A. Praeger, Inc., 1963, p. 53.
[11] *New York Times,* December 19, 1963.

an effective government, the leadership edge of the Common Market could be shifted from Paris to Bonn.

In sum, the EEC is a highly egalitarian union, in which comparatively strong system-elites operate. The elite-members do not make significant extra-utilitarian contributions or draw a disproportionate share of the utilitarian benefits of the system. Their main power differential is expressed in matters concerning the inclusion of new members in the Community and in the political sphere.

It is in line with our hypothesis that consensus and commitment to the Community are highest in the utilitarian sphere, in which the elite members exercise little of their power, and lower regarding questions of new membership and political unification, wherein these elites have a greater tendency to exercise their influence. When the Community faced its biggest crisis, over French rejection of British membership, the progress of unification was greatly slowed down. When the accelerated pace of the precrisis years was revised early in 1964, following the formulation of a common agricultural policy in December 1963 and an antiinflation policy in April 1964, the initiative and progress came again from the utilitarian, and not the political, sphere. The reason the EEC does not lack decisiveness in the utilitarian sphere, despite little or no elite action by any member, is that the central organs of the Community effectively perform the elite role. As the leadership in the political sphere became more divided between two elites with the accession of Erhard, progress in this sphere was slowed down.

Should Britain join the union, the stability of the power structure is likely to be much further reduced. While, on the one hand, a new pool of civil servants with a long tradition of impartiality would be available, on the other hand, the member-elite structure, our earlier theoretical considerations suggest, would be significantly disrupted. The EEC now has two member-elites, which are in general—though declining—agreement and coalition. The presence of a third elite-member, Britain, would open the Pandora's box of a three-elite structure alluded to above.[12] Even now, when Britain as an outsider cannot directly challenge the member-elites over the leadership posi-

[12] See below, p. 288.

tion, British policy places strains on the union and on the two-elite French-German coalition by trying to play Germany against France. The success of the EEC during its first five years rests in part, we suggest, upon a combination of a highly egalitarian union and a two-elite structure, in which one elite has an edge and the other is in general supportive of and not challenging to the position and policy of the superior one. Should Britain join the EEC, the succeeding years would provide an opportunity to test our proposition that a tri-elite structure would be considerably more conflict-prone and less successful. But then, the French-German coalition can be weakened not just by a new member-elite, but also by the acts of an external one, which brings us to the role of the United States in the process of European unification.

Internalization of American Controls

In the partially destroyed Europe of 1945 and during the following period of reconstruction, the United States played the role of an elite that provided resources, initiative, and direction. The United States carried out this role in part as the leading member of American-European organizations, such as NATO; in part as a half-external elite, as in the Organization for European Economic Cooperation (OEEC), in which the United States was only an associate member; and in part as a fully external elite, as a contributor to the European Coal and Steel Community (ECSC). The reason the United States could be an internal and an external elite at the same time is that the postwar evolution of international cooperation proceeded on at least two levels: that of European regional cooperation, to which the United States was an external elite, and that of Atlantic or Western-bloc integration, with respect to which the United States was an internal elite. The evolution of Atlantic unification will not be discussed here; it suffices to say that unification on the two levels did not develop in the same way; as part of Europe become more integrated, the integration of the Atlantic region did not substantially increase.[13] With an increased level of integration and extent of scope,

[13] For a discussion of the author's viewpoint on Atlantic unification, *Winning Without War.* Garden City, N.Y.: Doubleday & Company, Inc., 1964, chap. 2.

the European union gradually internalized functions that the United States performed and controlled as an external elite. This internalization took place on three major fronts: economic, military, and foreign policy. The EEC directly internalized only economic functions and powers, but its unification had important effects on two other, less advanced, internalization processes.

European economic cooperation in the postwar period was initially an outgrowth of the Marshall Plan. In his first public discussion of the Plan, in a speech on June 5, 1947, United States Secretary of State George C. Marshall emphasized that before the United States could offer assistance, "There must be some agreement *among* the countries of Europe as to the requirements of the situation and the part these countries themselves will take."[14] In July 1947, the representatives of 16 European nations met in Paris to form the Committee of European Economic Cooperation to draft such a plan. This was completed the following two months and included provisions for cooperation in the reduction of tariffs and the removal of other barriers to free trade and intercountry mobility of people.[15] Only after the United States representatives examined this plan did Congress in April 1948 adopt the Foreign Assistance Act. Thereafter, the European states set up the OEEC, in which the United States and Canada were associate members, to plan the allocation and use of American funds and other measures for economic cooperation. European unification was thus in part initiated and financially supported by an external elite. Participation in the OEEC increased the utilitarian assets available to the European participants without either necessitating cost to them or requiring a reallocation among them. This step toward unification was thus rewarding and comparatively "painless."

In the 1949 OEEC Council meetings, it became evident that the organization would continue to function after the cessation of American aid and efforts to further European cooperation. As the OEEC became less oriented toward satisfying the conditions of a grant and more interested in the direct benefits of economic cooperation, it

[14] Stephen S. Goodspeed, *The Nature and Function of International Organization.* New York: Oxford University Press, 1959, p. 569.
[15] *International Organization,* p. 569.

explicitly advocated decreased dependency on the United States. One of the most successful steps in this direction was the formation by the OEEC of the European Payments Union (EPU) in July 1950. The EPU was a European organization: although its policy was set and supervised by the OEEC Council, it had only European members, and it was thus one step removed from American influence. Moreover, the purpose of the EPU was to enable the European states to trade more with each other and to decrease their imports from the United States and hence their need for borrowing or receiving American dollars as grants. This was largely achieved in the following six years. It was the formation of the OEEC and the successful operation of the EPU that provided a foundation for the formation in 1952 of the European Coal and Steel Community, the immediate forerunner and takeoff base of the EEC.

While the ECSC was, even more than the EPU, a strictly European organization, the United States in 1954 contributed to its success by granting it a loan of $100 million through the Import-Export Bank. The effect of the loan was further increased, as it served to make available additional credit in Switzerland. These funds were used to facilitate the adjustment of the member-countries to the ECSC by providing the financing to modernize plants and mines; to retrain workers, especially Italian steel workers and miners in Sardinia; and to increase the attractiveness of the Schuman Plan to labor by financing housing projects, especially in Germany.[16] Thus once more the external elite contributed assets to internal allocation that made a unification step more rewarding and less demanding. But unlike the more continuous flow of Marshall Plan funds, this 1954 contribution to the ECSC was the only significant economic support afforded by the United States.

By the late fifties, with the rapid pace of recovery and economic growth, Europe was not only independent of direct American aid, but was asked to come to the assistance of the United States when the dollar crisis become more acute in 1960.[17] European cartoonists

[16] Ernst B. Haas, *The Uniting of Europe.* Stanford, Calif.: Stanford University Press, 1958, pp. 69, 92–93.

[17] For a discussion of disturbances in the balance of payments, see Don D. Humphrey, *The United States and the Common Market.* New York: Frederick A. Praeger, Inc., 1962, pp. 98–122. See also Robert Triffin, *Gold and the Dollar Crisis,* revised edition. New Haven, Conn.: Yale University Press, 1961.

could not resist portraying the patron coming to ask for charity from those who were yesterday on his relief list. In the economic area, the process of moving away from the aid and hence the implied influence of the external elite was more or less complete. A disproportional part of Western international commitments, especially defense, were still borne by the United States. While, for instance, the United States spent about 10 percent of its GNP in 1963 on defense, France spent only 5 percent and the percentage of the other EEC countries was even lower. But many Europeans did not regard these commitments as "theirs," and the trend was also toward reducing these shared undertakings.

Similar but less extensive shifts have occurred in military and foreign policy. These need be discussed here only briefly, since many of the issues are far broader than an analysis of the evolution of the EEC. Immediately following World War II, European defense was almost exclusively dependent upon American military forces and atomic weapons. An effort to form a European defense alliance by Britain, France, and the Benelux countries, the 1948 Brussels Treaty Organization, soon proved to be inadequate without major American assistance. This inadequacy led in 1949 to the North Atlantic Treaty, the basis of NATO, an undertaking largely financed by the United States and under the supreme command of an American general.

In the next decade, European contributions to NATO grew. At the same time their control of allied policy increased, but did not reach a level considered satisfactory to many Europeans.[18] A new effort to establish an exclusively European defense organization, the European Defense Community (EDC), was made in the early fifties. The planned EDC, although mainly intended to allow French control of German rearmament, would also have reduced the role of the United States in the European military picture. It was defeated in 1954 for reasons discussed below. The failure of the EDC was followed by efforts to revive the for-Europeans-only Brussels Treaty Organization and by the inclusion of Germany and Italy in the newly formed

[18] On the changing balance between Europe and America during the period here considered, see Alastair Buchan, *NATO in the 1960's,* New York: Frederick A. Praeger, Inc., 1960, pp. 34–45.

Western European Union in May 1955. But this organization by itself had little practical value.[19]

In the middle and late fifties it became increasingly evident that even if such a European defense organization had succeeded, Europe would still have been dependent on the American nuclear deterrent as the major source of its protection. Since then, the tendency to internalize the functions of the external elite has found a new expression in efforts to provide national nuclear forces, first by France, and as considered from time to time by West Germany. Britain was the first to develop a national deterrent, though its commitment to its development varied over the years. In the period between 1962 and early 1964, the United Kingdom's enthusiasm for a national deterrent was on the decline. Germany did not have nuclear weapons, but France actively continued to form its *force de frappe,* which strained its relations with the United States. By 1964, de Gaulle's France had sharply reduced its NATO ties, aiming to make itself, and the Europe that followed its leadership, more autonomous in military matters.

As of 1962, the partial internalization of the military function by France became highly relevant to the EEC. A nuclear deterrent requires a complex and expensive military capability. The economic success of the EEC gave rise to the idea that the Community, or part of it, might serve as the economic base of a European nuclear force with or without Britain, inside or outside NATO, but under less or no American control. To the degree that other EEC members might not be willing to accept this, France seemed to favor the building of a French deterrent rather than an EEC force.[20]

Seeking to maintain the Atlantic Alliance and its leadership of the West, attempting to check de Gaulle's control of Europe, and anxious to prevent the spread of nuclear weapons, the United States offered the Europeans a small, shared American-European nuclear force, usually referred to as the MLF (multilateral force). After some hesitation, Germany accepted the proposal with growing enthusiasm and declared its willingness to bear up to 67 percent of the European

[19] See Hans A. Schmitt, *The Path to European Union.* Baton Rouge, La.: Louisiana State University Press, 1962, pp. 225–229.
[20] Walter Lippmann, *Western Unity and the Common Market.* Boston, Mass.: Little, Brown & Company, 1962, pp. 19 ff.

expense involved. France completely refused to participate. The United States thus blocked the incipient military alliance of Germany and France, and limited the extension of the European internalization of this sector.

By 1964, the future of the MLF was very uncertain. In many ways it still could lead to a European rather than an Atlantic force. But while Germany moves toward a "special relationship" with the United States in military matters and France maintains a national deterrent, and reduces its military ties to the United States, European unification led by the French and the Germans cannot but suffer directly in scope (by regarding military internalization) and indirectly in other sectors as well as in the level of integration.

There is generally only a limited use for an independent nuclear force in the absence of an independent foreign policy. Until now, the EEC as such has had little foreign policy of its own. Still, since late 1959 (with few exceptions), the foreign ministers of the Six have met at three-month intervals to discuss common problems, from Berlin to the Congo. Much attention has been paid to the fact that France follows more and more a foreign policy of its own, in refusing to accede to the treaty for the partial cessation of nuclear tests, in recognizing Communist China, in favoring neutralization of Vietnam, etc. Less attention has been paid to the fact that on several foreign policy matters France and West Germany take a rather similar position. Germany, for instance, was extremely reluctant to sign the same test ban treaty France refused to sign. Germany and France favor a more firm policy on Berlin than does the United States. In matters of foreign trade, the EEC as a whole is developing collective representation; ambassadors are accredited to the EEC. In the near future all commercial treaties with nonmembers will have to be negotiated through the EEC. This will require the development of a foreign policy, at least on such matters as the extent and terms of trade with members of the Soviet bloc, Africa, Latin America, and other areas. Here, too, there are signs of a difference in approach between the United States and the EEC. The United States favors the elimination of trade barriers on items of which it and the EEC produce more than 80 percent of the global total, and favors world price stabilization efforts on items explored by Latin America and some other areas. The EEC, however, favors a comparatively more protectionist policy, coupled with special concessions to those African states with which its members have some political ties, that is, with most of the former French, Belgian, and Italian colonies. These differences in foreign economic policy between the United States and the EEC were often represented in the American press in 1963 and 1964 as reflecting the French position, and thus, in turn, the personal views and preferences of President de Gaulle. Actually, to the United States' surprise, the Six formed a joint policy and a united front in the "Kennedy round" of negotiations on tariff cuts and in the 1964 Trade and Development conference in Geneva.[21] While Germany again tended to favor the American position, for instance regarding the level of external tariffs, it was more in line with the Community and with French leadership in these trade matters than it was in military ones. In short, whole the development of an independent foreign policy on the EEC level is limited, the trend is in the same direction: a reduction of United States influence over European policy and the internalization of the control of this sphere of action by the EEC as a union or by its leading members.

THE EXTERNAL ELITE AND THE INTERNAL POWER STRUCTURE

How did the United States use its influence in Europe during the period it served as an effective elite? In general, it favored unification. It provided financial support for the ECSC and moral support for the EEC and it exerted pressure on Britain to join the EEC rather than establish a rival bloc, the European Free Trade Association (EFTA).[22] It objected to the participation of neutral members (especially Sweden and Switzerland, and to a lesser degree Austria) in the EEC,[23] as part of its efforts to tie the Community as closely as possible to the Western bloc and its leadership. While this policy was opposed to certain extensions of the union, it was not aimed against

[21] On U.S. surprise, see Peter Forbath, "Coming to Terms with the Common Market," *The Reporter,* June 20, 1963, p. 26.

[22] See U. W. Kitzinger, *The Challenge of the Common Market.* Oxford: Basil Blackwell, 1962 second edition, pp. 109ff.

[23] *New York Times,* April 4, 1962.

the union itself, and it might in fact turn out to have been supportive of the existing union by limiting the number of new members. A flood of new ones might have "diluted" the integrating power to the subminimal point. (This problem is further discussed below.)

In terms of its support for specific countries, the United States influence was in line with the emerging power structure in one case and not in two others. As early as the late forties, the United States realized the important role Germany was going to play in the recovery of Europe and helped Germany to regain a place in the European Community.[24] It supported German rearmament and the inclusion of Germany in NATO and the WEU. Since Germany today is a major NATO force, with troops totaling 12 divisions committed to the alliance,[25] and since it is perhaps the most important power in central Europe, the direction of United States influence and the trend of postwar European history supported each other.

The same cannot be said for American relations with Britain and France. The United States has treated Britain as a major power and as a close ally, deserving of special consideration and trust.[26] France under the Fourth Republic, with an unstable government, a large Communist party, a war in Algeria, and fewer cultural ties to the United States, was treated as a weak expower and regarded with some suspicion. Not only did the United States share nuclear secrets with Britain alone, but it often consulted the British government before taking an important step in the international arena without consulting France or even informing the French about an impending change of policy.

In retrospect this seems like a miscalculation since France's power has grown much stronger under the leadership of de Gaulle, while that of the United Kingdom was never as high as was implied by American policies—and has declined further with the slow prog-

---

[24] See *Britain in Western Europe,* Chatham House Study Group Report, Royal Institute of International Affairs. London: Oxford University Press, 1956, pp. 25 ff.

[25] This total amounts to about half the ground strength of NATO forces; Germany is the largest single national contributor to the conventional strength of the alliance.

[26] An obvious illustration of this occurred in 1958 when Congress amended the McMahon Act to permit sharing American nuclear knowledge with Britain, but not with France or any other state.

ress of EFTA, the success of the EEC, and the sluggish economy at home.

American policies, to the degree that they were inconsistent with European power trends, made the admission of Britain more difficult and strained relations within the EEC. France, as an internal leader of the union endeavoring to reduce American influence in Europe, did not want the most trusted ally of the former external elite in the EEC.[27] De Gaulle pointed out to a visiting group of deputies on January 24, 1963, that Britain disqualified itself as a European power at Nassau by allowing one of the vital attributes of its national sovereignty, the British nuclear deterrent, to become dependent on the United States, and by allowing the United States unilaterally to cancel its earlier commitments to deliver Skybolt missiles without even a protest from London. Britain in Europe, the General said, would be like a "traveling salesman" of United States interests.[28] The other EEC states, especially the Netherlands and Italy and, as of 1964, Germany, objected to the French position, responding in part to American prodding. By early 1964, it was not clear to what degree the union had been strained by the difference in American and French viewpoints; nor could it be determined at this stage whether United States influence would, in the end, be found to have limited European unification (by unwittingly helping to keep the British out) or enhanced it (by helping to prevent the excessive internal strain that British membership might have caused), if indeed it had any lasting effect at all. Whatever the answer to these questions, United States influence over the policy of the EEC in economic matters had declined; it was inferior to French influence; and it was not in line with the West European or EEC power structure. (It is possible, however, that in the post–de Gaulle period this structure could change or

[27] De Gaulle is on record as saying, in June 1962: "You speak to me of Europe. I prefer Europe to NATO, and among all the forms of Europe it is that of the Six I like best." Cited in *Manchester Guardian Weekly*, February 14, 1963, p. 2.

[28] Edmond Taylor, "After Brussels," *The Reporter*, February 14, 1963, pp. 29–30. See also Miriam Camp, *Britain and the European Community*. London: Oxford University Press, 1964, and Edward Whiting Fox, "The France of Charles de Gaulle," *Current History*, vol. 47 (1964), pp. 332–338.

possibly be changed, to fit the 1963–1964 American policy.) The union seemed strong enough by 1964 to weather the resulting strain, as long as it was not weakened by other processes.[29]

INTEGRATING POWER: AN EFFECTIVE COMPOSITION

IDENTITIVE POWER IS ADDED TO UTILITARIAN

An examination of the general increase in the integrating power of the EEC from 1957 through 1963 shows not that one power was enlarged as another declined, but that both utilitarian and identitive integrating power increased. (The EEC has but minuscule coercive power.[30]) The following analysis attempts to demonstrate that while both kinds of power have increased, identitive power increased more. When the EEC went into effect early in 1958, identitive power was small and the main integrating power was utilitarian. By the end of 1963, the Community had a significant identitive power; the utilitarian power was still the larger,[31] but by then it shared the integrating task with a strong identitive one.

The EEC was initiated after the efforts to form a common market

[29] "Agreements, cartels and financial interpenetrations make up the cement which binds the Common Market together, and this is a mortar strong enough to weather all political storms." Jean Daniel, "Can de Gaulle Do It?", *The New Republic,* March 2, 1963, p. 9. For an outstanding analysis of the effect of military policy on the unification of Europe, see Raymond Aron, Le Grand Débat. Paris: Calmann-Levy, 1963, esp. chap. 5.

[30] Both the ECSC High Authority and the EEC Commission might place levies on various products and fine parties (including nations and corporations), for violations of their rulings. National or municipal police forces would enforce these, as well as the rulings of the Court of Justice, directly—that is without the need for approval of the national governments—if fines should not be voluntarily paid. Thus the Community does have some coercive power, although it has not yet played an active role in the context of the power used. Hence it is not further discussed here; on the coercive power of the EEC, see Article 192 of the Treaty of Rome.

[31] These powers cannot be measured with any precision, but it would seem that the EEC could pursue unification, at least for a while, without much of the identitive power that has been accumulated; while this would seem impossible without the utilitarian power. In this sense, the utilitarian power was "larger."

among the 16 members of the OEEC had failed, following the success of the Benelux union, and as a direct outcome of the spillover
and success of the ECSC. All these were utilitarian organizations.
The 16-member OEEC was too heterogeneous to serve as the instrument of a broad-scope unification; Britain especially could not rec-
oncile its position with the supranational tendencies of many of the
Continental states. The fair success of the Benelux union was encouraging; it provided an example for the planners of the EEC, and
prepared the ground by partially unifying three of its future members. An agreement to form a similar utilitarian union among France,
Italy, and the Benelux states in 1949 was never put into effect.[32]
Negotiations were later expanded to include West Germany, both
because France felt that the best way to control a resurgent Germany
was to have it within rather than an outside a European union and
because of the success of the ECSC (in which Germany was a member), which set many procedural precedents for the EEC.

The ECSC, formed in 1952, initiated the successful unification of
the coal and steel sectors of the Six. Between 1952 and 1960, the
output of products subject to the ECSC increased by 35 percent, but
intra-Community trade in the same products increased by 200 percent. In 1952, only 16 percent of these products were traded in the
Community; by 1960; this proportion rose to about 33 percent.[33]
Moreover, the ECSC also triggered a spill-over process that generated other processes bringing pressures for further utilitarian unification.[34] In order to form a free market for these industries within
the limits of the Community, it was necessary to remove frontier
charges and other discriminatory national transportation rates, since
otherwise these could serve as an indirect means for a government
to subsidize its coal or steel industry. A Community-wide, long-run
policy on coal production could not be developed effectively without
some Community policy on other sources of energy, especially—it
was believed at that time—in the new field of atomic power. This
led to the formation of Euratom, a sharing of atomic research and

[32] This was the project referred to as "FRITALUX."
[33] Richard Mayne, "European Integration in the New Europe: A Statistical
Approach," *Daedalus,* vol. 93 (1964), p. 121.
[34] Haas, *Uniting of Europe,* pp. 103–110; 291 ff.

planning on the Community level for the development and use of atomic energy. Because of the extensive effects that the steel and coal industries have on the level of economic activity in general, the evolving ECSC made apparent the desirability of forming common fiscal, countercyclical, and investment policies. In short, the freeing of trade in the products of these two industries triggered processes that stimulated expansion in the scope of utilitarian unification.

The spill-over affected not just the utilitarian structures of the member societies. The ECSC has a supranational system-elite, the High Authority. The labor unions of the six countries realized the need to work together to present their positions before the High Authority, as did the steel and coal producers of the member states. A parallel development took place in regard to the political parties of the Six, with Conservatives, Social Democrats, and Liberals establishing various organs for mutual cooperation on matters relating to the ECSC.[35] Thus national interest groups became, to a degree, transnational.

The main support for the ECSC, as far as interest groups are concerned, initially came from the industrialists, especially of the larger industries (other than the French). In order to win the support of labor and to equalize working conditions to allow competition under equal conditions, the ECSC worked toward harmonization throughout the Community by *upward leveling.* This approach looks to the best conditions in any one of the member states as the standard toward which to advance the working conditions of the others. Thus, the work week was shortest in France, wages highest in Luxembourg, paid vacations most extensive in Belgium, and so forth. Moreover, a loan from the United States was used, in part, to ease the adjustment of workers, who had to learn new skills because of the effects of the ECSC, by providing for their retraining and mobility. A number of housing projects for workers was begun, and research on industrial health and safety was undertaken.[36] In short, allocation of utilitarian assets obtained from the outside "cushioned" the adjustment to the

[35] William Diebold, Jr., *The Schuman Plan.* New York: Frederick A. Praeger, Inc., 1959, pp. 458 ff.
[36] *The Schuman Plan,* pp. 432–433.

ECSC and increased the support of the labor unions for the unification process.[37]

The utilitarian power, in particular that generated by the success of the ECSC and its economic and administrative spill-over effects, both helped to initiate the EEC and was supportive of its development since 1957. Like the ECSC, the EEC, rather than forcing a reallocation of utilitarian assets among its members, augmented the assets of all participants. The average growth rate was an unusually high 14 percent for 1959, 7.9 percent for 1960, 5.2 percent for 1961, 4.9 percent for 1962, and about 4 percent in 1963. (On the average, growth was more than twice that of the United States or Britain in the same period.)

This economic growth cannot be credited exclusively to the formation of the EEC. In part, it was due to the general economic growth of the member countries that had already been begun in the preceding period.[38] Growth was also due, in part, to internal changes in the member countries unrelated to the formation of the EEC, such as the return of de Gaulle to power in 1958. De Gaulle's return led to the stabilization of the French government, the devaluation of the franc by about 17 percent, a checking of increasing wages and prices, elimination of the large costs of the war in Algeria, and other measures. In part, however, growth seems to have been due to the increased intercountry trade stimulated by the EEC. In the first four years of the Community, this trade increased by 72 percent, while trade with EFTA countries increased by only 36 percent and trade with the rest of the world (not including overseas associates of the EEC) by 25 percent. In 1962, trade within the Community increased by 14 percent, imports from nonmember countries by 8 percent, and exports by only 6 percent.

One of the main effects attributed to increased international trade is that the intense competition forces the closing of less efficient

[37] See Haas, *Uniting of Europe,* chap. 10, *passim,* on supranational trade unions and their positions on European integration as they evolved in the ECSC; and Diebold, *The Schuman Plan,* pp. 427–467. See also R. Colin Beever, *European Unity and the Trade Union Movements.* Leyden: A. W. Sythoff, 1960.

[38] The industrial product of France and Germany increased by about 50 percent between 1953 and 1958, following a return of these countries to pre–World War II production levels.

Table 11 IMPORTS OF EEC COUNTRIES
(FIGURES ARE IN MILLIONS OF U.S. $)

From:	1958	1959	1960	1961	1958–1961
Each other	$556	$674	$ 846	$ 976	+72 percent
EFTA	301	325	372	410	+36 percent
Rest of world	916	914	1109	1147	+25 percent

Source: EEC General Statistical Bulletin.

plants, creates a better division of labor among the countries involved, and, as a result, benefits the economies of all. Actually, because of general prosperity, there was a full employment of means of production in the EEC and few enterprises were eliminated by the increased competition. (Among the few exceptions are the coal mines. Quite a few high cost pits were closed in Belgium, West Germany, and France. Between 1958 and 1963, the coal labor force was reduced by about 25 percent.) The members' economies probably gained, though, by the granting of larger amounts of new business to more efficient producers and by the full employment that was sustained throughout the period.

While it is extremely difficult to determine the extent of utilitarian gains generated by the large increase in trade, two facts stand out: (a) For the period studied, the formation of the EEC coincided with, and in all likelihood contributed to, the economic growth and general prosperity of the member countries; and (b) in the public mind this prosperity became more closely associated with the formation of the EEC than economic analysis would demonstrate. That is, the citizens and elites of the member-states believed that they were benefiting from the union.[39] A survey taken in 1963 showed that three out of five EEC citizens felt that their living conditions had improved since the inception of the Community.[40] In other words, there was and is a

[39] The cautious tone adopted by the author on this question reflects the fact that the economic growth of member countries and trade among them was higher in pre-EEC years than since its initiation. See Alexander Lamfalussy, "Europe's Progress: Due to Common Market?" *Lloyds Bank Review* (October 1961), New Series, no. 62, pp. 1–16.

[40] *European Community,* January 1964, no. 68, p. 10. There is no direct evidence that they credited the EEC for this growth.

myth of utilitarian benefits above and beyond the actual utilitarian integrating power. This belief is part of the general myth of the Common Market, as the EEC is popularly referred to, and is a major source of its identitive power.

European Myth: Limited Identitive Power

The concept of an economic community for Europe was at no time purely utilitarian. Ideas of European unification, not excluding federation on the model of the United States, were frequently mentioned in the latter part of World War II by leaders of the European governments-in-exile in London. A union of free Europe was held as a counterideology to Hitler's new order and provided a release from the frustrations of the collapse of the national defense systems on the Continent. In 1944, the leaders of the resistance movements of eight countries met in Geneva to discuss the postwar unification of Europe. In the years immediately following 1945, the unification idea had a considerable following on the Continent. In May 1948, the various national groups held a congress at The Hague, which led to the formation of the European movement. European unification was favored by Churchill, Adenauer, Italian Prime Minister Alcide de Gasperi, Paul-Henri Spaak of Belgium, and many others. It is important to note, however, that initially the movement failed. The weakness of the Council of Europe formed in 1949 and the failure in 1954 to form the European Defense Community and a European Political Community led to a decline of the European movement and the general feeling that little would come of it. A decade had passed since World War II. The surviving ECSC was thought to be of minor importance compared to the dream of a federated Western Europe. The failure of the EDC and the EPC in 1954 and the related upsurge of national suspicions brought the indentitive power of the European movement to a low point. Nor was the formation of the EEC in 1957 greeted with the same enthusiasm it evoked several years later. Initially many questioned whether it would succeed.[41] Even after the

[41] Even a highly sophisticated study expressed some doubt that the timetable of the Treaty of Rome would be kept by 1970, and commented that this would be especially difficult in the early years. The study estimated the average annual growth rate of the Six, assuming the success of the EEC, would be 3.1 percent

Treaty of Rome had come into effect, Britain still thought that remaining outside would be more beneficial than joining the EEC, unless London's terms were accepted. It was only in 1960 and even more in 1961, when the success of the EEC had become increasingly apparent (developments well reflected in the British turnabout), that there was a major revival of the European myth and a new focus, not on federation, here and now, but on gradual expansion of a partial economic union toward political unification.

As of the early sixties the European Community myth was flourishing; numerous values had become tied to what was, after all, hardly more than an evolving customs union. The myth was tied to the hope that the Community presented the possibility of "overcoming the disastrous political divisions inherited from the past"; it was related to the concept of a "new Europe" that would once again export "its own ideas of political organization"; it envisaged the basis for a new relationship between Europe and the developing areas; and the EEC's effective regional organization was believed to provide, through the fostering of increased international cooperation, "some hope of survival in the nuclear age."[42]

Finally, while the EEC was at the outset clearly designed as an economic union, by 1962, the stress on political unification had regained part of its lost appeal. In the following two years, it became common to interpret the Treaty of Rome as if its original intention were to lay the groundwork for political unification. "We are not in business at all, we are in politics," said Walter Hallstein in a speech to a joint Harvard-M.I.T. meeting on May 22, 1961. It should be noted that many of the drafters of the treaty kept the goal of political unification clearly in mind but out of sight. Although the preamble of the treaty includes such vague language as ". . . to establish the foundation of a closer union among European people," this is hardly a very strong or explicit commitment to political unification. Of much greater immediate concern to the founders of the EEC was the goal specified in Article 2:

---

for 1955–1970. The actual EEC figure for its first four years was more than double this estimate. Economist Intelligence Unit Ltd., *Britain and Europe.* London: 1957, p. 2 and p. 10.

[42] The quoted portions are from Pryce, *Political Future,* pp. 10–11.

It shall be the aim of the community, by establishing a Common Market and progressively approximating the economic policies of the Member States, to promote . . . a harmonious development of economic activities, an increased stability, an accelerated raising of the standard of living and closer relations between its Member States.

The major sociopolitical groups that favored the formation of the EEC in 1957 and most members of the parliaments that ratified the treaty neither foresaw a development toward full political unification nor were they committed to it. Even the "Europeans" have been surprised.[43]

The myth of success that supports the growth in level and scope of the EEC, it should be noted, is much more fragile than has often been assumed. The idea of a united Europe, while popular in some intellectual circles and among the younger generation, has neither deep nor extensive roots. Surely there are many values the Europeans have in common and that could become tied to *Europa,* as the emerging union is occasionally referred to; but the Europeans have had such common values for many generations without unification, and the process of actively relating these values to the EEC has not advanced very much. Educational systems and other indentitive mechanisms, from mass media to religious organizations, excluding to a degree the Catholic Church, are still largely national, not supra-national.

The fragility of the myth of the EEC was demonstrated when de Gaulle vetoed the membership of Britain in the EEC. What one day was a successful union, full of self-confidence and a sense of progress, became on January 14, 1963, one whose participants referred to as having just died. "This is a black day for Europe. The Common Market is now only a mechanism and no longer a living thing," stated no less a man than Ludwig Erhard. A Ruhr industrialist revealed that the "vetoing of Britain was a deep and painful psychological shock."[44] The cautious chairman of the Common Market, Walter

---

[43] "It is only now that the political implications of this are beginning to appear. Although those who were responsible for the original concept of the Community believed from the start that the merging of economic sovereignty was only the first phase of a process which had a political objective, even they have been surprised by the speed of events." Pryce, *Political Future,* p. 9.

[44] *Time,* September 6, 1963, p. 82.

Hallstein, referred to a "crisis of confidence." For the following 11 months, until the formulation of a common agricultural policy in December 1963, the EEC made little progress, and only in 1964 did it gradually recover part of its earlier buoyancy. The 1963 crisis left a deep scar, which makes a future crisis of confidence even more likely to undermine the identitive power of the EEC. The fact that one political leader, in a single act, could inflict so deep a wound on the morale of the union seems to support our suggestion that, by 1963, the evolution of identitive power of the EEC, while impressive compared to the mid- and even the late fifties, still has a long way to go by absolute standards.

Nevertheless, sponsors of the European movement are continuing their efforts, and the mechanisms through which the myth evolves are many. Two outstanding charismatic leaders of Europe, de Gaulle and Adenauer, lend their support to it. Numerous highly flattering publications of the EEC in Western countries have made the dream of its success a source of identitive gratification for its citizens.

The growing European myth is, however, by no means the only source of the increasing identitive power of the EEC. There have also been increases in intercountry travel and communication, and the greater number of contacts among the citizens of the six countries supports the evolution of a community feeling. Border restrictions have been largely removed. The number of tourists has grown, and cultural programs bring together the citizens (especially the young) and the leaders of the Six. Unification of educational systems is difficult and slow, but progress has been made. There are now European Schools at Brussels, Luxembourg, Varese (Italy), Karlsruhe (Germany), and Mol (Belgium), although these serve mainly the large staffs of the various European organizations. National textbooks are being revised to exchange "self consciousness and bias for a wider objectivity" and European geography textbooks and European maps have been circulated, though most books are still nationalistic.[45] Citizens of EEC countries learn each others' languages. More Frenchmen speak German than English; more Italians speak

[45] Danielle Hegmann, "European Schools Broaden Educational Frontiers," *European Community,* April 1964, p. 9.

French than English; and, in a 1963 Reader's Digest survey,[46] of the 45 percent of the Dutchmen who had a second language, the majority spoke German. As far as traveling is concerned, between 1960 and 1963, 30 percent of the interviewed Dutchmen and 17 percent of the Belgians had been to Germany, and 12 percent of the Dutchmen and 25 percent of Belgians, to France. In comparison, less than 4 percent of these nationals visited Britain in the same period.

By 1963, about 564,000 persons earned their main income in an EEC country other than the one of which they were citizens; we should, however, note that there was often little "mixing" between these workers and the citizens of the countries in which they worked. In the development of intra-Community tourism, trade, friendships, and school exchange, as well as in most other aspects of the unification process, the fact stands out that the member countries are from one land bloc, in which distances are small and means of transportation and communication, compared to those of underdeveloped countries or earlier periods, are highly efficient. Proximity seems so important that non-EEC members, Switzerland and Austria, trade more with their EEC neighbors over the tariff wall than with their fellow EFTA countries, which are more removed geographically. Driving a car from one EEC country to another seems to be highly common; but going to Britain or Sweden, which involves crossing a narrow water passage, is less common. No water stretches separate EEC members from each other. Water seems somehow still a barrier that turns such a trip into something like the difference between a local and a long distance telephone call.

The effect of the increased contact among Common Market countries is well illustrated by the findings of Daniel Lerner, who studied the attitudes of French business leaders toward the EEC. He found that those who had no export business were in favor of the EEC in a ratio of 2:1; among those who had some exports, the ratio was 3:1; and among those whose business was over half export the ratio was 6:1. This might have been explained by interests in stable international relations and other economic reasons, but Lerner showed that

[46] Figures refer to a sample studied. See U. W. Kitzinger, *The New Europeans*. The Reader's Digest Association, Ltd., 1963, p. 14.

"exposure" to citizens of other countries was a major factor. Those who exported more also traveled more abroad, read more foreign publications, and received more foreign visitors at home, and hence were less "nationalistic."[47]

Finally, the supranational institutions, spirit, and symbols developed by the growing "settlements" of European civil servants, especially in Brussels and Strasbourg, have a direct effect. The truly European effective organs servicing all member-states provide a focus of identification for the European-minded citizens of the Six. No less important to the success of the EEC was the fact that both identitive and utilitarian integrating power was effectively used.

COMMUNICATION, RESPONSIVENESS, AND REPRESENTATION

Integrating power might increase and a union still be de-unified, particularly if the system-elites attempt to push through a unification program that exceeds the pace and scope that even the growing integrating power can support. Part of the success of the EEC, at least up to 1964, was due to the effective communication between the various power groups in the Community and the system-elites, and to the high (but not overly high) responsiveness of the Economic Commission.

The main institutionalized channel of communication between the various countries, with their interest groups, and the organs of the EEC is through their representation in Brussels. This is not limited to the monthly meetings of the Council of Ministers. Member states have permanent representatives in Brussels who are in close contact with the commission, and the respective countries are represented on various committees such as the Social and Economic Committee, and the one for transportation. In addition, large groups of experts in Brussels who are attached to the national delegations, while committed to their professional reference groups and somewhat "European" in spirit, are instructed in a general way to represent national

[47] Daniel Lerner, "French Business Leaders Look at EDC: A Preliminary Report," *Public Opinion Quarterly,* vol. 20 (1956), pp. 212–221. See also Louis Kriesberg, "German Public Opinion and the European Coal and Steel Community," *Public Opinion Quarterly,* vol. 23 (1959), pp. 28–42.

viewpoints. Moreover, members of the commission regularly visit the national capitals of the Six. In short, there is much communication between national centers and that of the Community.

Less developed and less regular are the contacts between the Community and the various interest groups from business to labor, from free professionals to farmers. Although they are represented in the Economic and Social Committee, this forum is too large and too heterogeneous to be of appreciable effectiveness as a medium of communication. In addition, there is informal communication between the Economic Commission and the national interest groups and the 200-odd Community-wide assumptions that have been organized during the first five years of the EEC. So far, however, these groups have been more concerned with articulating their intercountry interests, such as establishing subsidiaries and exchanging information, than with significant efforts to influence the Community on a supranational level. These groups, because of the limited agreement among them, are frequently not ready for such efforts. Their influence on the center of the EEC (it has no official capital as yet) will probably increase as the commission moves from such "negative" steps as reducing tariffs to "positive" ones such as setting the support level of prices of agricultural products. Meanwhile, the major channel for national interest and political groups is indirect, through the national governments.[48]

There is one other channel through which political groups can communicate their views to Brussels—the European Parliamentary Assembly (EPA). This organ is composed of members appointed by the national governments from among the parliamentarians of the respective countries; opposition parties are also represented. The EPA has, according to the treaty, "powers of deliberation and control" (Article 137). It receives and discusses the annual report of the Economic Commission; it can also address oral and written questions to the commission, which the latter is obliged to answer. Fi-

[48] "In terms of political activity, most economic interest groups have continued to rely for the most part on traditionally developed channels of access to national policy-making concerns, which still retain major decision-making authority." Lindberg, "Political Dynamics," p. 182.

nally, the EPA can force the resignation of the commissioners by a two-thirds "no confidence" vote. This power, however, is not very effective, since were it to be used other than very infrequently it would weaken the whole system. The assembly is seeking the power to force the resignation of individual commissioners in order to gain a more effective control, but this has not been granted to date. The commissioners are appointed by the national governments for four-year periods. Although there are certain matters on which the commission must consult the assembly, the final decision is in the hands of the council, which is neither responsible to the EPA nor required to consult it. In this sense, the assembly's main functions are recommendation and debate.[49]

The question is raised whether lacking responsibility to an elected body the commission is responsive enough to the public at large and to the politically effective national groups. This is important since the commission has, at least in the short run, an advantage over the council. On most matters the commission alone can initiate proposals, which the council can amend only unanimously. Though the council can refuse to discuss a commission proposal and thus in effect require its reformulation, this is more a veto power than an active or positive one.[50] Hence the commission could, at least temporarily, set a course that would be out of line with the views of the public, the interest groups, and the national governments ("temporarily," because in such a case the national governments would probably not reappoint the commissioners). By initiating Community action that does not command adequate support (or for which sufficient backing had not been gained), the commission might generate such strains that political groups would put pressure on their govern-

[49] See Eric Stein, "The European Parliamentary Assembly: Techniques of Emerging Political Control," *International Organization,* vol. 13 (1959), pp. 233–254; and Dusan Sidjanski, "Aspects Fédératifs de la Communauté Européene." Paper presented to the Sixth World Congress of the International Political Science Association, Geneva, September 21–25, 1964.

[50] Gebhard Bebz, "The Balance of Power in the European Communities," *Annuaire Européen,* vol. 5 (1959), pp. 70–71; and Leon N. Lindberg, "Decision-Making and Integration in the European Community." Paper presented to the annual meeting of the American Political Science Association, Chicago: September 9–12, 1964.

ments to withdraw or reduce their commitments to the Community. In any event, it is argued, it is undemocratic to have a bureaucracy act without being responsible to an elected body, even if the commission could "get away" with such action without undermining the Community.

For a more responsive commission and accelerated unification, the European movement favors (a) uniting the three executive agencies (High Authority, Economic Commission, and Euratom Commission); (b) electing the European Parliament by direct universal suffrage, which would focus public opinion and the politically effective groups on the supranational legislature and away from the national ones; (c) making the commission and the council fully responsible before the European Parliament, in order to establish democratic control of the "Eurocrats."[51] In general, the "Europeans" feel that the time is ripe for a renewal of the effort toward political unification, not excluding federation. Actually the suggested constitutional changes would go a long way toward putting it into effect.

The above suggestions must be evaluated with the following questions in mind: how responsive is the commission as it is? Is high or higher responsiveness desirable, especially at this stage? Is the West European Community ready for federation?

So far, the commission has been quite responsive to the member-governments, as well as to national and "supranational" pressure groups.[52] The commission, for instance, delayed public discussions of EEC agricultural policy until after the 1961 German elections, since it was expected that the German farmers would resist unification of this sector, and the Christian Democratic Union, the ruling party, draws much of its support from the farmers. On the other hand, the commission accelerated its endeavors on behalf of this policy in response to riots by French farmers, who are expected to benefit from the opening of the German market to their products.

A similar approach was taken with regard to anticartel measures.

---

[51] See Stein, "European Parliamentary Assembly," and Kitzinger, *The Challenge,* pp. 71–74.

[52] Actually, the "Europeans," especially in the EPA, have criticized the Commission for being *too* responsive and not sufficiently willing to resist such pressures.

Big industries in Western Europe are especially powerful and are less accustomed to government control than are those in, for example, the United States. Moreover, many of these industries were among the first and strongest supporters of the ECSC and the EEC. The political realism of the commission is reflected in its not insisting on the introduction of anticartel measures; practically no steps were taken in the first five years.[53] This is not because there was no need to do so. Many large corporations merged or formed other kinds of ties, and these control sizeable parts of the EEC market (including Belgium's Geavaert with Germany's Agfa; the Netherlands' Phillips and Germany's Siemens, Germany's Bleyle and France's Giller, Renault and Italy's Alfa Romeo). All told, there are about 30,000 marketing and manufacturing agreements.

In short, the commission seems to be quite responsive to political pressures and realities within the Six. It seems that to the degree that the responsiveness of the Economic Commission is less than maximum, this may have some advantages for unification. The member governments use the commission to introduce motions they consider necessary but which, for political reasons, they are reluctant to initiate, such as measures which affect the subsidies given to the farmers. When such measures are taken by the commission, a national government can "blame" the pressures of the other governments and that of the commission for having to agree to an unpopular step or policy. If the commission were more dependent upon popular support, its operation could not have these salutary effects. In this context it is also to be noted that the commission, unlike the established national civil services, is composed of many young experts and administrators whose innovative ideas could not be as freely exercised were it not for their relative isolation from political pressures. Thus, a certain degree of unresponsiveness by the commission

[53] The Treaty of Rome set the date for the application of the antitrust articles as "not later than January 1, 1961; however, as late as February 1963 it was not clear how or when these provisions were to be implemented. Moreover, the language of the Treaty does not make it clear whether those who hold dominant Market positions are to be 'banned or blessed.' " *The Christian Science Monitor,* February 14, 1963, p. 12. As an earlier source has phrased the problem, "[The Treaty] prohibits centralization, price fixing, market sharing, and similar practices *unless* they contribute to improvements in production and distribution, or to technical and economic progress." Economist Intelligence Unit, p. 3.

is not necessarily detrimental to the Community's long-run interests and future growth.

If the EPA were able to force the resignation of individual commissioners, this would not only violate the principle of collective responsibility but also might render the executive organs of the EEC quite unstable. Moreover, at least as long as the EPA is not a directly elected body but is chiefly composed of "European"-minded legislators, who are often recruited from among the federalist members of the national parliaments, the EPA might prod the commission toward a much more supranational policy than the citizens (and probably the governments) of the European Community are ready to adopt. It seems to us that the present balance, with a "radical" assembly that has chiefly identitive power, a council that is *comparatively* slow going, and a commission midway between, is effective. It allows the commission to forward unification without unduly rushing it.

It might be countered that without an effective Community parliament the EEC is a government by technocrats and bureaucrats and that this is undemocratic no matter how efficient it might seem or be. Moreover, the lack of control by an elected body makes the commission more attentive to organized interest groups than to the public at large. Were the commission responsible to a popularly elected parliament, it would become more responsive to the general public. Such a parliament would also be less "radical" than the EPA, since it would be more responsive to voters and interest groups. The manner in which parliamentarians are now selected by the national governments accounts in part for the "radical" tendencies of the EPA. Being a member of the EPA, while a source of symbolic gratification, places the strain of extra work on busy politicians and reduces the time available for their participation in national politics and the maintenance of their contacts with their constituencies. Some national parliamentarians spend up to 100 days a year on various "European" duties.[54] Hence these members of national assemblies who are more supranationally oriented either because of their constituencies or their individual commitments, are more likely to seek ap-

[54] Stein, "European Parliamentary Assembly," p. 240.

pointment and to be sent to the EPA than are others.[55] This would disappear once the parliament is directly elected, although the more "European" politicians would still be more likely to seek supranational rather than national offices.

Assuming for a moment that it is desirable to follow the "European" proposals, the main question remains: Is Europe ready for federation? So far, Europe has been unified mainly through the building of separate organs of intercountry cooperation for each function that was unified. NATO and the Western European Union are the military instruments; OECD and the European Development Fund, the instruments of European and Atlantic cooperation in matters concerning foreign aid; Euratom and CERN (Centre Européen de Recherche Nucléaire) in the fields of research and development of fissionable material, and so forth. Gradually a host of organizations has evolved; these differ in the range of their membership, in their degree of supranational authority, and in their relations to the EPA.

The question is, in what direction does this development point? Some view this web of limited-purpose organizations as a new form of international system that goes beyond "functional" international organization in the significance and number of the functions internationally served and in the authority of the system-elites, but does not directly engage the politically explosive issues of sovereignty and constitutions that a supranational federation would evoke. These authorities point out that international cooperation could well continue to evolve without superimposing on these agencies a supranational government and legislature.[56] For different reasons and drawing on different philosophies, both de Gaulle and Erhard take this point.[57]

In contrast, the federalists view the emergence of a web of limited-purpose organizations as an intermediary step, and suggest that a multiorganizational structure does not allow for enough communication and responsiveness. They point to the fact that there is no one center for settling conflicts over jurisdiction and substantive issues

[55] Reported by Pryce, *Political Future,* pp. 20 and 39.
[56] *Political Future,* pp. 70–74.
[57] *New York Times,* November 21, 1962.

or for building a general consensus, unless a full community is institutionalized. Both Jean Monnet and Walter Hallstein hold this view.[58]
This argument cannot be separated from the question of what the
"terminal" degree of the Community's unification ought to be. As
is obvious, the integrating power that suffices to bring about and
sustain a limited unification might not be adequate for a more extensive one. The questions that arise are how much integrating power is
needed for various levels of unification; and does the EEC now command it?

INTEGRATING POWER: A DYNAMIC PERSPECTIVE

POWERS REQUIRED VERSUS POWERS AVAILABLE

The dynamic relation between the amount of integrating power
available and the level of integration and scope of European unification is best studied in the full perspective of the postwar years rather
than the limited period of 1958 to 1964. The postwar period might
be divided as follows: (a) the immediate postwar years, 1945 to
1951; (b) the period of the ECSC, the forerunner of the EEC, 1952
to 1957; (c) the first six years of the EEC, 1958 to early 1964; and
(d) the following five to seven years, during which the EEC is to
complete its economic integration and when the question of its political shape will probably be decided.

In the first postwar years, the discrepancy between the integrating
powers available and the level of integration and scope of European
unification aimed at by various leaders was enormous; the failure of
their efforts was almost complete. The level of integrating power
was very low; it drew mainly on American support through the Marshall plan, the shared Soviet threat, and vague "European" ideals
that were not particularly widely shared. Churchill's call for Euro-

---

[58] Monnet has long argued that only an economy developed on a continental,
not a national, scale can ensure continued progress for Western Europe. Arnold
J. Zurcher, *The Struggle to Unite Europe 1940–1958.* New York: New York
University Press, 1958, p. 183. See also Ingo Reuss, "Die Europa-Union Im
Integration," *Europäische Wirtschaft,* vol. 2 (1959), pp. 474–476.

pean unification in his speech at Zurich in September 1946 was without appreciable effect. The appeals of other European leaders were similarly received. The various nations were concerned with the restoration of their heavily damaged economies, and were reluctant to share scarce resources with neighboring states that might have been more severely disadvantaged.

In the immediate postwar years, some attempts were made to bring about a "United States of Europe"; at the time there was little identitive or utilitarian integrating power available. In 1947, an international committee for the coordination of the movements for a United Europe was established, to bring together a large number of pro-integration groups. This committee organized the 1948 Hague Congress, which called for the formation of a directly elected European Assembly as a supreme political organ, reflecting the maximalist nature of the movement. As a result of this congress, a statute was signed in May 1949, creating the Council of Europe, in which ten countries initially participated.[59] The council was expected to forward unification in all areas (except defense matters, which presumably were handled by existing organizations, the Brussels Treaty Organization and later NATO). The aim of the council, according to Article 1 of its statute, was "to achieve a greater unity between its members for the purpose of safeguarding and realizing the ideals and principles which are their common heritage and facilitating their economic and social "progress," through "common action in economic, social, cultural, scientific, legal and administrative matters. . . ."[60]

The Council of Europe never "took off" for a variety of reasons. Britain objected to any supranational measures, especially those that touched upon political matters which many continentals favored. The council formed was left with only advisory capacities and no supranational authority; thus it was both weak initially and lacking in

[59] Included were the five Brussels Treaty states (France, Britain and Benelux) and Denmark, Eire, Italy, Norway, and Sweden.
[60] See Arthur H. Robertson, *The Council of Europe.* New York: Frederick A. Praeger, Inc., 1956, pp. 11ff. The text of the statute is reprinted in Zurcher, *Struggle to Unite Europe,* pp. 224–235. For a highly favorable view of the contribution of the Council of Europe to the growth of European cooperation, see Volney D. Hurd, *The Council of Europe.* New York: Manhattan, 1958.

ability to trigger a spill-over process; it found itself with a maximal assignment and with minimal powers. In short, the council aimed very high and accomplished very little.[61] It might even be said that it had some negative results, since it frustrated many members of the European movement who had supported its creation and envisaged it as the first pivotal step toward a United States of Europe. It has been pointed out that although many of the representatives who participated in the inauguration of the council were federalist-oriented, the new organ appeared ideal to those who would "limit" Europe, especially the British, Norwegians, and Danes, "who felt that Strasbourg was as far as united Europe should go."[62] Hence, the Hague Congress of 1948 did not give rise to anything approaching a major movement toward European union.

The organized following of the movement was still small in the early fifties, and "according to one estimate, the leadership in each country (was) exercised by five to ten people . . . a total of 60 to 80 persons for the whole of Europe."[63] At this same time (January 1952) it was estimated that the aggregate European membership of the movement did not exceed 80,000; in other words, Europeans outside a narrow circle were largely indifferent to the European movement.[64]

The second period (1952–1957) was one of increasing utilitarian integrating power, a result of the formation and successful development of the ECSC. The ECSC, with only six states, was fairly homogeneous; "obstructionist" Britain was not included; it had some supranational powers from the outset and was aiming low. The goal was multinational harmonization of only two industries, steel and coal, rather than of whole economies. It was quite successful; the common market for coal and steel was relatively effective in increasing productivity and trade among the member states. The ECSC also,

[61] This point is elaborated in the author's "European Unification: A Strategy of Change," *World Politics,* vol. 16 (1963), pp. 32–51.

[62] Zurcher, *Struggle to Unite Europe,* p. 47. For a quite different and interesting view of this period, see Gerda Zellentin, *Die Kommunisten und die Einigung Europas,* Frankfurt A/M: Athenäum Verlag, 1964.

[63] Michael T. Florinsky, *Integrated Europe?* New York: The Macmillan Company, 1955, pp. 112–114.

[64] *Integrated Europe?,* pp. 112–114.

by contributing to the reconciliation of France and Germany, and by triggering the spill-over processes discussed earlier, served as a stepping-stone toward the economic and political unification of Europe.

Still, integrating power was not high and identitive power was rather low. Although the ECSC was functioning well, by 1954 it had raised little "European" enthusiasm. It was in this year that a second attempt was made to form a broadly encompassing European union to parallel the ECSC in the military and political spheres by forming a European Defense Community (EDC) to be followed by a European Political Community (EPC) among the same six countries, the members of the ECSC. The aim of the EDC was to provide a supranational defense structure based on an integrated European army under a permanent European command. Article 38 of the EDC treaty draft provided for the proposed EPC, which looked toward full federation of the member states in a democratic state.

Both attempts to expand the scope of European unification failed when the French Assembly did not ratify the EDC treaty. The main reason both why the EDC was suggested in the first place and why it failed was that by 1954 the identitive power of the European ideal was not strong enough to overcome national loyalties, suspicions, and fears of other nations, especially the fear of Germany. The EDC was suggested as a means to avoid national German rearmament and failed because the safeguards against it, even in the EDC, were considered unsatisfactory by the French Assembly. Several other factors were also responsible, such as the thaw in the Cold War following the death of Stalin, the end of the Korean conflict, and the unfavorable British reaction to the treaty. (One French critic compared the prospect of an EDC without Britain to being "locked in a closet with fifty million Germans.") But these factors need not concern us here and do not alter our major conclusion that the failure of the EDC and the EPC is ultimately attributable to the lack of integrating power to support wider political unification at this stage. Raymond Aron expressed the sentiment of the period when he wrote:

The name Europe distinguishes a continent or a civilization, but not an economic or political unit . . . national passions are supposed to be on the

way to extinction . . . but they are replaced by ideological passions . . .
The European idea is empty, it has neither the transcendence of Messianic
ideologies nor the immanence of concrete patriotism. It was created by intellectuals, and that fact accounts at once for its genuine appeal to the mind
and its feeble echo in the heart.[65]

The second period, then, was one in which limited power was used
successfully to carry out a limited unification and one in which an
effort to generate a much more demanding unification failed.[66]

In the third period (1958–1964), that of the EEC, the identitive
and utilitarian integrating powers were built up, as discussed above.
The powers sufficed to carry a gradual extension of economic unification and, by the end of the period, to meet some economic-political
issues that earlier could not be handled collectively. The buildup of
integrating powers both allowed for and was itself strengthened by
the acceleration in the reduction of internal customs walls and in the
removal of quantitative restrictions. In January 1961 and again in
July 1962, customs rates were reduced ahead of schedule. Quotas
were almost wholly abolished by 1962, after a little more than 4
years instead of the 12 to 15 years planned in 1957. By 1962, the
EEC was strong enough to approach the question of agricultural policy, and it also took the first steps toward the formation of an anticartel tax and an investment policy. Moreover, cautious preliminary
steps toward some degree of political unification were taken in July
1961, including setting up a committee to draft statutes for closer
political ties. (The negotiations concerning these steps were suspended while the British application for membership was pending
and during the crisis that its rejection generated, but were resumed
in 1964.) The third period, as previously indicated, was thus one in
which integrating power and the level of integration and scope increased gradually and hand-in-hand, but in which the power needed
for federation was still far from available; nor was such a step at-

[65] *The Century of Total War.* Boston: The Beacon Press, 1955, pp. 313, 316.
[66] For discussions of this period that generally support our conclusions, see
Daniel Lerner and Raymond Aron (eds.), *France Defeats EDC.* New York: Frederick A. Praeger, Inc., 1957, and K. W. Haesele, *Europas Letzter Weg.* Frankfurt: A. M. Knaff, 1958.

tempted. Before the problems the EEC will face in the next period can be reviewed, another look at the third period, with regard to the strategy of unification employed, is called for.

A Gradualist Strategy

In many ways the turning point in the development of European unification came in 1955, when the efforts to form the EEC were begun at the Messina conference of the foreign ministers of the Six. It was then that the level of unification aimed at and the level of integrating power that existed and could be recruited were brought into balance. Such a balance of aims and means may result from some combination of a blind trial-and-error of historical forces; or be an accidental equilibrium that follows other, earlier, less effective combinations; or be the consequence of a deliberately designed strategy compatible with the dynamics of ongoing sociopolitical processes. The latter seems largely to have been the case here. While it is not suggested that all the ramifications of later developments in the unification process were foreseen by the framers of the Treaty of Rome, the success of the EEC rests at least in part upon the step-by-step or gradualist strategy adopted by its founders. The treaty amplifies close targets and underplays more remote and more difficult goals, allowing time for adjustments to new arrangements and to the partial loss of sovereignty that the new institutions entail.

The personality and mode of operation of Jean Monnet are to a significant degree responsible for the inauguration of this gradualist strategy and its continuing development. According to reports, he combines enthusiastic leadership with the tactics of an astute politician who learned to recognize the limits within which unification can progress. After the initial overestimation of the power of the European movement and the failure of earlier, more ambitious efforts, Monnet and his group redesigned their program toward the scaling-down of the pace of unification. A carefully worked out plan for a customs union to be accomplished in 12 to 15 years, which hopefully would lead to economic unification and eventually to political union, replaced the earlier slogans of "Federation Now" and

"No Europe Without a Common Sovereign." The "Europeans" decided to rely upon the spill-over effects of a gradual process rather than an impulsive assault on the windmills of sovereignty.

The political method of Monnet and his group was to work within the existing framework of governments rather than to endeavor to appeal directly to the people, as many federalists advocate. Monnet resigned his position as president of the ECSC High Authority in 1955 to organize a private organization called (in contrast to its gradualist strategy) the Action Committee for the United States of Europe.[67] The Action Committee is composed of some 40-odd European leaders representing major political parties and trade unions within the Community; it occasionally issues position papers relating to unification, but mainly it works informally through contacts with central political figures. It is not implied that Monnet and his groups have single-handedly set the policy and pace of European unification, but to the degree that their advice and the views of many others who share the gradualist position were followed—to the degree, that is, that the matching of aims and means, of plans and powers, was a deliberate policy—the success of the EEC was a consequence of a strategy of gradual change, and not the result of historic accident.

The Treaty of Rome itself contains a gradualist strategy, as is manifest from a review of several of its specific provisions: (a) the elimination of tariffs among the member countries over a 12- to 15-year period; (b) the gradual removal of qualitative trade controls; (c) the step-by-step harmonization of external tariffs; (d) the delaying of the formation of a common agricultural policy until the first stage is completed; (e) the formation of shared economic policies on various matters at an unspecified time; (f) the establishment of a Community organ, the Economic Commission, with the power to initiate and formulate proposals but leaving the exclusive power to approve these in control of the multinational Council of Ministers. Thus almost all the changes and adjustments the members were expected to

[67] A joint declaration of the Action Committee at its December 1962 meeting in Paris, on the one hand urges the EEC to "speed up the unification of Europe" while on the other hand it recognizes that "one must not aim at solving all problems at once." *Bulletin from the European Community,* no. 59, January 1963, p. 8.

make under the treaty were divided into numerous small steps. Of particular interest is the gradualist approach to the problem of the augmentation of the supranational power of the Community, as reflected in the voting patterns that became applicable as the union advanced from one stage to another. Although the term is never used, a trend toward supranationality is implied in the treaty, in that decisions must be reached by a unanimous vote in the first stage, by a qualified majority in the second, and by a qualified majority on a greater number of issues in the third.

Not only does the treaty include the above described provisions, but allowance is also made for a "locking-in" system that renders regression difficult. While the transition from the first to the second stage requires unanimous agreement, later transitions toward completion of the adjustment process require no decision and are automatic. Only a unanimous decision of all members can delay the initiation of the third stage or the completion of the process. Thus not only does no country have a veto on progress, but each has a veto against regression; any one state can prevent a legitimate retreat once the first stage is completed.

While a gradualist strategy clearly implies that the method of policy implementation will be a step-by-step approach, it by no means precludes a rapid advance from one step to another. Actually at least one time after the union had built up its integrating power, the EEC chose to use these provisions to accelerate its program in order to further strengthen its institutions in the face of an anticipated external threat. In 1960, British pressures to form a European free trade area, to include the EEC countries, began to mount. The "Europeans" and the Economic Commission feared that this would "dilute" the EEC in a larger bloc. To make their union less "reversible," the commission initiated two rounds of tariff reduction and removal of trade quotas ahead of schedule and engaged in several other "binding" acts.

SECTOR UNIFICATION: REALLOCATION AFTER INTEGRATION

During the first stage of the implementation of the Treaty of Rome, the reallocation of economic assets was minimized, and this phase of adjustment among the member-units was postponed until efforts to build up community sentiments, institutions, and integrating power had advanced. With the continuation of prosperity, high employment, an accelerated economic growth, and steadily increasing intercountry trade, a generally rewarding background was present. As suggested above, the degree to which the EEC as such can be credited with all these achievements is not subject to precise measurement. However, the facts remain that it did not reverse or impede prosperity, and most Europeans thought it did more for them than was probably the case. Thus, in addition to the benefits of real economic rewards, the EEC gave rise to a myth of success that was supportive of the Community's institutions and gratifying to its adherents.

Unification was expected to satisfy many of the specific interests of various national economic groups. Italian labor expected free access to employment sources in other member states; France, Italy, and the Netherlands expected an increased export of their agricultural products to Germany; German industry expected a larger free market for its products, and so forth. Similarly, it had wide political support. The conservative-Catholic parties supported the formation of the EEC from the outset. Most industrialists, although initially cautious, were soon pressing for an accelerated liberalization of the market as large increases in their production capacity resulted from their effort to meet the anticipated needs of the EEC market. The support of the Socialists and of the non-Communist labor unions was won with promises of full employment and upward leveling of working conditions, as mentioned above. Since the expectations of both management and labor were fulfilled and since only a few businesses had to be discontinued and only a very small percentage of the labor force retrained, as far as these groups were concerned the first five years of the EEC brought a clear increase in their utilitarian assets. To this was added the "bonus" of identitive gratification of active participation in the new Europe. In short, business and labor benefited from increase allocation. The only large sector, it seemed, that could not be satisfied without depriving the other sectors was the farm sector.

The EEC is committed to the development of a common agricultural policy by the terms of the Treaty of Rome; the objectives include increasing agricultural productivity, ensuring a fair standard of living for the agricultural population, stabilizing markets, and formulating reasonable consumer prices. As in other modern industrial economies, the agricultural sector of the EEC countries, which is relatively inefficient compared to the American one, is protected from market forces. There are many important differences in the nature of the agricultural sectors of the Six: differences in their problems, in the way they were traditionally treated, and in the way they now expect to be treated. All these matters, the details of which are highly complex, need not concern us here. The main point for the present discussion is that, in general, the agricultural sectors of the Six are the beneficiaries of member governments' policies of stocking crop surpluses and guaranteeing a minimum income for the farmers, and otherwise maintaining a near parity of the income of farmers with that of industrial workers. These policies require some funneling of funds to the agricultural sector, as the percentage of labor involved in agriculture is much larger than their relative contributions to the national incomes of the Six. In other words, through political pressures the farm sector obtains various state subsidies and other aids that increase taxes or consumer prices, or both. This amounts to a partial reallocation of the national income by the governments in favor of the farmers. Reversing this pattern and reducing the oversized farm sector would have largely alienated a major part of the Community before it was safely launched. Hence, although Italy, the Netherlands, and particularly France—the countries with the relatively more efficient farmers—were anxious to include agriculture in the EEC program, it was agreed that the formation of a common farm policy should be delayed until the end of the first stage, that is, until the integrating power of the EEC had been augmented. The goal of the common policy was allowed to embrace the catch-all hope "that farmers should receive as much money as possible, and consumers get their food as cheaply as possible, and that these two desirable but conflicting objectives should be brought about by almost any known method."[68]

[68] Cited in Brooks, "The Common Market," p. 47.

The agricultural dilemma is to a great degree a French-German problem. About half the arable land in the EEC is in France, and the French farm sector is by far the largest producer in the Community. On the other hand, the German farm sector is largely composed of small units operating at high costs, and a common market in food-stuffs would entail a drastic readjustment for the German farmers.[69] It has been estimated that close to a million German farmers would have to leave their farms over the next three decades if the program of free movement of foods and labor throughout the EEC advocated by the Economic Commission in 1964 were implemented. Because of these facts and the differences in the size of the farm sectors in the member countries, a crisis occurred late in 1961, when the EEC finally undertook to reach a common agricultural policy. The Treaty of Rome provided that "member states shall gradually develop the common agricultural policy during the transition period and shall establish it not later than at the end of that period" (Article 40).[70] Any member had the right to halt the transition to the second stage unless this was done. After a lengthy and difficult negotiation period, a shared agricultural policy was agreed upon and the EEC moved into the second stage.[71]

The technical details of the policy are of little relevance here; however, its political nature is of much interest. It was agreed that national subsidies and other aids to the farmers would be gradually replaced by a unified EEC system of price support, and that the exact level of these supports would not be immediately specified. During a seven-year transition period, European farmers would be provided with Community mechanisms needed for their adjustment to the EEC economy, "with the double purpose of stabilizing prices and

[69] U. W. Kitzinger, *The Challenge,* p. 30.

[70] On the problems as viewed during this period, see *Agricultural Policy in the European Economic Community,* Occasional Paper No. 1. London: Political and Economic Planning, November 21, 1958; and Alan D. Robinson, *Dutch Organized Agriculture in International Politics.* The Hague: Martinus Nighoff, 1961.

[71] Claire Sterling, "The Common Market: How Big Will It Grow?", *The Reporter,* November 8, 1962, p. 38. See also Memorandum of the EEC Commission on the Action Program for the Second Stage, European Community Information Service Bulletin, October 24, 1962, pp. 39ff.

guaranteeing farmers a normal income."[72] Thus, European agriculture is to be treated as the agriculture of a single community with no internal restrictions or duties, and at the same time will be protected from world competition.

The details of the common agricultural policy of the Community, especially how protectionist it will be, are as yet unclear. It has been agreed that the Community will collect levies on imported foodstuffs and use this income to finance subsidies to the farmers, although the level of these subsidies was not specified by 1964. If the subsidies are to be high, most of the burden of adjustment will be shifted to outsiders (such as American farmers), who will be driven out of the German market in order to permit import of farm products from other EEC countries, particularly from France. In this case, the consumers will continue to pay similar high prices for foodstuffs as before.

If the subsidies are to be low, the Community farmers in general, and especially the more inefficient ones, will have to shift to different occupations. Outsiders will not be much affected and consumers will be able to purchase their foodstuffs at lower prices.

In the case of high subsidies, little intra-EEC reallocation will occur. French farmers will be satisfied at the expense of outsiders. In the second case, reallocation will take place; farmers will be shifted from the country to the cities, consumers will be able to buy less expensive goods, and many German peasants will have to change their occupations to the benefit of French and other EEC farmers. Thus, in the first case, reallocation would be avoided once more by maintaining internal satisfaction at the cost of outsiders; while in the second case, some reallocation would be achieved, assuming that the now safely launched Community can withstand the tensions that reallocation inevitably involves. The actual policy will probably follow some kind of compromise between these two alternatives; but still, one will be able to characterize it as largely reallocative or not.[73]

---

[72] *France and Europe* (pamphlet). New York: Ambassade de France, Service de Presse et d'Information, March 1962, p. 36.

[73] See *European Community,* September 1962, pp. 3–5. See also Edwin L. Dale, Jr., "The Knife at Europe's Throat," *The New Republic,* December 1, 1962, pp. 12–13.

History cannot be rerun, but there is little doubt that persistent attempts to form an "internal" reallocation policy before the signing of the Treaty of Rome, before European unification had progressed, and before the Economic Commission had been formed, would probably have prevented the very initiation of the EEC. It may also be of interest to note that, late in 1961, when the EEC began to form its agricultural policy it still could not squarely face the question of reallocation; instead, the process was to be gradual. First, it was agreed that subsidies to the farmers would be continued; second, the subsidies would be provided by the Community under the supervision of the commission rather than by the national governments, thus partially removing the question from the national power centers that are subject to the direct pressures of the farmers. Finally, the formation of the farm policy itself was divided into several stages, one delayed until 1964.

Through various other devices, the Community provided for smaller groups than the farmers, such as miners and shipbuilders, groups that were likely to suffer disproportionately from the unification process. The Social Fund finances the retraining of displaced workers and their resettlement, as well as some unemployment benefits for the adjustment period. (By 1963, the reemployment of 183,000 workers was effected. In the coal industry alone, 130,000 men were assisted, though the shifting was greatly eased by the fact that the EEC countries, including Northern Italy, were labor-starved in this period. The EEC actually imports workers from Spain and Turkey.) The European Investment Bank assisted the development of the more backward regions in the Community for a limited period. (By 1963, loans totaling $233 million were issued.) Finally, the escape clauses built into the treaty enable the commission to allow a delay in the reduction of a particular tariff or other protectionist device when dislocation in one industry or country is severe, and hence to stretch out the transition period (Article 226). In January 1963, for instance, France was allowed to impose a 12 percent duty to stem the influx of cheaper Italian refrigerators, while Germany was permitted to impose a tariff on French candy, as imports of this had increased by 516 percent as compared to 1960. All these measures surely reduced the resistance to unification and enhanced the success of the EEC. Not only was the extent of reallocation reduced and part of the cost of adjustment "unloaded" on outsiders, but also significant reallocation was delayed until integration was sufficiently increased to withstand the strains reallocation invariably generates. Thus, using effectively its growing integrating power, the unification of the six European countries continued to grow.

THE NEXT YEARS: HARMONIZATION OR FEDERATION?

The EEC faces the fourth period in the years remaining until 1970. There are many observers who accept uncritically the EEC myth and who expect this time to be one of accelerated unification; a United Europe or *Europa* is frequently mentioned. It is this very myth and optimism, which in the past contributed significantly to the success of the EEC, that might now become an adverse factor. It seems to draw the EEC toward higher unification efforts than the present integrating power, even if it continues to grow, could support; and it attracts more members than the Community might be able to absorb.

The EEC, even if only the present six countries are to be members, faces a considerably more difficult period than the preceding one. On the economic side alone, the second series of reductions of internal customs duties by the remaining 50 percent will be more difficult than the first for two reasons. First, because some products have been overprotected. Hence, the removal of only half of the tariff might still not have meant exposure to the challenge of competition. The removal of remaining duties, down to zero, will test the ability of such producers to compete.

Second, because several sectors that found or expected to find the transition to a common market difficult were allowed temporary protection during the first period. These sectors will now have to be liberalized as their deferments are exhausted. While in the first phase the Community largely succeeded in avoiding clashes with major interest groups and concentrated primarily on the removal of tariff barriers for what was considered the mutual benefit of most groups and member countries, it has now reached a stage at which the interests of many groups are threatened. The farmers, particularly in Germany, but also in Belgium and France, have already protested against the common agricultural policy the Community started to put into effect in July 1962.[74] The important coal sector is dissatisfied with the Community's energy policy. Moreover, there seems to be a growing resentment in national capitals against the mushrooming supranational authority of the commission; the more the power of the EEC grows, the more the national bureaucracies feel threatened. The highly favorable economic climate that prevailed during the first five years is unlikely to continue. By late 1962, economists were for the first time expecting a recession in the Community.[75] Later, a concern for a price inflation set in. As real wages increased in 1963 by 8 percent in France, 15 percent in Italy, and 6.5 percent in inflation-conscious Germany, consumer prices rose about 18 percent in Italy and 23 percent in France in the four years following the foundation of the EEC. While both recession and runaway inflation might be averted if the members were to take such steps as were recommended by the Community or if similar measures were taken by members on their own, continuation of the 1958–1963 rapid economic growth without inflation is nonetheless unlikely.

In 1962, the EEC growth rate was already down to about 5 percent, the lowest since the EEC was begun. It was about 4 percent in 1963. In other words, the Community might face a slow economic growth or a period of "high stagnation" similar to the one that the United States has experienced in the early sixties. This would create a quite different climate for the mutual concessions the members have continuously to make to allow the formulation and expansion of a Community policy. It could shatter the myth of perennial success and lessen the effect of the reservoir of good will that is an important factor in inter-Six negotiations. In recent years, each country has received some concessions from the others and there is hence some degree of mutual obligation; and in view of the public support for the EEC there is some unwillingness on the part of any one state, including France, to retard the evolution of the union. Once a few sharp disagreements have occurred, however, this pattern may

[74] *Economist,* November 3, 1962, p. 448.
[75] *New York Times,* September 17, 1962.

quickly be broken. (It took about 15 months before the Community partially recovered from the crisis over the rejection of Britain.)

The prospects of a crisis, whether of a deep recession, long stagnation, or runaway inflation, could lead to an accelerated effort to build up the Community and provide more rather than less power for its supranational organs. The experiences of the 1930s suggest that international cooperation is preferable to having each state attempt to deal with economic problems on its own. While it is difficult to predict what the reaction to a future crisis will be, it must be noted that, in 1958, when the ECSC was faced with an excess of coal stocks, a partial nationalist regression occurred.[76] Member countries did not follow High Authority policy and did not close inefficient mines as planned or remove protection as required. This was a setback to the work of the ECSC and created a deep crisis of morale from which the ECSC did not fully recover. The events relating to the coal glut crisis did not gain wide public attention at the time, since the EEC's implementation was initiated in 1958 and became the focus of public interest. If the EEC should face a nationalist regression, this would be much more difficult to ignore.

The community is aware of these dangers. In order to counter a recession, stimulate economic growth, foster unification, and continue to build the "closer union" the Treaty of Rome envisions, the Action Program was proposed by the commission in November 1962. The program spells out a sequence of specific steps which would lead, by 1968, to the supranational formulation (and, to a degree, supranational control) of economic policy of the member countries.[77] As a first step, it proposes that the governors of the central banks of the member states meet regularly in Brussels to harmonize their monetary policies; later, this group will become the board of a supranational central bank. Simultaneously, a council of financial ministers of the Six will be developed to formulate jointly other aspects of economic policy, the employment policy of the member countries, and the eventual creation of a European currency. In prac-

[76] J. E. Meade, H. H. Liesner, and S. J. Wells, *Case Studies in European Economic Union.* London: Oxford University Press, 1962, pp. 248 ff.
[77] See *Memorandum of the Commission on the Action Programme for the Second Stage,* Brussels, October 27, 1962 Com. (62) 300.

tice, this would concentrate much of the regulation of the economies of the Six in the hands of Community organs.

It is impossible to determine whether the integrating power possessed by the Community is sufficient to carry out all or most of the unification steps suggested by the Action Program; the initial reaction to the program was somewhat negative and nationalist. The governors of the central banks were reluctant to accept the idea of regular meetings for harmonization;[78] de Gaulle remains skeptical of supranational organizations and favors stabilization of the EEC on a basis of more intergovernmental coordination;[79] Erhard, who is committed more to a policy of laissez-faire, criticized the plan for implying too much regulation.[80] In mid-February 1964, when the finance ministers of the EEC initiated steps toward unification of the tax systems of the Community, which involve compromises on matters concerning basic ideological and political principles of the member nations, one observer suggested that "this week may be remembered as the week the finance ministers bit off more than the Common Market can chew. The community may then choke to death as the result."[81] In mid-April 1964, the Community agreed in principle on adopting a common antiinflation program that required further harmonization of the policies of the Six. The merger of the executive bodies of the ECSC, Euratom, and the EEC seemed to be bringing the joint executive commission closer to a federal organ. In short, there are some signs that the commission is attempting to bring about more unification than can be supported by the integrating power likely to be available in the near future.

The Economic Commission is by no means the only source of pressure that might overload the unification process with more than the available power can carry. We have noted above the pressures of the European Parliamentary Assembly and the "Europeans" toward similar actions. No less important is the very success of the Euro-

[78] *New York Times,* December 15, 1962.

[79] For his general views on this matter, see his speech of October 7, 1960; see also *Political Economic Planning: France and the European Community,* Occasional Paper No. 11, p. 14.

[80] *New York Times,* November 21, 1962.

[81] Edward J. O'Toole, "Europe Tax Step Held Imperative," *New York Times,* February 16, 1964.

pean Community, which has attracted eleven new applicants. Britain, Denmark, Norway, and Ireland applied for full membership; Spain, Portugal, Turkey, Sweden, Austria, and Switzerland applied for the status of "associate" member, which was granted to Greece in 1962 and to Turkey in 1963. Most of these applications were suspended when Britain's application was rejected. But at least those of non-EFTA countries will probably be reactivated.

These applications carry three dangers: (a) they may sharply split the Community among those members that favor expansion and those that seek to limit the EEC, especially if British membership is reconsidered; (b) new members may increase the heterogeneity of the Community and hence make consensus formation more difficult by adding Protestant countries to a largely Catholic union, underdeveloped states to a developed group, and authoritarian regimes to more democratic ones; (c) finally, they may initiate an internal struggle for leadership, especially if Britain enters.[82]

Crucial for the later 1960s are the differences in viewpoints concerning the form that political institutions are to take. De Gaulle favors an intergovernmental structure, serviced by national bureaucracies, in which the Six would harmonize policies but make decisions by unanimous vote and implement them through national governments. The January 1963 French-German Treaty of Cooperation provides for several such organs.[83] The French viewpoint might later be modified and de Gaulle might accept decisions in the realm of political affairs made by a weighted majority with a greater role for the supranational bureaucracy, as he already is committed to do in economic matters. Still, the process of political unification might be arrested short of replacing the six governments by one as long as the Community's superior authority would be an intergovernmental, not federal, authority. This is a crucial difference that separates de Gaulle's vision from those held by the majority of the members of the Economic Commission and the European movement. The latter

[82] On the problems of trifold leadership, see below, p. 288.

[83] Text of the Treaty between the French Republic and the Federal Republic of Germany of January 22, 1963. New York: Ambassade de France, Service de Presse et d'Information. See also Altiero Spinelli, "De Gaulle's Plan," *The Atlantic Community Quarterly,* vol. 1 (1963), p. 395.

favor the building of a united European executive and legislature, not just a "harmonized" one.

By early 1964, new statements in favor of an advance toward political unification were made. De Gaulle declared that a major task was "the union of Europe, including as soon as possible the regular and organized cooperation of Germany, Italy, the Netherlands, Belgium, Luxembourg and France in the domain of politics, defense and culture, as will be the case in that of economics."[84] Erhard, who became more interested in political union since he became Chancellor and sees a chance for Germany to lead the European Community, declared that "Europe must become a political force and achieve greater political unity."[85] But little was achieved in terms of actual steps. Following two summit meetings between the General and the Chancellor, it was by no means clear whether the vision of a united Europe and the spill-over processes emanating from the economic realm would prevail, or whether the divisive factors, especially in military and to a degree foreign policy questions, would take priority. Nor were the differences of opinion on how to proceed toward political union reconciled.

The initial difference of opinion is in itself not necessarily deunifying as long as some consensus is eventually reached. The main danger is that this consensus seems likely to be formed around the harmonization (or intergovernmental) approach rather than around that of supranational orientation (although the spill-over process might generate more support for the supranational one in later years).

The future of the EEC seems largely dependent upon whether it can be maintained on a basis of harmonization of political matters, that is, extensive coordination of national efforts, or whether it must keep progressing toward central supranational control in order not to regress in economic integration.

In our judgment, the single most important factor affecting the need for supranational regulation of the Community is the degree of economic unification attempted. If the major means of national regulation were given up, as extensive economic integration requires,

[84] *European Community,* February–March 1964, no. 69, p. 6.
[85] *European Community,* p. 6. See also *New York Times,* July 21, 1964.

there is little doubt that Community regulation would be necessary, and this would have to be based on Community decisions. This is a point of some importance, and should be emphasized. It seems to us that unification cannot be stabilized on any and all levels of integration; it either has to continue to grow or it will regress. Up to 1964, the EEC largely removed barriers, which is comparatively easy, but did relatively little to unify the mechanisms of economic control. It still was largely a customs union and not an economic one. Plans were made at this stage to complete the freedom of movement of goods, services, and manpower by January 1, 1966. The more such movement actually takes place, the larger will be the pressure to unify the economic controls—especially monetary and fiscal policies—or the pressure toward regression in the union. As one observer put it:

If, for example, manpower will move freely and will remain in great demand, why would the working man forego the tax advantages of one country to burden himself with the more stringent taxes of other Common Market countries?

And, if an automobile manufacturer becomes free to ship his cars throughout the community without restriction, why not operate from a base where the tax on net income would be one third less than in other Common Market nations? . . .

In biting into the Common Market's massive and pervasive tax problems . . . the financial ministers have committed the community to a mortal struggle with its own future. If the Common Market six are able to digest the tax harmonization program when its Executive Commission formally presents it next fall [1965], then genuine economic integration in Europe one day may become reality.[86]

The range and significance of decisions that will have to be made once economic policy is formulated on the Community level will, it seems, require both a permanent center rather than sporadic or even regular meetings of ministers and Community mechanisms for consensus formation to support the decision-making center. This would amount to a union government and parliament by whatever names they might be called. The integrating power the EEC now has and will in the near future command do not seem strong enough to carry

[86] O'Toole, "Europe Tax Step."

both new members (especially Britain) and greatly increased unification at the same time, especially if political unification is to be of the supranational type. To combat the dangers of overloading by limiting the scope or level of political unification, by harmonization rather than supranational integration, seems impossible: nor can unification come to rest at simply any stage. The choice seems to be between progressing to broader and higher levels of integration or regressing to a lower level. In the long run, high economic integration cannot be maintained without considerable political integration.

On the other hand, there are many more options with respect to the admission of new members; it is in this area that overloading can be reduced by limiting new members, in the next five or so years, to a few smaller countries, such as Denmark, Spain, and Austria, and excluding others, especially Britain. If a great increase of members takes place, particularly if Britain is included, unification would be seriously disadvantaged. It will not necessarily fall apart, but it will probably regress in scope and level of integration and become an inflated tariff union rather than a United States of Europe.

CHAPTER 8

In Comparative Perspective

———————•—•—•———————

The general inquiry as to under what conditions efforts to initiate a unification process succeed is here studied with two particular questions in mind: Who is unifying and by means of what kinds of power. More precisely, 17 propositions were formulated at the outset of Part Two of this volume to focus our attention on specific questions regarding the effect of various distributions and compositions of power on the success of unification. We now turn to reexamine these propositions[1] in light of the data presented. We see that some propositions have been strengthened, some have been weakened, and some require reformulation. All call for more research in this area.

The examination of our propositions in these concluding pages is made in a comparative perspective. By comparing the effects different power structures and various power combinations had on unification in the four cases, it seems that one can reach conclusions, however tentative, that are more objective and provide more insight than by studying just one case.

EFFECTIVE POWER DISTRIBUTIONS

EXTERNAL ELITES: THE PRICE OF INTERFERENCE

The search for the effects of various power distributions on unification opens with an examination of the effects of external elites, which is of interest both in itself and for understanding the role of

[1] We stress again that these propositions are not to be confused with the much broader analytical instrument, or paradigm, presented in Part One.

internal elites in unification processes. We expected external elites to enhance the success of unification if the application of their power coincides rather than conflicts with the power structure of the emerging union. (The assumption made here is that the external elites do not command enough power to change the distribution of power among the units participating in the unification process to fit the institutional structure they are fostering. This assumption is valid for all the cases at hand.) This proposition is strengthened by the data.

Two of the unification efforts—the Caribbean and the West European—were directly affected by external elites. In the West Indies, Britain was of considerable significance in initiating the union: had it not been for British insistence on federation as an institutional prerequisite for independence, British identitive influence on the island-elites, and British utilitarian inducements, in all probability no unification attempt would have been made by the ten islands. But despite the considerable influence Britain had in the West Indies, its efforts to establish a Caribbean federation were unsuccessful. By fostering an institutional structure that favored the weaker islands over the more powerful ones in such matters as representation in both the federal government and the legislature and the allocation of utilitarian assets, Britain undermined the federation it was trying to encourage. The identification of the leaders and people of the more powerful islands (Jamaica and Trinidad) with the Federation of the West Indies was damaged by the concentration of federal positions in the hands of small islanders. Britain itself, by exercising leadership in the area, drained part of the gratification of federal leadership, thereby impoverishing the elite-status for the larger islands which saw few rewards in this status under the best circumstances. The fact that identification with the ideas and symbols of the externally sponsored federation as well as the related concept of a "West Indian nation" did not penetrate much beyond a limited group of politicians and intellectuals was another source of weakness of the federation. Even the democratic institutions the islands owed to Britain worked against the federal plan; it was through these institutions that the unconvinced classes voted the federation out of existence. In short, the British-sponsored federation was not sufficiently adjusted to the local power structure, interests, and values to take root. Since there were factors other than Britain's misdirected influence that caused de-unification, it is futile to speculate on the fate of the federation had Britain allowed a federal structure to develop that would have given greater satisfaction to the utilitarian interests or status needs of Jamaica and Trinidad and reflected more closely their power relative to the weaker islands.

The unification of Western Europe after World War II was encouraged by an external elite—in this case, the United States, whose policy and influence were reflected in the allocation of the Marshall Plan funds and its NATO policy. Diplomatic, economic, and military (threats to withhold protection) pressures were used to encourage European unification. American influence was compatible with the evolving European power structure with regard to one unit but not with regard to two others. The United States correctly judged the postwar development of power in the region as far as the resurgence of West Germany was concerned, but it misjudged the relative roles of France and Britain.

The United States encouraged the acceptance of West Germany in the various Western organizations such as NATO, the OEEC, and the Council of Europe. The rapid reconstruction of Western Germany, its large contributions to NATO, its important albeit secondary role in the ECSC and the EEC, and its support of positions favored by America, suggest that the United States was "betting on the right horse." While it is true that the "horse" did so well in part because the United States was betting on it, Germany could by no means have attained its present status by virtue of American support alone, as the weak position of Britain, despite United States backing, shows. Thus, American assistance to Germany was an instance of an external elite endorsing a rising internal one, neither trying to erect nor to block such an elite. The United States position vis-à-vis France and Britain was much less in line with the evolution of postwar power relations in Europe.

Until 1958, the government of France was unstable, its economy was or seemed weak, its involvement in colonial wars debilitating, its Communist party large, and its internal security system defective. Under these conditions, the United States treated France as a rather minor ally. On the other hand, the United States showed a strong preference for Britain, to which it felt closely bound by historical, political, religious, ethnic, and cultural ties and by the experience of extensive cooperation during two World Wars. This favoring of Britain over France proved, after 1958, to be contrary to the evolving power structure in Western Europe. The EEC developed rapidly under French initiative, but the United States continued to follow its pre-1958 policy, as reflected in its sharing of nuclear secrets with Britain while continuing to deny them to France, and in frequent consultations with Macmillan but not with de Gaulle. This had a direct effect on the EEC: When the United States took steps, in 1962, to initiate a multinational nuclear force within NATO, the American president consulted at Nassau with the British prime minister but not with the French president. The invitation to participate in such a force was sent from the Nassau conference to France at the same time that it was sent to the much less influential NATO allies, without previous consultation. This was followed, very shortly, by de Gaulle's veto of British membership in the EEC. There were, of course, many reasons for de Gaulle's decision, but the continued American policy of diminution of France, coupled with preferential treatment of Britain and Britain's acceptance of its subordinate position toward the United States, seems to have played an important role.

The United States, an elite outside the EEC, anxious to have its trusted associate in the union, encouraged West Germany, Italy, and the Netherlands to seek Britain's admission, despite France's objection. Since these countries had reasons of their own to favor Britain's membership, they pressured France in 1963 by stalemating several EEC activities that particularly concerned France. A general crisis of confidence in the EEC ensued. The degree to which the United States had precipitated this crisis by siding with Britain becomes evident if we consider how different the situation would have been if United States had strongly backed France, and limited its support for Britain. This might have had many undesirable consequences for the United States and the West, but it would have been much less threatening to the EEC, at least as far as the levels of its integration and scope in 1963 were concerned.

In short, in this case as in the Federation of the West Indies, the application of power by the external elite in favor of a weaker unit over a stronger one had de-unifying effects on the union. In the West Indies, it led to the withdrawal of the stronger units and thus to the breakup of the federation; in the EEC it resulted in at least temporary exclusion of the weaker unit by the stronger one[2] at the price of considerable strain on the union. In both cases, the external elite worked not with but "around" the stronger member(s), and this policy had de-unifying effects.

The rise and fall of the UAR was not significantly affected by any external elite, and none controlled the development of the Nordic Council and other regional associations in this area. Hence these two cases are not "relevant" to our proposition. The study of the Nordic area suggests, however, that the proposition ought to be extended. Not only the influence of external elites but also that of external and competitive systems on unification should be considered.

Most countries are members of more than one international system and are in more than one international power field. The efforts of any country to increase the integration of one system in which it is a member, or to form a new system, are affected by the repercussions such activity has, or is expected to have, on the country's participation in other systems. This plural membership is especially significant when the multiaffiliations of the units of the system whose integration is under study are not identical, when the competitive systems are more integrated than the system the units are trying to build up, and when the units attempting to forward unification are comparatively weak. In the case of the Nordic countries, developments in NATO, the EFTA, the EEC, and other international systems—which crisscross the Nordic integration, though they were not sufficient to prevent its growth altogether. In the UAR, Nasser's African- and Islam-wide ambitions, as well as the role he sought to play in other Arab nations, limited his ability to respond to Syria's needs, and hence to those of the union. Limited by his progressive stance in other "circles," he did not feel that he could allow the "right deviation" in Syria to develop as much as the consolidation of the UAR seemed to have required. It would be of interest to examine the

---

[2] "Strong" and "weak" in the EEC context.

position of other weak units from this viewpoint, to see to what degree their plural affiliations affect their ability to form and maintain unions of their own. It seems that even the more powerful units cannot escape the disintegrating effects multiple membership in international systems has when membership is not identical and the systems are not highly harmonized.[3]

INTERNALIZATION: EVEN VERSUS UNEVEN

In the West Indies and in the EEC unification was accompanied by internalization, that is, by the transfer of functions and powers of control from the external elite to the union, to its internal elites or its members. In both instances internalization was uneven. Either the degree of internalization of various member units of the evolving union was not the same, or internalization in one sector was lower than in others. Both modes of uneven internalization had de-unifying effects. These findings, as we shall see, suggest an extension of our original proposition.

Britain, the colonial power that controlled the West Indian islands, allowed them gradually to acquire self-government. But most of the authority was transferred to the member units (island governments) rather than to the union (federal government), and the pace and extent of transfer were uneven for the various units. While Jamaica and Trinidad were granted a large degree of self-government, the small islands were still held in varying degrees of colonial control. This had de-unifying effects, since the more independent units were reluctant to increase their ties with units whose political autonomy was more limited than theirs; that is, the federation was feared as delaying independence. Also, some deunification was caused by transferring authority to the units rather than to the shared administrative structure, an effect that would have occurred even if all units gained self-control at an even pace.

In the years immediately following World War II, Western Europe was dependent for both its defense and its economic welfare on the United States. With the economic resurgence of West Germany and

---

[3] This problem has been examined in another context by the author. See "A Grand Design?", *Conflict Resolution,* vol. 7 (1963), pp. 155–163.

the reconstruction of the other countries, soon followed by prosperity, full employment, and continued rapid growth of national incomes and productivity, the United States lost a good part of its influence in the economic sector that it had as the provider of scarce dollars and investment funds. By 1960, it was the United States that needed Europe's monetary assistance to stem fears of a run on the dollar. This change was reflected in the transition from the OEEC, which the United States dominated (though it was only an associate member), to the European Payments Union in which the Europeans helped one another to do with fewer dollars, to the OECD, in which the Europeans cooperated with the United States, as more or less equal partners on matters such as international trade and foreign aid. Internalization of control of economic policy has been much advanced by the EEC, which forms its own economic policies, largely independent of the United States, regarding both tariff concessions (it is more protectionist than America would like it to be) and foreign aid (which it concentrates on Africa, largely disregarding the frontiers of the Cold War in Asia and Latin America).

While in matters of economic policy the EEC countries have gained a large degree of independence from America's influence and an increasing measure of self-regulation, their defense and foreign policies are still largely dependent on the United States. Frequent mention of shared NATO control of nuclear weapons, the MLF, and national deterrents notwithstanding, at the end of 1963 nuclear weapons for the defense of Europe were almost exclusively under American control. While economic matters were controlled by Europeans, according to their conception of Europe's interests, defense arrangements other than nuclear were either "Atlantic," that is, subject to considerable American control, or national, and thus altogether outside the realm of joint control—Atlantic or European. Thus, internalization was highly uneven. As far as the European Community was concerned, it had internalized much control over its economic matters but had only little say in matters concerning its defense and related questions of foreign policy.

In this context, France's efforts to develop a national nuclear deterrent, its decision to withdraw part of its forces from NATO control, its request for the removal of American nuclear-armed bombers from French soil, and its refusal to participate in the proposed NATO multilateral nuclear force, can be viewed as attempts to balance the internalization of powers of the various sectors by reducing American influence on matters of defense and foreign policy and increasing Europe's self-control.[4] Such internalization of control would make the economic, defense, and foreign-policy sectors of the European Community similar in scope, *to the degree that these matters will be placed under EEC control* and not transferred from Atlantic to national regulation. The first steps in this direction were taken by the Franco-German Treaty of Cooperation of January 1963, which covers matters of defense and foreign policy and which invites other EEC countries to join.

The tendency to balance the internalization of powers in various sectors has resulted in some strains within the EEC, since not all the members share the same outlook. *The weaker the units are, the more strongly they tend to be oriented to the external elite.* Pro-American sentiments are strongest in the Netherlands and Italy, weakest in France, and medium in West Germany. (The statement holds for the West Indies, where the small islands are more pro-British than the larger ones.) Because of these strains, widening the scope of the EEC to include noneconomic matters is not the only direction the evolution of this union might follow. The regulation of the economic sector and of the defense sector might be brought into balance by extending the economic sector rather than by "shrinking" the defense one; this would be achieved if the economic sector of the EEC were extended into an Atlantic, OECD trade area, to be coextensive with NATO. In any event, it appears that *there is pressure to make the economic, defense, and foreign policy sectors coextensive* now that the hegemony of the external elite has been broken.

We originally expected that, as the level of integration and scope of a union increased, the union would tend to internalize both the functions performed and the authority held by the external elite. Both the study of the West Indies and of the EEC support this general view; however, they suggest several additional points, particularly regarding the relationship of this proposition to the question of the

[4] These European defenses would be under French influence in a fashion similar to the Atlantic ones under American influence.

success of unification. In general, we expect internalization to enhance the success of a union, since the increased self-control that follows makes it more likely that the union's needs will be met than if it is controlled by an external elite. (This expectation, if all other things are equal, includes elite responsiveness. If the external elite is more responsive than the internal elite, the result will be quite different. Note, for instance, the de-unifying effects of the internalization of control in the Federation of Rhodesia and Nyasaland, as power shifted from the British Colonial Office to the hands of the white settlers, a shift that accelerated African secessionist pressures.[5])

Internalization strains unification rather than enhances it under three conditions, each of which constitutes a mode of imperfect internalization rather than one in which successful internalization in itself undermines the union: (a) The functions and powers internalized are taken over by member units from the external elite rather than by the union (for example, the islands, rather than the Federation of West Indies, take over from Britain; or France, rather than the European Community, takes over from the United States). (b) The effect of such member- rather than union-internalization is even more de-unifying if some members' gains are not matched by those of others. Such uneven internalization increases heterogeneity, a factor that seems to make unification more difficult. (c) If internalization is uneven among sectors, such as the economic and the military ones, the resulting strain might be resolved in two ways: (i) The less encompassing sector might be extended to become coextensive with the other one (for example, European economic unification to include all NATO countries). This requires the external elite of the less encompassing sector to become an internal one and probably to share some of its power with the internal elites of the emerging union. (ii) Internalization of control of the other sector(s), such as defense, by the less encompassing union to make it as independent of external control in these sectors as it is in the first one. This involves a further loss of control of the evolving union by the external elite.

The second solution seems more likely, since it is in line with the

---

[5] Edward M. Clegg, *Race and Politics, Partnership in the Federation of Rhodesia and Nyasaland.* London: Oxford University Press, 1960.

general tendency of newly formed polities to seek increased self-control rather than to blend the degree of self-control attained into larger power structures. The transition, though, is likely to strain the union, as those member units that are more committed to the external elite will seek to promote broader unification to safeguard their interests. Notwithstanding being weaker, they still might be strong enough to block the internalization of control of other sectors.

ELITISM REVISITED

The effect of the distribution of power within each union on the success and failure of unification is less clear than that of the changing power relation between external elites and member units. We expected that a union would be less successful the more elites it had. It would do best with one elite to guide the unification effort; it would do less well with two elites (since conflicts over leadership would be more likely than in monoelite unions), but as long as the two elites were in coalitions, unification could still be quite successful; unions with three elites or more, we expected, would face a high level of conflict, since coalitions of three partners are difficult to stabilize. Egalitarian unions, with no elites, were expected to "compensate" for their low decisiveness by a low level of conflict and a high level of member commitment and to do as well as more elitist unions.

At first glance, no such association between the internal distribution of power and the success of unification appears. The UAR fell apart though it had only one elite; the EEC is doing best with two elites; the Federation of the West Indies broke up, though it seems to have had two elites, as does the EEC. Only the Nordic union seems to fit the pattern: It is egalitarian, low on decisiveness, and high on commitment.

A closer examination suggests that the four cases do not contradict the propositions advanced. The most direct challenge to our propositions comes from the UAR. Though the immediate initiative to form the UAR came from Syria, the union was in line with the plans and efforts of Egypt, which dominated the UAR. Since the union appears to have had only one elite, its collapse seems to be in direct opposition to our expectation that monoelite unions would be more effective than multielite ones. It should, however, be remembered that no one factor makes or breaks a unification effort, and since this union was faced with other unfavorable circumstances, the emergence of a single elite could not have saved it. But while this is quite valid we should be able to show the beneficial effects of the monoelite structure. If it did not suffice to maintain the union, did it at least extend its life, serve to counter some de-unifying factors? The answer seems to be a negative one. It is not that having a monoelite did not help; rather, it is not as clear as it seems at first glance that the UAR had one elite. We already have seen that the initiative to form the union came from Syria, not Egypt, as the initiative to dissolve it did. Initiation is one of the defining characteristics of an elite and Egypt was clearly lacking in this ingredient. Second, Egypt did not have the required assets or the necessary responsiveness. Responsiveness is discussed below, but the question of assets should be discussed here. An elite is a unit that is willing and able to invest some of its assets in leadership. In the case in point, the elite was poor, the follower comparatively well off. Still, Egypt was initially willing to sacrifice some of her resources to ease Syria's introduction into the union and finance the institutions of the UAR. But as the amount of contributions needed grew rather than declined and it became apparent that Egypt's investment of utilitarian assets was not securing for it the identitive gratification of leadership, Egypt's investments in the union were sharply curtailed. Thus it lost the second characteristic of an elite. It was at this stage that the UAR fell apart. Had Egypt been more affluent, such a curtailment of its investment in the union might not have been decided or at least have been implemented more gradually. Egypt, being poor, unrewarded for past sacrifices, and unwilling to invest additional resources by mid-1961, left the UAR, technically speaking, without an elite unit. The study of the UAR shows once more that it takes not just the will but also sufficient assets for a unit to maintain its position as an elite. In this sense, the UAR had no full-fledged elite: Egypt did not have the assets and lost the will.

To a large degree, the decline of the external elite of the West Indies did not coincide with the emergence of an internal one. The two potential elites of the West Indies were in conflict and hence neutralized much of their respective influence; moreover, they were less willing to spend their assets on unification than even Egypt was. Conflict marked the relations between Jamaica and Trinidad. Separated by a thousand miles, following noncomplementary economic policies (Jamaica was strongly protectionist while Trinidad supported a free-trade policy), differing in history (Trinidad was a Spanish possession and had been extensively settled by French farmers; Jamaica, though originally Spanish, had been little colonized by Spain and had been a British colony for over 300 years) and in ethnic composition (Trinidad has a large and powerful East Indian minority), they struggled with each other over leadership of the federation. It is not possible to determine to what extent this conflict weakened the already weak federation, but it is safe to state that it further reduced the already small regards of leadership. Basically, neither Jamaica nor Trinidad was anxious to make the sacrifices required by leadership; each was aiming to use its resources for its own development. Jamaica and Trinidad were largely uninterested in an elite position and its obligations; and to the degree that they were interested, competition with each other and with the retreating but still active external elite, Britain, undermined whatever reward federal leadership might have had to offer. In other words, Jamaica and Trinidad had the assets but not the will to be the elites of the federation.[6]

The situation in the EEC fits the propositions advanced once we recall that the EEC is not to be viewed as a two-elite structure, but one that is comparatively egalitarian in utilitarian matters and elitist in political ones. The new element the EEC introduces is that of the system-elite. We need to augment our propositions by stating that the *most effective unions are expected to be ruled by system-elites rather than by member-elites.* A system-elite combines the decisiveness found in member-elites with the ability to generate commitment found in egalitarian unions; the decisiveness is gained from the existence of one superior center of decision-making, while commitments

[6] Note that most of the population lives on the two larger islands, hence carrying the Little Eight would have been less difficult than if the population had been evenly distributed. Note also that foreign aid was available to alleviate this task.

are generated because the system-elite is representing all the members of the union as well as the union as a collectivity. (At least it is more likely to do so successfully than any member-elite.)

As far as utilitarian exchanges are concerned, the EEC—in the period studied—was highly egalitarian; all members benefited about equally from the exchanges. The center of utilitarian power that emerged was located largely in a system-elite, in part in the supranational Economic Commission and in part in the Community-oriented though intergovernmental Council of Ministers. In political matters, especially those concerning the question of membership and the expansion of unification into noneconomic sectors, initiative was clearly in France's hands, with West Germany as the second elite. On most issues, during the time of the period under study, the two elites were in agreement. They formed a leadership coalition within the political realm, though France had an edge in influence over Germany. This is reflected in France's more frequent initiation of programs, most of which were accepted, and in the intellectual leadership it provided for the Economic Commission. France's power edge and greater initiative further solidified the power structure of the EEC by clearly indicating who was at the top of the hierarchy. (However, as is common in such relations, some alienation developed in the secondary elite which, in the long run, especially if Germany's power grows relative to France's, might generate considerable strain. If a third elite-country is to join this union, we expect an intense power conflict.[7])

We expected egalitarian unions to be less decisive than elitist ones but more capable of generating commitment. The EEC casts an interesting light on this proposition. In utilitarian matters, in which this union was egalitarian, the commitments of the members to the union were high; at the same time, there were some complaints about a lack of decisiveness. While the union often reduced tariffs ahead of schedule and abolished quotas in four instead of 12 years, the difficulties accompanying the establishment of a common agricultural policy were enormous, the introduction of anticartel measures as proved indecisive, the implementation of a program of free mobility

---

[7] See *supra*, chap. 7, for our arguments in support of this position.

of labor has been slow, etc. Most steps that were taken involved many rounds of consultations, conferences, and committee meetings, as well as talks between the national delegations and the commission. (Still the EEC, even in these matters, was less indecisive than the Nordic union.)

On the other hand, in political matters there was much more decisiveness; in 1960, de Gaulle almost single-handedly blocked discussions of plans for supranational political unification and advanced intergovernmental ones,[8] as he blocked British entry to the EEC early in 1963. This decisiveness was accompanied by a lack of consultation and some alienation of the other five members. (The fact that Germany, as the secondary elite, was often consulted made the union's political leadership less elitist and provided its leadership with some European rather than merely French flavor.) In short, the union showed on the one side egalitarianism coupled with high commitment but some indecisiveness and, on the other hand, decisive elitism coupled with some alienation. Our proposition, derived from studies of interpersonal relations and small group behavior, is thus supported by these data on international relations.

The Nordic Council and other Nordic regional associations are highly egalitarian. While Sweden is more affluent than the other members and twice as large in population as the next largest member, it has shown relatively few elite tendencies in the period under study. It did take the initiative in various unification efforts such as the Nordic defense alliance and the Nordic common market, but it did not have the power or the inclination to advance them effectively. Again, in line with the proposition advanced, the commitment of members to the Nordic union was high but its decisiveness was low. Long negotiations frequently led to nothing more than recommendations that were not implemented or to resolutions to appoint one more study group to investigate once more the matter at hand. Even comparatively unimportant matters such as which side of the road to drive on or agreement on penalties for drunken driving involved years of consultation before a proposal was formulated, and even then, as in the case of the examples just cited, no action was taken

[8] Roy Pryce, *The Political Future of the European Community.* London: John Marshband, Ltd., 1962, pp. 42–44.

by the member-governments for fairly long periods of time. Many factors other than the egalitarian structure account for this indecisiveness, but the lack of regional leadership played its role and the absence of a system-elite seems an important factor in inhibiting decisiveness.

In short, after examining the four attempts at unification, we hold even more strongly than before that in order for a union to grow and succeed, there must be an elite-unit that has command of the needed assets *and* the will to invest them in unification. Egypt did not have sufficient assets and lost the will; Jamaica and Trinidad lacked the will more than the assets. Thus, the failure of unification in these two cases can be accounted for in part by the lack of an effective elite. The data also indicate the value of elite *coalitions* as against the damage caused by elite *conflict,* a dimension not included in our original proposition. The political evolution of the EEC was propelled by the French-German coalition while the West Indies suffered from conflicts between Jamaica and Trinidad, to the degree that they were active as federal elites at all. Egalitarian unions, like the Nordic one, or the EEC in utilitarian matters, score higher in building up and maintaining commitment than in decisiveness. The EEC was more decisive than the Nordic union because it had a system-elite that allowed both more decisiveness and more commitment than would have been possible otherwise. On the other hand, the EEC is not as fully effective as a union with a strong system-elite might be, because the member-elites of the EEC have not submitted themselves to the system-elite even in utilitarian matters. The future success of this union might be significantly enhanced by the growth of the system-elite, and largely undermined by new member-elites or a change from coalition to conflict in the relations between the two member-elites.

Our initial propositions have not been contradicted; however, the data suggested three extensions. We learned that a union might be elitist in one sector and egalitarian in another. The effects in each sector seem to be in line with our propositions. Second, system-elites seem to allow a union to increase both its decisiveness and its ability to build up and maintain the members' commitment. The stronger the system-elite is, vis-à-vis the member-elites, the more we would expect a unification effort to succeed. Finally, while three-member elite systems seem to us to be conflict-prone, the effect of a dual-elite structure on the success of a unification drive is determined largely by whether the elites are in conflict or coalition.

HARMONIZATION VERSUS INTEGRATION

Action in unison, the essence of a union, needs to be guided; units do not act in unison unless there is some investment in coordination. Coordination might be obtained by an external elite, a subject discussed above, or through either harmonization of the member-units or the development of a center of decision-making, identification, and control of force—that is, integration. Harmonization and integration are processes that might better be understood as pure definitions, as the two extreme ends of a continuum that consists of different ratios of one over the other. International systems might then be characterized as more integrated and less harmonized, or as less integrated and more harmonized. The EEC, for instance, due to the supranational elements of the Economic Commission, is more integrated and less harmonized than the Nordic union, which produces action in unison largely through harmonization.

The essence of the difference between high integration and high harmonization is that in the first case the units are partially fused together to form one system (for example, a nation out of tribes), while in the latter the units maintain their autonomy but work together. This is not the same difference as that between having and not having sovereignty, for having sovereignty does not imply coordination or acting in unison. *The difference between harmonization and integration is that between two modes of cooperation:* one that draws on a center of power above and beyond the member-units and one that seeks to do without it through interaction between the power centers of the member units. In the world of finance this is the difference between plans for setting up an international bank and plans seeking to improve the coordination between the central banks of nation-states.

In general, political scientists studying international relations tend to apply the harmonization model since it fits into the balance-of-power tradition and since they realize it is difficult to form supranational centers. Without questioning the assumption that in the period of nationalism it is easier to attain harmonization than integration, it seems to us on theoretical grounds that "harmonized" unions will be on the average less stable than "integrated" ones, and that harmonized unions will tend to have a much smaller scope of activities carried out in unison than integrated ones. This we expect to be the case, as a broad scope requires much cooperation that is difficult to attain by harmonization which is more cumbersome and slow than integration and is less reliable and predictable, since it is easier under harmonization not to follow an agreed-upon joint policy.

This is not to suggest that harmonization is more voluntaristic and hence more likely to maintain the commitment of the participants; on the contrary, one of the virtues of integration is that it builds up a center of power with which the participants can identify (an identification that is transferred to the union and its policies) and around which transnational interest groups can be formed that in turn ease the problem of forming a regional consensus. In short, we expect that no broad and stable unification will be attained without integration.

The data on the EEC and the Nordic union, which bear on this question, seem as far as it goes to support our position. The dynamic quality of the EEC unification, in the period under study, is due in part to the existence of supranational elements in the administration of the Community, elements that are lacking in the Nordic area. The absence of this source of identitive power seems to be a major factor in limiting regional unification in the Nordic countries.[9]

It is important to realize that in addition to the usual difficulties in controlling for other factors, the comparison is not a full one because, while the Nordic area is almost purely harmonized (to the degree it acts in unison) the EEC is not exclusively or even largely a supranational system. The EEC combines harmonization and integration, giving considerable weight to harmonization. If the EEC in the long run fails to amount to much more than the Nordic union, this might be due to factors that have nothing to do with the question

[9] Details will be found *supra*, p. 252ff.

at hand (for example, American pressures or de Gaulle's personality), or it might be due to the limited—rather than excessive—reliance on supranational centers. We have not yet had a group of *nation*-states trying a full-fledged or even an extensive regional supranational system.

A short comment on the role of institutions is called for. The difference between harmonization and integration is in part one of the institutional modes in which elite efforts to advance unification are molded. The question hence arises of how important differences in institutional structure are. Will a group of units that is "ready" for unification succeed with any institutional structure or will it not at least pick the one suited for its needs and capacity? Does not the reliance on harmonization largely reflect the lack of willingness of the unit-elites to submit to a supranational center? While we agree that institutional modes cannot form unions of units that are not predisposed when leadership and integrating power is lacking, we suggest—and the data seem to support this suggestion—that differences in institutional structure have an independent effect (see *supra,* p. 258ff.). The willingness of the units to accept supranational elites is not a static given; it can be changed by the efforts of various elites and the experience of successful supranational institutions.

Second, *the impact of supranational institutions is largest when other conditions for unification are favorable and least when they are not favorable.* That is, while in general they have only a limited independent effect, when the conditions are favorable the "right" institutional structure might provide the marginal difference between success and failure; actually under favorable conditions full success of unification without an integrated center is impossible.

Finally, it seems to us that the material presented here has justified the distinction between the institutional aspects of interstate systems and the more sociological aspects. We did identify the concept of a union not as a legal or institutional concept but as a sociopolitical reality whose earmark is acting in unison. Hence in our terms there might be a union without any formal regional structure, as the Nordic union was before the Nordic Council was established; or there might be a formal regional structure without the sociopolitical foundation of a union, a situation approximated in the West Indies in the last months of the federation; or there might be a formal structure that is more or less in accordance with the sociopolitical basis. In these terms, it makes sense to state that the institutional structure is more (or less) "advanced" than the union, and that the experience of a particular institutional structure strengthens (in the EEC) or weakens (in the West Indies) the union. In a sense, the disbandment of a particular institutional structure does not necessarily spell the end of an underlying union, as seems to be the case in the UAR. All these distinctions and propositions cannot be expressed if we fuse the legal, institutional, and sociopolitical concepts of union.

EFFECTIVE COMPOSITIONS

INTEGRATING POWER, SCOPE, AND LEVEL OF INTEGRATION

There was, as expected, a close relationship between the *level* and *scope* of integration attained and the *kinds* and *amounts* of integrating *power* available. In the West Indies, the utilitarian integrating power was weak. Despite an long, though intermittent, effort few island illusion structures developed. Further, the islands agreed only to a limited expansion of these structures with federation. Utilitarian exchanges among the islands were meager: the interisland trade amounted to about 2 percent of the total trade; freedom of labor mobility was opposed; there was no federal currency and only a very limited federal budget. Hence, the utilitarian losses that a secessionist unit faced were minimal.

Identitive power of the West Indian union was low, as identification of the average citizen with his island was considerably greater than his indentification with the federation or the "West Indian Nation," which was an intellectual artifice that had little mass appeal. The low utilitarian integrating power of the federation declined further as the more affluent units' development programs succeeded, while the other units, which were initially much worse off, remained in poverty. The increased ability of the larger islands to gain assets from the United States, not tied to federation, further reduced their dependence on British aid which was vaguely related to membership in the federation. The federation's threat to reallocated assets in favor of the smaller and poorer units at the expense of the larger islands created for these more affluent islands a utilitarian interest in secession. When the break came, there was no indigenous coercive power—no federal military or police force—that could, even if desired, delay secession until other kinds of integrating power could be built up. Nor did Britain employ its forces.

The initial efforts to bring about this federation aimed at a low scope and low level of integration, since the lack of integrating power to carry a more highly integrated union was recognized. Moreover, several adjustments were made to further reduce the scope of the federal structure to meet the low level of existing support. But as integrating power declined rather than grew under the anemic federal experience, it reached a level that was too weak to sustain even the low scope of this institutional framework, and the federation collapsed.

Utilitarian ties in the UAR were stronger than in the West Indies, at least in the sense that Egyptians gained increased control of the administrative structure of Syria, its foreign trade, and many of its industries. Interregional contacts were limited because of the discontiguous territory and differences in utilitarian structure and policies. The declining contributions of Egypt to Syria in the last year of the UAR further reduced the utilitarian ties. Attempts to reallocate assets in Syria accelerated the flight of capital from that country, thus weakening the economy which was suffering from a third year of drought and creating a deep economic crisis in the last year of the union. While some general indentitive commitments to the union continued to exist, as part of a general and vague spirit of Pan-Arabism, the specific commitments of Syrians to Egypt or to the institutional framework of the UAR were much weakened. The use of force, briefly attempted, probably could have kept the parts together for a while, but this was difficult because of the discontiguous territory, the small Egyptian force stationed in Syria, and the incomplete control of Syria's army by Nasser's men. Also, there was little inclination to apply force on a great scale. In this way, while the integrating power was reduced below the level necessary to maintain the 1958 union, the level of integration was not reduced so far as to make future attempts at unification too difficult. By averting a showdown, Nasser avoided the imprinting of a more bitter anti-European feeling upon Syrian consciousness. Whatever the future might bring, the union of 1958–1961, though provided with greater integrating power than the Federation of the West Indies, needed still more to maintain its much broader scope; and this was not available.

The Nordic countries are related by weak utilitarian-administrative ties that rest on informal intergovernmental cooperation coupled with some formal cooperation achieved through the Nordic Council and frequent intergovernmental meetings and consultations. There are only a few joint Nordic enterprises such as Scandinavian Air Service. Nordic trade constitutes a small fraction of the international trade of the area. The ceiling on the growth of utilitarian Nordic cooperation is largely a product of the dissimilar utilitarian ties that the Nordic countries have with non-Nordic countries and systems (Finland with Russia, Denmark with West Germany). Note, however, that Sweden is relatively less dependent on such ties. While indentitive similarities are high, they have limited actual (as distinct from potential) integrating value. They are not tied to any regional center of power and the Nordic Council is more a symbol of the relative unimportance of regional institutions and their weakness than a focus of identification. The ideology of Nordic cooperation far exceeds the scope and level of regional integration; even on the ideological level, regionalism is partially neutralized by nationalist commitments reflected in stereotyped suspicions of Sweden and rejection of supranationalism. There is no center of coercion. The low level of integration of the Nordic area can be maintained by small amounts of integrating power, and this is available; a decline or rise of this power is more likely to be a consequence of processes in other systems than the Nordic one, though some internal evolution is not to be excluded.

The EEC built up its utilitarian exchanges rather rapidly and its utilitarian structure more gradually, but quite effectively. Actually, its level of utilitarian integration is approaching a point at which some political unification will probably be required. While the initiation and growth of the EEC were largely supported by utilitarian power, these developments were enhanced by the presence of, and preexisting identitive commitments to, the idea of European unification, which the EEC has drawn upon and been able to expand. It had, and so far has needed, little coercive power. As the amount of integrating power available grew, the level and scope of integration increased. Agriculture was included; questions of tax and monetary policy were approached, etc. Whether this will lead to excessive optimism about European integration and to the extension of the EEC's institutional framework and activities before the requisite integrating power to support them is built up, is an open question.

It is hardly surprising that the more utilitarian and identitive power supporting a particular unification effort, the farther it advances, and vice versa. Several more specific questions and statements regarding the relationship between power and the level and scope of integration are suggested by the data.

As for identitive power, the data suggest that cultural similarities do not necessarily produce identitive integrating power and hence a high level and scope of integration. Units that have similar cultures, religions, languages, etc.—as the Arab countries or the Nordic ones—might not only fail to act in unison (that is, not form a union) because some *other* (non-identitive) factors work against unification and neutralize the beneficial effects of similarities in identitive assets; moreover they might not apply these assets toward building up such identitive power because of divisive *identitive* elements (for example, in the Nordic area, the historical memories of Swedish overlordship) or because the identitive assets are not related ("specified" technically) to a union. The fact that most Latin American elites (except in Brazil) speak Spanish does not assure that they will use it to build up mutual understanding and regional unions, and the fact that most Arabs are Moslems does not as a matter of course lead all Moslems to strive to come under the roof of one political union. Quite a few West Indians saw in their region a more cultural and anthropological than political concept. Even where identitive assets are tied to a political union, they do not necessarily support the one that exists; actually they might agitate for a quite different union. Thus the Syrian *Baaths* were probably as committed to Arab unity as Nasser, if not more so, but after they fell out of favor with Nasser and were eased out of power positions in Syria, they—while continuing to believe in Arab unity—were highly alienated from the UAR. What is needed is a consensus of support for the particular union, including an acceptance of its basic institutional features (for example, its unitary structure).

To be effective, the ideas that are legitimating a particular political institution, through which the process of unification is to be implemented, must also be positive and not just symbols of rejection. An "anti" ideology (such as anticolonialism) provides a convenient meeting ground for many people and groups that adhere to a variety of beliefs and have a variance of interests, but such an agreement tends to be unstable. Perhaps precisely because no genuine consensus is worked out in a purely antiideology as is necessary when a positive platform is agreed upon, the effectiveness of a pure antiideology is limited to the range of objects it rejects and to the period during which the external pressure (the target of antisymbols) is felt. Effective social movements—and unifications often have a movement aspect—require a positive ideology. One of the main limitations of the West Indian "nationhood," on the strictly ideological level, was that its political content (as distinct from its cultural one) was meager and largely "anti."

Even when the positive content is available, to be effective it must be accepted by the majority of the politically active citizens. When some elements of democracy are observed, there is always the potential danger that the lack of a broad basis of identitive commitments to a union will be exploited by an opposition to bring about secession. It seems that a program of education, in the broadest sense of the term including adult education and some forms of propaganda, is necessary to develop such a basis for a unification ideology. This was a weak spot of the Federation of the West Indies. Whether the "European" idea has really penetrated enough to provide the identitive power needed to support a European integration broad in scope, leading toward a political community, remains to be seen.

The limits of *charisma* are also to be examined in this context. There seems to be a wide belief, largely among the lay followers of public affairs but not altogether absent among professional analysts, that charismatic leadership can move identitive mountains, generating whatever commitment mass support of a reform or a unification movement requires. Actually, sociological analysis suggests that there are sharp structural limitations to the conditions under which charismatic leadership appears and the direction it can go. Our data illustrate this point. Nasser is a charismatic leader, and his *charisma,* as expected, engendered support of the union. His Union Day visits to Syria, his handing out land to the peasants, etc. were effective gestures. Still he could not generate anything like sufficient identitive power to support the UAR when other factors failed. Similarly, it makes for a good narrative but little historical validity to see Monnet as the "father" of the Common Market, unless we mean father in the literal sense of a man who conceived a union but had to find a "womb" in which it was to be planted and in which it would grow beyond his power and control. Actually, most of Monnet's ideas failed and it was only after drastic revisions of his initial ideas toward a much more gradualist approach, after half a dozen structural factors had been changed and several processes over which he had no control advanced, that the EEC was launched and progressed. The defeat of the highly charismatic Manley by the not less charismatic Bustamente in the referendum in Jamaica in 1961, which precipitated the secession of Jamaica and the disbandment of the West Indian federation, shows another limit of the charismatic leader—he can be neutralized by countercharismatics. Which of the two (or more) charismatics will win in such a contest is determined more by the structural factors (for example, to what degree did education predispose Jamaican voters to favor unification) than by who is a greater charismatic.[10]

Other statements, made here initially, regarding the effects of coercive power and the timing of showdowns, could not be explored, because of limitations of the data. Coercion was not used in three of the four cases. On the basis of the cases studied, we can speculate that the lack of force hastened the de-unification of the Federation of the West Indies (surely the Federation of Rhodesia and Nyasaland lasted much longer, under otherwise much less favorable circumstances, by relying considerably on force). The limited use of coer-

---

[10] Two chapters devoted to charisma and structure are included in the author's *A Comparative Analysis of Complex Organizations,* chaps. 9 and 10.

cive power in the UAR (by Sarraj and his secret police) probably extended its life. Nasser's refraining from a showdown in the first period left the northern region of the UAR with an unstable power structure, as far as the member groups were concerned. In particular, the army and the conservative groups were neither rendered harmless nor was their cooperation won. On the other hand, the avoidance of a large-scale use of force when secession came, while allowing the disbandment of the UAR, left the door open for future unification.

The data cast some light on the "functional" approach. They suggest that in gradually building up the scope of a union, the critical questions are what sectors are tackled first and how extensive the functional effort in each of these sectors is. If they are low spill-over sectors, or if integration in high spill-over sectors is below the take-off point, a broad-scope unification process will not be primed. Thus the numerous cases of "harmonized" legislation of the Scandinavian countries, such as the codification of driving laws or welfare privileges, have little effect on future unification, as they concern matters that generate only little if any new unification pressure. Scandinavian spokesmen will point dramatically to such measures as opening the door of these countries to all the citizens of the area, but actually little increase in labor movement has taken place and the rise in tourism is not significantly larger than in non-Nordic neighboring countries. Similarly, the unification measures taken by Syria and Egypt between 1955 and 1958 did little to prepare the ground for broader unification; though these measures were in the high spill-over military and economic sectors, the measures themselves were of such limited scope that they did not initiate a drawing together of the social structures of the two countries. Similarly, the sporadic efforts Britain made to build shared institutions for the West Indies were below the take-off point. On the other hand, integration of the coal and steel industries of six European countries seemed to have a considerably larger spill-over effect. In short, it seems that the "functional" approach in itself is neither valid nor false; it is not specific enough. The scope-broadening effect of functional integration depends on which sectors are selected and how much each is integrated.

COMMUNICATION, RESPONSIVENESS, AND REPRESENTATION

The existence of effective communication channels between member-units and the elite (or elites) and the responsiveness of the elite to the representation of politically effective groups, in relation to their power, were expected to enhance unification. We found that in one case there was not much of a center to communicate to and from or to be represented by; the union relied largely on informal, horizontal communication (the Nordic union). In the other two cases, representation was distorted, responsiveness, faulty, and—in line with our proposition—unification, unsuccessful (West Indies; UAR). The fourth one—the EEC—provides a case of effective communication, responsiveness, and representation; though unification here is successful, we shall see, the pattern is different from that we expected.

The Nordic union has no one center of decision-making or power. The Nordic Council, which is a consultative body, meets only for a short annual session. It does not even have a permanent secretariat. Though it can be convened between annual sessions, it was never felt necessary to do so. Actually the Nordic regional institutions are so sensitive to upward communications, so reluctant to move unless unanimity of support has been gained, that small minority groups can veto action by the system, though the action consists at best of making a recommendation to the member governments. The Nordic institutional structure plays, in effect, no role as an independent lever for unification. While thus the highest level of possible responsiveness is approximated, from the viewpoint of the advancement of unification this case actually reflects overresponsiveness. That is, less unification is attained than would be possible, all other things being equal, if the regional institutions were somewhat less responsive to upward communications and would instead show more leadership and generate more downward communication.

An abundance of informal and formal horizontal communication between the countries replaces to some degree the need for a regional organization and hence allows for more action-in-unison than one would expect from examining the limited and overresponsive institutional structure. In other words, to some degree, horizontal communication substitutes (or compensates) for the lack of elites, centers of regional power, and vertical communication. But it cannot fully substitute for these because there are limits on what horizontal communication "nets" can carry, in terms of loads and kinds of decisions. They also have fewer secondary-priming effects than regional organizations with decision-making centers of their own.

The only two significant barriers to communication between the ten West Indian islands and their federal government were the discontiguous territory and the paucity of facilities typical of an underdeveloped country. Lack of responsiveness was found in the British policy that did not recognize that the institutional structure that London was promoting for the federation was not compatible with its evolving power structure. In particular, the underrepresentation of Jamaica—corrected in part in a late stage of the life of the federation—and the barring, in effect, of the charismatic leaders of the two larger islands from federal office, was quite detrimental to the development of the federation. The lack of responsiveness of the federal government to the larger islands is reflected in the attempts to forward a federal tax policy, labor mobility, and other measures that were unacceptable to these islands.

The situation in the UAR is in part analogous to that of the West Indies, insofar as the unit that seceded was underrepresented in the union's government, which, in turn, was not responsive to the unit's needs, or, more precisely, was responsive for only a limited period. (And, as in the West Indies, the secessionist unit in the UAR was economically better off.) Moreover, Syria's underrepresentation was much higher than that of Jamaica and Trinidad. Not only was the union dominated by the Egyptians, but the government of Syria was also increasingly controlled by Egyptians. The media of upward communication, such as intelligence reports, did not suffice; the responsiveness of Nasser's government was faulty, both in the general strategy followed (see below), and in specific agrarian and commercial policies introduced. There is little question that Nasser and his staff knew about the rising alienation in Syria, but there is room for doubt whether they were aware of its scope and intensity. Intelligence reports are not backed by power (as compared to communications transmitted by political representatives); hence, they tend to inform rather than to generate pressure for response. Since it is the response that counts, rather than merely "being informed," our general contention that the role of communication in unification has been overemphasized and that of power underplayed is strengthened by developments in the UAR. Note, also, that groups that were initially cooped through representation, especially the *Baath,* were alienated when the institutional channels for the expression of their viewpoint and interests were closed. *Adequate representation seems to be a prerequisite for adequate responsiveness.*[11]

The secret of the success of the EEC lies in part in the way communication, responsiveness, and representation have been combined. There is considerable formal communication from the national capitals to the EEC headquarters and vice versa. It is transmitted in frequent meetings of the council and through continuous consultations of the commission with the permanent representatives of the Six and with the national interest groups. But these meetings and consultations, it should be noted, are also mechanisms by which the EEC's viewpoint is communicated to the national governments and not just devices for representing national and particularistic interests to the EEC. In addition, there is some informal consulting of government bureaucracies and EEC-wide pressure groups (such as farmers' associations, which cut across national boundaries), though both the transnational integration of these groups and the influence exerted by them in Brussels has been limited in the period under study. *In toto,* the commission appears to receive sufficient information on the needs of the member-nations (information that is based by power in the council, where the commission's proposals are subject to the approval or disapproval of national ministers) and of various interest groups (through national, multinational, and direct representation).

The commission is not, however, under any intensive pressure from these sources. It can, within the limits of the Treaty of Rome and the Community spirit, act as an independent lever to enhance unification. It cannot make the Six agree when there is no basis for

[11] This point has some bearing on the recent tendency of American students of developing nations to claim that a responsive government need not be democratic.

consensus, but it can elicit whatever latent consensus there may be (as it did for instance in the farm issue) and to some degree pioneer new steps to try to extend this consensus (as it did in formulating the 1962 Action Program). The commission, in pursuing these extension policies, has been careful not to overstep the bounds of national tolerance, despite pressure from the federalist European Parliamentary Assembly. While one might argue about this or that instance, the commission seems to provide, by and large, a clear example of an organ that is responsive and communicative, without being so responsive that no independent line or course of action can be pursued.

The commission is not under the direct and effective control of a parliamentary body or even of the national governments (which can only veto proposals but cannot initiate them; nor can they dismiss a commissioner in mid-term); this accounts, in part, for the commission's ability to resist pressures from interest groups and national administrations. Further, it is committed to the pursuit of the Community's interests as it conceives them and to the buildup of unification which provides ideological protection against nationalist pressures, though it is far from immune to them. At this initial stage of unification, such intermediate responsiveness seems conducive to greater unification. If the commission were subject to more extensive control by the national governments (some of which favor a less powerful system-elite), it would be unable to play the role it does in promoting unification; if it were less responsive to nationalist pressures, as the more extreme "Europeans" would have it, the commission would come into sharp conflict with the member-governments and alienate them to a degree that would prompt them to act to curb the commission's power. In short, while intermediate responsiveness might be undesirable from the viewpoint of values such as parliamentary responsibility and democracy (the commission being an appointed bureaucracy), intermediate responsiveness seems to be more effective than either high or low responsiveness from the viewpoint of the twin values of maintaining the members' commitments *and* advancing the level and scope of unification.

In short, the material suggests that extensive vertical communication and representation relative to the power of the participant units, coupled with intermediate responsiveness, as in the EEC, enhances unification most. High responsiveness, like that of the Nordic Council, might stalemate the responding organ; low responsiveness, as that of Nasser's "trusted" cabinet, might leave the elite free to stray beyond the bonds of tolerance of the member units to the detriment of the union.[12]

REACTIONS TO ALIENATION: SECESSION VERSUS REVOLT

We expected that the less integrated a system is, the greater the probability that alienated units will secede rather than attempt to gain control of the center to remove the source of their grievances. We expected this to be the case because the losses from secession incurred by an alienated unit and the advantages to be gained by controlling the power center are smaller the lower is the level of integration of a union. The price of secession is hence small and the rewards of revolution minor, since little "business" is conducted under the center's control. The EEC provides no evidence relevant to this point. The Nordic union has no center to be "captured"; in cases of dissatisfaction we would expect the disaffected members to try to reduce further their institutional ties rather than to try to gain control of the common associations (unless alienation is generated by the very limited capacity of these associations). The Syrians chose to secede rather than to try to capture the center of power of the UAR (the secession, of course, required taking over the unit—Syria—but not the power of the union). Taking over control of the union might seem an artificial alternative that small Syria would never consider. Actually, during the early days of the UAR, the Syrians expected to run the union because, they said, they were "smarter" than the Egyptians. The same holds for Jamaica and Trinidad; they chose to leave rather than to try to control the federation. (Trinidad, however, was willing to serve as the head of a unitary state of the east Caribbean, a situation in which it would have effective control of a more highly integrated union.) The preference for

[12] The responsiveness of the British and of the federal government of the West Indies to the larger islands was not adequate, though higher than Nasser's to Syria.

secession over revolution, at low levels of integration, is thus as fully supported by data as any statement can be from the material at hand. Of the four, the EEC is the only union which, if its integration continues to grow, we expect in the near future to reach a stage at which alienated parties will be more inclined to try to "take over" than to quit.

ASYMMETRIC EXCHANGES AND LEADERSHIP

The study of patterns of exchange was initiated with two "sensitizing" concepts rather than propositions. We made little use of the concept of "rate of exchange," defined by the amount of output a member has to provide for each unit of input it gains. Future study will determine if this concept is in itself of value. Coupled with the trifold classification of assets (or "substance of exchange"), as coercive, utilitarian, or identitive, it was helpful in highlighting the following point.

Elite-units that lead unifications seem not to seek to improve their positions by using their power to acquire more utilitarian assets from the union (from other units or from system transactions) than they invest in it; that is, contrary to a widely held belief, *their main interest in unification does not seem to be improving their utilitarian rates of exchange.* The data suggest the contrary; that leading a union, to the degree it is in the hands of a member-elite or an external elite (as distinguished from a system-elite), seems to require, on balance, investment of some utilitarian assets by the elite in exchange for some symbolic (identitive) gratification, such as that gained from the status of leadership. That is, if a full balance sheet could be drawn, it probably would show that the elite of a union invests more utilitarian assets in unification than any other member and derives from it more prestige and other symbolic gratification than any other member.

The Nordic countries' strong commitments to national sovereignty and their fears of Swedish superiority, caused by historical experience, may well account for the very limited symbolic reward available to Sweden as a potential elite of the contemporary Nordic union, and hence her rather reluctant attempts at leadership and limited investment in it. Still, Sweden provided more assets than the other countries in various joint enterprises (for example, SAS and the Norway-Swedish electrical project),[13] and would have been willing to provide even more (for instance, for a Nordic defense union in 1949) had the other Scandinavian countries been more willing to participate in such arrangements and recognize, and thus reward, Swedish leadership.

The balance sheet for the EEC is difficult to draw. By and large, utilitarian benefits and contributions of all members seem to be about even. In the period under study, France surely gained a disproportionate share of the symbolic rewards, though all members gained from the prestige the European Community enjoyed in the Western world. One could argue the case that France made an "extra" utilitarian contribution when it agreed to reduce the tariffs on industrial products before those on agriculture, in which it was much more interested. But this seemed only a temporary delay. Similarly, France's African associates received the major share of the funds the EEC Development Fund allotted, funds contributed by all six members. But at the same time, France is giving up, at least formally, its special ties to these associates; they are to become associates of the European Community. In short, little can be learned about the EEC from an analysis of the balance of exchanges, other than to state that it further strengthened our earlier statement that the EEC as a utilitarian union is basically an egalitarian union with no one country gaining from it or investing in it significantly more than the others. This of course may be one more reason for its success.

The UAR provides a good illustration of the price of leadership; poorer Egypt invested both assets and personnel in more affluent Syria to build up the first link of an Arab nation that would spread from the Atlantic Ocean to the Persian Gulf under Egypt's leadership. But it also shows the limits of an elite's toleration for asymmetric exchanges. As Syria—rejecting and rebelling—became more and more an embarrassment rather than a stepping-stone to the dream of Arab unity under Egypt, Egypt curtailed its contributions. Developments in the West Indies suggest that when the utilitarian contribu-

---

[13] If these assets are calculated on a per country and not a per capita basis.

tions the elite(s) are expected to make are large and the symbolic rewards are limited and not ensured (in this case, because of Britain's role, the conflict between the two larger islands over the elite status, and the small islands' monopolization of top federal posts), the exchange becomes too asymmetric and is rejected.

In sum, the twin concepts of rate and substance of exchange seem to be of some use, and the proposition about the asymmetric exchange of elites (utilitarian output, exchanged for symbolic input) seems to hold, at least for the initiation period, and as long as the asymmetry is not large. When the expected symbolic rewards are not forthcoming, the utilitarian investments are cut off.

A DYNAMIC PERSPECTIVE
OF INTEGRATING POWER

POWER REQUIREMENTS FOR GROWTH ARE
HIGHER THAN FOR MAINTENANCE

The fact that it requires less integrating power to stabilize the level and scope of a union than to expand it cannot be demonstrated till considerably more precise measurements of the variables concerned are developed, and the difficult methodological problems of comparative measurements are overcome.[14] Until then, all comparative statements, such as the following, are to be viewed as tentative. The West Indies and the UAR are beyond the consideration of the present proposition, since their level of integration and scope declined. That of the Nordic union increased after World War II and continued to grow somewhat in the period under study (1953–1964); by 1964, it was largely a stable union rather than a rising one. The level of the EEC and its scope, in comparison, grew continually in the period under study (1958–1964). A comparison of these two unions hence provides an opportunity to check our proposition.

The utilitarian power of the EEC was surely larger than that of the Nordic union; first of all, in terms of the proportion of trade that was intraunion (in 1961, it was 25 percent for the EEC and 20 per-

[14] On these problems, see my *A Comparative Analysis,* chap. 12.

cent for the Nordic countries). The EEC had a stronger utilitarian structure in its system-elite than the Nordic union, which relied on intergovernmental efforts and horizontal communication. Regarding the identitive power of the two unions, it seems safe to state that the Nordic people had greater feelings of kinship toward one another than the members of the EEC (compare, for instance, the attitude of Germans and Frenchmen to each other to that of Swedes and Norwegians). But affinity might not be activated as an identitive power to support a particular unification effort. It seems that the idea of Nordic unification had only limited active appeal to public imagination in the period at hand, while that of the European Community commaded greater enthusiasm. That is, the EEC, with less affinity, had more identitive power than the Nordic union. Finally, while the EEC had some coercive power, the Nordic union had none. Thus, to the degree that such statements can be verified at all, as expected, the growing EEC commanded more integrating power than the largely stable Nordic union.

MODERNIZATION AS PREDISPOSING TO UNIFICATION

The distinction between mature and premature unions, and between mature and overdue unions, was of little use in this study, though it might be too early to discard such distinctions. These concepts call attention to the state of the units and the system before a particular unification effort is launched—not with regard to the assets available for integrating purposes, but with regard to the degree to which the units themselves and the system are integrated, and in this sense predisposed to or against unification. When coupled with a comparative perspective, these concepts highlight one important problem that requires much more research.

Of the four unions studied, the two that succeeded are unions of modern countries; the two that failed are unions of traditional or transitional societies. If we look at cases other than those studied here, we find higher integration in Eastern Europe than in recent attempts at unification in Africa, Latin America, or Asia. It has already been suggested that regional integration is an effort developed countries may carry out, but underdeveloped are unlikely to accomplish.[15] In other words, while efforts to unify underdeveloped countries are often premature, advanced modernization predisposes to unification.

Several reasons can be given for this "prematurity" of unification efforts of underdeveloped countries. On the psychological level, one might refer to the association between the level of education of citizens and the extent of their horizon of information and identification. The illiterate's horizon tends to be his village, hardly his country.[16] A regional horizon, it is suggested, is far beyond him. The educated person, especially the college-trained, finds regional and even more extensive horizons more perceivable.[17] There is good reason to believe that such a restriction of horizon is common to many citizens of underdeveloped countries, but it is not clear what the effect of this restriction is on unification. Identification with the union is *required* only from politically active citizens, and those who are illiterate are rarely politically potent. Their consent for unification is hardly a prerequisite in these often authoritarian countries and, if it is needed, it can be mobilized by the leadership.

In the particular cases studied there is some evidence that restriction of horizons was one factor that hindered effective unification. In the Caribbean, the idea of a West Indian nation was largely limited to the more educated groups. When two charismatic leaders sought to resolve a personal and political difference between themselves and their parties by turning to the Jamaican voters, the majority of the voters—identifying with their island rather than with the federation and having been brought to believe that the interests of the two were in conflict—preferred to secede. Had their horizons been broader, the pro-federation party obviously would have had a better chance. Similarly, in the UAR, Nasser's ability to appeal to the peasants above the heads of the landlords in the name of Arab unity and Arab socialism required the peasants—especially in view of the economic

[15] Lincoln Gordon, "Economic Regionalism Reconsidered," *World Politics,* vol. 13 (1961), pp. 231–253.

[16] Lerner, *The Passing of Traditional Society,* pp. 48ff.

[17] William Evan, "An International Public Opinion Poll on Disarmament and Inspection by the People: A Study of Attitudes Toward Supranationalism," in Seymour Melman (ed.), *Inspection for Disarmament.* New York: Columbia University Press, 1958.

crisis in Syria—to have a more extensive horizon and time perspective than they had. This is one reason the secessionist coalition encountered no resistance on the part of the peasants and workers, who presumably were to be major beneficiaries of Nasser's reforms. The broader horizon of EEC and Nordic citizens seem to have helped these unions.[18]

A second reason that might be given for the incompatibility of unification and underdevelopment is that such countries lack citizens with the organizational and political skills required to handle regional unification. Again, the basic argument probably is valid; surely underdeveloped countries lack administrators and to a lesser degree skilled politicians (or, politicians of the calculative as against emotional type).[19] Still, leaders of these countries hold together nations of the size of India, federations with many tribes in their territories, such as Nigeria, and multiracial federations such as Malaya. It is hard to see why regional unions should require higher skills.

Note, though, that most of the underdeveloped nations were unified at least in part under colonial rule, so that some degree of unification existed before independence. As suggested above, it takes less power and perhaps fewer skills to maintain rather than to build up a union. Thus, the question of whether underdevelopment retards unification because the needed skills are lacking must be left open for future research. It is obvious, however, that the Economic Commission of the EEC and the Nordic Council found it comparatively easier to recruit effective administrators and calculative politicians than did the federal government of the West Indies. The latter's range of choice was particularly limited because of the provisions forbidding officials and politicians to hold both federal and island positions. The UAR surely did not have an abundance of administrators and calculative politicians, but this was hardly a factor in its lack of success; because of the authoritarian nature of the regime and the increased Egyptian staffing of Syrian positions, even those administrators and politicians available among the Syrians were not used.

[18] Arend Lipphart, "Tourist Traffic and Integration Potential," *Journal of Common Market Studies,* vol. 2 (1964), pp. 251–262.
[19] On the difference between these two types and the scarcity of one type versus the other, see Max F. Millikan and Donald L. M. Blackmer (eds.), *The Emerging Nations.* Boston: Little, Brown & Company, 1961, pp. 68ff.

A third argument accounting for the relationship between under-development and failures to unify is the preoccupation of underde-veloped countries with domestic problems. Brazil, for instance, could hardly be expected to lead a regional unification, as its atten-tion and resources are absorbed in the modernization of its large country. Surely such a preoccupation played a role in the secession of Jamaica and Trinidad. It also accounted in part for Egypt's impa-tience with Syria. But this argument assumes a necessary contradic-tion between the development of a country and regional unification. This might be the case for a country the size of Brazil, but for smaller countries, for instance the republics of Central America, the best chances for *national* development might well lie in a *regional* division of labor and cooperation, probably best attained by regional unification. Moreover, regional unification was initiated in Europe more to augment the development of nation-states than to replace it.[20]

Of all the tentative statements made in these concluding pages, those relating development to the "ability" to unify, are the most tentative. Limited horizons, lack of administrative and political skills, and preoccupation with domestic problems are such generic deficiencies that they seem quite inadequate to explain any particular phenomenon. We must nevertheless record that of the four unions studied, the two that succeeded were of developed countries and the two that failed were of underdeveloped. And, the effects of the dif-ferences in degree of development can be traced to one or more of these three deficiencies.

THE STAGE FOR ACCELERATION

Unifications rarely progress smoothly. When confronted with a "crisis" arising from the unification effort, elites in control are often faced with a decision that is close to a gamble. On the one hand, they might *decelerate* unification to allow more time for adjustment and to reduce the de-unifying pressures by curtailing the changes introduced. That is, they hope to reduce unification to the level the integrating power can carry. Or, the elites might marshal a grand

[20] This point is elaborated on in the author's "European Unification and Per-spectives on Sovereignty," *Daedalus,* vol. 92 (1963), pp. 498–520.

offensive to *accelerate* unification and bring it to a level at which, hopefully, new supportive power will arise (because new vested interests have become centered around the evolving structure, its values have become more visible, or less integrating power is necessary now that resistance has been broken). We expect *deceleration to be more effective when the union is premature,* that is, when resistance is high, and *acceleration more effective when the union is mature,* not to mention when it is overdue. What do the four cases studied show?

There is a generic difficulty in answering this question. It is difficult to determine the weight of this factor as against others. How much significance should be attributed to "basic, background factors"? How much to personal or interpersonal ones? How much to strategy? In general, we feel that no one factor determines the end result, but we would tend to grant greater weight to background factors. "Personalities" and strategies are important in realizing or wasting the potential of background factors, but they can alter them only to a limited degree.

The breakup of the federation of the West Indies can be attributed largely to "background" factors such as differences in per capita income and natural resources, the discontiguous territory, etc. In this context, the strategy followed did not help preserve the federation, but helped to destroy it. The fragile federation existed on a minimal basis, and a go-slow program was the only one the larger islands (on which the fate of the federation depended) were willing to tolerate. In 1956–1960, however, efforts were made by the small islands and by Britain to accelerate federal development and expand its scope, efforts that were undertaken as the larger islands were about to gain independence and thus increase their freedom of action. It was at this stage that federation became less tolerable to the larger islands, as they believed it would delay independence and would be a potential source of economic losses. When at this stage acceleration was attempted, the strain of unification passed the limit of tolerance of the larger islands. Last moment deceleration efforts came too late. The federation would probably have broken up sooner or later in any case, but its disbandment at this particular point was precipitated by acceleration efforts. This premature and weak federation might have lingered longer had no new demands been put on it; acceleration—in particular the prospects of a retroactive federal income tax—strained it to the breaking point.

Similarly, Egypt placed comparatively few demands on Syria in the first two years of the UAR. But as this go-slow policy did not yield the expected results—Syria was becoming more and more alienated from the union and secession was becoming a recognized danger—Nasser turned to a policy of acceleration. He tried to build a new basis of support among the Syrian masses (for example, through the National Union) and peasants (renewing the drive for agrarian reform) and to break the resistance of the powerful conservative groups in Syria by undermining their economic basis. But the conservative groups were challenged and highly alienated before their power was undermined and before the support of the masses could be developed and mobilized, that is, before new integrating power could be recruited. This is not to suggest that had Nasser maintained his earlier policy and slower unification pace, secession would have been avoided; but it would have been less likely to occur, or at least it might have been delayed. In sum, both these unions failed when, in a period of crisis, a go-slow strategy was replaced by acceleration.

The Nordic union consistently followed a go-slow strategy. When confronted with a deadlock, for instance, over the Nordic common market, it did not shift to an accelerated effort toward unification, but on the contrary, further slowed down till it came to an almost full standstill. One might suggest that this strategy saved the union from a de-unification crisis that might have resulted if Sweden and Denmark had tried to form a common market without Norway's full consent (for instance, by threatening Norway that they would form one of their own unless Norway agreed to a joint market). On the other hand, one ought to note that here deceleration of an already slow process practically halted unification. It is not possible to determine if this mature union could have done better with an acceleration policy, given the many and not coextensive affiliations of its members with other systems.

The EEC, much like the West Indies and the UAR, initially followed a gradualist and go-slow approach. That is, after the attempt

to launch European unification on a grand scale and at a rapid pace
failed, the initiators turned to the pursuit of integration on a more
limited basis, starting with the gradual unification of two sectors,
steel and coal. When this seemed successful, unification efforts were
extended to include significant proportions of the economies of the
Six. But the gradualist approach continued to be maintained and
considerable provision for deceleration was provided in case adverse
pressure mounted. After the successful initiation of this broader unification effort, the pace and scope of unification were accelerated:
tariff and quotas were reduced ahead of the maximal schedule, and
the Treaty was given a wider interpretation.

At first glance, it seems that the EEC followed the same pattern
as the UAR and the West Indies—a go-slow policy followed by acceleration—but with the opposite results. But a second look reveals
that this was not the case. The West Indies and the UAR *accelerated
at the moment of crisis,* that is, when the union and its integrating
power were strained. The EEC, on the other hand, *accelerated at the
moment of success,* as the amount of integrating power was growing
and in this sense a "surplus" was available. True, the initiators were
aware of potential crises they wished to avert by acceleration, but
they accelerated not in time of crisis but in anticipation of crisis.
Deceleration was more effective in crisis; acceleration, when unification was successful. Since premature unions are more likely to
face crises and mature and overdue ones to succeed, all other things
being equal, a go-slow (when necessary, decelerate) policy seems
more suitable to the first kind of union, and a rapid (when possible,
accelerate) pace, to the two others.

No Reallocation before Integration

Unification changes the power relations among the participating
units. Part of this change is an inevitable result of the process, part
is due to the deliberate effort of the founding elite or the emerging
power center to use unification for the purpose of introducing such
changes in the distribution of pwoer. The question arises as to
whether the reallocation of assets among the members is best preceded by growth of integration or whether such growth in integration

is best preceded by reallocation. ("Best" from the viewpoint of the potential success of unification.) The case for prior reallocation can be made in terms of the union's need for the means it requires in order to function (such as taxation), or by citing the desirability of rewarding the units and subunits that support unification and weakening or penalizing those that resist it by transferring assets from the resisters to the supporters. The case for delaying reallocation rests on the strains it imposes on the union. By building up integration first, by rewarding as many units and subunits as possible (for instance, by obtaining foreign aid), and by increasing their vested interest in the union, the chance of the union to withstand the strain of reallocation is increased.

The West Indies attempted reallocation before integration developed; this attempt precipitated the final breakdown of the federation. It might be of some interest to speculate what the building up of "integration before reallocation" would have entailed here. One major way every member of a union can be rewarded without anyone being deprived (that is, without reallocation) is if an external unit grants assets to the union. Such a grant is integrating as long as receiving it is conditional upon membership in the union. If members can receive their share of the grant even if they quit the union, a major source of utilitarian integrating power is lost. If they are more likely to receive it if they secede, or are likely to be able to keep a larger share for themselves if they do so, such assets have, of course, a de-unifying effect.

In the case of the West Indies, some such integrating power was provided by Britain in the foreign aid it gave to the federation as a federation. But it was not clear whether the aid to islands that might leave the federation would be stopped. Further, the aid was expected to be terminated gradually in any event. Moreover, the important subsidies on the sugar price were awarded before federation, during federation, and after it. Finally, since the federal structure was under the disproportional influence of the small islands, the larger islands expected to lose some of the aid channeled through the federation. By breaking away, Jamaica and Trinidad could hope to be in a better international bargaining position than they could achieve by staying in the union.

Assume for a moment that much of what happened had been reversed: assume that Britain increased its foreign aid after independence and granted it to the larger islands—as the federation's leaders—under the condition that the sum would be used in part (which would have been specified) for development of the small islands and in part for those of the larger ones; and that Britain agreed the aid would be continued for a considerable period if the federation were maintained and funds were allotted as agreed. Thus, for the larger islands, the federation would have been rewarding rather than penalizing and they could have expected that efforts to reduce the economic gap between themselves and the small islands would not slow down their own development. Assume also that the sugar subsidies and the American aid were given to the union, not to the units. The federation might still not have been saved, but the sharing of economic assets would have worked in its favor, while in reality they worked against it. Secession was a way of reallocation, of gaining more of the regional pie for the larger islands.

In the case of the UAR, Soviet foreign aid, given to both countries, could have played a similar role if given to Egypt as the leader of the union with an understanding that agreed proportions would be used to finance Syrian and joint projects. Actually, some aid was given in this way, but most Soviet aid was given directly to Egyptian projects such as the High Dam and to various Syrian ones, under the pre-UAR technical assistance agreement of 1957. There was no reason for Syria to believe that it would lose that aid in case of secession.

The situation in the Nordic union can be briefly characterized as one of no reallocation and little new integration, a combination that surely did not strain this union. The EEC quite systematically delayed reallocation until the integrating power was built up. This is best illustrated by the agreement to delay the formation of a common market in agricultural products; it can also be seen in focusing first on reduction of trade barriers, which was expected to benefit most citizens, and in allowing time for enthusiasm and shared institutions to evolve before turning, in the second stage, to some reallocation. Only in 1962 did the EEC approach, and with great caution, the questions of unification of tax structures and economic polities, and implementing anticartel measures—all steps that potentially involve considerable reallocation (depending on what policies are introduced and how consistently they are implemented). A close examination of the negotiations that preceded the ratification of the Treaty of Rome in 1955–1957, in which early reallocations were considered, suggests that the sides could not have faced significant reallocations at that stage, and probably not in the first years of the EEC.

In short, in the West Indies and the UAR—unions that failed—reallocations were attempted before integration developed; moreover, the stage in the histories of these unions at which the final crisis was precipitated was the stage at which accelerated reallocation was attempted. The Nordic union and the EEC succeeded; the former made no attempts at reallocation, the latter delayed them until the integrating power increased. Moreover, the delay seems directly related to the success of the EEC in the first stage of its unification efforts. How long a delay is necessary before reallocation can be introduced without unduly straining a union is, like most questions raised in these pages, a subject that requires more research. It is, for instance, still not clear that the EEC waited long enough, that is, allowed for sufficient integration before major reallocations were attempted.

Unification, like all social processes, is a complex phenomenon affected by many factors and forces. Practically all contemporary unifications, not only those studied here, have either already failed, or are still in the first stages of development. Hence, our study of necessity developed from a discussion of the conditions of initiation and the first steps of unification. Focusing on distribution and composition of power, on leaders and forces was more a question of choice. The study of other factors, we hope, will follow. In the next decades many more unification efforts are to be expected, and as nations' experience with and study of unification grows, their ability to direct this important process, rather than remain subject to its oscillation, will hopefully also increase. As stated in the Introduction, our aspiration is to contribute not just to a better understanding of the process of unification but also to the understanding of how better to unify.

GLOSSARY OF CONCEPTS

Allocate—(see *Typology of Functional Problems*)

Assets—possessions that a unit or system has, regardless of those other units may have.

Authority—legitimate power; that is, power whose exercise is viewed as just by those toward whom it is applied.

Coercive—(see *Typology of Assets and Powers*)

Communication—transmission of symbols from an actor(s) to others.

Community—a social unit that has self-sufficient integrative mechanisms; that is, the maintenance of its existence and form is provided for by its own processes and is not dependent upon those of external systems or member-units. A *political community* is a community that possesses three kinds of integration: (a) it has an effective control over the use of the means of violence (though it may "delegate" some of this monopoly to member-units); (b) it has a center of decision-making that is able to affect significantly the allocation of resources and rewards throughout the community; and (c) it is the dominant focus of political identification for the large majority of politically aware citizens.

Culture—the symbolic inheritance given by one generation to another; includes religion, secular ideologies, language, arts, etc.

De-unification—the process by which the bonds among the units of a system are weakened. See also *Unification*.

Dominant Function—the function in which a unit invests more resources, manpower, energy, and which its members value more highly than all other functions the given unit serves.

Downward Communication—refers to communication that flows from the elites to member-units; upward—from members to the elite.

Elite (or Elite-unit)—refers to a unit that devotes a comparatively high proportion of its assets to guide a process and lead other units to support it. The elite might be a member of the system (member-elite), an outsider (external elite), or a unit of the system (system-elite).

Elitism—the degree to which power is concentrated in the hands of one or a few units, as against a more or less equal distribution among many.

329

External Elite—(see *Elite*)

Identitive—(see *Typology of Assets and Powers, Typology of Functional Problems*)

Integrate—(see *Typology of Functional Problems*)

Integration—the ability of a unit or system to maintain itself in the face of internal and external challenges.

Internalization—the process by means of which control of a system is taken over by member-elites from external elite-units.

Lieutenant Unit—a unit whose power status is lower than that of the elite unit(s) and higher than that of the follower(s).

Mature Unifications—unifications in which the level of vested interests in the unit is medium to low, in which there is no unit-control of coercion, or only a limited one, and in which the population's identification with the units is weak and progressively weakening. *Overdue unifications* are ones in which there are widely felt needs for more interunit, union-wide regulation. *Premature unification* occurs when the populations of the member-units have strong vested interests in the regulation of utilitarian processes, on the unit rather than the system level; they desire unit-control of coercive power and strongly identify with the units as compared to the system.

Member Elite—(see *Elite*)

Monofunctional Organizations—consultative bodies whose decision-making powers are sharply limited either by the rule of unanimity, or by the nonbinding nature of the resolutions passed, or by both; and whose decision-making scope is limited to one or a few spheres (e.g., postal services, or health, or labor, etc.) and to functions that are not essential to the survival of the member units or their ability to pursue their national interests.

Overdue—(see *Mature Unifications*)

Political Community—(see *Community*)

Power—a unit's capacity to induce or influence another unit to carry out directives or any other norms it (the first unit) supports.

Powers—(see *Typology of Assets and Powers*)

Premature—(see *Mature Unifications*)

Scope—measured in terms of the number of social sectors of the member-units into which the shared system penetrates (e.g. only military, both military and economic) and in terms of the importance of these sectors to the survival of the units and the realization of their interests (e.g. postal service versus defense alliance).

Secondary Priming (Spill-over)—unification in one sector triggers a similar process in others, rather than a triggering by any external force.

Social Sector—all the activities of a social unit that serve a particular function of that unit.

Solidifiers—factors that are operative in the advanced and final stages of a process but ineffective in the initiation or early stages.

Supranational—refers to inter-state systems that have a center in which decisions binding the member units are made, and in which the identification of the politically conscious citizens with the comment units (the nations) is high and of the secular-"historical" type.

System—changes in the action of one unit affect actions in others, and these latter changes in turn have repercussions on the unit or units in which or from which the change was initiated.

System-Elite—(see *Elite*)

Typology of Assets and Powers—*Utilitarian assets* include economic possessions, technical and administrative capabilities, manpower, etc. *Utilitarian power* is generated when these assets of a unit are allocated or exchanged in such a fashion as to allow it to bring another unit to comply with norms it upholds, or with those the system upholds for its members. *Coercive power* (or *force*) results when coercive assets are used by one unit to impose its will or norms on the others, or by the system to impose its norms on the member units. *Coercion* is used to refer to the use of the means of violence, and not to pressure in a more generic sense as is sometimes done. *Identitive assets* is used to refer to characteristics of a unit or units that might be used to build up an identitive power. The assets are turned into power when a member unit or the system (through its representatives) succeeds in establishing that a particular course of action which it wishes other units or all member units to follow is consistent with, or an expression of, the values to which the participants of these units are committed.

Typology of Functional Problems—a union that has matured into a political community will share and centrally regulate activities that answer functional problems of all four types: *adapt* to its ecological and social environment, *allocate* means and rewards among its subunits, *integrate* its subunits into one polity, and establish as well as reinforce the *identitive* commitments of its members.

Unbalanced Systems—systems in which integration on one score is significantly higher than on the others.

Unification—the process by which the bonds among the units of a system are strengthened.

Union—a group of countries that act in unison, on a continuous rather than *ad hoc* basis, on a wide range of matters, and on matters more important to their interest than is the case in typical International Organizations.

Utilitarian—(see *Typology of Assets and Powers*)

SUBJECT INDEX

acceleration strategy:
  in European Economic Commu-
    nity, 271
  in Federation of the West Indies,
    322
  as integrating power, 31
  in mature unions, 82, 95
  in United Arab Republic, 129–33.
    See also dynamic perspective
Adams, Sir Grantley, 152, 156, 175,
  182
Adenauer, Konrad, 235, 255
Albania, 29
amalgamated communities, 56–57
Amer, Field Marshal, 112, 113, 120,
  126
American-European nuclear force,
  242, 243
Arab League, 32n, 98
Argentina, 40
Asali, Sabri al-, 102
assets, 38–39, 42, 220
  coercive, 39
  identitive, 39
  utilitarian, 38
Aswan, High Dam, 98
Australia, 24, 29, 83
Austria, 23
authority, defined, 8n

Baghdad Pact, 49, 98
Barbados, 140

as member of Federation of the
  West Indies, 149ff
Belgium, 35
  as member of European Economic
    Community, 231ff
Benelux, 21, 23, 31, 231
Bizi, General Afif al, 102n
blocs:
  control of violence by, 7
  decision making by, 8
  integration in, 8
Baath, 98ff
Brazil, 17, 40
British Commonwealth, 24, 25, 36,
  46, 78
British Guiana, 144, 154, 182
British Honduras, 144, 154
British Virgin Islands, 170
Bustamente, Alexander, 143, 147,
  151, 156, 177, 179, 181, 182, 308

Canada, 24, 29, 34
Caribbean Commission, 32, 91, 142
Central America, 27
  Federation of, 46
Central American Common Market,
  18, 24, 47
Central Treaty Organization
  (CENTO), 48, 49, 50
Ceylon, 29
charismatic power, 39n, 307–8
Chile, 40

333

Thailand, 36
Treaty of Rome, 20, 26, 32, 230, 231, 261n, 269, 270, 275, 279
Trinidad:
  economic importance of, 158–65
  in Federation of the West Indies, 141ff
  resistance to federation by, 145

unbalanced system, 11
unification, 3
  modernization of country as predisposition to, 318–21
  sequences of, 58–60
  termination state of, 60–63.
  See also integrating power, integrated sectors
union, defined, 12
Union of African States, 13, 28, 35, 36
Union of South Africa, 25, 35
Union of Soviet Socialist Republics, 10, 77, 79
unit, defined, 3, 83–88
unit integration, 17–18
unit properties, 16–33
  analytical, 19–27. *See also* heterogeneity
  individual, 16–18
United Arab Republic, 40, 98ff
  dynamic perspective of acceleration, 129–33, 323–24
  reallocation of subunits, 133, 326–27
  economic effects of unification on, 113–16
  effective composition in, 122–28, 303–17
  asymmetric exchange, 316
  coercive power, 124, 309
  communication and responsiveness, 125–28, 311–12

identitive power, 107, 122, 306–7
secession, 119–21, 314
utilitarian power, 107, 123, 304–5
effective distribution in, 103–7, 286–302
  elitism, 103–6, 289, 294–95
first efforts to form, 99–103
five-year plan of, 134–36
governing body of, 109
preunification state of, 98–107
shared properties of, 104–5
trade in, 116
United Nations, 7n, 43
United States, 10, 21–22, 24, 48, 49
  as elite, in European Economic Community, 238–46, 287
Upper Volta, 28
utilitarian assets, 38
utilitarian power, 37–40, 41, 72
  in European Economic Community, 247–52
  in Federation of the West Indies, 153–66
  in Nordic Council, 203–11
  in United Arab Republic, 107, 123, 304–5

Warsaw Treaty Organization, 10, 23
West Indies, 29
  Federation of. *See* Federation of the West Indies
Williams, Dr. Eric, 147, 151, 152, 156, 163, 180, 181
Windward Islands, 140, 141, 149, 171

Yemen, 99, 109
Yugoslavia, 77

Zanzibar, 26

AUTHOR INDEX

343